D0853733

940.54 Devlin 862802
Devlin, Gerard M.
Silent wings

862802
$27.95

## Brooke County Public Library
### Wellsburg, W. Va.

1.  Books may be kept two weeks and may
be renewed once for the same period, except
7 day books and magazines.

2.  A fine is charged for each day a book is
not returned according to the above rule.  No
book will be issued to any person incurring
such a fine until it has been paid.

3.  All injuries to books beyond reasonable
wear and all losses shall be made good to the
satisfaction of the Librarian.

4.  Each borrower is held responsible for all
books charged on his card and for all fines ac-
cruing on the same.

6/86      6/86

Brooke County Library
945 Main Street
Wellsburg, W. Va. 26070

Atlanta County Library
945 Main Street

The Saga of the U.S. Army and Marine
Combat Glider Pilots During World War II

# SILENT
# WINGS

## GERARD M. DEVLIN

Introduction by Lieutenant General
Sir Napier Crookenden

Foreword by
General William C. Westmoreland

St. Martin's Press
New York

SILENT WINGS. Copyright © 1985 by Gerard M. Devlin. All rights reserved.
Printed in the United States of America. No part of this book may be used or
reproduced in any manner whatsoever without written permission except in
the case of brief quotations embodied in critical articles or reviews. For
information, address St. Martin's Press, 175 Fifth Avenue, New York, N.Y.
10010.

Maps by Paul Costa

Library of Congress Cataloging in Publication Data

Devlin, Gerard M.
    Silent wings.

    Includes index.
    1. World War, 1939-1945—Aerial operations,
American.    2. Gliders (Aeronautics)    I. Title.
D790.D39 1985      940.54/4973      85-12535
ISBN 0-312-72460-8

First Published in Great Britain by W. H. Allen

10  9  8  7  6  5  4  3  2

940.54
Devlin

862802      6/86      6/86

Grateful acknowledgement is made for permission to reprint material from the following:

Excerpt from *Seven Came Through* by Edward V. Rickenbacker. Copyright © 1943 by Doubleday & Co., Inc. Reprinted by permission of publisher.

Excerpt from *Defeat Into Victory* by William J. Slim. Copyright © 1961 by Field Marshal the Viscount Slim. Reprinted by permission of Harold Ober Associates, Inc.

Excerpt from *The U.S. Army in World War II: Sicily and the Surrender of Italy* by Martin Blumenson. Copyright © 1965. Reprinted by permission of the Office of the Chief of Military History, Department of the Army.

Excerpt from the *St. Louis Post-Dispatch* of May 4, 1975. Reprinted by permission of the *St. Louis Post-Dispatch*.

Excerpt from *The Glider War* by James E. Mrazek. Copyright © 1975 by James E. Mrazek. Reprinted by permission of St. Martin's Press, Inc., New York.

Excerpt from *Military Heritage of America* by Col. R. Ernest Dupuy and Trevor N. Dupuy, copyright © 1956. Reprinted by permission of McGraw-Hill Book Company.

Excerpts from *History of the Second World* by Captain B. H. Liddell Hart. Copyright © 1970. Reprinted by permission of G. P. Putnam's Sons.

Excerpts from *Back To Mandalay* by Lowell Thomas. Copyright © 1951. Reprinted by permission of the estate of Lowell Thomas.

Excerpts from *A Bridge Too Far* by Cornelius Ryan. Copyright © 1974. Reprinted by permission of Simon & Schuster, Inc.

For the glider pilots who courageously flew those fragile, motorless aircraft with reckless abandon. And for the glider mechanics who laboured long and hard to keep them flying.

*and*

For my mother, Anna Marie Devlin, who suffered and worried through World War I, World War II, the Korean War and the Vietnam War while her husband and sons were in combat.

People that fly airplanes are fool enough, but anyone that gets into one of those gliders is a damn fool.

Colonel Philip G. Cochran
Commanding Officer, 1st Air Commando Group

Glider pilots were the most uninhibited individualists in the army. There seemed to be something about flying a glider, or being selected for that job, that freed a man from the ordinary restraints of army life. Those who wanted to fight, fought like lions. Those who wanted to get back to Brussels managed to get there before anyone else. Once their gliders had landed or crashed, there was no flying for them to do. After each airborne operation it had been recommended that the glider pilots be organized into units, trained in infantry tactics, and given a job on the ground. They were usually right up front when the need was greatest. But they successfully defied all such attempts at organization.

*Rendezvous With Destiny,*
History of the 101st Airborne Division

# Contents

# Foreword

WORLD WAR II SAW the introduction of many revolutionary and formidable types of military aircraft. Not the least of those was the combat glider, the only aircraft built to crash.

The intrepid pilots who flew the gliders were as unique as their motorless flying machines. Never before in history had any nation produced aviators whose duty it was deliberately to crashland, and then go on to fight as combat infantrymen. They were no ordinary fighters. Their battlefields were behind enemy lines.

Every landing was a genuine do-or-die situation for the glider pilots. It was their awesome responsibility to repeatedly risk their lives by landing heavily laden aircraft containing combat soldiers and equipment in unfamiliar fields deep within enemy-held territory, often in total darkness. They were the only aviators during World War II who had no motors, no parachutes, and no second chances.

Despite their remarkable achievements on a number of battlefields, the glider pilots have been the least heralded heroes of World War II. Strangely, their accomplishments have remained one of the least known events of that war.

Here, for the first time, is the complete story of the glider pilots who, in a brief period, had to master not only the aircraft they flew, but the tactics required for the extremely complex and hazardous business of arriving on a distant battlefield from the sky.

*William C. Westmoreland*
General, U.S. Army, Retired
Charleston, South Carolina
January 1985

# Introduction

GERARD DEVLIN HAS WRITTEN a fascinating history of glider pilots in combat, clearly based on a great deal of detailed research and informed by his affection and admiration for the men who flew the gliders – and their passengers – into battle.

It is of equal interest to both British and American readers for several reasons. In the first place the book describes in some detail how the United States glider force was developed, a story in which the difficulties encountered were much the same as those met by British Airborne Forces in their struggle to expand. Both the United States Army Air Corps and the Royal Air Force were reluctant to allow any diversion of effort from the bombing offensives against Germany and later Japan, and the figures of aircraft production in the United States illustrate this clearly. To take one year, for example, in 1943 the Americans produced the astonishing totals of 28,362 bomber aircraft and 24,005 fighters, but only 7,013 transport aircraft.

In glider production the United States Airborne Command suffered too from a wide diversity of manufacturers and continuous changes in policy, although the final figure of 14,612 gliders produced in America looks handsome enough beside the British total of 5,935. Perhaps I may quote Colonel Josiah Dalbey, Chief of Staff, U.S. Airborne Command, whose words in October 1943 could have been echoed in Britain: 'one of our basic troubles has been the failure to properly evaluate this new weapon from the topside down . . . both the R.A.F. in England and the A.A.F. here are extremely apathetic towards anything airborne.'

This book is also a reminder of the 43 years of close co-operation and mutual affection between U.S. and British Airborne Forces. In June 1942 Brigadier General William C. Lee, the 'Father' of U.S. Airborne Forces, flew to England, met the founder of the British

Airborne Forces, Major-General 'Boy' Browning and visited the British, Polish, Free French, Norwegian, Belgian and Dutch units on parachute training in the U.K. The two men struck up a mutual friendship, discussed together the need for Airborne divisions of all arms and set up a two-way flow of ideas and men which continues to the present day.

British and American Airborne Forces shared the same sort of dangers, triumphs and disasters in successive World War II campaigns – North Africa, Sicily, Normandy, Holland and the Rhine. The Airborne Divisions of both countries were good fighting units by any standards and, even after all their advantages of manpower selection and special training have been discounted, they had a certain recipe for success in battle and a special pride in being Airborne, which the parachute units of both nations still show in the very different conditions of the 1980s.

My own first contact with U.S. Airborne Forces was in 1943, when I was brigade major of the 6th Airlanding Brigade in the British 6th Airborne Division on Salisbury Plain. Just to the north of us around Newbury were units of the U.S. 101st Airborne Division and after one enjoyable riot in Devizes, with about a hundred men of each Division fighting over a girl, both divisions established cordial relations. In the D-Day fighting in Normandy I was impressed by the extraordinary good fortune of the British glider landings, both in the dark at 3 a.m. on that 6 June, when 48 out of 68 Horsas landed safely on Landing Zone N and later in daylight that evening when, in the second lift for the Division of 258 tug and glider combinations, 248 Horsa and Hamilcar gliders brought safely in to LZN and W two battalions of the 6th Airlanding Brigade.

In sharp contrast, the second lift for the US 82nd Airborne Division, due to land on LZW, came down in the face of intense fire from the German 795th Ost Battalion, who still held the northern flank of the landing zone, and suffered heavy casualties. This was simply the fortune of war, but a curious sidelight on those far-off days is that British glider pilots liked to fly the Horsa and had full confidence in it, whereas the American glider pilots preferred their own Waco or CG4A.

By 24 March 1945, and the crossing of the Rhine by General Matthew Ridgway's XVIIIth Airborne Corps, I was commanding the British 9th Parachute Battalion. The two Airborne Divisions, the United States 17th and the British 6th, flew into battle together and I shall never forget the sight and feel of that immense aerial armada. At Wavre in Belgium our long column of aircraft from the North-West joined with the skytrain of the 17th Division, coming up out of the South-West. Looking out of our starboard windows I could see their aircraft stretching back for miles, while from the open door on our portside the aircraft and gliders of our own division were still coming up over the horizon from England – and ahead, the two streams of aircraft, each nine ships wide, were flying steadily on, side by side, towards Germany. Above and beside us wheeled the hundreds of fighters of our close escort, and soon I could see ahead of us the great curve of the River Rhine north of Wesel and our dropping zone beyond it.

These and many other unforgettable moments will be conjured up by Gerard Devlin in this remarkable book, but perhaps from reading it I shall retain two lasting impressions – the extraordinary capacity of the American people to improvise, to 'get on with it' and to produce the goods, and the outstanding courage and skill of both American and British glider pilots.

*Sir Napier Crookenden KCB, DSO, OBE*
Lieutenant-General, British Army, Retired
Kent, England
February 1985

# Acknowledgements

I WISH TO THANK J. Garth 'Bud' Caldwell of the National World War II Glider Pilots Association for suggesting that I write this book.

At the outset, I must acknowledge Captain Ralph S. Barnaby, U.S.N., holder of America's Soaring Certificate No. 1 (issued to him in 1911 by the F.A.I.), naval aviator, aeronautical engineer, artist, author, sculptor, aviation history authority extraordinaire, and four-term President of the Soaring Society of America. In personal interviews Captain Barnaby kindly reminisced at great length with me about the very early days of soaring and aviation in the United States and in Europe; his association with the Wright Brothers, Amelia Earhart, Charles Lindbergh, and other aviation greats; his historic 1930 experimental glider descent from the belly of the airship U.S.S. *Los Angeles*; and his work with military gliders during World War II. Without his valuable assistance this book never could have been written.

I am also deeply grateful to John Robinson, one of only two Americans ever to become a three-time winner of the National Soaring Competitions, and the first person in the world to complete the 'Diamond C' – still the greatest soaring achievement worldwide – for the comprehensive explanations of how he staged the first glider flying demonstrations for General Hap Arnold, and how he instructed the first classes of military students to be trained at Elmira and Twentynine Palms. Thanks to him, I was able to finally untangle the confused and poorly documented story of how America trained her glider pilots.

Next I must thank Tip Randolph, National Secretary of the World War II Glider Pilots Association, and his wife, Ginney, for helping me locate present and former members of the Association who participated in battle actions described in this book. There were many times that I called them late at night, but they never complained. William K. Horn, the Association's historian and editor of its excellent publication, 'Silent Wings', was also of great assistance in putting me in touch with veteran glider pilots, and providing me with a wealth of information and photos that had been buried away since the early days of World War II. For his continuous support throughout the writing of this book, and his kind permission to use the title 'Silent Wings', I am most grateful.

I also want to express my appreciation to the following U.S. Army officers who were the wartime commanders of the units indicated: General Matthew B. Ridgway, XVIII Airborne Corps and 82nd Airborne Division; Lieutenant General Joseph M. Swing, 11th Airborne Division; Lieutenant General James M. Gavin, 82nd Airborne Division; Major General William M. Miley, 17th Airborne Division; Major General Joseph Harper, 327th Glider Infantry Regiment, and Lieutenant Colonel Henry A. Burgess, who commanded Task Force Gypsy on Luzon during the final airborne operation of World War II. These men gave freely of their time in answering my questions concerning various battles, or took time from their busy schedules to grant me interviews.

Among the many former military glider pilots contributing to the book I would like to thank in particular the following: Bard Coatsworth, for his words of encouragement and for sending rare, out-of-print books dealing with gliders, and who painstakingly explained in writing and with detailed drawings the method used by powered airplanes to snatch a grounded glider into flight; William T. Sampson II, for enlightening me about the early days of military glider training, and for teaching me the rudiments of glider flying while seated in my living room; Arthur C. Furchgott, for sending instructional booklets that he used while teaching glider flying in 1943 at South Plains Army Air Field in Texas; the late Michael C. Murphy, for granting me an interview in Florida at a time when he was not feeling well, and for taking time to answer my many long letters concerning the early development of the American military glider programme and combat glider tactics; Richard A. Flood, who, during the period 1943–1945 was supervisor of glider and power pilot flight and ground school training at Laurinburg-Maxton Army Air Field, North Carolina, for sending detailed information concerning development of the glider pick-up system and other experiments conducted during the war years; Colonel Ellsworth P. Curry, wartime base commander of Laurinburg-Maxton, for explaining combat training operations at that glider centre; Lieutenant Colonel Ernest A. LaSalle, wartime commander of the Glider Mechanics School at Sheppard Army Air Field, Texas, and inventor of numerous glider safety devices and retrieval systems, for technical information pertaining to all American gliders; Earl Rishel, for allowing me to borrow his flight log books and photo albums; George 'Pete' Buckley, for coming to my aid on several occasions with the answer to vital questions that no one else could answer, and for loaning me books from his personal library; Earl F. Simson, David S. Kaufman, and Robert J. Meer, for sending information about operations on New Guinea and Biak Island; Wolfram Sexauer for material about his Biak-to-Leyte flight in a CG-13A glider that was carrying a general's staff car; and Walter A. Barker, who flew a glider across the Rhine two days prior to Operation Varsity to pick up wounded soldiers and return them to hospitals in France, for providing blueprints of his special aircraft and information about his mercy mission.

For sending me a wealth of material about the training of their illustrious 1st Air Commando Group in the United States and in India, plus the Group's subsequent combat actions in Burma, I am most grateful to: Generals John R. Alison and Robert N. Trubey; Lieutenant Colonels Robert E. Moist and Donald E. Seese; Captain Neal J. Blush; Charles B. Turner; and Thomas Hight. A special word of thanks to Bob Bovey, historian of the 1st Air Commando Veterans Association, who, even though he was recovering from surgery at the time, kindly sent names and addresses of glider pilots who took part in Operation Thursday and other combat operations in Burma.

My thanks also go to these other contributors: Colonel Floyd J. Sweet, a veteran World War II glider pilot himself, and designer of the CG-15A glider, president of the National Soaring Museum, past president of the Soaring Society of America, and the nation's foremost authority on American military gliders, for granting me an interview at his home in Virginia, and for providing information that I requested during several subsequent phone calls; Kenneth W. Decker and John S. McCollom, two of the three persons who survived the Shangri-La Valley crash, for the time and information they gave during interviews; Cecil E. Walter, leader of the parachute element during the rescue in the valley, for interviews in which he detailed the entire rescue operation; Henry Palmer, one of the glider pilots who participated in the rescue flight from the valley; Harry N. Perl, one of two survivors of the September 1943 crash of the MC-1 glider, for sharing with me his experiences during that air disaster; Colonel Harry W. Generous, who was chief of staff of the IX Troop Carrier Command in England during World War II, for detailed documentation about the organization of troop carrier units, and especially for providing me with a complete after-action report of Operation Varsity; Command Sergeant Major Arthur E. Provost, one of those rare soldiers who is both parachute- and glider-qualified, for detailing his participation in Operation Tarheel, the last training manoeuvre in which gliders were employed in the United States; Mark Swanson, former assembly foreman at the Ford Motor Company's Kingsford, Michigan, glider plant, for patiently explaining how Ford built gliders; Roger W. Griswold II, designer of the famous Griswold Nose crash-protection device that saved many a glider pilot's life, for allowing me to borrow rare photos of his inventions; Colonel James M. Mrazek, who is himself an author and former glider infantryman, for assisting me in contacting veterans of the 1st Air Commando Group; Virginia Fritcher, for sending copies of postwar newspapers containing advertisements offering crated CG-4A gliders to the public for $75.00 each; Dennis Davies, for providing definitive information regarding weapons and equipment used by American, British, and German forces during World War II; and Al Clarke for allowing me to use his copy machine at will.

I was assisted greatly during the writing of the Fighting Falcon episode by several citizens in Greenville, Michigan, where that famous glider was manufactured by the Gibson Refrigeration Company. Dave Higbie, assistant editor of the *Daily News*, and Sandy Main, the paper's news production editor, both sent copies of articles printed on that day in 1943 when the glider was christened at Black Field. H.O. 'Bill' Williams of the Flat River Historical Society also sent more newspaper items and some original photos. William J. Delp, who was an employee of Gibson Refrigeration during the war years until he entered the U.S. Army, kindly sent a number of interesting documents about the Fighting Falcon and put me in touch with five of the former students who helped raise the funds used to purchase the glider. And from his home in Texas, Colonel Alvin E. Robinson, the man who piloted the airplane that towed the Fighting Falcon on D-Day, related to me his frightening experiences during the trip across the Channel to France and back again through flak-filled skies to England. For all the valuable assistance provided by those fine people, I am very grateful.

Librarians continue to be among the nicest people on earth. In every library and museum I visited, I was always given great assistance by uncomplaining research librarians who dug through files, and climbed tall book racks, to locate books for me. I am especially indebted to Josephine Weaver at the Fort Devens, Massachusetts, library, and to Edith McEvoy and Ruth Ferrel at the Nashua, New Hampshire, public library.

Among the countless other people who have helped in various ways, I must acknowledge the reverend Father Gerard Thuring of Groesbeek, Holland, who sent information concerning precise locations of glider landing zones used by American forces during Operation Market-Garden.

My thanks also go to Lorraine V. Travis, Secretary of the British Mule Society in England, and Major P. G. Malins, MBE, MC, of the British Army, for providing me with detailed information concerning the numbers and types of mules used in Burma by Brigadier Orde Wingate and his gallant Chindits.

I must also express my appreciation to Captain Hans Distelmeir of Germany's *Luftlande-Fliegerkameradschaft* (a World War II glider pilot veteran association), who is a survivor of the historic glider attack on Fort Eben Emael in Belgium. At the 1980 reunion in Atlanta of the National World War II Glider Pilots Association, Captain Distelmeir graciously granted my request for an interview during which he taught me how to correctly pronounce the name of that Belgian fortress.

There were a great many glider pilots who took time to answer my requests for photos to accompany the manuscript. Space does not permit me to list all of their names, but I am grateful to them all. Several other people and organizations also helped with photos. Those who deserve special mention are Bob Storck, archivist of the Vintage Sailplane Association, and editor of its excellent *Bungee Cord* magazine; Shirley Sliwa, Director of the National Soaring Museum; Stu Vogt at the 101st Airborne Division's museum at Fort Campbell, Kentucky; and the 11th, 17th, 82nd and 101st Airborne Division Associations.

For continuous words of encouragement during the four years that it took to write this book, my thanks go to my son, Mike; my daughters, Deanna-Lyn and Patricia; their husbands, Paul and

Robert; my brother, Arthur, who is himself an author; my sister, Marie, and her husband, Don. My thanks also go to my agent, Paul Gitlin; and to Jared Kieling, senior editor at St. Martin's, and his colleague, Janet Vultee, both of whom deserve a commendation medal for the excellent job they did in polishing the jagged edges of my manuscript.

Above all others who gave me encouragement and assistance stands my wife, Leona. She organized and collated research, typed all but one chapter, and was my constant source of strength.

As happened during the writing of my previous work on World War II, *Paratrooper!*, published in 1979, there were a great many times during the writing of this book that I was unable to come up with the right word or phrase to complete an important paragraph. On each of those occasions, I put my pen down on my desk and prayed to the Almighty and his Blessed Mother for assistance. They never let me down.

*Gerard M. Devlin*
Nashua, New Hampshire

# Chapter 1

## *Evolution of the Glider*

FOR THOUSANDS OF YEARS WHILE man attempted to achieve his overpowering aspiration to fly like a bird, historians and storytellers glorified the exploits of two Greeks, Daedalus and his son Icarus.

According to an ancient Greek legend, Daedalus and Icarus were being held in a prison on the island of Crete by King Minos when they plotted to escape on wings they had secretly made of feathers held in place by wax. Just prior to take-off, Daedalus instructed his son to fly low over the water until they reached safety on the island of Sicily. However, shortly after they had glided over the prison walls Icarus became so thrilled with his newfound ability to fly that he ignored his father's advice and flew higher and higher above the water. He eventually flew so high that the heat of the sun melted the wax on his wings, causing them to shed their feathers; Icarus plunged into the sea and drowned. Meanwhile, Daedalus continued on to Sicily where he glided to earth unaware of the disaster that had overtaken his son. Though the story of Daedalus and his son is only a myth there is considerable irony in it, because both the islands of Crete and Sicily were to be the scenes of large motorless combat glider assault landings during World War II.

Succeeding generations of would-be bird-men apparently were not frightened by this example of flying's initial 50 per cent safety record. Inspired by the success of Daedalus, a large number of experimenters throughout history tried to emulate him by constructing wings of wood, covered either by feathers or cloth. Upon completing their inventions they would proceed to the nearest high place, usually a cliff or tall building, and leap into space – to be seriously injured or killed.

With regularity the first experimenters fell to their deaths much like the mythical Icarus. Even one of the early kings of England had to pay the terrible price of aviation pioneering. In the year 863 B.C. a

[1]

man named Bladud became the ninth king of England. Documents record that he founded a university at Stamford in Lincolnshire and built the city of Bath where he reputedly summoned magical powers to create the hot springs found there today. Whatever mystical power King Bladud may have had deserted him when he jumped off the top of the Temple of Apollo in what was then called Trinaventum and is now known as London. With a pair of feather-covered wings as his only visible means of support, the good king fell like a stone and crashed into the courtyard of the temple where he broke his neck and died. He was succeeded to the throne by his son, King Lear.

For centuries following King Bladud's untimely death the world's greatest thinkers, scientists, and most imaginative engineers tried to find the key to successful bird-like flight. All of those early experimenters believed that flight could be achieved with a well-designed ornithopter, a man-powered, flapping-wing device. Accordingly they continued to build many variations of the basic lightweight mechanical wings which netted them only broken bones and funerals during their experimental flight trials.

It was Italy's brilliant Leonardo da Vinci, painter of the Mona Lisa, architect, scientist and creator of more mechanical inventions than nearly any other person in history who first discovered that man's dream of imitating the flight of birds with only arm-powered wing-flapping mechanisms had been doomed to failure from the beginning. England's King Bladud had been dead nearly 2,000 years when, in the year A.D. 1505, Leonardo turned his talents as an artist and inventor to the job of solving the riddle of human flight. Possessing a then unequalled knowledge of the anatomy both of the human body and numerous species of birds, he designed several aircraft, one of which was a sort of manpowered hang glider.

Leonardo's unique invention had rigid inboard wings and moveable outer sections of wings that could be made to flap by means of an arrangement of cables, pulleys and pivots. Instead of using just the inadequate power of a man's arms, Leonardo's invention had the pilot lying prone beneath it in a harness so that he could generate power and maintain control in flight by briskly moving both arms and legs. With only minor modifications, modern hang gliders are replicas of Leonardo's original design.

There is no evidence to suggest that Leonardo actually conducted test flights with his numerous aircraft designs. All of his highly ingenious creations, with detailed sketches and written explanations

[2]

of their workings, were confined to the pages of numerous manuscripts that he left. They are still being marvelled at by scholars and scientists.

History's first true bird-man ever to successfully fly in a controllable aircraft did not make his appearance until nearly 400 years after Leonardo's time. This remarkable individual was a German mechanical engineer, Otto Lilienthal.

Lilienthal was 42 years old when in 1890 his book *Der Vogelflug als Grundlage für Fliegerkunst* (Bird Flight as the Basis of Aviation) was published. It was a voluminous work based on findings he had made during ten years of carefully observing the flight of every type of bird, from sparrows to the majestic eagles of Germany. One of the first findings in the book was Lilienthal's correct determination that the human body simply did not possess the required muscle structure nor dexterity to successfully imitate the rapid flapping of a bird's wings in flight. Starting in the same year he set about designing his own flying machine. Rather than experiment with yet another ornithopter, Lilienthal concentrated his efforts on designing a series of rigid, single-wing gliders.

The U.S. Army had just completed the last of its campaigns against the American Indians when, in the spring 1891, Lilienthal began flight experiments on a hill near Berlin with the first of his gliders. It was constructed of slender peeled branches, cut from young willow trees, and covered with waxed linen cloth. Assisted by his younger brother Gustav, Otto hiked to the top of the hill carrying his rigid glider, which had a small tail section affixed to it. After a short rest on the hill's summit, Otto picked up the glider, faced into the wind, and began running down the hillside clutching the wooden braces positioned in the open middle section of the wing. He had only run about 15 yards when he felt himself being lifted free of the earth. Once airborne he quickly tucked his legs up as high as he could and held on for dear life to his invention as it carried him down the hill.

Lilienthal's first test glides were unimpressive; they lasted only a few seconds, during which time he sailed downhill only a few feet and sustained skinned knees and body bruises upon landing. However, by the end of that summer he managed to stretch his downhill glides to a distance of 50 feet and had developed a technique which enabled him to land on his feet without injuring himself or his fragile glider.

[3]

Starting in 1894, Lilienthal experimented with biplane (double wing) gliders that afforded him a greater degree of control in flight and enabled him to lengthen his downhill glides to 100 yards at altitudes approaching 50 feet. The moderate success of his hang gliders made Lilienthal obsessed with the idea that with further modification to his inventions he would be able to duplicate the dexterity of a bird. He eventually made over 2,000 glides in search of the key to bird-like flight.

Returning in 1896 to his basic rigid single-wing gliders, Lilienthal began a series of experimental flights, the object of which was to fly a complete 360 degree circle. By this time, he had taught himself how to make maximum use of prevailing winds while in flight and to accomplish slight turning manoeuvres by shifting the weight of his suspended body in the direction he wished to travel. It was during one of those hazardous turning movements on August 9, 1896, that a sharp breeze from an unexpected quarter caused his glider to stall (lose its lift) at an altitude of 50 feet. Though he struggled violently to recover from the stall he was unable to do so and crashed. He died the next day at a hospital in Berlin. Lilienthal's last words to his family were prophetic for future generations of bird-men: 'Sacrifices must be made.'

Fortunately for those who were to follow him, Lilienthal had kept detailed records of his experiments and inventions and had always cheerfully permitted anyone who wished to do so to observe and photograph him while he carried out exhaustive test flights from hilltops around Berlin.

Lilienthal's hang glider flying experiments were continued in England by Percy Pilcher, a 29-year-old Scotsman who had visited him in Germany and had observed several of his glider flights. Back at his home in Eynsford, Kent, in England, Pilcher eventually built a series of four hang gliders that he christened the Bat, the Beetle, the Gull, and the Hawk. Each was patterned after Lilienthal's models, but Pilcher used bamboo in the construction of his gliders and affixed an undercarriage with wheels to the final Hawk model. The addition of the undercarriage and wheels enabled the Hawk to be towed into the air by a team of wildly galloping horses. Using his unique launch method, Pilcher managed to achieve controlled glides in excess of 300 yards down and across windswept valleys near his home.

On September 30, 1899, Pilcher was conducting some horse-towed launch experiments with the Hawk glider at Lord Braye's home near Market Harborough when a bamboo strut in the tail section broke. Pilcher crashed and was so seriously injured that he died two days later without regaining consciousness. With the demise of both Lilienthal and Pilcher, serious experimentation with aviation in Europe ceased for nearly ten years.

In the United States, meanwhile, Lilienthal had an imitator in the person of Octave Chanute, a well-to-do engineer whose speciality was bridge building. Using engineering data he had accumulated during years spent designing bridges Chanute restructured Lilienthal's basic monoplane hang glider wing. In 1896 he introduced the braced biplane formula with its wing bays and incorporated structural refinements that were mathematically correct and produced a more rigid set of wings. Chanute was 63 years old in 1896 when he began his aviation design experiments, so he left the test flying to younger assistants who achieved moderate success with his many innovative hang glider models. Aside from his significant contribution to the perfection of glider wings, Chanute is best remembered in aviation history as a generous patron of those younger than he who were trying to achieve true flight. He gave freely of his time and money to others who were struggling to find the key to prolonged flight.

Starting in 1899, two brothers from Dayton, Ohio – Orville and Wilbur Wright – began a series of experiments with gliders that were to culminate in the conquest of the air four years later. Inspired by Lilienthal, encouraged by Chanute, and confident of their own ability, the Wrights read everything in print about flying and then cautiously began their experiments.

The Wright brothers knew when they began experimenting in 1899 that the problem of true flight was not how to get into the air; that had already been done by Lilienthal. The greatest problem, as they then saw it, was controlling an aircraft once it became airborne. They first constructed a small-scale kite-glider with only a five-foot wing span. Structurally, this model glider was very similar to Chanute's larger, rigid-biplane gliders and had a fixed vertical tailplane for longitudinal stability. The chief difference between their glider and Chanute's was the fact that they had built into it a series of wires with which they could control the direction of flight by warping (twisting) the wingtips rather than having to shift the weight of the pilot's body as Lilienthal had to do.

Satisfied with results obtained from their model, the brothers next

[5]

built a full-scale man-carrying glider. It too was similar to Chanute's biplane but had an elevator mounted in front of the wing and no tail section. They named this aircraft No. 1 Glider and, in the autumn of 1900, travelled with it to Kitty Hawk, a sandy, windblown town located on North Carolina's outer banks along the Atlantic shoreline. There they began a series of test flights during which first one and then the other brother would lie on the bottom wing of the glider as it skimmed above the sand, riding brisk breezes blowing across from Albemarle Sound. By the fall of that same year they had each completed dozens of glides and had concluded that many refinements were needed if they were to achieve controlled flight.

For the next two years the Wrights travelled between their laboratory in Dayton and Kitty Hawk, where they conducted extensive flight tests with new and larger gliders. Through trial and error, they gradually mastered the problems of balance and control.

In their No. 3 glider, which they perfected in October of 1902, the Wright brothers incorporated all structural refinements and flight control devices they had experimented with in previous models. During the last six days of their stay along the breezy shores of North Carolina that year they managed to make more than 375 glides, some of them lasting 15 seconds, while hovering nearly six feet above the ground, and covering distances up to 350 feet. Had they wanted to, the Wrights could have continued to perfect the art of soaring, but their ambition was to build a powered aircraft.

As history records, the world's then two best glider pilots returned to Kitty Hawk in 1903, bringing with them a unique aircraft that they had christened *Flyer I*. A further refinement of their No. 3 glider, *Flyer I* was equipped with a 12-horsepower, four-cylinder engine and two propellers which the Wrights had designed and built at their Dayton laboratory. After rehearsing their routine at Kitty Hawk with a motorless glider, they successfully launched *Flyer I* at 10:35 a.m. on December 17, with Orville at its controls. It was the world's first powered, sustained, and controlled flight. With the engine chattering noisily at his side, Orville raised the elevator, bringing the machine up to an altitude of 10 feet. Immediately thereafter it dipped, climbed again, then darted for the ground, coming to rest in the soft sand. The flight lasted only 12 seconds, during which Orville travelled 120 feet – less than the wingspan of a modern-day four-engined jetliner. But brief as it was, that epic flight was to change the course of history.

Even though he was caught up in the new world of powered flight, Orville Wright never forgot his first love of soaring. In 1911 he returned to Kitty Hawk to test an automatic stabilizing device. On October 24, he was launched into a 40 mph wind aboard a glider equipped with the new stabilizing device. To his astonishment, and that of ground observers, Orville managed to remain aloft for 9 minutes and 45 seconds. It was a soaring record that would stand for a decade.

Despite all the publicity being directed at the Wright brothers because of their revolutionary accomplishments in the field of controlled motorized flight, there were still those in America who persisted in experimentation with gliders during the early 1900s. Most notable among them was Professor John J. Montgomery of the Santa Clara Jesuit College in California. In 1904, Montgomery designed and built a tandem wing glider that had wing torque controls, plus a rudder and elevator. After making a few refinements and conducting some low-altitude flying experiments with it himself, Montgomery decided to show his invention to the public. With the aid of Ed Unger, a prominent west coast balloonist, Montgomery hired a circus trapeze artist to act as the pilot of his glider. On April 29, 1905, 15,000 people packed themselves into the Santa Clara fairgrounds to witness the first high altitude flight of the glider which Montgomery had named the *Santa Clara*. The flight plan called for the *Santa Clara* to be hauled aloft suspended beneath one of Unger's gigantic smoke-belching balloons, then cut loose to glide back to earth. As the wide-eyed crowd stood watching, Daniel Maloney, a 130-pound circus acrobat clad in bright red trunks, climbed into the pilot's seat suspended beneath the Santa Clara. Ground crew members quickly untied the balloon's restraining ropes and Maloney began waving to the crowd as he was carried aloft.

Many of those standing in the crowd watching Maloney go up were convinced that they were looking at a man who was about to die. But unlike his observers, Maloney was full of confidence in the glider and his ability to control it in flight. Upon reaching the planned altitude of 4,000 feet, Maloney cut the *Santa Clara* loose from the balloon and began his descent. The crowd held its breath for the first few seconds but then broke into applause as Maloney deftly piloted the aircraft through a series of graceful turns. A few minutes after releasing himself from the balloon Maloney landed the *Santa Clara* less than a mile away from his launch site.

[7]

Thrilled by the total success of his first glider, Professor Mont-gomery built four more just like it and took them on an exhibition tour up and down the coast of California that summer. Things went well at first, but then disaster struck. On July 18, 1905, Maloney had just cut his glider away from a balloon when one of its tail braces broke in two. A split second later one of the wings folded in half and the glider began its plunge to earth. Hundreds of horrified people in the crowd screamed as Maloney crashed to his death only a few feet in front of them. Maloney became the third glider pilot in modern times to die, after Otto Lilienthal and Percy Pilcher. But by no means was he to be the last. Six years later, Montgomery himself was killed when he fell to earth from an altitude of only 20 feet while conducting an experimental glider flight.

Yet the death of Maloney and rapid advances being made by the Wright brothers in powered flying machines did little to dampen the enthusiasm of glider advocates. By 1909, several glider manufactur-ing plants had sprung up across the United States. In the November 1910 edition of *Aeronautics: The American Magazine of Aerial Loco-motion*, there appeared an advertisement by the C. and A. Whitman Company, a large manufacturer of airplanes located on Staten Island in New York. Two photos accompanied the advertisement. One showed a complete aircraft parked in front of the Staten Island factory. The other was of a man flying a Whitman hang glider.

In the same issue of the magazine there was also a news article concerning the Church Aeroplane Company of Brooklyn, New York, that had sold one of its glider products to D. A. Kramer, a local bicycle racing champion. The article stated that Mr. Kramer 'has been making some very successful flights, and has been towed by an automobile, and when reaching 75 or 80 feet, cutting loose and gliding several hundred feet to the ground.'

Whatever interest there might have been in gliding was overshad-owed by events during World War I. Throughout that terrible conflict newspapers in England, France, Germany and the United States were filled with stories detailing the heroics of brave young pilots who flew warplanes and killed each other in the sky above France. When the war finally ended, the victorious allied nations concentrated their efforts on refining some of their combat aircraft and developing commercial aviation industries in their respective countries.

In their drive to build bigger, faster and higher-flying aircraft with

[8]

which to equip their blossoming commercial aviation companies, the victors of World War I paid virtually no attention to the development of gliders. Meanwhile in the defeated nation of Germany, interest in gliders could not have been greater.

## Chapter 2

# *Better Late Than Never*

FOR MANY YEARS, EVEN BEFORE the outbreak of World War I, the Germans had displayed considerable skill in the development of gliders. But during the war years of 1914–1918 they had focused their attention on the exploits of the young airmen flying powered combat airplanes on both the Western and Eastern fronts.

A sudden return to glider flying was generated early in 1919 when Germany was obliged to sign the Treaty of Versailles. Under the harsh military provisions of that treaty Germany was required to cut its six-million-man army down to a caretaker force of 100,000 troops, completely deactivate its air force, and immediately scrap all of its powered warplanes. The treaty made absolutely no mention of the use of gliders.

As early as the summer of 1919 active glider flying clubs began springing up all over Germany. Virtually all of those clubs equipped themselves with the Zögling (student), a new type of primary training glider which had been manufactured for sale to the public. The Zögling was far different from previous hang glider models in that it had a single long central landing skid upon which the pilot sat with his legs extended horizontally. Crude hand and foot controls enabled the pilot to manoeuvre in flight.

The Zögling and its pilot were launched by a shock cord device resembling a gigantic slingshot. The shock cord itself was a 200 foot length of stretchable rubberized rope that had a small metal ring positioned at its midpoint.[1] When the time came for launch, the metal ring was affixed to an inverted hook on the nose of the glider. Two men acted as anchors, holding the glider in place with a short length of non-stretchable hemp rope attached to its tail. Then, at a command given by the launch director, two teams of men would walk the ends of the shock cord away from the glider at an angle until it formed a taut V. While holding the wing of the glider level himself,

[10]

the launch director would next command the men holding the ends of the taut shock cord to first walk and then run away from the glider until they stretched the cord nearly to its breaking point. At that time the launch director would signal the two men straining at the tail to release their grips, and the glider would be catapulted into the air.[2] As the glider passed over the heads of the launch crew gravity would cause the shock cord ring to disengage itself from the nose hook, allowing the cord to fall to the ground and be gathered up.

By 1920, sufficient design and construction of new gliders had been completed in Germany to cause Oskur Ursinius, editor of the popular, Frankfurt-based *Flugsport* (Sport Flying) magazine, to sponsor the country's first national glider flying competitions. The site selected by Ursinius for the competitions was Mount Wasserkuppe, a 3,117-foot peak situated in the Rohn Mountains only a few miles from what is now the border separating East and West Germany. Some previous experimental glider flying had been conducted on the windblown slopes of Mount Wasserkuppe as early as 1913. But starting in 1920, that mountain was to rapidly become the cradle of German glider developments and the mecca of worldwide soaring enthusiasts.

To encourage participation in the first national contest, *Flugsport* magazine advertised that the event would be held during the months of August and September when the climate and prevailing winds on Mount Wasserkuppe would be at their best. As a further enticement, the magazine offered cash prizes to glider pilots who could make the longest and greatest number of flights, and to glider designers who could produce the glider with the best glide ratio.

A total of 24 young German glider pilots gathered at the first competition in 1920 to demonstrate their flying skill, exchange ideas, and try to win one of the many cash prizes. They brought with them a collection of aircraft ranging in style from the old Lilienthal hang gliders to variations of the more modern Zögling models. Things proceeded quite nicely during the month of August with officials keeping records of each contestant's long glides down the slopes of Mount Wasserkuppe. The great enthusiasm that existed during the first half of the meet was dampened somewhat by an accident involving one of the youngest contestants, 20-year-old Eugene von Loessl. While gliding down the slopes at an altitude of only 15 feet, his fragile glider was overturned by a sudden strong gust of wind. Unable to regain control at that low altitude, the young man fell into a pile of boulders and was killed.

[11]

Whatever hopes the other contestants entertained for winning some of the cash prizes were brushed aside with the appearance of Wolfgang Klemperer during the sixth week of the meet. Klemperer was a seasoned power pilot and a veteran of combat service with the German air force during World War I. He had brought to Mount Wasserkuppe a sleek new glider of revolutionary design that had been constructed by a group of students at the Aachen Institute of Technology under the supervision of Professor Erich von Karmen. Named the Schwarzer Teufel (Black Devil), Klemperer's glider was a cantilever low-wing monoplane with a fully enclosed, streamlined fuselage and a cockpit equipped with a control stick and rudder pedals. Fastened to the underside of the glider were two long wooden ski-like landing skids cushioned by rubber pads to ensure soft landings.

Klemperer and his talented associates from Aachen managed to win most of the 1920 prize money with the Black Devil glider. His most outstanding flight that year consisted of a shock cord launch from the summit of Mount Wasserkuppe followed by a record-setting 6,006-foot glide straight down the slopes into an adjoining valley.

Aviation history was made again in 1921 during the second German national glider competition at Mount Wasserkuppe. With the exception of Klemperer's distance record set the year before, all previous glider flights had been of relatively short duration and had been flown in a generally straight line down the slopes of the mountain. But at the 1921 meet there appeared Fredric Harth, the glider pilot who is credited with mastering the art of slope soaring and putting an end to the era, for the Germans at least, of simple downhill skysliding.

Harth brought to the 1921 meet a refined lightweight glider similar in appearance to the one in which Klemperer had made his record flight the preceding year. Harth had built his glider with the assistance of Willi Messerschmitt, a then unknown 23-year-old aircraft designer who would later give Germany the Messerschmitt Bf 109, one of the most deadly fighter planes ever to see combat during World War II. The main difference between Harth's glider and all of its predecessors was that it had several special features designed into it which gave it a theretofore unheard of 1 to 16 glide ratio. That is to say, for every foot of altitude it lost during flight it would fly 16 feet forward.

[12]

While at the controls of his glider, Harth managed to fly across the widest part of the mountain where he effortlessly rode the invisible crest of wind being deflected upward by the smooth broad slopes. Meet officials stood watching in amazement as Harth repeatedly banked and circled his glider so as to continue riding the brisk slope winds. Some 21½ minutes after he had been launched, Harth finally landed to the cheers of other contestants, and even the meet officials, all of whom recognized that the new art of slope soaring had been mastered right before their eyes.

Though they had not yet found the key which would unlock the mystery of true soaring flight, the early remarkable achievements of German glider pilots at Mount Wasserkuppe, and their subsequent publication throughout Germany, made glider flying one of the most popular sports in that country as early as 1921. All of the young German glider pilots looked upon their sport as an enjoyable hobby. But there were other Germans who viewed the increasingly growing number of glider clubs as excellent sources of power pilot candidates when and if the day came when Germany could re-form a powered combat air force.

One military-minded German civilian who held that view was Hermann Göring, a highly decorated World War I fighter ace with 22 kills to his credit, who was still smarting over his country's defeat in that war. Along with many of his friends and countrymen, Göring looked forward to the day when Germany would again take up arms to avenge the defeat it had suffered in World War I. Göring and others like him made no secret of their militaristic aims for the future. Early in 1922 when Captain Edward V. Rickenbacker went to Berlin on business, he was entertained by four German ex-fighter pilots who had fought against him in France. One of those four pilots was Göring. In his book, *Seven Came Through*, Rickenbacker had this to say concerning a conversation he had with Göring during their 1922 meeting:

> Göring said something I still remember. He said: Our whole future is in the air. And it is by air power that we are going to recapture the German empire. To accomplish this we will do three things. First, we will teach gliding as a sport to all our young men. Then we will build up commercial aviation. Finally we will create the skeleton of a military air force. When the time comes, we will put all three together – and the German empire will be reborn.[3]

At the time Göring made his ominous forecast of future world events to Rickenbacker, he was an embittered World War I veteran

[13]

employed as a sales representative for a German parachute manufacturing firm. As such he was powerless to change the desperate situation his country was in. However, elsewhere in Berlin at that time there was another distinguished veteran of World War I who had already set in motion a series of events which would eventually lead to the rebirth of German military and industrial might. That man was General Hans von Seeckt, head of the meagre 100,000-man Reichswehr army allowed Germany by the allied nations.

Along with all other German combat veterans of World War I, Von Seeckt had been greatly angered by the harsh political and military provisions of the Treaty of Versailles. As commander of the Reichswehr, Von Seeckt was determined to do everything within his power to see that Germany would not forever remain isolated in international politics and an impotent, second-class military power, as was the wish of the allied nations. From the moment he assumed command of the Reichswehr in 1920, the general began conspiring to use its members as a cadre for the new German army when the time was ripe for its rebirth and expansion.

Under inflexible guidelines established by Von Seeckt, only the most highly educated sergeants and officers who had proven themselves to be effective leaders and courageous under fire during World War I were permitted to remain on active duty in his greatly reduced peacetime Reichswehr. Jews, communists, socialists, and even outspoken democrats were all automatically excluded without regard for their previous military service, no matter how exemplary it might have been. Once he had selected the members of his private club, the general saw to it that their food and living conditions were improved, pay was increased, and that emphasis was placed on sports and other recreational activities for the troops. Von Seeckt next established a series of military schools and rigorous training exercises that all members of the Reichswehr were required to attend on a frequent basis. Thus, within a few months of its formation in 1920, the elite cadre force that was the Reichswehr had begun a vigorous training and educational course which its commander felt would prepare it to serve Germany well in better days to come.

In 1921 Von Seeckt, without the knowledge of the German government, negotiated a clandestine mutual military assistance pact with an unlikely ally, the Soviet Union, against whom Germany had fought bitterly during World War I. The pact had been made at the request of Nikolai Lenin, leader of the successful communist revolution of 1917 in Russia. Under the terms of the pact, German military and civilian advisers would assist Russia in rebuilding her armaments industry and modernizing her army along the lines of the highly efficient German military forces. In return, the Reichswehr would receive periodic secret shipments of Russian-manufactured heavy offensive weapons, which it was forbidden to have under the Treaty of Versailles. Another provision of the pact permitted the Reichswehr to send selected officers to Russia to receive training on the aircraft, tanks, and heavy artillery being developed there by German weapons experts.

Numerous American, British and French military observers were stationed in Germany for the sole purpose of enforcing the terms of the Treaty of Versailles. General Von Seeckt and his associates in the Reichswehr Ministry had to exercise extreme caution and deception to keep their deal with the Russians secret. At Von Seeckt's direction, a select group of staff officers set up business in an isolated area of his Berlin headquarters building in September of 1921. Operating under the cover name of Sondergruppe R (Special Group R), those staff officers coordinated the many secret German manufacturing and military assistance programmes going on inside Russia. During that same month, Von Seeckt sent Colonel Oskar von Niedermayer to Russia in civilian clothes to open an office there called Zentrale Moskau (Moscow Central). Von Niedermayer's role was essentially that of an unofficial German army military attaché. Just as quickly as he opened his place of business in Moscow, Von Niedermayer energetically went about his duty of coordinating activities of all Germans then operating in Russia.

The secret collaboration that had existed for a year between Germany and Russia was formalized in 1922 when those two countries signed the Treaty of Rapallo. Ostensibly the treaty was a formal renewal of friendship between the two countries. By signing the treaty, each party agreed to a mutual renunciation of war reparations claims, establishment of German–Russian trade, and the immediate resumption of diplomatic relations. Germany's surprise announcement of the treaty's signing shocked the nations of Europe, all of whom rightly thought that no good would come to them because of it. On its surface, the Treaty of Rapallo contained nothing frightful to the Allies, but a secret protocol formally legalized the existing year-old mutual military assistance pact between Germany and the Soviet Union.

[15]

Thus several teams of German military and civilian advisers had been providing technical know-how to Russian military and industrial leaders when, in 1923, the Soviet government began encouraging its citizens to take an active interest in glider flying. A government-sponsored national glider meet was held that year in Russia. Though only nine gliders participated in that first meet, their nationally publicized meagre accomplishments served to stimulate an avid interest in gliders throughout Russia. Within the next few years, glider flying would gradually become a popular sport in the Soviet Union.

Starting in 1923 the Allied Control Commission that had been closely monitoring all German activities since 1920 began to relax some of the more stringent provisions of the Treaty of Versailles which had been retarding Germany's industrial recovery from World War I. One of the first things the commission did was to allow Germany a limited revival of its civilian aircraft industry. In less than a year, German airplane manufacturers were turning out small and large aircraft which they marketed not only in Germany but in many foreign countries. This rebirth provided a great stimulus to the air-minded youth of the country. As early as 1926, high-schools throughout Germany had glider clubs with experienced teachers who had been trained at the Mount Wasserkuppe gliding centre. Under the direction of these skilled instructors, thousands of young Germans trained on gliders to become future pilots of powered airplanes.

One of the acknowledged leaders of Germany's glider design, research and flying techniques during the mid-1920s was Professor Walter Georgii of the Rohn Rossitten Gesellschaaft Research Institute. During World War I, Georgii had served in the German Air Force's England Geschwader which had bombed London. An avid exponent of his country's early glider accomplishments, Professor Georgii managed to send small groups of German glider-flying instructors to Belgium, France, Hungary, Russia, and the United States as early as 1925 for the purpose of spreading the gospel and creating international interest in gliders. As a result of visits by those German instructors, interest in glider flying increased in some countries during the mid-1920s. But nowhere did it approach the popularity it enjoyed in Germany.

Today it is well known to pilots of motorless sailplanes that invisible cells of warm air, called thermal bubbles, continuously rise from heated surfaces of the earth, and that those cells grow larger as they rise into the atmosphere. But in 1926 what little there was then known of thermal dynamics had been limited to theoretical assumptions by meteorologists such as Professor Georgii. From his personal observations, Georgii knew that slow-moving cumulous clouds were visible evidence of air in motion and that dark cumulonimbus storm clouds produced violent updrafts inside their seething interiors powerful enough to rip the wings off an airplane. Starting in 1926, Georgii embarked upon a series of studies aimed at proving his theory that the same invisible air currents which gave motion to the clouds could also provide considerable lift to well-designed sailplanes and thereby give them an excellent chance of escaping from the restrictions of earthbound contour flying.

Another of Professor Georgii's theories was that advancing cold fronts swept across the earth like giant brooms, forcing warmer air in front of them to be sharply driven upward. This theory was proven conclusively by Johannes Nehring, an experienced pilot of both gliders and powered airplanes. At Georgii's request, Nehring flew a powered airplane into the squall line of an advancing cold front on June 29, 1928, turned off his engine, and continued flying for 15 minutes without losing altitude. From this experiment, Georgii deduced that sailplanes flown by skilled glider pilots should be capable of travelling in those same updrafts for as long and as far as the pilot dared to go.

An Austrian Jew named Robert Kronfeld made aviation history the following year when he proved what was to be for glider pilots the most significant of Professor Georgii's theories. It was a mild spring day on May 15, 1929, when Kronfeld was launched from Mount Wasserkuppe at the controls of his sophisticated Wien (Vienna) sailplane. Having observed a giant grouping of cumulous clouds drifting toward his launch site, Kronfeld had taken off in search of the rising thermal cells that Professor Georgii predicted would provide adequate lift to sailplane pilots looking for long distance flights. True to Georgii's predictions, Kronfeld felt his sailplane being gently lifted upward by the rising warm-air thermals beneath the clouds. By putting his sailplane through a series of spiralling turns inside the thermals, Kronfeld climbed to 6,700 feet, where he began a record-breaking flight that ended several hours later, 102 kilometres away from his take-off point. That historic flight by Kronfeld served to mark the point at which soaring was finally freed from the earth's contours.

[17]

A few days later, Kronfeld put on a parachute before climbing into his sailplane to prove Professor Georgii's danger-filled theory concerning sailplanes being capable of riding convective warm air currents swept forward by advancing cold fronts. Flying in cold air just ahead of the advancing squall line of a rainstorm, Kronfeld could hear loud thunder as he felt a strong surge of invisible power propel his sailplane forward and upward into warmer air. For the next four and one-half hours Kronfeld darted eastward across Germany just ahead of the rolling storm. Darkness eventually forced him to land at Hermsdorf, some 85 miles distant from Mount Wasserkuppe. For the second time that week this courageous pilot had made aviation history.

While all of these revolutionary glider and sailplane developments had been taking place in Germany during the 1920s, progress with those same types of aircraft had been extremely slow in the United States. Unlike the Germans who had been forced to use gliders as their only means of flying, the Americans were free to develop powered aircraft and had become so involved with them that they all but forgot gliders and glider flying. In June of 1922, the U.S. Air Service (forerunner of today's U.S. Air Force) conducted a few experiments at McCook Field in Ohio with miniature pilotless gliders that were then being considered for use as targets for airplanes and ground anti-aircraft guns. During those experiments, the small three-foot-long gliders were carried aloft on the upper wing of powered biplanes. Upon entering the target area, the pilot of the biplane would release the glider and then quickly fly away to safety as waiting attack airplanes or ground artillery commenced firing at it. Though the small free-flying glider performed its target duty well, it had one serious drawback. It could remain airborne for only a few minutes before either gravity or a direct hit forced it to the ground. For that reason the U.S. Air Service discarded miniature gliders in favour of large sleeve-shaped canvas targets that could be towed across the target area for several hours at a time.

Also at McCook Field in 1922, the U.S. Air Service experimented with a full-sized, single place glider designed by Jean A. Roche, a French-born American. But like the miniature gliders, Roche's creation was unable to remain airborne for a respectable length of time so the flight experiments were cancelled.

For those relatively few Americans who had an interest in gliders during the early 1920s, there was no national coordinating agency

[18]

such as the Germans then enjoyed. What little new glider design and construction took place in America was conducted by individuals who forged ahead without benefit of knowledge gained from similar experiments taking place in other states.

The most energetic glider experimenter on the west coast during the 1920s was William Hawley Bowlus. Originally from Illinois, Bowlus had moved to California with his family in 1909 at the age of 13. He had only been in California a year when he developed an interest in aviation and began building a series of biplane gliders of his own design. Following a tour of duty as an aircraft mechanic with the U.S. Air Service in France during World War I, he returned to civilian life and was subsequently employed by Ryan Aircraft Company in San Diego. Bowlus was plant manager of Ryan Aircraft in 1927 when the firm received a telegram from a Charles A. Lindbergh who was then an unknown air mail pilot. In his telegram, Lindbergh asked Ryan Aircraft if it could, in only 60 days, build a single engine airplane in which he intended to fly alone across the Atlantic Ocean. Ryan replied in the affirmative and, with Bowlus personally in charge of every detail of its construction, delivered the *Spirit of St. Louis* to Lindbergh within the required 60 days. Many special features incorporated into the design of that unique aircraft were originated by Bowlus.

While still employed by Ryan, Bowlus build his first sailplane, the *Falcon*, during his spare time at home. On October 19, 1929, he established an American soaring record with his aircraft by slope soaring for one hour and twenty-one minutes above Point Loma near San Diego. Shortly after that record flight, he left Ryan Aircraft and opened his own Bowlus Sailplane Company Limited. It was in a Bowlus sailplane that Charles Lindbergh won the ninth F.A.I. (Fédération Aéronautique Internationale) 'C' Soaring Certificate to be issued in the United States. With only a minimum of instruction in glider flying from Bowlus himself, Lindbergh took off on January 29, 1930, and soared above Point Loma for nearly an hour before gliding to a perfect landing. Not to be outdone by her famous husband, Anne Lindbergh, who was an accomplished flyer herself, took off in a Bowlus sailplane one week later from Soledad Mountain near San Diego and became the first woman in America to win a F.A.I. 'C' Soaring Certificate. Her certificate bears the number 10 and the signature of Orville Wright who was then serving as chairman of the National Aeronautic Association of the United States.

[19]

The first attempt by Americans to establish a nationwide glider pilot organization similar to the one the Germans had established in 1920 was finally made during the summer of 1929, when the National Glider Association was formed in Detroit with W. B. Mayo as its first president. Mayo's principal assistant in Detroit was Robert T. Walker, who was also the chief engineer of the aviation branch of the Ford Motor Company. One of the first things Mayo did as president of the National Glider Association was to begin a methodical search for an ideal location in the United States where the First National Glider contest could be held the following year.

Mayo initially thought of holding the contest right in Detroit because the financing necessary to support the enterprise was already available in that city. However, as a glider enthusiast himself, Mayo knew that it would take a lot more than money to produce a good contest. Suitable terrain and weather conditions were just as essential, and Walker knew that Detroit had neither.

Living in Akron, Ohio, at this time was Wolfgang Klemperer, winner of Germany's first national gliding contest. For the past several years, Klemperer had been employed as a design engineer in the Goodyear Rubber Company's aviation department. Because of Klemperer's longstanding reputation as a glider expert, Walter Mayo contacted him and asked him to help select a suitable site for America's first national glider contest. Klemperer agreed and immediately undertook the study of topographical maps of many likely areas in Tennessee, Virginia, Ohio, Vermont, Connecticut, Pennsylvania, and the Finger Lakes region of western New York State.

During his visit to the New York area, Klemperer was entertained by two men prominent in the field of aviation. One of them was Sherman P. Vorhees of Elmira. Vorhees was chairman of the aviation committee of the Elmira Association of Commerce and also the director of schools for the General Aviation Company based at Elmira's Southport airport. The other man was Warren E. Eaton of Norwich, New York. During World War I, Eaton had won the Distinguished Service Cross while serving as a fighter pilot in France with the famed 103rd Aero Squadron. Following the war he returned to his family's pharmaceutical company but was soon back in the business of flying as the owner-manager of the Norwich airport. Among several aircraft he owned and often flew was a primary glider. Vorhees and Eaton took Klemperer on an extensive tour by car and airplane of several excellent glider take-off and landing sites at

[20]

Elmira. On the second day of his tour Klemperer became convinced that, of all the other areas he had previously inspected in the United States, Elmira was the most suitable location for glider flying in general and the best spot in the country for the first national competitions. Later that evening he sent a telegram to Walter Mayo in Detroit recommending Elmira. Mayo accepted the recommendation and soon started the wheels in motion for the contest to be held there.

Plans for a September 1930 national glider meeting at Elmira were still being discussed by the National Glider Association when the U.S. Navy decided to conduct an experiment of its own with a glider. Prior to that time, none of the armed services could envision any possible military use for a glider or soaring aircraft. But the U.S. Navy had come around to thinking that a glider might be of some use in conjunction with experiments it was then conducting with its fleet of enormous rigid airships.

The chief problem then faced by the skipper of an airship away from its base during foul weather was finding a suitable alternative emergency mooring site well outside the storm area. Whenever this situation occurred, it was the duty of the Airship Landing Officer to strap on an emergency parachute and jump to the ground with it. If the officer survived the parachute descent he next had to round up a crew of civilian volunteers who would grab on to ropes lowered from the airship and tie it down to whatever fixed or heavy objects they could reach. Though parachutes did provide a means of getting the landing officers to the ground during emergency situations, the navy considered them too risky for use at low altitudes and began looking to the glider as a more reliable vehicle for descents from all altitudes.

Late in December of 1929, the navy began preparations for the experimental release of a glider from an airship in flight. There being no suitable American glider available for the test, the navy purchased a German Prüffling (Graduate) secondary glider and mated it to the underside of the airship U.S.S. *Los Angeles* at Lakehurst Naval Air Station, located about 10 miles from the Atlantic Ocean in New Jersey. Successful ground testing of the glider release mechanism had just been completed when, on the bitter cold day of January 31, 1930, the *Los Angeles* began slowly climbing into the sky with the glider attached to her belly. When she reached the planned glider release altitude of 3,000 feet, her skipper levelled her off and steered directly into a brisk breeze blowing in off the ocean. The airspeed indicator of the *Los Angeles* had just reached 30 knots when the intrepid test pilot of the glider, U.S. Navy Lieutenant Ralph Stanton Barnaby, began to climb down a ladder leading from the wheelhouse to the glider. Having rehearsed his ladder descent many times prior to take-off, Barnaby experienced no difficulty manoeuvring himself into the open cockpit of the glider.

The U.S. Navy could not have picked a more qualified or dedicated test pilot than Lieutenant Barnaby for this dangerous experiment. Born on January 21, 1893, in Meadville, Pennsylvania, Barnaby was a career naval officer with a deep love of flying. His flying days stretched as far back as 1909, when he had successfully flown a hang glider that he had designed and built himself. In designing that glider, Barnaby was guided by photographs and newspaper articles that had been published about Otto Lilienthal, who had been killed in a soaring accident in Germany only 13 years previously. Later as a high-school student Barnaby had skipped a full week of classes to attend the second International Air Races held in Belmont Park on Long Island. While at Belmont Park, he was hired by Orville and Wilbur Wright to perform light maintenance work on their Baby Grand airplane that participated in the races.

Barnaby had entered the navy in 1917 when the United States became involved in World War I, and he had been pursuing a career as an aeronautical engineer. He had achieved national fame for a historic aviation feat only five months before the experimental flight that he was about to make from the belly of the *Los Angeles*. On August 18, 1929, at the soaring school operated by The American Motorless Aviation Corporation at South Wellfleet on Cape Cod, Massachusetts, Barnaby had managed to soar up and down the shoreline for 15 minutes and 6 seconds, breaking Orville Wright's record of 9 minutes and 45 seconds set at Kitty Hawk on October 24, 1911. For that record achievement Barnaby was presented the first F.A.I. 'C' Soaring Certificate ever to be issued to an American glider pilot. A few weeks later William H. Bowlus earned licence No. 2 out in California.

Barnaby had only been in the glider – still attached to the belly of the *Los Angeles* – for a few minutes when he felt his hands and feet growing numb from the intense cold being generated by the combined speed of the airship and a brisk breeze blowing in off the ocean. For a moment he considered cancelling the experiment because he doubted he would be able to operate the foot and hand controls of the glider with his nearly frozen limbs. But having got

[22]

that far he decided to continue rather than disappoint the airship crew and teams of ground observers who had come all the way from Washington.

Shaking from the bitter cold now, Barnaby managed to keep his eyes on the airspeed indicator of the glider. When it reached 40 knots he signalled the Engineering Officer, positioned only eight feet above his head in the wheelhouse, to trip the release mechanism. Much to Barnaby's relief the glider immediately dropped free of the mother ship. It responded perfectly as he put it through a series of descending turns. Thirteen minutes after he had been released from the airship, Barnaby skidded the glider to a halt in a snow-covered area beside the air station's main runway. Though his experiment had demonstrated that the glider was a reliable means of emergency transportation for airship landing officers, only one other such flight was conducted by the navy. What little military success the glider briefly enjoyed with the U.S. Navy in 1930 was soon forgotten when other experimentation conducted that same year proved the feasibility of hooking and unhooking powered airplanes to airships in flight. The next two airships to be commissioned by the navy, the *Akron* and the *Macon*, were both equipped to carry airplanes which could be launched and retrieved in flight.[4]

By the time Lieutenant Barnaby made his successful test glider flight from the belly of the *Los Angeles*, the art of towing gliders by airplanes had been fully perfected not only in the United States but in Germany and Russia as well. Only two months after Barnaby's flight from the airship, Frank Hawks, a nationally known airplane racing pilot, took off in California at the controls of a utility glider being towed at the end of a 500-foot rope trailing a Waco biplane bound for New York. This first coast-to-coast flight by a towed glider was strictly a publicity gimmick, the purpose of which was to awaken the nation's interest in cargo carrying gliders. The plan called for Hawks to deliver a sack of U.S. Mail to New York aboard the *Eaglet*, a red, white, and blue glider that had been manufactured by the Franklin Glider Corporation. After taking off from San Diego on March 30, the *Eaglet* made several stopovers at large airports on the way to New York, where crowds saw it land and take off again with its cargo. It was raining in New York when the *Eaglet* arrived there on April 7, 1930, at the end of its cross-country flight. Hawks cut the *Eaglet* loose from the tow-ship at 4,000 feet and glided to a smooth landing 16 minutes later before a cheering crowd of soaked onlookers. Immediately upon climbing out of the *Eaglet*, Hawks ceremoniously handed the sack of week-old mail to a waiting representative of the New York Post Office. Successful though it was, this first public demonstration of the cargo-carrying capabilities offered by utility gliders received virtually no press coverage. Except for a few local newspaper stories it received at stopover points along the way to New York, the remarkable flight of the *Eaglet* went largely unnoticed by the American public.[5]

What little general interest the American public then had in gliders was increased ever so slightly by the moderately good press coverage given the country's first national glider contest held at Elmira, New York, during the period September 21 to October 5, 1930. A total of 24 pilots turned up at Elmira to fly 14 gliders. When the contest ended, the United States had its own first national soaring champion in Albert E. Hastings of Los Angeles, California. Second place was won by Warren E. Eaton.

By 1931 the American glider movement had blossomed, despite the fact that the country was then still in a severe economic depression, because gliders offered an inexpensive means of sport flying to many thousands of air enthusiasts who could not afford to operate powered airplanes. And even though the entire country had fallen on hard times, no fewer than 10 companies managed to stay in business throughout the Great Depression by selling glider kits through the mail.

A considerable boost was given to the growing American glider movement in March of 1931 by Wolfram Hirth, one of Germany's best-known glider pilots. Earlier, in January, Hirth had approached both the New York City Police and Parks departments requesting their permission to fly his glider along Manhattan's Riverside Drive. The purpose of the flight, said Hirth, was to garner some publicity for the sport. After giving his written assurance that he would not fly beyond the limits of 150th and 172nd streets, Hirth received the required permits for the flight to take place on March 12. With the assistance of 20 men pulling an extra long shock cord, Hirth was launched out over the Hudson River at noontime from a small park located at 161st Street and Riverside Drive. Dozens of policemen held the huge crowd back as newspaper photographers snapped pictures of Hirth's glider rising in the upcurrents of air blowing over the Hudson River.

A mere 10 seconds after launch, Hirth had reached an altitude of

100 feet. Thirty seconds later he was looking down at the top of 12- and 15-storey buildings. When his altimeter registered 600 feet above the launch site, Hirth took off on a brief excursion down to 150th Street and back up to 172nd Street, keeping his promise to stay within those two limits. Finally, after 45 minutes of flying above the buildings of Manhattan, Hirth landed his glider smoothly and without incident beside the Hudson.

Following Hirth's spectacular promotional flight in New York, a number of American soaring enthusiasts began setting flight endurance records at various points around the country. In Hawaii, meanwhile, U.S. Air Corps Second Lieutenant John C. Crain set out to break all existing flight endurance records in a glider he had designed and built himself. Crain was then stationed at Wheeler Field on the island of Oahu. Since glider flying was not then officially sanctioned by any of the services, Crain had to make his record-breaking attempt during off-duty hours dressed in civilian clothes. With three chocolate bars and a canteen of black coffee stowed under the seat of his open cockpit glider, he was launched into the air from a cleared pineapple field overlooking Honolulu at 2:35 p.m. on Saturday, July 25, 1931. Supported by strong sea breezes being deflected upward by the steep cliffs along the edges of the island, Crain easily managed to stay aloft throughout the afternoon. Two of his friends, Lieutenants William A. Cocke and William J. Scott, shouted words of encouragement from below.

There was only a faint glimmer of daylight left from the setting sun when Lieutenant Crain began to turn his glider away from the cliffs toward the landing field. Just then his friend Lieutenant Scott yelled up the news that an officer from the nearby battery of the 64th Coast Artillery Regiment had offered to provide searchlight illumination of the dangerous cliffs if he wanted to attempt remaining aloft throughout the night and land in the morning. Though he had not made preparations for such a long flight, Crain immediately yelled back, 'Have them turn on the searchlights, I'll give it a try.'

The long night hours dragged by as Crain fought to remain awake and keep his glider from crashing into the illuminated cliffs. All searchlights were turned off at sunrise when it was expected that Crain would land. But to the amazement of his sleepy-eyed friends on the ground, Crain ignored their pleas that he land at once before exhaustion and disaster overtook him. Finally, at 7:12 a.m., he set the glider down in the same field he had been launched from the preceding day. Unfortunately for Lieutenant Crain, he had not arranged for official observers to witness what turned out to be his record overnight soaring flight of 16 hours and 38 minutes. His great feat of endurance flying was therefore ruled ineligible for entry into the record books.

During the summer of 1931, glider flying became a favourite sport of off-duty servicemen stationed at isolated military bases around the United States and overseas. Having very few off-duty recreational activities available to them at their bases, hundreds of servicemen chipped in with friends to purchase primary training gliders which were then still being sold in kit form by American airplane manufacturers. Being complete novices at glider flying, many of those servicemen were seriously injured in crashes while attempting to teach themselves how to fly their fragile aircraft. This resulted in an order being issued that year by Secretary of War Patrick J. Hurley forbidding all forms of glider flying by off-duty military personnel.

Nearly every state in the union could boast of its own glider club in 1932 when the National Glider Association went out of business and was immediately replaced by the Soaring Society of America. With Warren E. Eaton as its first president, the Soaring Society of America was formed specifically to organize the country's third annual soaring contest to be held in July of 1932 at Elmira. However, the society remained in existence following that contest and soon became nationally recognized as the chief representative of soaring and gliding in the United States. Under Eaton's direction the organization flourished and its membership grew. Because of its demonstrated leadership of the American sport glider movement, the Soaring Society of America was granted authority in 1932 by the Fédération Aéronautique Internationale to officially document all soaring and gliding records established in the United States.

Early in 1933, the U.S. Navy decided to incorporate glider flying into the primary flying course it was then giving to naval aviation cadets at Pensacola, Florida. The navy made that decision based on a suggestion offered by its own Lieutenant Barnaby, the glider pilot who had made headlines three years earlier with his daring experimental flight from the U.S.S. *Los Angeles*. It was Barnaby's opinion that a powered airplane was nothing more than an expensive glider with a gasoline engine mounted on it, and that when it quit running at several thousand feet up in the sky the pilot ought to know how to land it rather than abandon it to be ruined in a destructive crash.

[26]

Because of his reputation as the foremost military authority on glider flying, Barnaby was chosen to be the chief of glider instruction at Pensacola. He reported for duty in June of 1933 to set up the programme and to personally train his instructors. Throughout 1934 and 1935, selected members of each new class reporting to Pensacola for flight training underwent a month-long course in glider flying before moving into powered airplanes. Barnaby's glider programme was well received by both students and faculty at Pensacola. But in 1936 the programme had to be discontinued when the navy decided that the additional time and money being devoted to gliders was a luxury it could not afford during the Great Depression. It would take the passage of another five years and the coming of World War II before American military authorities would again be forced to experiment with gliders.

The ruggedly handsome Richard C. DuPont, a descendant of E. I. DuPont, founder of the giant DuPont Chemical Company, had been one of the first to join the Soaring Society of America when it was formed back in 1932. Unlike most Americans living in those lean Depression years, Richard DuPont was a man of considerable means who could easily afford to purchase the most sophisticated soaring aircraft then being manufactured in Germany. Because of his personal wealth and courage he was able almost singlehandedly to carry the burden of American soaring throughout the Depression when the majority of Americans thought they were wealthy if they had but a few dollars to spend on food to feed themselves. On June 25, 1934, at the age of 21, DuPont made American soaring history when he was launched from Harris Hill in Elmira, New York, and soared non-stop 158 miles to Basking Ridge, New Jersey. Long-distance sport soaring finally came of age in America with that record-setting flight by DuPont.

Ironically the first member of the fast-growing Soaring Society of America to die in a glider crash was its first president, Warren Eaton. On December 1, 1934, Eaton fell to his death from the glider he was piloting during a flying demonstration in Miami, Florida. He was replaced as president by Lieutenant Ralph S. Barnaby, U.S. Navy, who was then still teaching at Pensacola.

Later in 1934, Richard DuPont became America's fourth national soaring champion at Elmira. He won that title a second time in 1935, and nearly won it the third time in a row in 1936 but lost to 22-year-old Charles 'Chet' Decker who became champion that year.

[27]

Strange as it may seem, Decker won the championship in the *Albatross*, a used glider that had been sold to him by DuPont. Finally in 1937 DuPont realized his ambition to become the first three-time winner of the American national soaring competitions at Elmira. He won the championship that year in the *Mimimoa*, a sleek new German-built gull-winged sailplane designed by Wolfram Hirth, the same man who had piloted a glider over Manhattan in 1931.

DuPont became the third president of the Soaring Society of America in 1937. Shortly thereafter he installed his friend and fellow soaring enthusiast, Lewin B. Barringer, as general manager of the society. Though neither of them knew it at that time, both DuPont and Barringer would play vital roles in the future American military glider programme.

In far off Russia, meanwhile, many developments in both glider and soaring aircraft design had been taking place unbeknownst to the outside world. Starting in 1931, the Soviet government had decided to greatly expand its gliding and soaring programmes. At the Ninth Party Congress, held in January of that year, the Communist League of Youth passed a resolution urging all young Russians to take part in the expansion of existing glider programmes so that Mother Russia might capture as many soaring records as was humanly possible. Upon passage of that resolution, the government started construction of a glider factory near Moscow and convened a meeting in Koktabel where 80 of Russia's top aircraft designers assembled to discuss glider designs for the future. Of the many structural glider designs studied by that group, only seven were selected for construction and flight tests in the spring of 1932.

In what was a minor production miracle, the Russians had all seven prototype gliders available for testing right on schedule in 1932. During those tests Vladimir Stepanchenok established a new Russian soaring record by looping a G-9 glider 115 times during a single flight. Other Soviet pilots performed newly developed aerobatic manoeuvres and participated in long-distance airplane tows.

The undisputed star of the 1932 Soviet glider trials was the TsK Komsula, the world's first four-place transport glider capable of being towed by large airplanes. This unique aircraft had been specially designed by G. F. Groschev for long-distance hauling of either passengers or cargo. Two years later, in 1934, the Moscow glider factory produced another of Groschev's creations, the GN-4 glider which could comfortably carry five passengers in an enclosed cabin. Spurred on by these successes, the Russians started building larger transport gliders during the mid-1930s. Meanwhile the glider movement had become so popular in the Soviet Union that by October of 1934 ten gliding schools had been established and 57,000 Russians had become licensed glider pilots.

By 1935, the modernized Soviet military forces contained several battalions of parachute infantry that had conducted mass jump training exercises in the Moscow, Kiev and Belorussian military districts. Concurrent with the development of those parachute forces, the military institute at Leningrad produced a glider so large that it could comfortably seat 18 passengers. Elsewhere in Russia during this same period a bomber was refuelled in mid-air for the first time in history, using a rubber hose from a two-seat experimental G-14 fuel glider it was towing. The Russians were understandably proud of their new parachute units and large transport gliders – so much so that they displayed them to the interested eyes of visiting officers from the newly reborn German armed forces.

Ever since Adolf Hitler had become Chancellor of Germany on January 30, 1933, he had contrived to secretly build up a strong air force. Within a few months of assuming office, Hitler created a 'ministry of aviation' and placed his political croney, World War I fighter ace Hermann Göring, in charge of it. Working with great speed, Göring managed to quietly organize skeleton command and staff sections of clandestine Luftwaffe units under the noses of foreign military observers in Berlin.

Using less secrecy than was required for his undercover military units, Göring publicly gave orders in 1934 for the involuntary placement of all civilian glider clubs into the Deutsche Luftsport Verbund, a newly created subsidiary of his air ministry. The man Göring selected to head this new organization was an old comrade of his, Colonel Bruno Loerzer, who had shot down 45 Allied airplanes during World War I. Under Loerzer's direction, glider flying became a sport with a point in Germany. What had formerly been an enjoyable hobby was now a rigidly controlled, state-supported training activity, the object of which was to produce pilots for the soon-to-be-unveiled powered combat squadrons of the Luftwaffe.

Large black swastikas, the emblem of the Nazi party, had long been painted on tail sections of German sport gliders when in March of 1935 Hitler startled the world by bringing his Luftwaffe units out into the open, complete with their own new dark blue uniforms and flying badges. Simultaneously, he defiantly announced that Germany no longer considered itself bound by provisions of the Treaty of Versailles and, from that day forward, there would be compulsory military service in Germany.

The Allies did nothing to prevent Hitler from rearming Germany. Thousands of young men who had learned to fly gliders during the early 1930s eagerly joined Luftwaffe squadrons. One of those new glider-trained recruits was 23-year-old Adolf Galland, who soon became a fighter pilot. Later, in 1937, Galland would see his first aerial combat in Spain with the Condor Legion.[6] Still later, during World War II, he would become, at the age of 29, the youngest general ever to serve in the German armed forces and would be promoted to the post of commanding general of the Fighter Arm. While rising through the ranks he would shoot down no fewer than 103 Allied aircraft.

Military cooperation between Germany and the Soviet Union was still quite strong when, in September of 1936, Luftwaffe Colonel Kurt Student, the future father of Germany's World War II airborne troops, arrived in Moscow on official business. Student had great respect for the Russian air force. During World War I he had been a fighter pilot on both the Western and Eastern fronts. It was while he was flying on the Eastern Front that he had been shot down and seriously wounded by a Russian airman. Along with other selected officers, Student had remained on active duty in the Reichswehr since 1918. At the time of his trip to Moscow he was serving as chief of the German aviation experimental unit whose function it was to determine what type of equipment and aircraft should be a part of the new Luftwaffe. The main purpose of his visit to the Soviet Union was to see what military hardware and tactics the Russians had developed during the past few years.

Upon returning to Berlin, Colonel Student submitted a detailed report to his superiors concerning a massive 1,500-man parachute drop and some large transport gliders he had seen in Russia. Based on a recommendation contained in his report, the Luftwaffe opened its own jump school at Stendal early in 1937. Not quite a year later, Student was promoted to brigadier general and given command of the 7th Air Division, Germany's first experimental airborne division. Following numerous tactical training exercises, Student determined that the best task organization for his division was three parachute regiments consisting of three battalions each, and a separate battalion of engineer troops.

[30]

Further field testing with his new division convinced Student that he needed a vehicle which could deliver heavy weapons into airheads to be held by his lightly armed parachute troops. (The term 'airhead' refers to a specified geographical area within enemy territory which is to be seized by the attacking airborne forces and held to ensure the continuous delivery of reinforcements and material by air.) He thought of using gliders, but his idea was laughed at by general staff officers in Berlin. It was not until October 1938, when Student had been elevated to major general rank and appointed Inspector of Airborne Forces, that he was able to pursue the notion of using gliders. He did so at the Darmstadt Airborne Experimental Centre, which was also under his control as the Inspector of Airborne Forces. Working in cooperation with aviation technicians provided by General Ernst Udet, chief of the Luftwaffe's Technicians Office, Student and his airborne troops began final experimentation at Darmstadt in November 1938 with a glider designed in 1932 by Dr. Alexander Lippisch and Professor Walter Georgii as a flying observatory for high altitude meteorological tests. When first flown as a civilian aircraft in 1932, the glider had been designated the OBS Flying Observatory. Because of its large size the glider had eventually attracted the attention of General Hans Jeschonnek (chief of the Plans and Operations Division on the Luftwaffe General Staff) and of General Udet, both of whom exerted pressure for development of an even larger model capable of carrying armed combat troops. The development of the troop transport glider, classified as secret, had been assigned to Hans Jacobs, an aircraft designer on the staff of the Deutsche Forschungsanhalt Für Segelflug (DFS), a subsidiary of the Rohen Research Institute. By January 1937, Jacobs and his associates had perfected what was designated the DFS 230, a very large glider that looked like an airplane without an engine. Weighing 1,800 pounds, the DFS 230 had a wingspan of 72 feet and a length of 37.5 feet. It was flown by a single pilot and could carry nine fully equipped soldiers or 2,800 pounds of cargo.

Designed to be towed by the three-motored Ju 52, workhorse of the Luftwaffe, the DFS 230 had a steel tubing framework covered by fabric. Its wings were constructed of stressed plywood with spoilers located on their upper surfaces to steepen the angle of glide. On take-off, the glider jettisoned its set of front wheels; it would land on a single ski-like skid extending from its nose to about the midpoint of its belly. The Germans, unlike other nations during World War II,

[31]

considered all of their gliders to be combat aircraft. Accordingly, they armed the DFS 230 with a light machine gun to protect itself in flight and to cover ground debarkation of passengers in enemy territory.

Flight and field landing tests of the DFS 230 glider were completed at Darmstadt in February of 1939 by General Student and his airborne troops. Initially, Student was not favourably impressed by the DFS 230, but he eventually became convinced that it would be a good vehicle for long-distance transporting of both troops and equipment. Shortly after those tests, the DFS 230 was ordered into production. Manufacturing contracts were signed by officers of the Gothaer Waggonfabrik, the same company that had built the gigantic twin-engined Gotha G-IV bombers used to terrorize London and Paris during World War I. At the time this company received the glider contract it was manufacturing rail-road passenger and cargo cars.

General Student had still been in the final phases of testing his parachute troops and the DFS 230 glider when, late in 1939, he received orders directly from Adolf Hitler to prepare his airborne troops for battle. Having easily subdued Poland by force of arms that September, Hitler was making preparations to launch a massive surprise attack in the spring of 1940 against Belgium, Holland and France. Hitler had kept the existence of his new airborne units secret during operations in Poland. But he planned to make maximum use of their surprise and shock effect during his forthcoming assault against the West.

German staff officers whose duty it was to prepare detailed written plans for the attack against the West were personally instructed by Hitler concerning objectives to be seized by Student's airborne troops. At Hitler's direction, several parachute and air landing zones were plotted at key points in Holland and Belgium. Though all objectives were deep behind enemy lines and promised to produce hard fighting, none guaranteed more difficulty than the one plotted at Fort Eban Emael, Belgium's seemingly impregnable bastion positioned along the Albert Canal just forward of the Meuse River. The fort lay squarely in the path of the panzer columns that were scheduled to burst out of Germany on the opening day of the assault and penetrate to the Meuse River in Belgium. Once safely across bridges spanning the Meuse, the tanks were to begin their long northerly strategic thrust to outflank the Maginot Line in France.

[32]

Completed only in 1935 and equipped with the most modern military weapons, Fort Eban Emael consisted of six reinforced concrete walls enclosing a large grassy area measuring 800 by 1,000 yards. Atop the walls were several machine gun bunkers and anti-aircraft artillery cupolas, each of which had protected searchlights for illuminating night targets. Scattered around the grassy interior area of the fort were twelve huge steel-plated rotating cupolas and reinforced concrete casemates. Each contained heavy artillery pieces which could deliver aimed fire not only on roads leading to the fort and surrounding towns but on all approaches to bridges crossing the Meuse River located to the flanks and rear of the fort. A force of 780 Belgian soldiers under the command of Major Fritz Lucien Jottrand manned the fort. When not on duty they lived in spacious, air-conditioned underground quarters deep beneath the artillery blockhouses resting on the grassy plain. Jottrand's troops could walk to any part of the fort through an elaborate system of underground tunnels.

Hitler and his staff officers reckoned that it would be nearly impossible for conventional ground units to capture Fort Eban Emael in less than two weeks' time. So an exceptionally bold plan for the capture of the fort and its nearby bridges was conceived by Hitler himself. It called for three assault parties, code-named Iron, Concrete and Steel, to land by glider on O-Day (the German equivalent of D-Day) to capture bridges crossing the Meuse River at Canne, Vroenhoven, and Veldwezelt respectively. Simultaneously, a fourth assault party, code-named Granite, would land in gliders on the large grassy plain inside Fort Eban Emael and overpower the defenders before they had time to react.

The mission of capturing Fort Eban Emael and the nearby bridges crossing the Meuse River was assigned to a small force from General Student's 7th Air Division code-named Assault Group Koch. Named for its commander, Captain Walter Koch, the force consisted of only one company of paratroopers from the 1st Parachute Regiment and a paratroop engineer platoon led by Lieutenant Rudolf Witzig. Preparations for what was to be the first gliderborne assault in the history of warfare began in November 1939 deep within the secluded German military training area of Hildesheim. Splitting the paratroop company into three detachments, Captain Koch had each group rehearse numerous glider landings and ground assaults on dummy wooden bridges simulating the real ones crossing the Meuse

[33]

in Belgium. Elsewhere in that same training area Lieutenant Witzig, leader of the assault party that was to land inside the fort, had his troops rehearse attacks on wooden blockhouses laid out in the exact pattern that appeared in aerial photos taken of the fort by German spy planes.

Winter passed into spring and, on May 10, 1940, Hitler loosed his armed forces against the West. Starting at 4:30 a.m. that day, forty-one Ju52s each towing a fully loaded DFS 230 glider began taking off in darkness from Cologne's two airfields, Butweilerhof on the left bank of the Rhine River and Ostheim on the right bank. In ten minutes, Task Force Koch was airborne and heading for its objectives in Belgium. Every detail of this daring gliderborne attack had been worked out to perfection. Plans called for the Ju52s to follow a 45-mile-long string of ground navigation beacons that would lead them westward to the German frontier city of Aachen. There, at an altitude of 8,500 feet, all of the DFS 230s were to be released just as the morning sun would be sending its first rays across the country-side. Having a glide ratio of 12 to 1, the DFS 230s were then expected to silently glide down to their assigned objectives some 20 miles inside Belgium, unheralded by the noise of the Ju52s engines.

As so often happens during the execution of well-laid plans, Task Force Koch experienced trouble shortly after take-off. The pilot of the Ju 52 towing the last of eleven gliders belonging to Granite – the force that was to land inside Fort Eban Emael – suddenly noticed the blue exhaust flames of another airplane that appeared to be on a collision course with him. He instinctively put his airplane into a steep dive to avoid a crash but in so doing snapped the glider tow-rope in two. The dumbfounded glider pilot, seeing that his tow-rope had broken for no apparent reason, banked hard to his left in the darkness and guided the DFS 230 down to a remarkably smooth landing on the outskirts of Cologne. Ordinarily, such a mishap caused no great alarm to the task force commander, because accidents are expected and planned for during training and combat missions. However, the glider that had just become separated from the flock contained Lieutenant Witzig, the officer who was supposed to lead the assault of Fort Eban Emael.

Enraged at being sidelined, Witzig shouted orders at his men to start chopping down the few trees at the end of the meadow so that another airplane might land and lift them off again to catch up with the task force. Then he ran to a nearby road, commandeered the first

[34]

vehicle that came along, and raced back to his departure airport.

Lieutenant Witzig was still at the airport, frantically trying to round up another tow-plane, when the remaining ten gliders carrying his assault party began skidding quietly to a halt inside the walled expanse of grass that was the roof of Fort Eban Emael. Before the stunned Belgian defenders could react, Witzig's troops burst out of the gliders with guns blazing and ran toward their designated cupola and casemate targets. Several teams of the attacking Germans were carrying shaped charges, a newly developed explosive device which could blast a hole through steel plates and reinforced concrete. Covered by machine-gun fire from their gliders, the Germans climbed on top of the casemates and cupolas where they emplaced the shaped charges and lit the fuses. Seconds later the explosives detonated, killing several occupants of the targets and sending jets of molten steel deep into the bowels of the fort. Having thus destroyed all of the casemates and cupolas within minutes of their arrival, Witzig's troops attacked the wall defences from inside the fort. A wild shoot-out ensued at close quarters, and the Germans quickly overpowered the dazed Belgians. Only 20 minutes after landing, Witzig's troops had accomplished the impossible by neutralizing the fortress at a cost of only six dead and 20 wounded. A state of confusion still existed inside the fort as late as 8:30 that same morning when a lone Ju52 appeared overhead towing a glider. Suddenly the glider parted company with the Ju52 and dived sharply down to a hard landing inside the fort. Out of it stepped a red-faced Lieutenant Witzig, still in a great state of anger, to belatedly take command of his troops.

Meanwhile outside the fort, 30 DFS 230s carrying Captain Koch and the other three German glider assault parties had landed along the Meuse River to seize the bridges at Vroenhoven, Canne and Veldewezelt. Only at Canne did the Germans fail to rapidly carry out their mission; an alert Belgian sergeant there had blown up the bridge when he saw the gliders landing. The other two bridges were captured intact in less than a half hour at a cost to the attacking Germans of 15 killed and 39 wounded. Later that same morning, long German tank columns rumbled past Fort Eban Emael unmolested, crossing secured bridges over the Meuse on the first leg of their deep thrust into northern France.

For sheer audacity and shock effect, nothing like the swift glider-borne assault carried out so effectively by Storm Group Koch had ever before happened in any war. Nevertheless, Hitler chose to keep its sensational battle accomplishments secret so that he might use gliders again in the future with equal success.

Hitler personally decorated all paratroopers who had demonstrated heroism in and around Fort Eban Emael in Belgium. But photographs of those medal presentations appeared in German newspapers alongside others showing airborne troops who had seen combat in Holland, giving the impression to civilians that their honours had been earned in that country and not in Belgium.

The tight security lid that was clamped on events at Fort Eban Emael by Hitler was loosened following the collapse of France in June 1940. It was then that Hitler gave permission for Japanese and other selected foreign military attachés to be taken on a guided tour of the battlefields in the west where his German forces had been so victorious. Shortly after that tour, the U.S. Military Intelligence Division of the War Department received reliable information that German gliderborne forces had quickly captured Belgium's vital Fort Eban Emael during the same time that other parachute and air landing units had been enjoying great success up in Holland. Not yet at war themselves, the Americans failed to grasp the importance of the glider as a combat weapon and did nothing with the intelligence report except to file it.

The Americans did, however, see some possibilities for parachute troop units in their own army. On June 25, 1940, a call went out for volunteers from the 29th Infantry Regiment stationed at Fort Benning, Georgia, to serve in a test platoon that would conduct experimental parachute jumps. Two weeks later the test platoon of infantry volunteers began its jump training at Fort Benning's small airfield under the supervision of U.S. Army Air Corps parachuting instructors.

Japanese generals were so impressed by the startling accomplishments of German airborne divisions that they began experimentation with both parachute and glider troop units only one month after the fall of Fort Eban Emael. Later in 1940 the Japanese army would activate two airborne infantry divisions, each containing one regiment of parachute troops and two regiments of glider troops.[7]

British civil and military authorities had also been greatly impressed by the dazzling efficiency of German airborne divisions. Much to his credit, Prime Minister Winston Churchill reacted quickly to the German initiative in this newest form of warfare. In

June of 1940 he ordered the creation of a 5,000-man parachute force and an experimental glider unit. Later that same month the General Aircraft Company Ltd. began constructing the first transport glider to be produced on the Allied side during World War II. Designated the Hotspur Mark I, it was a mid-wing cantilever monoplane with a wingspan of 62 feet and an overall length of 39.7 feet. In addition to the pilot it could carry seven fully equipped troops, two less than the German DFS 230 glider employed at Fort Eban Emael.

With virtually all of western Europe now in his grip, Hitler issued his famous Führer Directive No. 16 on July 16, 1940, dealing with preparations for a landing operation on English soil. Code-named Seelöwe (Sea Lion), this operation was to be spearheaded by his now much favoured parachute and glider troops. The issuance of this directive prompted the design of two new impressive cargo gliders that were incorporated into the German aircraft inventory very early in the war. First of these was the Messerschmitt Me 321, still the largest operational glider ever built. Aptly nicknamed the Gigant (Giant) by its German designers, this immense glider had a wingspan of 181 feet, was 93 feet long, and could carry an incredible 24 tons of cargo, or a Pz. Kw IV tank,[8] or 200 fully equipped troops. Test flown for the first time on February 21, 1941, the Me 321 performed satisfactorily, but its four-engined Ju 290 tow-plane ate up over 4,000 feet of runway before getting it airborne.

In an attempt to get their huge glider into the sky more quickly, the Germans began experimenting with two very unusual launch methods. First they tried hitching three twin-engined Me 110 fighters (like three horses to a single carriage) by two ropes to the nose of the glider. That method proved unsatisfactory because power differences between the tow-planes nearly pulled the glider apart while in flight.

The Germans next developed a unique glider tug called the He 111Z. This odd-looking aircraft was actually two twin-engined Heinkel He 111 bombers that had been fused together at their wingtips. A fifth engine had been grafted onto the wing junction, and the pilot sat in the port fuselage. Given the name of Zwilling (twin), the He 111Z proved to be the perfect tug for the Me 321 glider.

Far smaller than the Me 321 Giant was the versatile high-winged, twin-boom Gotha Go 242 glider. Capable of carrying either four tons of cargo or 22 combat troops, the Go 242 had a wingspan of 79 feet and an overall length of 52.5 feet. Bulky equipment such as artillery

[37]

pieces and light trucks could be loaded in the central cargo nacelle through the rear of the fuselage, which was hinged at the top and could be raised to facilitate rapid loading and unloading. When the invasion of England eventually had to be cancelled, both the Me 321 and the Go 242 gliders were deployed to the Russian front and used there in great numbers to haul weapons, ammunition, troops, and even horses into the forward combat areas.

Throughout the summer of 1940, during which the Germans, the Japanese, and the beleaguered British were making such great strides in the development of their glider programmes, none of the American armed forces had a single glider. Nor did any of them contemplate ever using them, for any purpose. Alarmed by the rise of dictators in Europe, the bombing of England by the Luftwaffe, and darkening war clouds in the Far East, the Americans were then too caught up in a frantic manufacturing race to arm themselves and their allies with powered airplanes even to consider gliders.

As the political and military situation around the globe worsened during the first months of 1941, more and more intelligence reports filtered into the U.S. War Department about the rapidly expanding German glider programme. With each passing day, the likelihood of American involvement in the war was growing stronger. On Tuesday, February 25, 1941, Major General Henry H. 'Hap' Arnold, Chief of Army Air Force, finally announced that, 'In view of certain information received from abroad, a study should be initiated on developing a glider that could be towed by an aircraft.'[9]

A staff officer in Arnold's headquarters, learning of his boss's decision, casually remarked to a friend, 'Based on what we've been hearing for a long while around here about the German glider programme, it looks like we've got a lot of catching up to do.' Overhearing this remark, General Arnold shot back, 'Yes, we are indeed getting a late start. But better late than never. Now let's get going!'

With those words of General Arnold's the most controversial training and procurement programmes ever to be undertaken by any of the American armed services, before or after World War II, got under way.

# Chapter 3

## *Growing Pains*

OFFICIALS OF THE AIR CORPS'S experimental aircraft test centre at Wright Field in Ohio were already overworked when, on March 4, 1941, they received an urgent classified memorandum from General Arnold's office in Washington. In the opening paragraph Arnold said that he wanted a team of flight engineers to design a glider capable of 'transporting personnel and *matériel* and seizing objectives that cannot normally be reached by conventional ground units.'[1]

In what was an obvious plan to copy German military glider developments, Arnold went on to say that the glider had to be capable of being towed either singly or in pairs, and of carrying between 12 and 15 troops plus four portable machine guns with 500 rounds of ammunition for each gun, or an equivalent weight in cargo. The anticipated mission of such a glider, said Arnold, would be to land self-contained combat teams behind enemy lines.

Design engineers at Wright Field were beginning their conferences concerning this 15-place glider when a second classified memo arrived from General Arnold's office. This one directed procurement officers at Wright Field to place immediate orders with civilian aircraft manufacturers for experimental models of 2, 8 and 15-place gliders. Such a great sense of urgency as this second memo conveyed did not seem unusual to officials at Wright Field. By this time they were accustomed to everything associated with the blossoming American national defence programme being on a rush basis. What distressed them was the memo's last paragraph, which stipulated that glider production orders could be placed only with civilian companies not already manufacturing powered aircraft. General Arnold had inserted that restrictive clause in the memo to ensure uninterrupted production at the large aircraft companies which were expanding to meet demands of both the American defence effort and the European war. Despite this obstacle placed before them, procurement officers at Wright Field managed as quickly as March 8 to send letters containing detailed engineering requirements for 2, 8, and 15-place gliders to 11 small aircraft manufacturing companies. The letters invited each of the companies to build and submit prototypes for evaluation at Wright Field.

It is surprising that of the eleven companies contacted, only four of them (Bowlus Sailplanes, Inc., of San Fernando, California; Frankfort Sailplane Company of Joliet, Illinois; St. Louis Aircraft Corporation of St. Louis, Missouri; and Waco Aircraft Company of Troy, Ohio) sent positive replies. Most of those who declined sent lengthy explanations of previous production commitments or said that the 15-place glider was too large for their facilities. A few of the manufacturers were less diplomatic and said bluntly that they did not want to get involved in a chancy experimental venture associated with large transport gliders whose airworthiness was unproven. These first rejections in what would become a series of rebuffs by established aircraft manufacturers were merely the earliest of the many obstacles which would retard the development of the fledgling American glider programme.

As the four interested companies prepared their estimates of cost and delivery times for experimental glider models, General Arnold and several influential members of the U.S. Congress flew to Elmira, New York, for a one-day cram course on gliders and glider-flying techniques. There they were guests of the Elmira Area Soaring Corporation, a glider flying school that had just opened for business. Arnold and the congressmen witnessed a series of impressive demonstrations, including a single-engined Stearman airplane towing three Schweizer 2-place sailplanes. The glider flights that day were supervised by the school's chief instructor, John Robinson, winner of the 1940 United States National Soaring Competitions held at Elmira.[2]

Impressed by what he saw at Elmira, General Arnold returned to Washington pondering the fact that the Army Air Forces were heading into a complex glider development programme without benefit of any military experience. Thanks to its peacetime neglect of the military potential of gliders, and the existing 10-year-old ban on glider flying by off-duty personnel, the Army Air Forces had no one amongst their ranks to whom they could turn for advice about transport gliders.

In an effort to obtain at least some detailed knowledge of glider flying, Arnold fired off another memorandum to officials at Wright

Field. This one directed them to negotiate a contract with the Elmira Area Soaring Corporation for it to send John Robinson and other members of its faculty to Wright Field for the purpose of drawing up a programme of glider flying instruction for military power pilots. By the end of April, Robinson and his associates had travelled to Wright Field where they prepared a detailed 30-hour flying programme that met with the approval of military authorities there.

At Wright Field the development of gliders and their procurement from civilian manufacturers was a function of the Aircraft Laboratory, a part of the Experimental Engineering Section. The Glider Branch of the Aircraft Laboratory was commanded by Major Frederick R. Dent, Jr., a 1929 graduate of West Point and an accomplished power airplane test pilot. By the middle of May, Dent's organization had ordered 10 gliders (eight 2-place, one 8-place, and one 15-place) for static and experimental tests from the four manufacturers willing to do business with Wright Field. With all of those gliders scheduled for a June delivery, Dent sent a letter to General Arnold's office in Washington saying that glider pilots would have to be trained in order to carry on future development and service testing.

In response to Dent's letter, orders were issued from Washington for Dent and 11 other power pilots to take the 30-hour glider flying course put together by the civilian soaring champion, John Robinson. Dent and half of the officers would receive their training at Elmira, New York, from the Elmira Soaring Corporation; the other half would be trained in Lockport, Illinois, by the Lewis School of Aeronautics. Both groups were ordered to commence their training on June 1.

Before Major Dent and the other power pilots could begin their glider flying lessons, dramatic events occurred in the Balkans which were to have a profound influence on the embryonic American glider and parachute programmes. Mussolini had launched a massive ground and air attack against neutral Greece without first coordinating the operation with his German allies. Within three weeks after Italian troops began their assault from across the Albanian border, Greek forces commanded by General Alexandros Papagos had driven them back. Fearing a complete rout of his army, Mussolini appealed to Hitler for troop transport planes to ferry reinforcements to Albania. Hitler granted the request, but despite the arrival of reinforcements, Mussolini's infantry divisions could not get their stalled attack rolling again.

Rugged Greek mountain troops were threatening deeper attacks into Albania when Mussolini went to see Hitler a second time, for military assistance. By this time Hitler was furious with Mussolini, both for the ineptness of his troops and for his having caused British air and ground forces commanded by General Sir Henry M. Wilson to land in Greece to assist in the defence of the country. Hitler did not want British bombers on Greek airfields where they could strike the Rumanian oil fields he intended to use to fuel his panzers and airplanes during the surprise attack he was planning to launch against the Soviet Union in May. A detailed review of the deteriorating Italian position in Albania, and the rapid build-up of British warplanes in Greece, convinced Hitler to make his fateful decision to postpone the assault against Russia and attack Greece.

At dawn on April 6, 1941, a German combined air and ground force punched its way through the Metaxis Line in northern Greece. Picking up speed as they moved south toward the capital city of Athens, the German spearhead forces rolled over the Greek and British troops that got in their way. By April 20, the tactical situation became hopeless, and Papagos generously suggested to Wilson that all British forces be evacuated from Greece before his army disintegrated completely under the German onslaught. Three days later the Greek Army capitulated. With a portion of his courageous British Expeditionary Force rearguard detachment left behind to fend off German thrusts at historic Thermopylae Pass, Wilson ordered his remaining troops to withdraw to several seaports near Athens and on the Peloponnesus. For the next five nights the Royal Navy conducted a difficult and heroic Dunkirk-like evacuation, taking severe punishment from the Luftwaffe in the process.

Once they broke through the stubborn British defenders at Thermopylae Pass, German motorized infantry units raced south toward the seaports in pursuit of withdrawing Greek and British forces. In order for the withdrawing Greek and British units to get to the Peloponnesus and the Royal Navy's evacuation ships waiting there, they had to cross over the big iron bridge spanning the Corinth Canal. The German high command decided to stop the flow of traffic over that bridge by seizing control of it with a daring glider and parachute assault.

Shortly after daybreak on April 26, British troops defending the bridge at Corinth were subjected to an intense bombing and strafing attack by the Luftwaffe. The last dive bomber was just leaving when six DFS 230 gliders containing 36 German paratroopers cut loose from their tow-planes. Three of the gliders landed at the north end of the bridge; the other three skidded to a halt at the southern end. Before the stunned defenders could react, the Germans seized control of the bridge. Moments later, 40 planeloads of German paratroopers jumped near the bridge and began rounding up 2,371 Greek and British troops. The cost to the German airborne force was 63 killed, 158 wounded and 16 missing in action.

The swift German victory at the bridge suddenly went up in smoke when somewhere in the distance an unknown Greek or British soldier aimed his weapon in the general direction of the bridge and fired what has got to be the luckiest chance hit of the war. The round landed in a pile of demolitions that German paratroopers had just finished removing from the span, setting off a gigantic explosion. The blast dropped the bridge neatly into the canal along with several of the paratroopers who were standing on it congratulating themselves for having captured it intact.

The destruction of the Corinth bridge enabled the majority of Greek and British troops already across it to escape capture. In a dramatic rescue operation performed virtually under the noses of the pursuing Germans, the Royal Navy managed to evacuate a total of 50,662 troops from ports in Athens and on the Peloponnesus. Evacuees from Greece were deposited on Crete, a Greek-owned island 160 miles south of the mainland.

Although they stood victorious on the southern shores of the mainland, the Germans had not yet fought their final battle for control of Greece. With Crete still in British hands, RAF bombers stationed there could still reach Rumania's oil fields. For the Germans, it became essential that Crete be taken.

On the map, Crete resembles a large east-west sausage with a slight bulge in its middle. Measuring 170 miles long and 40 miles wide, it is the largest island in the Aegean Sea. Four chains of rugged mountain ranges, the smallest of which averages 4,500 feet in height, run the full length of Crete. Strategically placed along the northern shore of the island were three airfields with natural deep water harbours nearby. Because of its natural ruggedness the terrain of Crete heavily favoured the defending force.

For a brief period while his troops had been still fighting on the mainland of Greece, Hitler was of the opinion that Crete was not worth taking. His main objection to attacking Crete was that most of the air and ground force resources that would have to be committed

[43]

there were already scheduled for participation in the surprise invasion of Russia due to start on May 15. But argument from his Luftwaffe tactical advisers concerning the dangers posed by British bombers based on the island gradually brought him around to giving serious consideration to its capture. What little doubt remained in Hitler's mind was dispelled by General Kurt Student, the commanding general of all German airborne forces. During a visit to Hitler's headquarters on April 21, Student convinced his Führer that his airborne forces, operating alone, could capture Crete.

The plan that Student presented to Hitler called for glider and parachute forces to simultaneously seize all three airfields on the north coast of Crete. Once the airfields were in German hands, mountain infantry troops would be flown in to spread out like expanding oil spots until all three airfields overlapped. They would then push up and over the island's mountainous terrain to its southern shore, completing the capture. Hitler approved Student's plan and set May 20 as the date of the attack. Student was allotted 25,000 troops. Except for a few small Italian patrol boats, there would be no naval support. The airborne troops were going to have to capture Crete all by themselves.

The commander of all British Commonwealth troops on Crete was a stout-hearted New Zealander, Major General Bernard Freyberg. At 52, Freyberg was already a living legend because of his numerous feats of personal valour during World War I and the more recent battles against Rommel's Afrika Korps in Libya. During his encounters with German troops in two world wars, Freyberg had thus far been awarded the Victoria Cross and had been wounded in action no less than 12 times.

With the Royal Navy in control of the waters around Crete, Freyberg knew that any attack would have to come by air and be directed against one or more of the island's three north shore airfields. Because the Germans had already tipped their hand by employing airborne troops at Corinth, and the British spies on the mainland were reporting the arrival of many additional German airborne units, Freyberg knew what to expect. He accordingly disposed his combined British Commonwealth and Greek forces about the island, giving primary attention to the three airfields.

Well before first light on May 20 some 500 German transport planes and 74 DFS 230 gliders carrying paratroopers of the 7th Airborne Division started taking off for Crete from scattered airfields on the Greek mainland. In accordance with German airborne tactical doctrine, the gliders and their tugs preceded the paratroop planes. Generalleutnant Wilhelm Seussman, commanding general of the 7th Airborne Division, had chosen to personally lead the attack by riding in the glider positioned at the head of the flying column.

With typical German military efficiency the many separate sections of the flying column smoothly rendezvoused south of Athens just as the sun appeared on the horizon and headed out over the Aegean Sea for Crete. The column had been over water but a few moments when the glider in which General Seussman was riding could be seen to be going through a series of rapid diving and climbing manoeuvres. Unable to withstand the excessive stress of that porpoising action, the wings of the glider began twisting. A few moments later they both collapsed and the glider plunged into the sea. There were no survivors. The 7th Airborne Division continued flying toward Crete without its commanding general, whose death proved to be an omen of impending disaster for his division.

At his command post on Crete, General Freyberg had grown very suspicious. Ever since first light Luftwaffe planes had been conducting heavier than usual bombing attacks against the three airfields situated along the northern coast of the island. Shortly after 6:00 a.m. he placed all units on red alert and then waited for the next German move.

It came at 7:15 a.m. when a force consisting of 32 DFS 230 gliders began landing on and around Maleme, the westernmost airfield on the island. All of these German troops were under the command of Major Walter Koch, the same officer who had led the highly successful attack on Fort Eban Emael and its nearby bridges in Belgium. Unfortunately for Koch, this mission was to be very unlike the good times he experienced in Belgium. All around the airfield at Maleme were well-camouflaged New Zealand soldiers, heavily armed with automatic weapons. Koch's troops were just starting to climb out of their gliders when the New Zealanders opened fire. In seconds whole platoons of Germans were killed and their gliders set on fire.

Koch and his surviving troopers were still pinned down at Maleme when at 7:45 a.m. an almost endless stream of German planes appeared overhead and began dropping paratroopers directly into the murderous hail of New Zealand machine gun bullets. Hundreds

[45]

of paratroopers were killed before getting free of their harnesses. Yet in spite of these appalling losses a few of the determined attackers managed to gain a toehold on the airport before noon.

Fighting at Maleme had raged on into the afternoon when word reached Freyberg's headquarters that additional German glider and parachute troops were landing at Heraklion and Canea, Crete's other two airfields. The reports stated that German casualties at all three airfields were extremely heavy. In his situation report, the British commander at Heraklion stated that his defending troops found it nearly impossible to move among their positions because of all the dead and dying German paratroopers lying on the ground. But still the drops continued.

Darkness finally fell across Crete giving the badly mauled Germans a chance to recover slightly from the pounding they had endured all day long. During the night the New Zealand commander at Maleme lost radio contact with his forward units and his higher headquarters. This led him to wrongfully assume that his front line companies had been overrun. Knowing that his battalion was dangerously low on ammunition he ordered an immediate withdrawal of all units he could contact by foot messenger. His instructions were for all units to pull back to a point south of the airfield where he hoped to stop the Germans in the morning.

At dawn the disbelieving Germans at Maleme were thrilled to see that their enemy was gone. Word of the retreat was radioed back to General Student's headquarters in Athens. Later that same morning dozens of Ju 52 transports landed under fire at Maleme. Pilots kept their engines running as platoons of mountain infantrymen hastily disembarked and dispersed themselves along the sides of the concrete runways. As soon as the last soldier hit the concrete, the planes took off for the mainland to pick up troops of the second wave.

On the second day of the battle the tide began to turn in favour of the reinforced German airborne troops at Maleme. Resupplied with ammunition brought in by the airplanes, they launched vigorous attacks to enlarge their airhead so that additional reinforcements could be airlanded behind them. The same thing was happening at the other two airfields.

On the sixth day of the battle, May 26, General Freyberg radioed a message to his superiors in Egypt: 'In my opinion the limit of endurance has been reached by the troops under my command . . . our position here is hopeless.'[3] Coming as it did from such a fearless

[46]

combat leader, Freyberg's dire verdict went unquestioned at headquarters in Egypt, and starting on the 28th the Royal Navy began yet another heroic evacuation under constant air attack. A total of 15,000 British troops were safely evacuated to Egypt.

In what has been properly described by historians as one of the most surprising and courageous exploits of the war, Crete had been captured entirely by airborne forces. But the price had been horrendous. Of the 13,000 German troops that jumped and glided onto the island, 5,140 had been either killed or wounded in action. Luftwaffe aircraft losses were also very high. Of the 350 planes destroyed during the attack, half had been Ju 52 transports that would be sorely needed later in Russia. Hitler was so distressed by the casualty figures that he vowed never again to employ his airborne forces in large numbers.

Because of Hitler's decision against further massive glider and parachute attacks, and the exceedingly high casualties suffered there, Crete has become known as the graveyard of the German airborne. And much has been written about what might have happened if Hitler had not needed to send some of his finest troops to Greece in the first place to finish what Mussolini started. In the original timetable for Operation Barbarossa, the surprise attack on the Soviet Union, Hitler had planned to start his assault forces moving eastward in mid-May. He estimated that within six weeks of summer campaigning his combat veteran forces would bring the Russian Army to its knees, thus forcing the Soviet Union to surrender. However, operations in Greece obliged him to delay the start of Barbarossa by some seven weeks. As a result, when his attacking divisions were only approaching the outskirts of Moscow and Leningrad, the first early snows of what was to be the coldest Russian winter in many years were already starting to fall.

Unaware of the true extent of casualties suffered by the Germans on Crete, American and British strategists saw only the results. A lightly armed airborne force had flown nearly two hundred miles over the sea, attacked an enormous, mountainous island that was defended by a force over twice its own size, and had captured it in only eight days. The British and the Americans agreed that these results were both alarming and impressive. Here at last was proof positive that gliders could be used for something other than Sunday afternoon joy rides.

American and British military authorities were just beginning their study of the airborne assault techniques used by the Germans on Crete when, on June 1, the first 12 American power pilots to undergo glider flying training received their initial lessons at Elmira, New York, and Lockport, Illinois. At Elmira, Major Dent and his group received their instruction from John Robinson, who started them off in single-place Franklin utility gliders. The glider was towed across open fields by a car with the pilot required to keep the glider on the ground even though he had sufficient speed to fly. When he had mastered the glider's foot and hand steering controls the student was permitted to gradually climb to a maximum of 500 feet where he released the tow-rope to practise approaches and spot landings on the school's runway. After eight hours of flying time in the Franklin gliders, instruction was shifted to the 2-place Schweizer sailplanes. In the Schweizers, the students sat in the front cockpit, with the instructor behind them in the rear cockpit. After demonstrating flying proficiency the students were allowed to make solo flights in these sailplanes. Later, dual sailplane tows were made behind a Waco trainer airplane with a 220 horsepower Continental engine. Each student also completed eight hours as pilot of the Waco tug plane. The last part of the instruction programme consisted of a cross-country solo glider flight that ended at an airport 40 miles south of Elmira. A similar training programme was followed at the school at Illinois. Upon completion of their three week glider flying programme, both groups of officers returned to their parent units.

This early period of the American glider programme was characterized by the absence of a detailed plan for the future. In Washington the top military brass were now thoroughly convinced that the time had come for the American military forces to establish some sort of a glider echelon of its own, similar to the one the Germans had used so effectively in Belgium and now in Greece. However, as late as the end of June none of the military services could agree on the doctrine for employment of gliders, the composition of units to be formed, or the number of troops to be transported in the glider echelon.

The absence of firm planning guidance from the Army's Plans and Operations Division during this period of uncertainty angered General Arnold. He alone foresaw the enormous difficulties that would befall his service when it would be called upon – and soon – to suddenly produce pilots for the glider echelon then being discussed in Washington. As the Army's top airman and a former flying

[48]

instructor himself, Arnold knew that it would take considerable time to develop a staff of trained instructors. On July 7 he took the first step, ordering his chief of staff, Brigadier General Carl Spaatz, to expedite the preparation of a directive outlining requirements for 150 officer power pilots to be trained as glider instructors. Pearl Harbor was then exactly five months away.

On August 28, Arnold received from Spaatz a three-part plan concerning the glider pilot programme. Part one contained a recommendation for 21 of the 150 officer power pilots to start receiving their training during the last week of September at the Elmira Area Soaring Corporation's school in New York. In part two of his plan, Spaatz pointed out that the intensely cold New York winters made that state a poor location for year-round flying training of any type. He suggested that the balance of the 150 pilots be trained at some other civilian glider flying contract schools in the south and west where prevailing mild winter weather conditions would be more conducive to rapid progress in the glider programme.

In part three of his plan Spaatz had anticipated that the training of pilots would be necessary on a far larger scale once Washington decided on the ultimate size of the glider echelon. Painfully aware that the Army Air Force had no one in its ranks to conduct that training in the event of rapid expansion of the glider programme, Spaatz recommended that all elementary glider flying instruction be administered by civilian contract schools. He also recommended that one advanced military-run glider school be later activated with its flying instructors, key personnel, and cadre being comprised of the 150 officer power pilots that would undergo the initial elementary glider flying instruction at civilian schools.

Only four days after receiving Spaatz's plan, Arnold gave approval to all of its recommendations. Administrative machinery for the completion of the 150 Officer Power Pilot Programme was quickly put in motion. By the middle of September the officers to be trained by the Elmira Area Soaring Corporation had been selected, and a contract had been signed with the Twentynine Palms Air Academy in California for the training of the balance of the officers. According to the terms of that contract, the Twentynine Palms Air Academy was to start training its first class of military officers on November 30, 1941, and the final class in March 1942. With procurement of military gliders just getting under way, training at both the New York and California based schools was to be four weeks long during which

[49]

time each student was to be given 30 hours of flying time in sleek-bodied civilian sailplanes. As events were later to prove, the thermal soaring training that these officers received was of little value to them when they had to learn how to fly the larger military transport gliders.

Now that the groundwork had been laid for the 150 Officer Power Pilot Programme, and a final decision was expected shortly from the Army General Staff concerning the ultimate number of glider pilots needed, General Arnold began looking round for someone that he could bring to Washington to be in charge of the glider project. Having no one in uniform qualified to manage the project he selected a nationally prominent civilian soaring enthusiast, Lewin B. Barringer, who at that time was still serving as general manager of The Soaring Society of America at Elmira, New York, and as editor of the nationally circulated *Soaring Magazine*. Barringer was eminently qualified for the task of running the glider project. His own glider flying days stretched back to 1930. Only two years after his first flight he opened his own Wings Glider Flying School near Philadelphia. He first achieved national prominence on April 19, 1938, when he made what was for the Americans a record-setting soaring flight of 212 miles from Wichita Falls, Texas, to Tulsa, Oklahoma. More recently, he had gained international acclaim by soaring to a world record altitude mark of 14,960 feet over Sun Valley, Idaho, reaching an actual height of over 21,000 feet above sea level. In addition to his initial record-setting soaring feats, Barringer again had achieved international recognition in 1940 as the co-author of *Flight Without Power*, a book dealing with the history of glider flight and the current state of glider flying in Europe and the United States. Barringer accepted the job offer extended by General Arnold. On October 15, 1941, he reported to Washington where he assumed the newly created position of Glider Specialist in the Office of the Director of Air Support. Along with his title Barringer was given full charge of all matters pertaining to gliders. Later, in May 1942, he was given a direct commission at the rank of major by General Arnold.

Barringer was just getting settled into his new job in Washington when on Sunday, December 7, 1941, the Japanese plunged America into World War II with their sneak attack at Pearl Harbor in Hawaii. The masterfully planned and executed Japanese attack consisted of 363 planes launched from six aircraft carriers that had managed to steam unnoticed to within 275 miles of Hawaii. The first bombs fell at 7:55 a.m. just as the American base was coming to life for a quiet Sunday. When the last Japanese carrier plane flew away at 10:00 a.m. it left behind the burning ruins of the U.S. Navy's Pacific Battle Fleet which had been at anchor in the harbour. On nearby airfields over 200 U.S. Army and Navy airplanes were destroyed where they had been parked, close together so as to make them easier to guard against sabotage. A total of 2,403 Americans were dead, and an additional 1,178 lay wounded. Casualties suffered by the Japanese during their devastating attack were slight. They lost 29 planes, 6 midget submarines which had played a minor role in the attack, and 100 lives. Three days after Pearl Harbor the Japanese followed up their initial battle success against American forces in the Pacific by conducting a combined air and amphibious infantry invasion of the Philippines. By that time both Germany and Italy had declared war on the United States.

The rush of world events following Pearl Harbor brought a gigantic and immediate expansion of all American military forces. Concurrent with that expansion, enormous pressure was placed on American industry to equip the fighting troops with everything from .45 calibre pistols to battleships and four-engined B-17 bombers. On December 20 – only two weeks after Pearl Harbor – the total number of required glider pilots was suddenly set at 1,000. This upward leap in what was to have been a gradual programme was brought about by a requirement given to the Army Air Forces by the Army General Staff to 'provide air transport by means of troop airplanes and gliders for one air-borne [sic] division at the earliest practical date.'[4] Since tactics and operating techniques of airborne divisions were then still in the experimental stage, Army Air Forces staff officers in Washington had made an educated guess that approximately 75 per cent of the personnel and equipment of a standard 14,000-man infantry division could be carried in gliders and the remaining 25 per cent could ride in the tow-planes. In order to transport the division, therefore, 1,000 gliders and 292 transport planes would be required. Half of the gliders were to be 8-place types transporting 3,500 troops, and the other half would be 15-place types carrying 7,000 troops. In what was to prove to be a grievous planning error, those same staff officers estimated that four 8-place or three 15-place fully loaded gliders could be towed behind a single transport plane filled with troops.

[51]

Even at this early date the Army Air Forces saw that the expanding glider pilot programme would seriously interfere with its likewise expanding power pilot training requirements. From the very beginning of the glider programme it was expected that all glider pilots would be commissioned power pilot officers who already had graduated from the Air Corps Flying School system. However, with the country at war, 1,000 power pilots could not be spared for the glider programme. Colonel Earl L. Naiden, the Chief of the Army Air Forces Training Division, had been anticipating just such an emergency officer pilot shortage situation. On December 27 he suggested to General Arnold that selected volunteer active duty enlisted men be permitted to enter the glider pilot programme provided that they had never been 'washed out' of a military flying school and could meet these qualifications: 1) previous aviation experience that included completion of the Civil Aeronautics Administration (CAA) primary or secondary powered aircraft flying courses, or 2) at least 30 hours of flying time at the controls of a civilian glider, and 3) be able to pass the same rigid physical examination given to military power pilot candidates. Naiden also suggested that all qualified enlisted men go through the training in their current ranks and upon graduation receive an immediate promotion to the rank of staff sergeant. Arnold bought Naiden's suggestions. Effective February 19, 1942, enlisted men were allowed to apply for glider pilot training.

Administrative machinery for the 1,000 Glider Pilot Programme was just beginning to run smoothly when on April 1 General Arnold announced that he was quadrupling the glider programme by raising the number of pilots needed to 4,200. Five weeks later, the Army Air Forces staff was still working night and day ironing out the many problems associated with the 4,200 Glider Pilot Programme when General Arnold staggered everyone by announcing a 6,000 Glider Pilot Programme.

Now that the scope of the programme had been widened substantially, the Army Air Forces found itself hard pressed to find enough qualified military applicants willing to volunteer for the training. A letter was sent out from Washington on May 11, 1942, to the commanding officers of every U.S. Army base in the continental United States. This letter outlined the enormity of the programme and instructed commanders to see to it that all of their eligible personnel were encouraged to apply for glider pilot training at once. It also

[52]

detailed a new set of prerequisites for applicants. Effective immediately, glider pilot training was open to all officers and enlisted men who were citizens, 18 to 35 years of age, and who had not been eliminated from a military or civilian flying school. (The upper age limit for those wishing to apply for power pilot training was then 26 years.) Applicants also had to be able to pass a less rigid physical exam for flying duty and have one of the following types of aerial experience: a) Holder of a currently effective Airman Certificate, private grade or higher, b) Holder of a lapsed Airman Certificate, provided that such certificate did not lapse prior to January 1, 1942, or c) Have completed 200 or more glider flights. The letter closed by stating that officers and enlisted men would go through the training programme in their current ranks, and that upon graduation the enlisted men would be promoted to the grade of staff sergeant. Officers, meanwhile, would retain the rank in which they began the training.

Only five days after this letter was issued from Washington it was amended and the qualifications were further reduced so as to tap a large reservoir of prospective volunteers. The period of lapse of the Airman's Certificate was pushed back to January 1, 1941, and those applicants who had been washed out of power schools would be permitted to apply provided they had flown as principal pilot or student pilot for at least 50 hours in military aircraft.

But even this lessening of the requirements failed to produce the expected flood of volunteers from among the active duty military units. When it became apparent that the required personnel could not be procured from within the military establishment, the Army Air Forces turned to the Civil Aeronautics Administration (progenitor of the Federal Aviation Agency) for help in tapping the last remaining sources of experienced airmen in the United States. By the end of May the CAA had sent a letter to the 85,000 civilians who had an active Airman Certificate on file in Washington, inviting them to participate in the vastly expanded glider pilot training programme. If the prospective trainee expressed an interest, and if the applicant's qualifications indicated adequate aerial experience and met all of the general requirements, the CAA certified him as being 'generally suited for glider pilot training'. Upon presentation of the CAA certification form to his local Army recruiting office, the applicant was accepted for enlistment and sent to one of 17 Air Force bases scattered around the country.[5] At those bases the candidates were given either the Army General Classification Test on which a minimum score of 110 was necessary for qualification, or the Aviation Cadet Mental Screening Test. Ordinarily the latter test had a passing score of 80 for those wishing to attend power pilot training. But for the glider programme the score had been lowered to 65. Applicants who successfully passed these initial mental screening tests were then administered the physical examination for flying duty. If they passed both the mental and physical exams, the applicants were enlisted in the Air Corps in the rank of private and attached to the base where they were initially processed to await assignment to a glider training school. Those who failed the exams were permitted to return home at government expense.

Panic began to grip General Arnold and his entire staff during the first week in June when progress reports revealed that the tremendous combined procurement effort being put forth by the Army Director of Personnel, the Adjutant General, and the CAA was still not producing even the minimum required number of volunteers. So critical was the situation that General Arnold actually gave consideration to dispensing with the military tradition of asking for volunteers for hazardous flying duty and ordering non-volunteers into the programme. An emergency meeting was convened on June 10 in Washington to discuss alternative ways of solving the shortage.

During that conference a number of radical personnel policies were established. Chief among them was the decision to permit both civilian and military applicants who had no flying experience whatsoever, but who otherwise conformed to the present requirements, to enter the programme. This was indeed a departure from the day when only officer graduates of military flying schools were considered qualified for this same training.

Under the new set of rules, applicants without previous flying experience would be classified as Class B students. Before reporting for glider pilot training, all Class B students were to receive an eight-week block of instruction during which they would be taught how to fly a light-powered airplane and to become proficient in making dead-stick landings during daylight and darkness. Meanwhile, applicants with previous experience were designated Class A students and would be entered directly into a glider flying school as soon as possible. Along with the establishment of the Class A and B student types there was a general lowering of the physical qualifications. Applicants were to be certified as physically qualified pro-

[54]

vided they could successfully pass an examination for general flying duty with a substandard visual acuity of 20-100, correctable to 20-20. Certain applicants with colour blindness were also allowed into the programme provided their cases were not extreme.

Military authorities spent considerable time and money publicizing the greatly revised glider pilot training programme. All company first sergeants were required to make frequent announcements at troop formations about the programme and its promises of quick promotion to the rank of staff sergeant. And by the end of June the U.S. Army Recruiting Publicity Bureau had published an attractive seven-page pamphlet titled 'New Flying Opportunities – Be a Glider Pilot in the U.S. Army.' Widely distributed all across America to flying clubs, at sporting events, on college campuses and even in barbershops, the pamphlet had this to say about glider pilot training: 'It's a he-man's job for men who want to serve their country in the air.' In concise paragraphs it also spelled out all the physical and mental prerequisites for the training and gave detailed information on how and where to apply for it. Emblazoned across the last page were the words, 'Soar to Victory as a Glider Pilot in the U.S. Army Air Forces.'

The nationwide distribution of pamphlets coincided with the beginning of a combined war bond sales and military recruitment drive. Jointly planned by the U.S. Treasury Department and the Army Air Forces, the drive was to start in Washington, D.C., and then go on tour to a number of large cities throughout the country. A sort of travelling military road show, called the Air Cavalcade, was to be the main attraction of the drive. It consisted of an imposing collection of the newest American fighters and bombers, a borrowed British Spitfire, plus a German Messerschmitt 109 fighter that had been captured by British ground forces in North Africa. The general plan was for the Air Cavalcade to travel around to easily accessible civilian airports so that large numbers of young Americans could see the array of airplanes at close range and be inspired to join the Air Corps. Meanwhile, war bonds and stamps would be sold as admission tickets to the huge crowds of people that were sure to gather at the airports to view the war planes. It was presumed by everyone associated with the drive that the sleek new P-39 and P-40 fighter airplanes would be the stars of the road show. But things didn't turn out that way.

Sensing an opportunity to focus national attention on the glider

[55]

pilot programme, Air Force officials in Washington decided, almost at the last moment, to add a glider to the road show. In this case the glider was a small 2-place Laister-Kauffman civilian sailplane that had been hurriedly purchased for use in the drive. Its pilot was to be Staff Sergeant William T. Sampson II. At the time he was chosen to participate in the Air Cavalcade, Sampson was still a student at Elmira, New York, in the first enlisted class of glider pilots to be trained by the U.S. Army. Only three days before the start of the drive in Washington, Sampson was abruptly pulled out of his training programme and rushed to Wright Field in Ohio. There he was given a quick familiarization course with the civilian sailplane he was to fly in the Air Cavalcade.

Sampson himself came from a long line of Navy men. He was named after his famous grandfather, Admiral William T. Sampson, who had been in command of the North Atlantic Squadron when it defeated the Spanish fleet under Admiral Pascual Cervera during the 1898 war with Spain. His father, too, was a career naval officer and had seen service on destroyers during World War I. Sampson had begun his glider flying career back in 1929 when, at the age of 16, he joined the Providence Gliding Club in Rhode Island. By 1931 he had a CAA commercial glider pilot licence, a CAA private licence for powered aircraft, and had won several trophies in glider flying competition.

Sunday, June 28, 1942, was opening day for the bond drive in the nation's capital. Attracted by news that the popular German-born film star, Marlene Dietrich, would be on hand to promote the sale of war bonds, a crowd of 50,000 people gathered at the Washington National Airport to watch the Air Cavalcade arrive from the sky. All of the big, powerful war planes had landed and were parked along the sides of the main runway when a lone Army L-1A, piloted by Lieutenant Luke Cartwright, arrived overhead pulling the tiny glider behind flown by Sergeant Sampson. Spotting his designated landing point, Sampson cut loose from the L-1A and began gracefully putting his noiseless aircraft through a series of intricate flying manoeuvres that normally would be difficult for a powered airplane to execute. With the awestruck crowd staring up at the glider, Sampson guided it skilfully to a silent landing right beside the other planes of the cavalcade. The crowd was so impressed by Sampson's show-stealing entrance that they rushed out to see him, leaving the war planes virtually unattended. And so it was to go at all the other airports that the Air Cavalcade visited during its two-month, 10,000-mile tour around the country.

Later that same afternoon a pre-arranged military ceremony was held at Washington National Airport. It consisted of the swearing into service of 500 youths on their way to Powered Aviation Cadet training in Texas. Seated in the V.I.P. section of the spectator bleachers with families of the new cadets were Marlene Dietrich, a number of military dignitaries, and the Air Cavalcade pilots. When the ceremony ended, Sergeant Sampson was suddenly called to the reviewing stand in front of the bleachers. Fear overtook him as he walked toward the reviewing stand thinking that he was going to be asked to give an extemporaneous speech to the cadets. His fears were calmed when he was told simply to stand at attention while Major Donald M. Hamilton of the U.S. Army Air Corps pinned onto his uniform the first pair of glider pilot wings ever to be presented to a U.S. Army glider pilot. At the conclusion of that brief ceremony, Sampson looked down at his silver wings and saw that they were, with one exception, identical to wings awarded military graduates of power pilot training. Mounted on the shield that is positioned in the centre of the wings was a large silver letter 'G'. Whenever a stranger would ask a glider pilot during World War II why that big letter 'G' was on his wings, he would reply, 'That G stands for *guts!*'

Fortunately, the combination of an intensified recruiting programme and lowering of physical and mental prerequisites did in the end obtain a sufficient number of applicants for glider pilot training without the Army Air Forces having to press non-volunteers into the programme. However, now that the pilot procurement problem had been solved the Army Air Forces found itself facing a far greater challenge in finding enough civilian glider flying schools to provide pilot training. The school problem had first surfaced in November 1941 when the Twentynine Palms Air Academy in California failed to open on schedule to begin training the first small class of the 150 Officers Programme. Due to unforeseen difficulties in hiring qualified instructors and rounding up a tiny fleet of sailplanes, the Twentynine Palms Air Academy did not matriculate the first officer class until January 19, 1942. When the size of the programme suddenly ballooned up to 6,000 pilots in May, a decision was made in Washington to greatly enlarge the number of civilian contract schools that would administer preliminary glider training to military students. But with there being only five gliding schools in the entire

[57]

country, none of which could accommodate more than a few students at a time, the military authorities had to settle for doing business with what were conveniently called Preliminary Light Airplane Gliding Schools. At those facilities, military students were required to take off at the controls of a light powered airplane accompanied by a civilian instructor. After circling back over the airport at a thousand feet the instructor would turn off the engine and require the student to land the aircraft as a glider. Just as soon as the wheels touched down the instructor would turn the power on again and the whole procedure would be repeated several times. A total of 18 such schools were in operation around the country by June 1942.[6]

Additional glider training schools also were opened that same summer in Okmulgee and Vanita, Oklahoma; Tucumcari, New Mexico; Wickenburg, Arizona: Port Morgan, Colorado; Pittsburgh, Kansas; Starkville, Mississippi; Greenville, South Carolina, and in the Texas cities of Amarillo, Dalhart, Hamilton, Lamesa and Waco. As the glider pilot programme continued to grow in size the Army Air Forces established advanced glider schools in Victorville, California; Stuttgart, Arkansas; Fort Sumner, New Mexico, and at the South Plains Army Air Base in Lubbock, Texas. However, as early as April of 1943 all advanced training was centralized at the latter base.

To provide at least some kind of training aircraft to the newly formed gliding schools the United States government began buying from civilian owners every available sailplane in the country. By August 1942 only 61 flyable sailplanes had been found and purchased for the sum of $86,690. Seeing that it could not possibly obtain enough sailplanes from civilian owners, the government began placing new construction orders for 2-place training gliders with the Air Glider, Schweizer, Laister-Kauffman, and Frankfort glider manufacturing companies. With the exception of Air Glider, all of these companies eventually delivered small 2-place sailplanes which were used extensively by military students until larger combat gliders became available from other manufacturers.

During this same period the U.S. Army decided to activate two airborne divisions. The two units selected to go airborne were the 82nd and 101st Infantry divisions, both of which originally had been formed during World War I but deactivated following that conflict. On August 15, 1942, the 82nd and 101st Airborne divisions were formally activated at Camp Claiborne in Louisiana. The initial composition of each division was two glider and one parachute infantry regiments, plus an assortment of glider and parachute artillery, engineer, medical, signal and ordnance sub-units. These two new Army airborne divisions were task organized to be lean and mean, each with a strength of 8,825 officers and men – slightly more than half the size of a standard infantry division.

While reviewing the limited progress that had been made thus far in the glider pilot programme, General Arnold came to the conclusion that the use of various small sailplanes purchased from civilians and the light powered 2-place airplanes were at best a stop-gap measure. Arnold reasoned that what the students really needed was a great number of larger training gliders which had the same general flying and landing characteristics as the big transport gliders they would eventually pilot into combat. Not knowing where to obtain such a glider in a hurry, Arnold turned to his friend, Charles I. Stanton, the civilian head of the Civil Aeronautics Administration (CAA) who was well known throughout military and civilian circles in Washington for his uncanny ability to solve knotty aviation problems quickly. Stanton had graduated with honours as an engineering student from Tufts University in 1917. And like Arnold, he had been a U.S. Army pilot during World War I.

As the CAA Administrator, Stanton had been supervising the government-sponsored Civilian Pilot Training Programme (CPTP) since 1939. In the CPTP, thousands of volunteer civilians were prepared for eventual military service by being taught how to fly small 2-place airplanes at dozens of civilian flying schools around the country that were under contract to, and supervised by, the CAA. Shortly after Pearl Harbor the CPTP was renamed the War Training Service (WTS), and its graduates went straight into military flying schools where they were trained to fly fighter and bomber aircraft. Because of its three year involvement with the training of civilians, the CAA had amassed an enormous fleet of Piper Cub, Aeronca Defender, and Taylorcraft Tandum light training airplanes. In reviewing Arnold's request for help, Stanton decided that the answer to the problem lay in his fleet of airplanes. Within a few hours of hearing from Arnold he made a number of sketches showing how a small powered plane could be converted into a makeshift glider with very few modifications. He started the process by removing the airplane's cowl and its 65-horsepower engine. In their place he drew in a third seat and a newly shaped nose section that had a tow-line device positioned on its front. The weight of the removed engine was compensated for by the addition of a third student, so the delicate balance of the aircraft would not be affected. Lastly, he sketched in a lowered landing gear that gave the aircraft a ground attitude almost identical to that of a large cargo glider.

Later that same day, Stanton called in two of the CAA's top engineers, Harold Hoekstra and Nelson Shapter, and asked them to review his sketches and double check his rough calculations for the conversion job. They returned a few hours later saying everything checked out perfectly. By this time the business day had come to an end in Washington, but Stanton remained in his office to telephone the vice president of Aeronca Aircraft Corporation, Lee H. Smith, to ask if Aeronca would be interested in converting some of its powered Defender airplanes into gliders similar to the one he had just designed on his desktop scratch pad. Smith replied in the affirmative and, only nine days later, delivered a prototype XTG-5 (*X* for experimental, *T* for training and *G* for glider) which was successfully test flown by Lewin Barringer, the head of the military glider programme. Once approved for mass production the redesigned civilian Aeronca Defender entered military service as the TG-5 training glider. In less than a month from the time that General Arnold first contacted Stanton for assistance, Aeronca had delivered 50 TG-5s to the civilian glider training schools.

Using Aeronca's TG-5 as a model, the Taylorcraft Aviation Corporation hurriedly converted 250 of its 2-place Taylorcraft Tandums into military service as the 3-place TG-6. The Piper Aircraft Corporation likewise followed suit by converting 250 of its famous Piper J3 Cub 2-place airplanes into 3-place TG-8s. As quickly as they rolled off the assembly lines, these TG-6s and TG-8s were hurriedly towed to the civilian contract flying schools for use by military students.

The rapid conversion project engineered by Charles I. Stanton was the most outstanding success in the trouble-plagued glider production programme of World War II. But even though he had wrought a production miracle, Stanton unknowingly created a greater problem than the one his miracle solved. By the end of October 1942 there were 10,294 students committed to glider pilot training. Aided by the plentiful supply of converted power planes, the civilian contract flying schools had by that time managed to graduate 5,585 students from their primary schools. But because so few of the larger combat gliders had been manufactured, nearly all of those 5,585 students had to be sent to military bases in Ohio,

Tennessee, Arkansas, and other states where they were assigned to personnel holding pools. There they were told that they would just have to stay put until big combat gliders were available for the next phase of their training. The accumulation of students in these pools created almost insurmountable morale problems and a loss of flying proficiency on the part of the glider students.

In the early days of the personnel procurement programme these students had been given glittering promises of training within six weeks of entry into service and rapid advancement in rank as the glider programme grew in size. But now they found themselves stuck at desolate bases with virtually nothing to do while the big gliders were manufactured. Weeks slipped into months. Living conditions soon became cramped with newcomers being required to sleep in tent areas where water and electrical facilities were practically nil. Fistfights were breaking out even among friends. Students started going AWOL (absent without leave) in large numbers, and there was a near mutinous atmosphere in every pool.

To remedy this volatile situation, the military authorities began shifting students to other bases where living conditions were more civilized, if only slightly. Furloughs of up to 30 days were granted to some students who had been in the pools the longest. To keep the men occupied, a series of physical training, weapons, firing, and infantry battle drills was instituted. A number of liaison airplanes were also delivered to bases having pools so that the students could maintain at least some of their flying proficiency. While these measures served to calm troubled waters, none of them had the morale raising effect of the news that came from Washington on November 21. On that date the Headquarters of the Army Air Forces announced that, effective immediately, all graduates of glider training would be promoted to flight officer (a rank no longer in use, but one which compares with the present day rank of warrant officer).

Eventually the big combat gliders that the students were awaiting began rolling off the assembly lines and the pools gradually dried up, but not before considerable damage had been done to the morale of thousands of waiting glider pilot students who came to feel they would have been better employed elsewhere fighting the war.

Sources of glider production were severely limited by strict orders from Washington to avoid interference with the paramount powered combat aircraft procurement programmes. This was a source of endless headaches to officials at Wright Field. No one there was more aware of the pressure being applied from on high than Brigadier General Kenneth B. Wolfe, Chief of the Production Division. In a telephone conversation with Colonel John W. Sessums of the Material Command in Washington, Wolfe plaintively remarked, 'We just can't get everything, so I comply with one order and disregard others. General Arnold has personally given me a direct order to meet established glider requirements, and I am going to get these gliders if I don't do anything else!'[7]

Of the four original aircraft manufacturing firms that agreed to do business with Wright Field, only the Waco Aircraft Company of Ohio was able to submit prototypes of 8- and 15-place combat gliders that managed to pass all structural and flight tests. In April 1943 Waco's 8-place CG-3A (C for Cargo, G for Glider) was formally accepted for production by military authorities. With a wingspan of 73 feet and a length of 48.5 feet, the CG-3A was a high-winged monoplane with strut braces. Its wings and empennage were made of wood, but the fuselage consisted of welded steel tubing covered with fabric. It came equipped with two types of landing gear, a fixed set of wheels for training purposes, and droppable wheels for operational use. The design gross weight of the CG-3A was 4,400 pounds, and it could be towed at 120 miles per hour. Some 100 CG-3As had already been manufactured and sent to glider pilot training centres when the Army Air Forces cancelled all further production orders in favour of the larger CG-4A glider.

Affectionately called 'the most forgiving ugly beast that ever flew' by World War II glider pilots, the 15-place CG-4A glider proved itself to be the undisputed workhorse of American airborne forces during that war. Actually, the CG-4A was little more than an enlarged CG-3A. Its wingspan was 83.6 feet and its overall length was 48 feet. In the CG-4A, though, the floor was made of honeycombed plywood, a construction technique that provided strength with minimal weight. The load-bearing capacity of its sturdy floor enabled the CG-4A to carry 4,060 pounds, which was 620 more pounds than the glider's own empty weight.

A unique feature of the CG-4A was that its entire nose section (including the pilot's compartment) swung upward, creating a 70 × 60 inch aperture leading into its cargo compartment. This facilitated the rapid loading and unloading of an assortment of heavy items ranging from a jeep with radio equipment, driver, radio operator and

[62]

one other soldier; or two soldiers and a jeep trailer loaded with combat supplies; or a 75mm pack howitzer with 25 rounds of ammunition and two artillerymen; to a small bulldozer and its operator.

Designed for two pilots who sat side by side, the CG-4A could be towed at a maximum safe speed of 150 miles per hour with a gross weight load of 7,500 pounds. The first CG-4As to be produced had a single control wheel mounted on a column that could be swung between the pilot and copilot seats. Later models provided each pilot with his own control wheel of the same size as an automobile steering wheel. In front of the pilots was an instrument panel containing an air speed indicator, an altimeter, a rate of climb indicator, and a bank and turn indicator. All of these instruments had originally been manufactured for use in powered airplanes where engine vibrations would keep the indicator needles from sticking. The glider pilots knew this, and while flying their vibrationless aircraft they frequently tapped all indicators to be sure they were giving correct readings. Early CG-4A production models had a primitive means of communication between glider and tug pilots. It consisted of a telephone wire wrapped around the tow-rope. Often the delicate telephone lines shorted out while being dragged along concrete runways during take-offs. Whenever that happened pilots of the tug-ships would, upon entering the glider release area, lower their wheels as a signal to the glider pilot to cut himself loose. Two-way radios eventually replaced this crude system.

The outside appearance of the CG-4A gave an illusion of simple construction. The final production models actually contained just over 70,000 parts. A total of 13,909 CG-4As were manufactured during World War II – more than the number of B-17, B-25 or B-26 bombers; P-38, P-39 or P40 fighters, or any of the C-46, C-47 or C-54 transport airplanes manufactured during that same time period.

It was not until June 20, 1942 – six weeks after the announcement of the 6,000 Glider Pilot Program – that the CG-4A was declared fit for mass production. By the end of July a total of 16 companies were given contracts to build CG-4As.[8] Of those 16 companies, four had no experience in manufacturing any type of aircraft: 1) Ward Furniture Manufacturing Company in Fort Smith, Arkansas, 2) Ridgefield Manufacturing Corporation in Ridgefield, New Jersey, a builder of plastic, wood and metal industrial exhibit and display items, 3) National Aircraft Corporation in Elwood, Indiana, previously a manufacturer of plywood airplane parts, and 4) Robertson

[63]

Aircraft Corporation in St. Louis, Missouri, formerly an aircraft training and service institution.

Of the remaining 12 companies, only the Waco Aircraft Company in Troy, Ohio; the Ford Motor Company in Detroit, Michigan; the Cessna Aircraft Company in Wichita, Kansas, and possibly the Timm Aircraft Company in Los Angeles, California, could draw upon extensive aeronautical experience in the execution of their glider contracts. Only Cessna and Ford had anything approaching what could be deemed adequate facilities and the organizational framework expected of a prime contractor attempting the production of so many aircraft. In brief, it was an unimposing industrial group which undertook the production of combat gliders being demanded by the Army Air Forces.

As the chief design contractor, Waco was made responsible by the U.S. Government for supplying extensive data to the other manufacturers of the CG-4A. With the exception of Cessna, all manufacturers signed an engineering and assistance licence agreement with Waco. Terms of that agreement obliged Waco to furnish all its CG-4A engineering data and production techniques to the other prime contractors. It also permitted prime contractors to send observers to the Waco plant to study production methods and secure newly developed engineering data. To protect Waco against labour pirating, the agreement had a provision forbidding attempts by prime contractors to induce Waco employees to leave their jobs in order to accept employment with them. For its engineering and production assistance, Waco charged each participating company $250 per glider on a stated quantity of gliders manufactured by each company. The number of gliders on which the fee was charged ranged from 20 to 230 and was determined by the size of the contract held by the participating company.

So as to obtain a high degree of standardization and interchangeability of parts on every CG-4A glider, the government asked the Bromley Engineering Company in Detroit to manufacture master jigs and fixtures to be supplied to all 16 companies that would be building the gliders. Bromley Engineering was in the midst of this when the Army Air Forces' over-anxious Material Centre in Washington wired all 16 companies to start building CG-4A gliders immediately. The companies were told that they could build their own production tools, jigs and fixtures, and were advised that interchangeability was unimportant compared to the vital need to build as many gliders as possible during the next three months. The Bromley Engineering contract, about 40 per cent complete in August of 1942, was terminated. The cancelled tooling programme cost the government approximately $647,000.

Confused by conflicting instructions from Washington, the 16 companies that had been selected to build CG-4A gliders spent the remainder of the summer of 1942 hiring and training workers, organizing production facilities, and purchasing materials.

The degree of expertise within the 16 companies in the CG-4A production effort ranged from very good to very poor during the war years. One company that received a poor rating by the Army Air Forces was the Babcock Aircraft Corporation in Deland, Florida. Babcock had been organized in May of 1939 to produce lightweight commercial airplanes. But because of manufacturing restrictions imposed by the National Defense Program of 1941, the company was forced to abandon its plans before it had completed building its first aircraft. When given a government contract in 1942 to manufacture CG-4A gliders, Babcock had only a few employees available with sufficient knowledge and experience to build aircraft. All of their other experienced hands had by then migrated to western states where other airplane companies were doing a booming business. To prepare itself for the large glider construction contract, Babcock had to hire local people whose only work experience had been in the Florida citrus groves.

Because its original plant was too small, Babcock leased the nearby Volusia County fairgrounds and buildings to use as a production facility. Having thus expended all of its working capital, Babcock was obliged to secure a 30 per cent advance payment from the government with which it started alterations in the run-down buildings scattered about the fairgrounds. By February 1943 all of Babcock's buildings were crowded to capacity with CG-4As in various stages of construction. At that point the company rented a huge circus tent, erected it in Deland, and started building gliders in it. Seven months later a storm destroyed the tent and the renting agency sued Babcock for $10,000 in damages to its property. Babcock was still reeling from the shock of the tent's destruction when the roofs of all the fairground buildings started leaking badly during a series of rainstorms.

Things were just starting to get back to normal at Babcock when difficulties arose with the two Air Corps officers stationed there to oversee production operations. Almost from the start of their stay at Babcock the two officers had been highly critical of what they saw and were now making little attempt to conceal their opinions from plant officials. Relations between the government and the company eventually became so strained that the contract was cancelled. At the time the contract was terminated, Babcock had built 54 gliders at a cost of nearly $51,000 apiece. By way of comparison, highly sophisticated P-51 Mustang fighters manufactured during that same period cost $58,824 each.

On the other end of the spectrum was the Ford Motor Company with its many years of experience in mass producing automobiles. As early as March 1942 five representatives from Ford had travelled to Wright Field where they approached military officials of the Aircraft Laboratory about getting their company involved in the budding glider programme. Negotiations resulted in a June contract with Ford for 1,000 CG-4A gliders. But even with all the resources at Ford's command, it is interesting to note that the company had delivered only six gliders by February 1943. This illustrates that the problems of getting into full production were not easily overcome, even by a manufacturing giant like Ford. Nevertheless, the government's experience with the variety of companies in this programme proved the wisdom of placing procurement orders with financially sound firms familiar with mass production techniques.

Ford established its glider plant in Kingsford, Michigan, where it had been manufacturing wooden-sided station wagons since 1931. The entire Kingsford facility was converted to glider production, with 4,500 people working around the clock in eight-hour shifts. During their peak production period the workers at Kingsford turned out eight gliders per day. Military inspectors at the plant would check each CG-4A after it had been fully assembled. If the gliders passed inspection they would then be disassembled by Ford employees and crated for rail shipment to glider training schools. Starting in 1944, this awkward shipping process was speeded up considerably when Ford cut a 120-foot-wide swath through wooded areas leading from its assembly line to the airport one mile away in Kingsford. Fully assembled gliders could then be pulled off the assembly line by Ford farm tractors and hauled through the woods to the airport. From there military airplanes would tow them to their destinations around the country.

The Kingsford plant eventually turned out 4,190 CG-4As, more than twice the number of gliders produced by any other company during the war. Ford's price tag of only $15,400 per CG-4A demonstrated the economy of streamlined and efficient mass production. Nearly all of the other 15 manufacturers of CG-4As charged Uncle Sam a minimum of $25,000 for their gliders.

Before the end of the war, the American glider programme involved 23 companies in 10 states in the development of experimental and combat models, and 22 more firms in 14 states in the manufacture of production models. So as to meet their delivery dates, many of the prime contractors had to subcontract much of their work to dozens of companies having even less experience than themselves in construction of aircraft. For example, the Steinway and Sons piano manufacturing firm built wings and tail surfaces for General Aircraft; the H. J. Heinz Pickle Company also supplied wings to G&A Aircraft and sparcap strips to Ford Motor Company. Meanwhile, the Anheuser-Busch brewery made inboard wing panels for Laister-Kauffmann. And in St. Louis the Gardner Metal Products Company, formerly a manufacturer of coffins, was fabricating steel fittings which connected CG-4A wing struts to the fuselage. The Robertson Aircraft Company, also of St. Louis, was the exclusive user of those steel fittings.

The tremendous frustration and pressure felt by military officers whose job it was to work with this multitude of inexperienced companies is best summed up by a statement that appeared in a memo issued by the Engineering Division at Wright Field in mid-1941:

> The prosecution of this project has been extremely difficult at times owing primarily to the fact that the companies interested have never before had any business with the Air Corps. It was necessary to laboriously, and at great expense of time and effort, bear with these model specifications, preparation of drawings, contract details and clauses, etc. In almost every case it was necessary to give the ultimate in personal attention to the representative or company official; and owing to the fact that the project appeared of enormous proportions to most of these people, it was necessary to 'stand by' during their period of 'making up their minds.' All of the foregoing adds up to the expenditure of a great deal of time and effort in the endeavour to give this project all possible expedited action.[9]

It is a little-known fact that during the time that the U.S. Army Air Forces was trying to get its glider programme off the ground, both the U.S. Marine Corps and its parent service, the U.S. Navy, were independently developing glider programmes. As early as October

[67]

1940 the Commandant of the Marine Corps, Major General Thomas Holcomb, had directed that one battalion of each Marine regiment be designated as 'air troops' and train for rapid movement aboard airplanes. Each of the air troop battalions, said Holcomb, was to contain one paratroop company and three air landing companies. As initially envisioned by Holcomb, the air landed companies were to be trained for operations only with powered aircraft. However, following the German airborne conquest of Crete in May 1941 he began giving consideration to equipping his air troop battalions with gliders so that they might have the capacity of employment in restricted areas where powered aircraft would not be able to land safely.

Just one month after the fall of Crete, the Marine Corps took its first step toward establishing its glider force by requesting the U.S. Navy's Bureau of Aeronautics to begin design studies on a glider that would be capable of transporting 12 fully armed Marines. In presenting its request to the Navy, the Marine Corps said that it wanted its glider to be able to: 1) take off and land on both water and land, 2) transport bulky equipment such as anti-tank guns, 3) be rigged for static line paratroop jumping, and 4) mount exterior machine guns for defensive and offensive use.

Design studies for the 12-place glider were underway when, early in July of 1941, a marine aviator, Lieutenant Eschol M. Mallory, was dispatched to observe U.S. Army glider pilot students undergoing flight training at the Elmira Area Soaring Corporation's glider school. One month later Mallory was sent out to Illinois where he conducted a brief inspection tour of two gliding schools, the Lewis School of Aeronautics in Lockport where Army students had been earlier trained, and the Motorless Flight Institute located in the south Chicago suburb of Harvey. At the completion of his tour Mallory submitted a report to General Holcomb, saying that the Lewis school was the larger and better of the two, in that it was capable of handling 20 students at a time in a nine-week course aimed at those with little or no previous flying experience. The Motorless Flight Institute, said Mallory, could only offer 25-35 glider flying hours in a four-week course that could accommodate but four experienced aviation students at a time.

Armed with Mallory's report, General Holcomb issued a late July 1941 call for volunteers in which he informed all marines that he was looking for 50 officers and 100 non-commissioned officers who wanted to become glider pilots. All officers through the grade of captain could apply, and no aviation experience was necessary for any applicant. Initially, all training would be given at civilian schools and would be restricted to officers until service schools could be established. Within two days after Holcomb's message was transmitted from Washington, all quotas were filled.

The task of procuring the gliders that would be flown by U.S. Marine pilots was the responsibility of Captain Marc A. Mitscher, U.S. Navy, the Assistant Chief of the Bureau of Naval Aeronautics. At Mitscher's direction, contracts were let with the Allied Aviation Corporation of Baltimore, Maryland, and the Bristol Aeronautical Corporation of New Haven, Connecticut, for prototype models of 12-place amphibious gliders. Although Mitscher had initiated the contracts in a timely manner, he and the U.S. Marines would be forced to endure agonizing months of waiting for even the slightest sign of progress in the delivery of prototypes, because these two manufacturers were without experience in building gliders of any sort.

Progress was so slow that it was not until October 1942 that the Bristol Aeronautical Corporation finally delivered a static test model of its XLRQ-1 amphibious 12-place glider. With a wingspan of 71 feet and length of 43.5 feet, the XLRQ-1 had a panelled plexiglass nose and roof section that extended back to the midpoint of the fuselage, giving crew and passengers an unrestricted field of vision. In May 1943 Bristol finally delivered a flight test model of this same glider. Shortly thereafter the U.S. Navy conducted limited flight tests with it using PBY-5A and J2F-5 aircraft as tow-planes. Meanwhile, the contract with Allied Aviation was cancelled before it had produced its first static test prototype glider model.

The Navy also let contracts during this same period for 24-place gliders with two light aircraft manufacturing firms, AGA Aviation Corporation of Willow Grove, Pennsylvania, and Snead and Company of Jersey City, New Jersey. AGA planned to build the XLRG-1 which was configured to accommodate a pilot, copilot, and 12 marines in its elevated centre nacelle, plus five more marines in each of its two outboard twin float pods. Snead and Company concurrently began working on its XLRH-1 twin-hulled floatwing model.

The 12- and 24-place gliders were still in their initial developmental stages when the U.S. Navy's Bureau of Aeronautics undertook a top secret project associated with the building of its XLRN-1, the biggest but least known glider to be produced by American industry during World War II. Constructed in rigid secrecy by the Naval Aircraft Factory in Johnsonville, Pennsylvania, the XLRN-1 was an enormous, high-wing cantilever monoplane made completely of wood. In many respects it was similar to England's giant Hamilcar glider which could transport a seven-ton Tetrarch Mark IV tank.[10] The wingspans of both gliders were 110 feet, but with an overall length of 67.5 feet the American glider was exactly one foot shorter than its British counterpart. The XLRN-1 had been designed for three possible modes of employment. One was as a transport capable of landing 80 combat troops. Another was a 3,000 gallon capacity gasoline and aviation fuel transporter. The third and final purpose of this glider was by far the most remarkable. Navy demolition experts planned to use it as a glide bomb to neutralize the heavily fortified German submarine pens along the northern shores of France. Up to that point in the war the submarine pens had withstood repeated air raids by the heaviest British and American bombers without the slightest sign of damage. The Navy figured on destroying the pens by having a glider pilot aboard the tow-plane who would cut the glider loose and then guide it by means of radio operated controls into the mouth of the submarine pen, where it would explode on contact. Only one XLRN-1 was built during the war. It was successfully test flown many times behind a four-engined Navy R5D airplane but was never employed in combat. The XLRN-1 was the only American glider to have slotted spoilers which could be activated to stand perpendicular above and below the wings for deceleration during landings.

A series of conferences was held in September 1941 at Headquarters Marine Corps in Washington to evaluate progress that had been made thus far in the glider programme. There emerged from those meetings a decision to do away with the earlier plan for establishing an air troops battalion in each regiment. In its place came a new plan to procure sufficient 12- and 24-place gliders to airlift two air infantry battalions. One battalion was to be stationed on the east coast of the United States and equipped with 12-place models while the other battalion would be stationed on the west coast with the larger gliders.

The first actual training of U.S. Marine Corps glider pilots got underway in November 1941 when four marine aviators, led by Lieutenant Colonel Vernon M. Guymon, enrolled at the Motorless Flight Institute in Harvey, Illinois. Eight other marine officers without previous flying experience entered the Lewis School of Aeronautics in nearby Lockport. By mid-December all 12 officers had graduated and been assigned to the headquarters of the Marine Base at Paris Island, South Carolina. There they began advanced training in six Schweizer 2-place sailplanes that had been purchased for use until the larger 12- and 24-place transport gliders could be manufactured.

With its glider force now gradually growing in size, the U.S. Marine Corps activated a new unit called Glider Group 71 in March 1942 and assigned all of its glider personnel to it. As a sub-unit of the Fleet Marine Force, Glider Group 71 was stationed at the Marine Corps Air Station on Paris Island. When things later started getting crowded on Paris Island during the wartime expansion of the corps a decision was made to relocate Glider Group 71 to another base having more elbow room. Tentative sites for the new home of the group were Eagle Mountain Lake, Texas; Edenton, North Carolina; Shawnee, Oklahoma; and Addison Point, Florida. Detailed inspections of all those locations revealed that the one in Texas was the most suitable for glider training. Construction crews began carving out a new camp at Eagle Mountain Lake in early October. Barely one month later Glider Group 71 left Paris Island for its new home in Texas.

A rapid decline of the U.S. Marine programme began in February 1943 when its commandant ordered that no further steps be taken with motorless aircraft until more pressing personnel needs in the Pacific battle areas were met. By this time not a single flyable 12- or 24-place glider had been delivered by any of the manufacturers, and the island-hopping pattern of operations in the Pacific had emerged. The Pacific island objectives were covered with thick jungle growth and unsuitable for airborne operations, and the commandant recognized that glider and paratroop units were luxuries the corps could ill afford. On June 24, 1943, he ordered the termination of the glider programme and the reassignment of Glider Group 71 personnel to existing marine aviation squadrons. The few 12-place gliders that had been delivered by that date were turned over to the U.S. Army Air Forces. For the remainder of the war the Eagle Mountain Lake glider facility in Texas was a night fighter training base. At the time of its deactivation Glider Group 71 had an assigned strength of 36 officers, 246 men and 21 gliders.

The three main American military services were mired in the trials

[71]

and tribulations of their infant glider programmes, while overseas great technological advances in the art of glider building were being made by their allies and enemies. As early as three months prior to their surprise attack on Pearl Harbor, the Japanese had produced and test flown their Ku-1 troop transport glider. Slightly smaller than its German counterpart, the DFS 230 glider, the Ku-1 was a high-winged twin-boomed aircraft that had a wingspan of 55 feet and was 32 feet long. Its troop carrying capacity was eight fully equipped soldiers, one fewer than that of the German glider. Later, in 1942, Japan also began developing its huge Ku-7 tank carrying glider. Nearly identical in appearance to the smaller twin-boomed German Go 242 glider, the Japanese Ku-7 had a wingspan of 114 feet, which was greater than even the U.S. Navy's big XLRN-1 or England's Hamilcar tank transporter glider. The Ku-1's ten-foot-wide central cargo nacelle could easily accommodate an 8-ton tank or 32 soldiers. Japan only built nine Ku-7s during the war. All of them were successfully test flown but none was used in combat.

Italy's armed forces were initially equipped in 1941 with borrowed German DFS 230 and Go 242 gliders. But by 1942 Italian aeronautical engineers had produced their extremely well-designed AL-12P attack and transport glider. Large, yet very sleek in appearance, the AL-12P had a 47-foot-long tubular body and a wing span of 70 feet. It could carry 12 troops or 2,700 pounds of cargo. The AL-12P was followed in 1943 by the larger TM-2 glider. Constructed entirely of wood, the TM-2 was designed to lift 8,800 pounds of cargo or 20 troops. On one of its first test flights the TM-2 spun out of control shortly after release from its tow-plane and crashed, killing its two pilots. Further flight testing of other TM-1s was in progress when Italy signed the armistice with the Allies. As one of only a few World War II gliders to be still in existence, a full-sized (wingspan 74.8 feet, length 42.5 feet) TM-2 is on permanent display in Italy's Milan Museum.

Elsewhere, the British had been very busy with their own advanced glider projects. Early in September 1941 they successfully test flew their all wooden Horsa glider that was to see extensive combat service during the war. Larger than America's later developed CG-4A glider, the Horsa had a wingspan of 88 feet, was 68 feet long, and could carry 28 troops (15 more than the CG-4A), plus a pilot and copilot. And it was while the U.S. Army Air Forces was still trying to figure out where it was going to get enough volunteers for its 1,000

[72]

Officer Glider Pilot Program that in March of 1942 the British conducted successful flight tests with the first of their giant tank carrying Hamilcar gliders. A total of 412 of these flying monsters were built during the war. Many of them saw combat service during Allied airborne operations in France, Holland and Germany.

As the first prototype models of the Horsa glider were undergoing initial flight trials in January of 1942, England activated an army organization called the Glider Pilot Regiment. Commanded by Colonel John F. Rock of the Royal Engineers, this newest of British regiments was comprised entirely of glider pilots organized into squads, platoons and companies and thoroughly trained to both fly gliders and fight as infantry. Because of its unique dual flying and ground fighting mission the Glider Pilot Regiment was, and still is, the only one of its kind to be formed by any military force in the world. When Colonel Rock was killed in a glider crash in late 1942, command of the regiment passed to Colonel George F. Chatterton.

Unlike their British counterparts, the American glider pilots were never task organized for ground fighting missions. As early as May 12, 1942, Brigadier General Lawrence S. Kuter, the Air Force Director of Individual Training, published a directive containing the first definition of the glider pilot's mission when a member of a combat team. The last paragraph of that directive stated: 'The role of the glider pilot in combat will be primarily to land his glider safely, expedite the rapid debarkation of his passengers, secure his glider on the ground, assure that transport which may land after the glider-borne [sic] troops have secured the airdrome or locality to permit reinforcement by transport-borne [sic] troops. The glider pilot will participate in ground combat only in exceptional circumstances or after his glider has been wrecked in landing.'[11]

Despite this official prohibition against their taking part in ground combat except in 'exceptional circumstances,' many American glider pilots intentionally found their way into some extraordinarily difficult combat situations during the war.

Several times throughout the course of World War II the Americans sent officers from their Wright Field glider centre to England to learn from, and exchange information with, their allies. The first such visit occurred in March of 1942 when newly promoted Colonel Frederick R. Dent Jr. conducted a two-week observation tour of British glider experimental and manufacturing facilities. As an experienced power pilot himself, Dent was accustomed to seeing

[73]

large military aircraft. But when his British hosts showed him their still secret giant Hamilcar tank-carrying glider he was awestruck by its huge size. Upon his return to Wright Field Dent described the Hamilcar to American flight engineers by saying, 'It was the biggest hunk of airplane I have ever seen put together.'[1]

Several such informational exchange trips had been made by the Americans when in March 1943 General Arnold dispatched his glider specialist, Major Lewin B. Barringer, to England to obtain detailed estimates of British production for that year. On its return from England the aircraft in which Barringer was a passenger disappeared without trace somewhere over the Caribbean Sea. When informed of Barringer's death, Arnold was visibly shaken, for he knew that America's most knowledgeable glider expert had died at the time his country needed him most. Finding himself back at square one, Arnold began looking around for someone to fill the big pair of shoes left behind by Barringer. It was not until April 20 that he signed on the prominent civilian soaring enthusiast, Richard C. DuPont. Barringer and DuPont had been close friends and had worked together extensively while they were both affiliated with the Soaring Society of America. Arnold gave DuPont the new title of Special Assistant for the Glider Programme, which accorded DuPont considerably more prestige than Barringer had enjoyed; it gave him the same degree of authority as any other assistant chief of air staff in the War Department when it came to matters concerning the glider programme.

Richard DuPont had been at his new job in Washington for exactly one month when the first large-scale training test of American glider pilots and gliders took place during the May 1943 manoeuvres of the 101st Airborne Division in the vicinity of Kershaw, South Carolina. Even at this late date, the tactical potential of the American CG-4A glider was still very much unknown. The stated purpose of the Kershaw manoeuvres, as they became known, was to determine if the big fully loaded CG-4As really could safely land troops and equipment in rough fields and farm pastures that first would be seized by paratroopers of the 101st Airborne Division. Airplanes for the manoeuvres were suppled by the 63rd, 375th and 403rd Troop Carrier Squadrons of the 50th Troop Carrier Wing. On opening day of the exercises, May 23, Colonel Robert F. Sink's 506th Parachute Infantry Regiment jumped on several drop zones near Kershaw and rapidly occupied key positions surrounding fields in which the gliders were to land. Paratroopers had just completed closing the ring around the landing zones when low-flying airplanes pulling CG-4As appeared on the horizon. Moments later those same gliders could be seen cutting loose from their tugs and thumping down on the ground where they rolled to a stop and began disgorging their cargoes of men and machines. During the rough landings several gliders were damaged as they collided with barbed wire fences and trees. Fortunately, the injuries to pilots and passengers were minimal. The low injury and damage rates influenced military umpires of the manoeuvres to say that the landing exercises had imparted 'great confidence in our glider pilots, in the gliders themselves, and in their being able to carry out tasks assigned to them.'[13]

Throughout this hectic period of U.S. development and pilot training, the American proponents of big transport gliders had been particularly anxious to prove their tactical value. But such vindication could only be achieved in combat. For the Americans, that day of reckoning was closer at hand than anyone realized in May of 1943.

# Chapter 4

## *Disaster Over Sicily*

ON JANUARY 19, 1943, while Allied troops were still locked in combat with Rommel's Afrika Korps in Tunisia, the American and British Combined Chiefs of Staff decided to launch Operation Husky – a joint airborne and amphibious invasion of Sicily – once victory had been achieved in Africa.

The Combined Chiefs had chosen Sicily as their initial re-entry point into Europe for a number of reasons, the most important one being their desire to knock Italy out of the war, thus placing a greater strategic burden on Germany. The loss of Sicily, they felt, would bring about the downfall of Mussolini's shaky regime and a complete collapse in the weakening Italian–German military alliance.

The Combined Chiefs knew that taking Sicily would be no easy matter. The largest island in the Mediterranean, it measures 9,815 square miles in area, about the same size as Belgium. Separated from the mainland of Italy only by the two-mile-wide Straits of Messina, Sicily was of great strategic value to the Axis forces. Scattered about the island were 30 airfields from which German planes had been ranging out to supply Rommel in Africa and to attack Allied shipping. As on the Axis-held island of Crete some 400 miles to the east, the terrain of Sicily favoured the defending force. Except for its gentle sandy shores and a few small areas along its south and east coasts, Sicily is covered by hills and mountains. An excellent road network crisscrossed the island, permitting the rapid movement of enemy reserves to any threatened point of its shoreline.

America's General Dwight D. Eisenhower was chosen to command all Allied troops going to Sicily. On January 23, while he was still directing combat operations in Northwest Africa, Ike's communications officer handed him the following top secret message, just transmitted from Casablanca where the Combined Chiefs were meeting with President Roosevelt and Prime Minister

[76]

Churchill: 'The Combined Chiefs of staff have resolved that an attack against Sicily will be launched in 1943 with the target date as the period of the favorable July moon.'[1]

Eisenhower and his planning staff interpreted 'favourable' to mean the period of the second quarter of the moon, when there would be sufficient moonlight early in the night for the airborne troops to drop and assemble, and complete darkness after midnight, when the moon had set, for naval convoys bearing the amphibious assault forces to approach Sicily undetected. Eisenhower selected the date of Saturday, July 10, 1943 as D-Day for Operation Husky.

Although D-Day for the invasion of Sicily was then some six months away, the Allies took swift action in setting up machinery to begin planning the mission. On February 2, with his forces moving steadily closer to Eisenhower's armies in Tunisia, England's renowned General Sir Harold Alexander was appointed deputy to Eisenhower. Under Alexander, a small headquarters, code-named Force 141, was set up in Algiers to begin detailed planning of the invasion of Sicily.

The amphibious assault forces allocated to attack Sicily were comprised of General George S. Patton's American Seventh Army and General Bernard L. Montgomery's British Eighth Army. According to preliminary plans worked out at Force 141 Headquarters, Montgomery's troops were to make the main attack on Sicily with a massive landing on the east coast just below the city of Syracuse. Once ashore, Monty was to take Syracuse quickly, then start working his way up the coast to seize the point of Messina and prevent Axis troops from escaping across the Straits of Messina to the mainland of Italy. Patton's forces were to make a supporting attack with a second amphibious assault along the south coast. From his southern beachhead, Patton was to attack across the island to seize Palermo and then swing east to link up with the British at Messina.

Both the British 1st and the American 82nd Airborne divisions were to take part in Operation Husky. Initial invasion plans called for each division to parachute into Sicily during the night of July 9–10, several hours ahead of the amphibious troops to secure key roads and bridges leading inland from the invasion beaches. At Force 141 Headquarters, the planning for employment of those two divisions was the responsibility of Lieutenant General Frederick Browning, a Grenadier Guards officer known throughout the British Army as the

[77]

father of its airborne troops. Working in conjunction with Browning was the senior American airborne adviser, Major General Joseph M. Swing, who had graduated from West Point with Eisenhower. Swing had been called to Africa from his U.S. assignment as commander of the newly activated 11th Airborne Division, then in training at Camp Mackall, North Carolina.

When the airborne plan for the support of Operation Husky was formulated early in March, it was to be strictly a parachute attack by American and British paratroopers into their respective zones of action along the south and east coasts of Sicily. Gliders were not even considered for use in the assault phase of the invasion. There were some tentative plans for American forces to use them several days after the amphibious assault troops had moved well inland, but only to transport supplies across the Mediterranean to capture airfields on Sicily. Since there was then no urgent need for gliders, authorities at Force 141 waited until the middle of March to request that 500 of them be shipped from the United States to Africa, where they would be prepared for use in follow-up resupply missions to Sicily late in July or possibly early August.

Unlike ruggedly built powered airplanes that could either be flown directly overseas or shipped to distant ports fully assembled on the decks of aircraft carriers, gliders had to be shipped unassembled in wooden crates. Just one CG-4A glider, for example, required five enormous wooden crates to be shipped overseas.[2] And again, unlike powered aircraft, which were ready for combat almost immediately upon reaching their destinations, the relatively delicate gliders required several days to be gently unloaded from cargo ships, uncrated, and painstakingly reassembled before they were ready for their test flights. This time-consuming shipping procedure was to be a source of considerable grief for the Allies throughout the war.

The task of assembling the gliders due to arrive at Casablanca and ferrying them forward to bases in Algeria was given to a detachment of 110 American glider pilots based in Egypt. During the last week in March, all glider pilots in Egypt were suddenly dispatched to Nouvian in Algeria to await the arrival of American ships bringing gliders to Africa.

All of those pilots were new to the business of glider flying; they had graduated from flight school just three months before. In fact, they had been out of glider school only two weeks when they became the first American glider pilots to be sent overseas during World War

[78]

II. On December 21, 1942, they had sailed out of Norfolk, Virginia, aboard the S.S. *Mariposa*, a former luxury liner that had been converted into a troopship. In order to avoid German airplanes and submarines operating in the Mediterranean, the *Mariposa* had sailed a roundabout course across the south Atlantic to the southern tip of Africa. Rounding the Cape of Good Hope, she had steamed a northerly course through the Indian Ocean, the Red Sea, and the Suez Canal. On February 1, 1943, after 43 days at sea, the seagoing glider pilots had stepped onto dry land at Port Tewfik, Egypt. They had been assigned to the 316th Troop Carrier Group, whose commander had given them the discouraging news that there were no gliders anywhere in Egypt for them to fly. Despite the lack of gliders, all of the pilots had been kept gainfully employed since their arrival in Egypt as copilots of the C-47 airplanes that were hauling combat supplies to Montgomery's Eighth Army fighting Rommel's Afrika Korps in the Western Desert and, on return flights, evacuating wounded British soldiers to hospitals in the rearward areas.

Upon their transfer to Algeria in March, the glider pilots were told that half their detachment would eventually be dispatched to the port of Casablanca in French Morocco, where they would supervise the unloading and reassembly of crated gliders arriving by ship. Once the gliders had been test flown, the pilots were to ferry them to airfields in Algeria where the other half of their detachment would prepare them for cargo-flying missions. But throughout the remainder of March and well into April, the pilots waited in vain for news that the ships had arrived from America. During that time they kept themselves occupied by flying five French civilian Avia 152-A secondary gliders that had been found at an airfield near Oran. However, the little French gliders afforded very little meaningful flying experience because they were too fragile to be towed by powered airplanes and had to be launched on short flights by means of a steel cable towed by a jeep. Throughout this generally unproductive training period none of the plans officers at Force 141 in Algeria became alarmed by the tardiness of cargo ships bringing the gliders from America. Since D-Day, re-supply missions were the only ones contemplated for the gliders, the plans officers giving their attention to the more urgent matter of organizing the complicated amphibious and parachute attacks to be launched against Sicily.

During the last week in May, however, gliders suddenly took on great importance. By that time hostilities had been concluded in

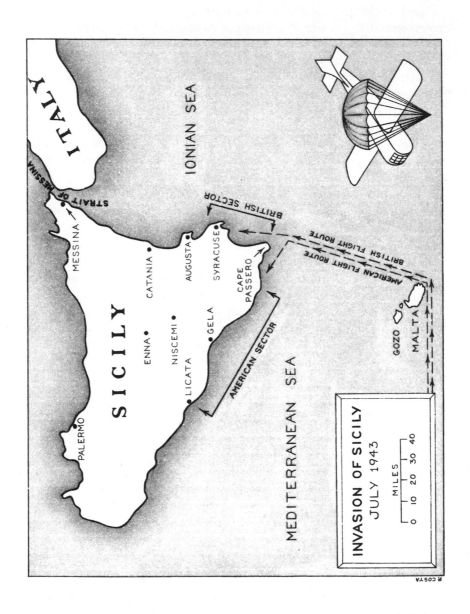

Africa, and the victorious Montgomery was able to conduct a detailed study of the plan that had been prepared at Force 141 for the employment of the British paratroopers who were to spearhead his attack on the east coast of Sicily. According to that plan, the paratroopers were to be dropped west of Syracuse at midnight on the night before D-Day to seize the Ponte Grande bridge, over which his forces had to march to capture Syracuse and subsequently Messina. While reviewing the airborne plan, Montgomery expressed some doubt about paratroop airplanes being able to find their drop zones on a dark night, deep in enemy territory. His chief worry was that the paratroopers might be widely scattered and unable to regroup in the darkness in time to seize their objectives. After reviewing the plan for nearly an hour, Montgomery surprised his entire staff by abruptly announcing that he wanted the airborne spearhead force to be landed not by parachute but by glider. Just as the Germans had done three years earlier in Belgium, Montgomery wanted his gliders to be landed in neat clusters so that his airborne assault troops could pour out of them in well-organized groups to seize the Ponte Grande bridge and advance into Syracuse.

Several of Montgomery's key advisers tried to talk him out of his startling decision. Group Captain T. B. Cooper of the Royal Air Force protested that night glider assaults were not a part of British airborne doctrine. Cooper said that to attempt a complicated night combat glider mission on such short notice with inexperienced crews and troops simply was not practicable. Though presented with a number of convincing arguments against the use of gliders, Montgomery stuck by his decision.

By this time, late in May, both the British 1st and the American 82nd Airborne divisions had been assembled in Northwest Africa. The British 1st Airborne Division was commanded by Major G. F. Hopkinson, who was later killed in action during ground fighting on the Italian mainland. Hopkinson's division consisted of the 1st and 2nd Parachute Brigades and glider unit titled the 1st Air Landing Brigade. The American 82nd Airborne Division was commanded by Major General Matthew B. Ridgway, who would survive the war and later succeed General MacArthur as commander of all United Nations troops in the Korean conflict. Ridgway's division had arrived in Africa from the United States on May 10. It consisted of the 504th and 505th Parachute Infantry regiments and the 325th Glider Infantry Regiment.

[81]

Attached to General Hopkinson's division, but not an integral part of it, was the 1st Battalion of the British Glider Pilot Regiment, commanded by Colonel George Chatterton. At this time Chatterton's regiment consisted of only two battalions. Its other battalion was still undergoing initial activation and training in England. With D-Day for Operation Husky only two and a half months away, General Hopkinson summoned Chatterton to his command post in Algiers and briefed him in person on the glider assault landing mission Montgomery had ordered. Chatterton was stunned by what he heard. After a few seconds of silence, he informed Hopkinson that his pilots were all recent graduates of glider school, with a maximum of eight hours' flying time, and had yet to participate in their first tactical landing exercise with troops. Very few of the pilots had ever flown a glider at night; night flying was not taught at the British glider flying school. Chatterton said that in fact it would be impossible for the pilots to participate in the mission because they had been hurriedly shipped to Africa without their tow planes and gliders.

The conversation became heated. It ended with General Hopkinson giving Colonel Chatterton a choice: accept the mission or be dismissed from command of his unit. Faced with the ugly possibility of dismissal just before a combat operation, Chatterton gritted his teeth, saluted the general, and strode out of his office to begin preparations for the night glider assault.

At the time Montgomery announced his decision to spearhead his Sicily landings with gliders, 240 American Waco CG-4As had arrived in Africa, but only 30 of them had been assembled and test-flown. An emergency was declared in the glider assembly centres, and once the crisis was realized, it was met. Gliders were immediately given priority over all other aircraft in Africa. Additional manpower was dispatched to the assembly centres, and round-the-clock assembly lines speeded up delivery schedules. Thus, by June 13, some 346 gliders had been assembled, test flown, and delivered to American and British airfields in Algeria and Tunisia. Meanwhile, however, irreplaceable training time had been lost. D-Day was now only a month away.

Two days after Montgomery's decision to use gliders, 30 of the American glider pilots who had been called out of Egypt were hastily dispatched to the British airborne base at Gouberine in Tunisia. The Americans were told that they were being sent to Tunisia to teach the British how to fly American gliders, and that since it was only a training assignment there was no need for them to take along combat clothing or equipment. Consequently they all arrived in Tunisia wearing semidress khaki uniforms. A few brought along their pistols, but that was the only combat equipment they took with them.

A welcoming committee of British glider pilots greeted the Americans at Gouberine and did their best to make the Yanks feel like fully-fledged members of the British Glider Pilot Regiment. With D-Day less than a month off, the Americans began their training programme at once, utilizing twenty Wacos that had been earlier delivered to Gouberine. Following a few days of lectures concerning fundamentals of loading the CG-4A and its flight characteristics, the American teachers took their earnest students for their first check rides. Towed by C-47s from the American 51st Troop Carrier Wing, several flights of Wacos climbed into the air over Gouberine with British glider pilots acting as copilots. On all succeeding flights the Americans flew as copilots, giving the British complete control from take-off to landing.

A major problem during the training programme was the complete lack of radio communications between the tow planes and gliders. In the rush and confusion at the glider assembly centres, all of the radio intercom sets had somehow been lost. Without this vital communication link the glider pilots had to watch the astrodome in the roof of their tug-ship for a hand signal from the crew chief indicating that it was time to cut loose and land. Finding that procedure too bothersome, the pilots worked out a new release signal: the tow-plane would lower its wheels when it was permissible to make the cutway. Even with these awkward procedures, the British glider pilots proved themselves to be fast learners, consistently displaying outstanding airmanship.

The first large-scale practice tactical formation mission with the gliders was conducted on June 14, when a flight of 54 Wacos with British pilots was towed over a 70-mile course and released to glide down onto Froha airfield. During that exercise, the pilots flew in four-plane formations spaced at two minute intervals. On June 20, glider mission 'Eve' was flown in a similar formation over a 100-mile course. Both of these exercises went well, but neither one could be regarded as a genuine combat training mission since the gliders had landed by daylight on smooth airport runways.

Immediately following the 'Eve' exercise, all glider training missions had to be halted so that the C-47s could be used elsewhere

[83]

for paratroop dropping rehearsals. The American glider pilots were upset by the sudden departure of the tow-planes; they felt that the British needed considerably more training in night flying and landing techniques. According to records kept by the Americans, the British pilots had thus far only accumulated an average of 4.5 hours of flying time in the Wacos, including 1.2 hours of night flying per student. Worst of all, the British still had not participated in a training exercise involving the mass release of gliders over water, either in daylight or at night.

With the arrival in late June of some Horsa gliders from England, the morale of British glider pilots at Gouberine was raised considerably. The Horsas had come to Tunisia as part of Operation Turkey Buzzard, an incredibly courageous undertaking that proved to be the greatest long-distance combat glider tow by any nation during the war. Conceived by Squadron Leader Wilkinson of the R.A.F., Operation Turkey Buzzard involved the towing of 30 Horsas by modified four-engined Halifax bombers all the way from England to Tunisia, a distance in excess of 2,400 air miles, with only one stop. To allow for safety during emergency ditching of gliders, both legs of the trip were to be flown during daylight hours. The first leg was a ten-hour non-stop over-water flight from Portreath in Cornwall to French Morocco, through skies known to contain marauding German aircraft. The second leg, lasting seven hours, took the Halifax tugs and gliders across the treacherous Atlas Mountains of northwestern Africa to their final destination in Tunisia. Before the first Halifax and Horsa combination had ever left England, Wilkinson grimly predicted that not all of them would survive both legs. His prediction proved to be all too true. Of the 30 Horsas taking part in the mission, only 19 made it to Tunisia. The rest were reported as having either been shot down by German fighters or forced to ditch at sea or in the mountains.

During the time that the American glider pilots had been instructing their eager students at Gouberdine, the Allied brass at Force 141 back in Algiers had been refining the original plan for employment of airborne troops during Operation Husky. In its final form, Husky contained four separate airborne operations, two of them British and two American. To achieve tactical surprise and to protect the airborne troops from enemy anti-aircraft guns, all four operations would take place during hours of darkness.

The British 1st Airborne Division would lead off the attack on the night before D-Day with an operation code-named 'Ladbroke.' As directed by Montgomery, Ladbroke was to be a massive glider assault by the 1st Air Landing Brigade, commanded by Brigadier Philip 'Pip' Hicks. Hicks and his troops were given the mission of landing just below Syracuse, the first of Montgomery's two main objectives on Sicily. The critical Ponte Grande bridge, half a mile southeast of the city, was to be captured by a *coup-de-main* party carried aboard eight gliders. Meanwhile, the remainder of the brigade was to land in other LZs (landing zones) east and south of the Ponte Grande. Their mission was to consolidate the hold on the bridge and then advance into Syracuse to secure the city and knock out coast artillery batteries that could deliver fire on the beaches to be used in the morning by the amphibious forces of the Eighth Army. Ladbroke was timed so that the gliders would be released from their tugs starting at 10:30 on the night before the initial amphibious assault landings. Then, just as the Germans had done so efficiently at Fort Eban Emael three years earlier, the British gliderborne troops would make a silent approach over the beaches into three large LZs where they would quietly dismount and seize their objectives before the enemy could react. Final linkup with the Eighth Army was planned for 7:30 a.m. on D-Day.

Hard on the heels of Ladbroke would come 'Husky Number One', the first American airborne mission. Not quite one hour after the British glider landings, Colonel James M. Gavin's reinforced 505th Regimental Combat Team[3] would make a parachute assault near Gela on the south coast. Gavin's mission at Gela was to secure all roads leading inland from the beaches and to occupy key points within his DZ (drop zone) so that it could be used again by the other parachute regiment of the 82nd Airborne Division.

'Husky Number Two', the second American operation, was scheduled to take place after beachheads had been well established on Sicily. Tentatively planned for the night of July 11, this mission called for the delivery of Colonel Reuben H. Tucker's 504th Parachute Combat Team[4] into the DZ already secured by Gavin's force.

'Fustian' was to be the fourth and final airborne operation during the invasion of Sicily, a combination parachute and glider assault to capture the vital Primasole Bridge spanning the Simento River south of Catania. Montgomery knew that just beyond Catania the rugged terrain of Sicily's east coast gives way to wide open flatlands leading up to Messina. His plan was to race across those flatlands and seize

[85]

Messina, cutting off the only escape route to the mainland for German and Italian troops.

To avoid the danger of friendly fire from the 1,405 Allied naval vessels taking part in the invasion, all four of these night airborne operations had to be flown over a circuitous route to Sicily. By that point in the war it was well known that shipboard gunners fired readily whenever an airplane came near them at night. As worked out by the planners at Force 141, all gliders and paratroop aircraft were to orbit over their departure airfields until they were in tactical formation for the flight to Sicily. Once the flight leaders were satisfied that their units were in good shape, they were to drop to within 200 feet of the water and take a heading that would bring them over the Cherigui Islands, and thence eastwards to Malta, their first main checkpoint. Searchlights on Malta would be turned on periodically to help them find the island.

At Malta, all aircraft were to turn left and head north for checkpoint 2, the southeast corner of Sicily. From there the British were to continue north to their objectives while the trailing Americans made a second left turn toward their DZ at Gela. The forecast promised moonlit conditions, favourable for night flying, but many pilots were concerned by the roundabout course. The straightline distance from the centre of their take-off fields in Tunisia to their target areas on Sicily was only 250 miles, but the complicated dogleg they were supposed to fly measured 450 miles, nearly twice as far. By daylight this might not have been a problem, but here they were supposed to maintain tight formation in near-blackout conditions only 200 feet above the water to avoid detection by enemy radio directional finders. To negotiate such a difficult route under those conditions would be a challenge even for pilots with far more experience than these young aviators and navigators.

With only three days remaining until D-Day, the 42 American flight instructors began packing for the return trip to Algeria. They had no sooner finished than an American colonel arrived at Gouberdine looking for volunteers to accompany the British into combat. Their job during the invasion, said the colonel, would be to fly as copilots in the Wacos and to be official observers of the British glider troops in combat. Once Sicily had been captured, they would rejoin their units in Africa, where they would brief other American glider pilots on combat landing techniques.

Thirty Americans volunteered for the mission and were put on

[86]

detached service with the British Glider Pilot Regiment. Knowing that the Americans had come to Tunisia without combat equipment, British supply sergeants quickly outfitted them with Sten guns and ammunition pouches. The only item the British were unable to provide was combat clothing. That proved to be only a minor problem; the Americans said they could fly and fight in the same khaki uniforms they had worn while teaching.

The hot African sun was just beginning to set on July 9 when 1,200 troops of Brigadier Hicks's 1st Air Landing Brigade began climbing into 136 Waco and eight Horsa gliders parked on six airfields clustered around Gouberdine. Meanwhile, tug-ships from the North African Air Force Troop Carrier Command (a mixed force of 111 American C-47s, 25 British Albemarles, and eight Halifaxes) began warming their engines, creating minor dust storms at each of the primitive airstrips. At exactly 6:42 p.m. the lead airplane at each airfield gunned its engines and roared down the runway with its heavily loaded glider in tow. Like parts of a well-oiled machine, each airplane-and-glider combination fed itself into the ground pattern and took off to attach itself to the tail of the long skytrain.

Earlier in the afternoon, intercom sets were hastily installed in about half of the Wacos during the final briefings of glider pilots and unit commanders at each of the airfields. It had been explained that only three glider LZs would be utilized on Sicily. LZ 1 and LZ 2 were close to the shoreline; into these two would go all of the Wacos carrying the assault troops who were to capture Syracuse and knock out its shore batteries. LZ 3 consisted of two strips of land between a quarter of a mile and a mile west of the brigade's primary objective, the Ponte Grande bridge. All of LZ 3 was reserved for the eight Horsas carrying the *coup-de-main* party, whose mission was to seize the bridge and prevent its destruction by enemy forces.

Because of the concentration of enemy anti-aircraft guns along the eastern, seaward edge of Syracuse, the approach to all three LZs would have to be made from the south of the city. Briefing officers told the tug pilots to take Sicily's Cape Ognina as the initial point for their final run, and to set their course one mile off its tip for the end of Cape Murro di Porco. Halfway between those two capes, and at a distance of 3,000 yards from the shoreline, all tug pilots were to release their gliders, then turn right and head back to Africa. Release altitude for Wacos going into LZ 1 was set at 1,500 feet and for those going into LZ 2 at 1,000 feet. Since the Waco CG-4A glider ordina-

[87]

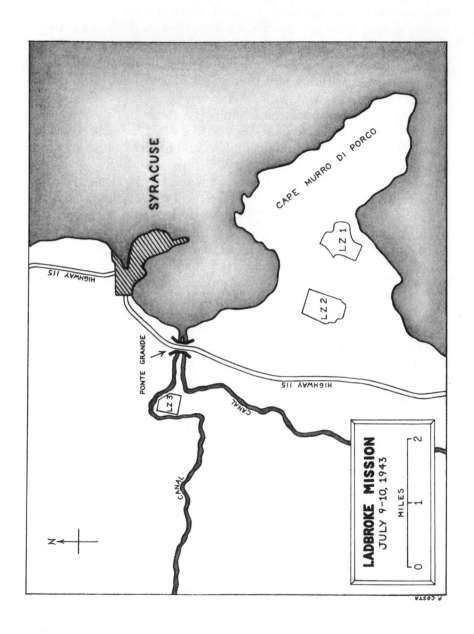

SYRACUSE

CAPE MURRO DI PORCO

LZ 1

LZ 2

HIGHWAY 115

HIGHWAY 115

PONTE GRANDE

LZ 3

CANAL

CANAL

**LADBROKE MISSION**
JULY 9–10, 1943

MILES

0        1        2

N

F. COSTA

arily could glide 14 times its altitude at release, the gliders bound for both LZs should be able to fly about two miles farther than would presumably be necessary. The heavier Horsa gliders going into LZ 3 would be released at 3,500 feet from their Halifax tugs.

The huge skytrain was still forming up over Tunisia when it began to have its first troubles. Six airplanes towing Wacos had to turn back because the gliders had somehow been improperly loaded and could not, in the opinion of their pilots, be safely towed all the way to the objective. Minutes after those aircraft left the skytrain, a seventh airplane was forced to turn back when a jeep in its glider broke loose from its tiedowns. Fortunately these mishaps occurred while there was still enough light to enable these drop-outs to land safely back at their departure airfields.

Reduced to 137 gliders and tugs, the several sections which made up the skytrain rendezvoused smoothly over the Kuriate Islands and set out towards Malta, 200 miles to the east. Everything was proceeding like clockwork, when, near the navigation checkpoint on Linosa, the skytrain hit extremely turbulent headwinds. The wind blew so strongly that it buffeted the tow-planes up and down, putting considerable physical strain on the glider pilots struggling to maintain position behind them.[5] With the sky growing darker and the ocean churning below, the glider pilots hung on for dear life as the weaving skytrain roared on toward Malta.

It was completely dark by the time the lead planes sighted Malta, where General Eisenhower had established his invasion headquarters. There the pilots sighted the six vertical white searchlight beams. Overhead, several British Spitfires provided protection against enemy fighters. Guided by the beacons, all aircraft rounded Malta's southeastern corner to begin the 70 mile leg to a point five miles off Cape Passero, the southernmost tip of Sicily. As Eisenhower stood watching the dim forms of gliders passing overhead, he rubbed his seven lucky coins and offered up a prayer to the Almighty for the safety of his troops and the success of Husky.

Flying in total darkness now, still buffeted by strong turbulence, the skytrain was making its way northward when a Horsa and two Wacos suddenly broke loose from their tugs, plunged into the ocean and vanished with all hands. Terrible as those three losses were, they could give no idea of the disaster that loomed ahead.

Waiting on Sicily for the Allies was a formidable Axis force – ten Italian and two German combat divisions totalling over 200,000 troops. All Axis forces were under the command of Italy's General Alfredo Guzzoni, a crusty veteran of World War I who had been called out of retirement to take charge on Sicily. Directly under Guzzoni, in command of German troops, was General Fridolin von Senger und Etterlin, a former Rhodes scholar recently returned from service as a panzer division commander on the Russian front. Because of the rough seas and blustery weather, General Guzzoni had given orders for his combat units to stand down for the remainder of the night and for anti-aircraft batteries along the shoreline to maintain only a minimum watch. When his orders had been transmitted, the 65-year-old general went to bed, confident of a quiet night's sleep.

After passing Malta, some segments of the approaching skytrain overran formations ahead of them in the darkness, and several tug-planes began drifting off course, and when Cape Passero came into view by dim moonlight they began climbing to the prescribed release altitude before turning onto the final leg which would lead them to the offshore glider release area. Many of the tug and glider pilots were worried by the time they reached the release altitude. The strong winds were causing dust storms down on the ground, and the roads and other landmarks that had shown up clearly in aerial photographs back in Tunisia were now obscured by rolling clouds of dust. The first seven tug-planes made their runs into the release area accurately and undetected. With precision, the glider pilots cut loose and began their descents into the murk, hoping for some sign – any sign – of their LZs.

The noise of the lead tug's motors had awakened the defenders before the second group of airplanes got into the release area with their gliders. Searchlights knifed through the sky and shore batteries began firing. In a matter of minutes the air was so full of flak, tracer bullets and brightly burning flares that the pilots of succeeding tugs and gliders found it hard to judge their position or even to see the shoreline. Confusion came quickly; several tugs broke formation and headed out to sea to get a better view of the shoreline. Two of those airplanes never found the release area; they flew back to Africa, taking their gliders with them. Further back in the skytrain some stragglers mistook other parts of the shoreline for their objective. Six gliders mistakenly landed between the tip of Cape Passero and Avola, 15 miles south of their LZs near Syracuse. Six others released in that same area came to grief in the ocean. One tug-plane completely overshot all three LZs and released its glider near Augusta, 15 miles north of Syracuse.

As his glider was about to enter the offshore release area, Flight Officer Samuel Fine, one of the 30 American instructor-volunteers, became concerned by the anti-aircraft fire over the objective. Another thing that worried Fine was the altitude of his tug-ship – it did not appear to be high enough for him to glide into his LZ once he had cut himself loose. Over the intercom he heard the voice of the tug pilot, Captain Willard E. Fawcett, telling him to cut loose. 'Sir, there's no way we can possibly reach the shoreline, let alone our LZ, from this altitude,' Fine called back. 'You're going to have to make a second pass and bring us in at 2,500 feet.' 'Okay,' replied Fawcett. 'But you better understand that if you don't release on the second pass, I'm going to cut you loose from this end.' With that transmission, the intercom fell silent. By the light of exploding flak shells Fine saw his tug begin a graceful turn back out over the ocean.

On the second pass, Fine's tug entered the release area flying parallel to the shoreline at 2,500 feet. With less than a minute remaining to release, both Fine and the British pilot beside him remarked at how much more intense the anti-aircraft fire had grown since the first pass. The increase in the volume of fire was a real worry to the 15 British soldiers seated behind the two pilots. All of a sudden it was time to cut loose. Fine reached up, tripped the release mechanism, and made his 90-degree turn into the teeth of the enemy shellfire. As he glided toward the shoreline, watching long streams of tracer bullets passing to his left and right, he remembered that in between each of those tracer rounds were five more bullets that he could not see. Miraculously, the glider passed over the shoreline without taking a hit. By the light of the moon, Fine made out a large field in front of him and headed for it. To his surprise the heavily loaded glider touched down lightly and began rolling smoothly across the field. When a large stone wall at the end of the field appeared, Fine hooked one of the wings on a tree, bringing the glider to a quick stop.

For a few seconds it was quiet. Fine and the British soldiers unfastened their safety belts and prepared to climb out. Then, from behind the stone wall, enemy riflemen began shooting at their glider. A bullet crashed through the windshield, striking Fine in his left shoulder and knocking him out of his seat. Picking himself up off the floor, he found that both of his knees were soaking wet. He thought that he must be losing an awful lot of blood. Running his hands down both legs, Fine discovered that it was not blood: one of the men had vomited during the tense approach to the LZ and Fine had knelt in the puddle.

The sergeant in charge of the passengers in Fine's glider yelled for everyone to dismount and start shooting back at the enemy. The first two men out of the glider began shooting in the direction of the stone wall, but their fire was not enough. One of the British soldiers hurrying out the door was severely wounded, and Fine was hit a second time as he was stepping out of the door. When all passengers had debarked they began blazing away at the stone wall. This time the volume of their combined fire forced the enemy to withdraw, and the senior sergeant directed his troops to shoulder their ammunition loads and started marching toward the Ponte Grande bridge. During the march the badly wounded man was placed at the rear of the column, where several men took turns carrying him.

Out over the ocean, other gliders were being released. Colonel Chatterton had on board his glider Brigadier Hicks, the commander of the air landing brigade, and several staff officers. Almost from the moment that he cut away from his tug, Chatterton knew he would be unable to glide all the way to shore. With his glider rapidly losing altitude, he steered toward what looked like the shoreline. A searchlight beam found him, and soon two machine guns were firing at his glider. As he turned to avoid the light, his right wing was shattered by a flak burst that sent the glider crashing into the ocean a few hundred yards offshore. Everyone on board managed to crawl up onto the one undamaged wing.

A shore-based searchlight swept across the water and came to rest on Chatterton's glider. Brigadier Hicks hissed, 'Keep still, everybody keep dead still.' There were several long bursts of machine gun fire, which passed somewhere overhead, and then the light moved on. Chatterton suggested they swim for shore, and one by one men slid into the water. Some 20 minutes later Chatterton and all of his passengers safely reached dry land where they gathered to plan their next move.

With the enemy forces now fully alerted and his own gliders so widely scattered, Colonel Chatterton became utterly dejected. However, his morale soon received a dramatic uplift when a small boat containing a squad of Special Air Service troops suddenly pulled up to the shoreline in front of him. Chatterton and all those with him joined these skilled British troops and advanced up the cliff in search of coastal batteries and pillboxes. During the night they disposed of several Italian strongpoints and rounded up 150 prisoners. Shortly after dawn, Chatterton's party linked up with other British forces who were advancing inland.

Two of the eight Horsas carrying the *coup-de-main* party were able to make it all the way into LZ 3. Riding aboard the first one was the commander of the party, Major Peter Ballinger, with a detachment of engineers and several boxes containing highly explosive bangalore torpedoes that were to be used in breaching barbed wire fences protecting the bridge. Just as Ballinger's glider was touching down, it was struck by a burst of tracer bullets which ignited the bangalore torpedoes. The force of the explosion scattered bodies for hundreds of feet.

Less than a minute later the second Horsa, piloted by Staff Sergeant John Galpin, landed in LZ 3 and rolled to a stop. Lieutenant Lawrence Withers and his platoon of South Staffordshire infantrymen debarked and dashed to the perimeter of the LZ to await the other seven gliders in their party. When a 15-minute wait failed to produce any newcomers, Withers decided to attack the Ponte Grande with his own small platoon. His plan was to assault the structure from both ends simultaneously. Making their way to the bridge under cover of darkness, Withers and half of his platoon swam across the river and approached the concrete pillbox at the north end undetected. Then, on a pre-arranged signal, Withers led the charge against the northern end of the bridge while the other half of his platoon assaulted the southern end. The sudden violence of the attack so unnerved the Italian defenders that they surrendered immediately without destroying the bridge. As they had rehearsed in Africa, British soldiers removed the Italians' demolition charges from the support girders and threw them into the river. Withers and his small band then consolidated their hold on the bridge throughout the remainder of the night as small groups of other British soldiers joined up with them.

Lieutenant Withers and his men were still setting up defensive positions around the Ponte Grande when Italian shore batteries that had been only partially manned when the first few gliders began landing sprang fully to life. Italian artillerymen went into well-rehearsed gunnery procedures, filling the sky with a murderously heavy volume of flak. Many incoming tug pilots took evasive action, swerving wide of the designated offshore release area and into other areas of their own choosing to release their gliders. Others tried to avoid the exploding flak shells by climbing a thousand feet before releasing their gliders. Still others tried sneaking into the release area well below the specified altitude.

The result of so many uncoordinated evasive manoeuvres was total confusion and, ultimately, disaster. Gliders that had been released at higher altitudes could be seen dropping through formations of gliders still being towed. There were mid-air collisions and near misses. Gliders that had been released, or forced to cut away too low, began splashing down in the ocean – 69 of the Wacos and three of the Horsas. Many of their heavily laden occupants drowned in seconds. Survivors from 56 of the ditched gliders testified later, with great bitterness, that their American tow-plane pilots cut them loose far short of the release area.

Having won a varsity letter with the Brown University swim team the previous year, Flight Officer Howard B. Johnson had been less concerned than most about the long flight over water to Sicily. Just off Syracuse, Sergeant Lee, the British pilot, had cut them loose from the tow-ship. Everything seemed to be going well during the approach to shore when Johnson suddenly heard a loud noise like a C-47 about to plough into the glider's starboard side. Fearing a mid-air collision, he yelled to Sergeant Lee, 'Pull up!' Lee pulled back on the controls, pitching the glider's nose up sharply. Although the quickness of the manoeuvre had avoided the collision, it had produced a stalling action which robbed the glider of the altitude needed for the final run into the LZ. Moments later Lee guided the glider to a perfect water landing only a few hundred yards from shore. Enemy riflemen had seen the glider touch down and begun shooting at it, wounding one of the eight British medics on board. With bullets splashing into the water a few feet from the glider's nose, Johnson, Lee and the eight medics jumped out the portside door and began swimming for deeper water to get away from the gunfire. When the firing stopped a short while later, Johnson and his group swam ashore. After wringing out their clothing, Johnson and Lee went inland in search of other members of the brigade, leaving the medics by the shoreline to assist injured troops.

Elsewhere in the darkness a glider containing Flight Officer Donald L. Daves, his British pilot and 13 South Staffordshire infantrymen began its descent. At the time of cut-off from the tug, neither Daves nor the British pilot had been able to see anything ahead of

[94]

them except flak and frightening streams of tracer bullets, but they figured that at any second land would appear dead ahead. When instead they saw whitecaps rushing up to meet them, Daves yelled over his shoulder, 'You guys back there better get ready for a water landing!' He had barely got the words out when the British pilot set the glider down smoothly in the sea. One of the infantrymen jumped to his feet and slashed a hole in the fabric roof with his bayonet. Calm prevailed as one by one the soldiers climbed out and distributed themselves on the wings. Their combined weight caused all but the tail of the glider to sink to a depth of about one foot, where it seemed to hover.

They tried to estimate how far out to sea they had landed. A few minutes of silent staring and a few more minutes of discussion produced a consensus that the shoreline was one mile distant. Two of the British soldiers peeled off their clothing and started swimming toward land; everyone else decided to remain with the partially submerged glider to await daylight.

Like so many glider pilots that night, Flight Officer Michael J. Samek of New York City knew from the moment his glider was cut loose that it would never make it to shore. As the glider descended through the darkness, both he and the British pilot beside him strained for a glimpse of the shoreline. But all they could see ahead were tracer bullets and exploding flak. The glider eventually ran out of sky and was guided by the British pilot to a smooth landing in the rolling sea. In a matter of seconds, Samek and all aboard had clambered out and were sitting on the wings trying to determine how far they were from shore. Though he could not actually see the shoreline, Samek was able to estimate its direction from the tracer bullets and searchlight beams. The glider was beginning to settle lower in the water. Samek and one of the British soldiers decided to try swimming ashore. The rest decided to remain with the glider.

Stripping off everything but his shorts and pistol belt, Samek got ready for the long swim. To keep his load light, he removed his pistol and holster and tossed them into the water, leaving only his canteen attached to his belt. He dived into the water alone and began swimming toward the light of the enemy guns. About half an hour later he swam up to another Waco floating in the water. Several survivors were clinging to its wings, but none of them could say how far away the beach might be. Determined to make it, Samek pushed himself off again. He had swum only a few hundred feet farther when he came upon another partially submerged Waco to which four survivors were clinging. Samek got a grip on the glider's plexiglass nose section and glanced down into the pilot's compartment. In the dim flicker of bursting flak shells he saw the body of a fellow New Yorker, Flight Officer Guiseppe Y. Capite, still strapped in the copilot's seat. Capite had apparently drowned when his glider crashed into the sea.

None of the survivors on this second glider knew the distance to land. Samek pushed off into the darkness once more. Another half hour of hard swimming brought him to a third Waco covered with survivors, likewise uncertain of where they were. Still in the water, Samek gave consideration to pushing off again. But his aching muscles told him he was on the threshold of exhaustion. With land apparently still far off, he knew that his chances of making it there alive were now very slim. He pulled himself up on the wing of the glider and sat down beside a cluster of soaking wet British soldiers who were shivering in the night breeze.

Samek, clad only in his shorts, was soon very cold himself, and he began shivering uncontrollably. With the help of a British soldier he tore a large section of canvas fabric from the wing and wrapped it around himself like a blanket. While doing so he inadvertently inflicted many small cuts on his back, arms, and legs with the razor-sharp bits of adhesive dope that had come off with the canvas. At first he did not notice the cuts, but as salt water dripped down over them he began to feel intense pain. As he sat there on the bobbing glider, Samek debated whether the cold night breeze or the salt in his wounds was causing him the greater agony.

When the British fleet started massing off the coast of Sicily in the early morning, lookouts aboard the warships were startled to see so many gliders floating in the water. News of the downed gliders was flashed throughout the fleet and all vessels were advised to be on the lookout for survivors. At daybreak, one of the British soldiers beside Samek sighted a ship in the distance; instantly everyone was yelling at it. Thrilled at the thought of rescue, Samek jumped to his feet along with the others and began waving his canvas blanket. Moments later a Dutch ship operating as part of the British fleet pulled alongside the glider and took its grateful survivors aboard. Dutchmen aboard the ship issued everyone dry sailor uniforms and plenty of hot chocolate.

Several miles away, meanwhile, a British cruiser H.M.S. *Mauritius* rescued Flight Officer Daves and the other waterlogged soldiers with him. The ship had arrived not a moment too soon. When Daves was picked up, the only part of his glider still above water was the tail section.

Colonel Chatterton, along with Brigadier Hicks and a group of British soldiers, had managed during the night to capture some 150 Italian soldiers. At daybreak the prisoners were herded into a farmyard where they were placed in a wooden pig sty. Climbing onto the roof of the sty, Chatterton looked out to sea; he could see the Allied fleet at anchor, still debarking amphibious troops and equipment. The sight of the fleet thrilled Chatterton; he knew that the all-important link-up would be made soon. But his elevated spirits were dashed when a British destroyer began firing at the farmhouse beside him. Fortunately one of the soldiers with Chatterton had a signal light with which he signalled the destroyer to shift its aim to a nearby Italian artillery position. Later that morning Chatterton met up with the amphibious troops as they came ashore.

Farther up the shoreline another British force, consisting of the 1st Air Landing Brigade's deputy commander, Colonel Jonah Jones, two glider pilots, and the staff and clerks of the brigade headquarters, was hiding in a deserted farmhouse. Earlier in the night they had made a smooth landing several miles distant from their appointed LZ. While making their way to the LZ area, they had come upon a well-defended shore battery consisting of five field guns protected by barbed wire. Realizing that it would be risky to attack the battery in the darkness without knowing the extent of its other defences, Jones decided to wait until he could get a better look at the position. Shortly after sunrise, Jones led a vigorous attack on the battery with his little band of clerks, glider pilots and staff officers. Some 30 minutes after the skirmish began, the Italians surrendered the battery to Jones.

The sun was just starting its climb into the Sicilian sky on D-Day when another group of British soldiers reached the Ponte Grande bridge to join up with Lieutenant Withers and his platoon, who were still holding out there. Among this latest batch of newcomers was the American glider pilot Flight Officer Samuel Fine, who had been twice wounded before even setting foot on Sicily. Soon the British force at the bridge swelled to a strength of eight officers and 65 enlisted men, many of whom, like Fine, had been wounded during their landings and travels to the bridge. At 8:00 a.m. a civilian car containing two men appeared in the distance, apparently racing straight for the bridge. A British rifleman guarding the main approach to the bridge signalled the car to stop, but it came on at high speed. Seeing that the car was not slowing down, the rifleman squeezed off a short burst at it with his Sten gun. The volley he fired killed the driver and wounded the passenger. With the body of the dead driver slumped over the wheel, the car veered sharply off to the side of the road and stopped. British medics carried the wounded man into the blockhouse at the north end of the bridge, where some Italian soldiers were being held prisoner, and bound up his wounds. As the medics were treating him, the man explained that he and his companion were two politicians who were trying to escape from Syracuse where other British soldiers were closing in on the city.

Toward 9:30 a.m. the troops at the Ponte Grande bridge began to get apprehensive. Before taking off from Africa they had been told that British tanks and infantry would link up with them at 7:30 a.m. on D-Day. While they were looking and listening for the tanks, an enemy mortar shell whistled in and exploded near the bridge, killing three men. Then came a blast of machine gun and rifle fire from a detachment of Italian infantry that could now be seen in the distance. The two sides exchanged fire for the next several hours, and the British casualties continued to mount.

Things got worse when the Italians wheeled a howitzer into place on a ridge overlooking the British positions around the Ponte Grande bridge. With an ear-splitting crash, the first howitzer shell struck the blockhouse containing the Italian prisoners, killing them all and sending chunks of concrete flying. Along with the howitzer fire, several machine guns raked the British positions. By 3:30 p.m. there were still no British tanks, and all but 15 of the stubborn defenders at the bridge had been either killed or wounded. Shortly thereafter the defenders ran out of ammunition. With their backs to the sea, they surrendered.

As he was marched away from the bridge with the British prisoners, Flight Officer Fine became despondent. During the final struggle to hold the bridge against the advancing enemy he had been wounded for the third time, and all he could foresee now was spending the duration of the war in an Italian prisoner of war camp. He was watching the Italian guards marching along beside him when he heard some of the British soldiers at the head of the column shouting. They had just sighted a British captain on the road 50 yards ahead of them and were trying to tell him to run before the Italians took him prisoner. Instead of running, the captain drew his pistol and jumped behind a tree by the side of the road. The first shot he fired struck the lead Italian guard between the eyes, killing him instantly. The other guards were so disconcerted by this marksmanship that they began shouting and running in among the prisoners, nearly dropping their rifles in the process. As two guards ran in front of him, Fine snatched their loosely held rifles out of their hands. Keeping one, he threw the other to the nearest British soldier. The two guards were still running for cover when Fine and his companion shot them with their own rifles. Fine and his partner then began shooting at others, now crouching together in a ditch, and to Fine's surprise the Italians surrendered. Fine and the British soldiers with him returned to the unguarded bridge and re-occupied it. Later that afternoon a link-up was effected at the bridge by troops of the British 5th Infantry Division of Montgomery's Eighth Army.

It is an amazing and almost damning fact that every one of the airplanes that had brought gliders to Sicily got safely back to Africa. But only 49 Wacos and five Horsas are known to have landed on Sicilian soil within a 10 mile radius of their LZs. Of those 49 Wacos, only two landed inside LZ 1 and one other in LZ 2. The Horsas fared little better than the Wacos: two of them were able to make it into LZ 3, but one was blown apart by a direct hit as it was preparing to land. Personnel losses on this first Allied glider assault mission of the war were appalling. Casualties would be reckoned a month after D-Day at 605 officers and men, of whom 326 were presumed to have drowned. The names of 88 British and 13 American glider pilots were listed among those presumed drowned.

Colonel Jim Gavin and his reinforced 505th Regimental Combat Team had begun the flight to Sicily some two hours after the British glider troops had taken off the previous night. Just as he was boarding his plane, Gavin had been told by a messenger that the surface wind speed at his objective was 35 miles per hour. Gavin knew that training jumps were called off when the wind exceeded 15 miles per hour.

Once in the air, Gavin's force formed into a stepped-up V-of-Vs formation, composed of nine C-47s per flight. Only the leading aircraft in each flight carried a competent navigator; the rest were to follow the leader. In all there were 226 paratroop planes spread out over 100 miles. To preserve complete secrecy, no pathfinder parties, ground signal lights, or radio beacons were to be employed on Sicily.

Brooke County Library
945 Main Street
Wellsburg, W. Va. 26070

6/86

5/86

862802

Pilots and jumpmasters would have to identify their DZs by eye from photographs, a task difficult during daylight training jumps and all but impossible during a night combat jump.

Enroute to Malta, the paratroop planes encountered the strong crosswinds that had plagued the glider pilots. Paratroop planes were blown so far off course that they missed even the searchlight beams on Malta and flew by the big island without seeing it. Some disorientated pilots realized their error, but the strict radio silence prevented them from asking other airplanes for directions. Those pilots who managed to spot Malta turned north toward Sicily, but many of these too were blown off course.

The farther they flew, the more unravelled the paratroop formations became. Instead of arriving off Sicily in an orderly formation, the widely scattered jump planes approached the island from every point of the compass. To make matters worse for both pilots and jumpmasters, a thick blanket of smoke from pre-invasion bombings covered much of the southern shoreline of Sicily, obscuring ground navigation references.

Standing in the open door of his rolling and pitching airplane, Colonel Gavin peered down into the darkness for some sign of his DZ. Suddenly the green jump light flicked on and he jumped into the night. Though Gavin had no way of knowing it when he made his bone-jarring landing, the plan for the dropping of his force had gone totally awry. Nearly all his troops were being dropped far outside of the DZ above Gela. He and his planeload had come to earth close to the town of Vittoria, nearly 20 miles east of the DZ. Comparatively speaking, Gavin was close to his DZ. A great many of his troops were then being dropped into the British zone, nearly 60 miles east of the DZ.

As succeeding flights of jump planes flew over the island, antiaircraft fire grew in intensity. Eight C-47s were blasted out of the sky as their paratroopers struggled to jump free before impact; 10 others were severely damaged. Three aircraft, unable to find their DZs or to penetrate the flak, returned to Africa without dropping their troops.

It was not until one o'clock in the morning that the last paratrooper slammed down into Sicily. Instead of having been dropped neatly inside the goose-egg-shaped DZ near Gala, Gavin and his combat team had been scattered all over the southeast corner of Sicily. A total of 127 planes had made drops at widely separated points in the hills above the beaches that were to be attacked in the morning by the

[100]

American 45th Infantry Division. Gavin himself was with one of those small groups. Twenty-three other planes dropped their sticks[6] into the British zone near Noto. The remaining planes, minus those shot down, managed to drop their sticks somewhere inside the 1st Infantry Division area where the DZ was located. Of the 3,405 troopers that had left Africa under his command, Gavin could not muster more than 20 on the ground four hours after the jump. As dawn approached and no more of his men appeared, Gavin began to wonder seriously if he was even on Sicily.

Small bands of Gavin's lost paratroopers were roaming through the hills, cutting telephone lines and ambushing enemy patrols when, at a little after three o'clock in the morning, Allied landing barges began putting thousands of infantrymen ashore. Resistance to the landings, although fierce, was spotty and brief. Well before first light the amphibious troops had fought their way inland and were trying to link up with paratroopers who were not there.

General Guzzoni, the Italian commander of Sicily, had been awake at his command post in Enna since before midnight. Numerous exaggerated reports were flowing in from the German and Italian units about widespread British glider attacks along the east coast and thousands of American paratroop landings on the east and south coasts. There was pandemonium in the Italian war room as staff officers plotted each new sighting on the big wall map. Obviously, the Allies were coming in strength. Still, old soldier Guzzoni remained calm, waiting for the last pieces of the puzzle to fall into place. By three-thirty in the morning, Guzzoni had confirmed reports of amphibious assaults and had reached the correct conclusion that the Allies had made two very large landings: the British in the east, and the Americans in the south. He then gave orders for counterattacks to be launched at dawn against both Allied beachheads.

Capitalizing on the confusion caused to the Axis forces by the miscarried glider and parachute landings, Generals Patton and Montgomery pushed inland vigorously with their amphibiously landed infantry and tank forces. By sunset on D-Day both generals had managed to beat back all counterattacks in their respective zones of action and had brought ashore nearly all the heavy hardware needed for the push to their final objective on the island.

Earlier in the day, while his divisions had been busy beating back German tank-led counterattacks, General Patton had sent a message to General Ridgway's command post near Gela ordering the 82nd Airborne Division to execute Husky Number One that night. Though he had already firmly established himself on Sicily, Patton wanted the remainder of Ridgway's paratroopers brought over from Africa to help strengthen the large American beachhead. The DZ to be used was the grassy Farello airstrip near Gela. Since that entire area had already been secured by Gavin's force, everyone in the chain of command considered this parachute reinforcement mission little more than a routine night training jump.

Every conceivable precaution was taken to ensure that Allied naval gunners and land-based army anti-aircraft artillery would hold their fire while the paratroop planes flew over the invasion area enroute to the DZ that night. Orders giving the precise time of the drops were transmitted to all units. General Ridgway himself visited several gun crews on the island to verify that the no-fire order had filtered down to the troops.

However, while Colonel Tucker's 504th Parachute Combat Team was flying toward Sicily that night, German airplanes made several harassing bombing runs along the south coast of the island. Their final attack began at 10:10 p.m. For the next half hour American anti-aircraft gunners at sea and on shore blazed away at the bombers, forcing them to break off their attacks. No sooner had the last German planes departed than the lead American paratroop planes arrived over the southeast corner of Sicily. There they made a left-hand turn to begin their final 25 mile leg, which passed directly over friendly troops. These first few planes were right on course, and at 10:40 p.m. paratroopers poured out of them and landed accurately inside the DZ.

The second group of planes was on final approach to the DZ when a machine-gunner on the ground began shooting at them. Other gunners, thinking that someone had just sighted more German planes, opened fire. Even ships out at sea joined in. Within seconds, hundreds of guns were blazing at the slow-flying jump planes, which, at their low altitude, were hard to miss.

Down on the ground, Generals Patton and Ridgway stood thunderstruck, helpless to stop the slaughter. Before their horrified eyes, six planes burst into fireballs and plunged to earth with paratroopers trapped inside. Several others pancaked into the sea where shipboard gunners shot them full of holes. Of the 144 planes that took part in this mission, 23 were never seen again. Aboard one of those planes had been Brigadier General Charles L. Keerans, Jr., the deputy commanding general of the 82nd Airborne Division. Not a qualified parachutist himself, the general had gone along on this mission simply to observe the drops and return to Africa with the empty planes. Keerans was the only American general killed during the invasion of Sicily.[7]

Over half of the airplanes that managed to limp back to Africa were so damaged that they could not be flown for months. Many contained the bodies of men still wearing their unused parachutes. Thirty-seven other planes had to be scrapped. Nearly all bore bullet holes and blotches of dried blood on the floors, grim testimony to what they had been through that night. By 7:15 the next morning, Colonel Tucker had managed to assemble only one artillery battery and one rifle company on the DZ. By nightfall a mere 550 of the 2,000 men that took off from Africa with him had been accounted for.

Grimmer still was the toll in human life. A total of 318 para-troopers had been either killed or wounded. And all of those casualties had been caused by Americans.

Although the three airborne operations that had been executed thus far during the invasion of Sicily had been nothing short of disastrous, both Generals Patton and Montgomery managed to make impressive ground gains against the defending German and Italian troops. During its first three days on Sicily, Montgomery's hard-charging Eighth Army fought its way up the hilly east coast, where it captured both Syracuse and Augusta against light opposition. By July 12, Montgomery was poised before the city of Catania, ready to begin what he felt was going to be a swift and decisive drive to capture Messina, only 60 miles farther up the coast. But as the British were preparing to continue their advance, they encountered stiff resistance from German mobile reserve units that had been hurriedly thrown in to interdict the coastal roads. When informed of the sudden appearance of German troops blocking his path Monty decided to launch Operation Fustian.

The primary purpose of Fustian was the seizure of the key Primo-sole Bridge leading into Catania, now behind German lines. Fustian called for Brigadier Gerald M. Lathbury's 1st Parachute Brigade to conduct a parachute assault on the bridge during the night of July 13-14. Some two hours after this parachute attack, a glider force consisting of eight Wacos and eleven Horsas loaded with artillery pieces, jeeps and other hardware were to land in two LZs near the

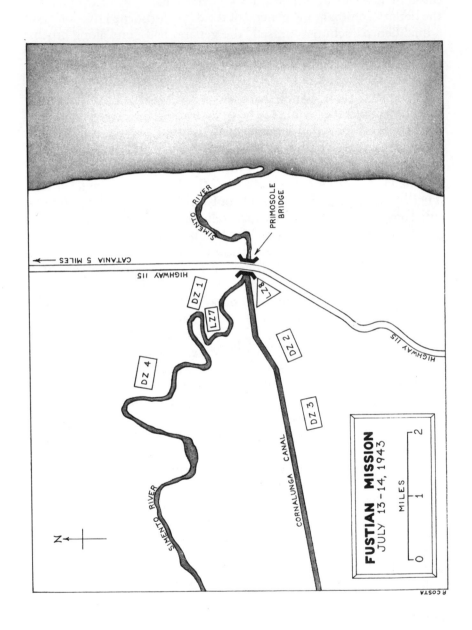

R COSTA

bridge to strengthen the airhead against enemy counterattacks. At first light on the 14th, Montgomery's tank-led infantry attack force was to punch its way through the German lines to link up with the airborne forces holding the bridge. Once German defences had been ruptured by air and ground attack, the Eighth Army was to press on up the coast and seize Messina.

Fustian was a unique airborne operation; it would be the first one conducted by any of the combatant nations during World War II in which small detachments of specially trained paratroop pathfinders would precede the main body of troops and gliders into the airhead. A half hour ahead of the main body, several teams of volunteers from the British 21st Independent Parachute Company would jump in to mark DZs and LZs with lights and radio beacons.

The lead pathfinder planes of Fustian began taking off from their airfields in Tunisia at 7:20 p.m. A half hour later, 124 American C-47s from the 51st Troop Carrier Wing and 11 Albemarles from the British 38th Wing left carrying a total of 1,856 paratroopers of Brigadier Lathbury's brigade. The pathfinders made it into the four DZs unscathed and began setting up their guidance devices at once.

The trailing main body of aircraft was not as fortunate as the pathfinders. Even before it arrived off the south coast of Sicily, three Albemarles near the end of the column were fired on by Allied ships. Real trouble began as the columns flew past Sicily's Cape Passero. There, some of the paratroop planes were mistaken by British warships for German torpedo bombers. Soon the sky was ablaze with anti-aircraft fire. The disaster suffered two nights earlier by American paratroopers on the south coast was being repeated here on the east coast. Eleven American planes filled with British paratroopers were shot out of the sky. Fifty other American planes were hit but managed to keep on flying. Pilots of another 27 aircraft at the end of the column turned back for Africa rather than risk flying their unarmoured, unarmed and inflammable transports through the friendly fire.

Other pilots continued up the coast until they felt it was safe to turn inland and attempt going back to locate their DZs. Guided by the pathfinders' beacons, several of these aircraft made accurate drops. Others mistakenly spread paratroopers all around the city of Catania.

The British paratroopers who had been dropped accurately at the bridge were astounded when they began bumping into German paratroopers walking around on their DZ. In one of the strangest coincidences of the war, German paratroopers had jumped only moments before the British, and both forces were using the same DZ. Unbeknownst to the British, the Germans had been flown in from the Italian mainland to jump and defend the bridge that the British were trying to capture. Both sides were completely confused by their chance meeting in the dark. Wild shoot-outs broke out at point blank range, with the British quickly gaining the upper hand. Once they had forced the Germans off the DZ the British got on with the business of attacking the Italian-held bridge.

The 19 gliders bringing heavy weapons and jeeps were due to arrive at one o'clock in the morning, by which time the situation around the bridge was expected to be well in hand. But because of the encounter with the German paratroopers, the British were just starting their attack on the bridge at that hour. The plan was for the Horsas to land in LZ 8, a triangle about 500 yards long with the bridge at its apex, and the Wacos to go into LZ 7, a 600-yard-long rectangle located in the bend of the river.

Like the paratroop planes that had preceded them, the gliders had their share of trouble during this mission. While enroute to Sicily one Horsa was accidentally released and vanished at sea. Four others were shot down by enemy gunners after releasing from their tow-planes. Three of the remaining Wacos made disastrous crash landings, and another three had the misfortune of landing in the midst of strong enemy defensive positions.

Only four gliders, all of them Horsas, made accurate landings inside their intended LZs. Occupants of those gliders had to postpone the unloading of their heavy weapons to lend a hand to the paratroopers who were still trying to capture the bridge. Heavy fighting raged on throughout the night, and it was not until 4:40 a.m. that the British finally captured the Primosole Bridge.

At noon a battalion of Germans arrived by truck from Catania to launch a counterattack against the bridge and its new owners. By 6:00 p.m., the Germans were using deadly accurate 88 mm guns to blast the British airborne troops from their positions on and around the bridge. The defenders soon ran out of ammunition – an occupational hazard for airborne troops – and were in danger of being overrun. Darkness was coming, and still there was no sign of the Eighth Army's tanks. Casualties were still mounting when Brigadier Lathbury, who had himself been wounded, gave the order to aban-

Near Berlin, Germany, 1891. History's first successful bird-man,
Otto Lilienthal, tests one of his earliest braced monoplane
gliders. Lilienthal managed to manoeuvre his gliders by
swinging his body to shift the centre of gravity. His method of
flight control is still used today by hang glider enthusiasts. *The
Smithsonian Institution*

Dure Park, Illinois, 1895. Test pilot August Heinz hang-glides down a breezy sand dune along Lake Michigan's shoreline with an experimental Chanute biplane glider. *The Smithsonian Institution*

Kitty Hawk, North Carolina, 1901. This is the second glider that the Wright Brothers built. Here, with his primitive aircraft at rest in the sand, Wilbur Wright practices shifting his body from side to side just as he will do to control it while in flight. *The Smithsonian Institution*

October 24, 1911, Kitty Hawk, North Carolina. Eight years after making aviation history with their Flyer I powered airplane, the Wright Brothers returned to Kitty Hawk to conduct more flight control experiments. With Orville at its controls, this glider remained aloft for 9 minutes and 45 seconds, setting a soaring record that remained unbroken for the next ten years. *The Smithsonian Institution*

Germany 1936. Civilians use a shock cord to launch a Prüffling glider. *Vintage Sailplane Association*

Ralph Stanton Barnaby, U.S. Navy, the only American officer who had experience with gliders at the outset of World War II. This photo was taken in 1941 before his promotion to captain.
*Ralph S. Barnaby*

Lakehurst Naval Air Station, New Jersey, January 31, 1930. This rare photograph was taken only seconds after the successful test drop of a glider from the belly of the airship, U.S.S. *Los Angeles*. The glider (visible in centre of photo) is being piloted by Lieutenant Commander Ralph S. Barnaby. *Ralph S. Barnaby*

Germany, 1935. A large group of civilian soaring enthusiasts gather at the Wasserkuppe for the annual competitions. *The Smithsonian Institution*

Germany, 1937. Members of a German civilian glider club enjoy a day of soaring at the famed Wasserkuppe. By this time civilian aircraft in Germany were required to display the swastika emblem of the Nazi Party. *Bundesarchiv*

March 12, 1931, New York City. Germany's soaring champion, Wolfram Hirth (standing beside cockpit), prepares to climb aboard his Darmstadt II sailplane for a shock-cord launch out over the Hudson River. *Soaring Society of America*

**TARGET GLIDER, AIR CORPS TYPE G-3**

CLOSE-UP SHOWING CONSTRUCTION

UNIVERSAL MOUNTING ON ATTACK AIRPLANE

The G-3 target glider has been used extensively in coast artillery anti-aircraft firing experiments and also in aerial gunnery experiments with pursuit airplanes at Selfridge Field.

During the early 1920s the U.S. Army Air Corps launched small gliders from powered biplanes for use as gunnery targets by other airplanes and anti-aircraft artillery. *U.S. Air Force*

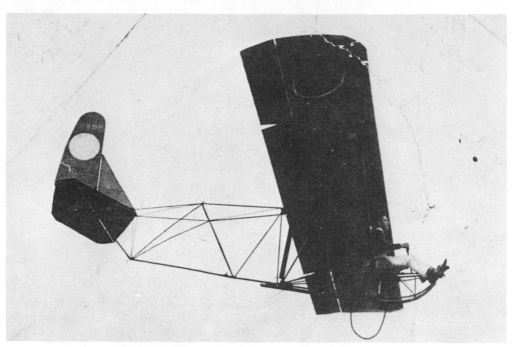

Livermore, California, May 24, 1936. Herbert J. Brown at the controls of a primary training glider that was built by the Terry Glider Company of San Francisco. Brown was then only 17 years old and a member of the Bay Cities Glider Club. During World War II he flew combat gliders in Europe. *Herbert J. Brown*

Close-up of the Luftwaffe's nine-passenger DSF-230 assault glider which saw extensive combat in Belgium, Holland, Greece, Crete and Russia. Cockpit canopy and fuselage side panels have been removed to illustrate how the cramped passengers sat astride a narrow wooden bench. Clamps along the bench held rifles secure until touchdown. The machine gun was used for defence in flight and to provide suppressive fire as passengers disembarked in objective areas. Germany was the only nation to equip its gliders with machine guns. Wheels could be jettisoned to permit landing on a central belly skid attached to spring-loaded shock absorbers. *Bundesarchiv*

General Kurt Student, father of Germany's World War II airborne
forces. *Imperial War Museum*

Germany's Me 321, the largest operational glider in history. It had a wingspan of 181 feet and could carry 200 troops or one Pz. Kw IV tank. *The Smithsonian Institution*

Belgium, May 12, 1941. Adolf Hitler (centre), poses with some of the victors of Fort Eben Emael after having just decorated each of them with the Iron Cross. From left to right: Lt. Delicia, Lt. Witzig (leader of the assault inside the fort), Captain Koch (commander of Assault Group Koch), Lt. Zierach, Adolf Hitler, Lt. Ringler, Lt. Meissner, Lt. Kiess, Lt. Altmann, and Lt. Jager. *Bundesarchiv*

Japan's Kokusai Ku-8-II glider. During World War II Japan manufactured over 700 of these 18-passenger combat gliders. Several of them were found abandoned at Nichols Field, near Manila, after the surrender of Japanese forces in the Philippines. *U.S. Air Force*

England, 1940. Two British Airspeed Hotspur gliders are in free flight just after cutting loose from their tow-ships. The all-wood Hotspur was the first transport glider produced by the Allies during World War II. It carried two pilots, one behind the other, and seven troops. Doors allowed passengers to enter and exit on both sides. The pilots boarded by way of a hinged plexiglass canopy. Hotspurs were used extensively for training by England's Glider Pilot Regiment, but none were ever used in combat. *Imperial War Museum*

England, 1942. This Albemarle is returning to base from a glider training mission in the midlands. Like all other British glider tugs during the war, the Albemarle was originally designed (in 1939) to be a bomber. Beginning in October of 1941, however, the Albemarles were converted into glider tugs and troop transports. Each was powered by two 1,590 hp Bristol XI 14-cylinder radial engines. Wingspan was 77 feet; length 59 feet, 11 inches. *Imperial War Museum*

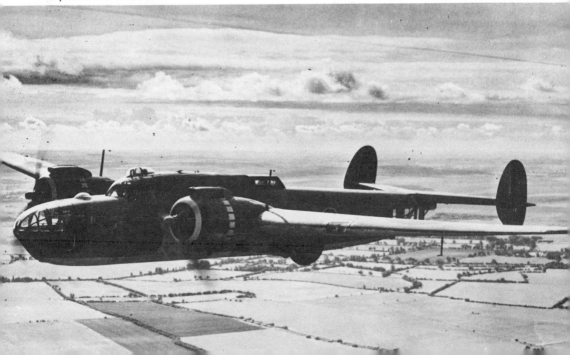

England's Hamilcar glider disgorging a Tetrarch tank. The Hamilcar was the largest glider built by the Allies. It had a wingspan of 110 feet and could carry one tank or 40 troops. Hamilcars saw service in Normandy, Holland, and Germany. *Imperial War Museum*

Laurinburg-Maxton Army Air Base, North Carolina, August 1944. General Henry H. Arnold (centre), the Commanding General of the U.S. Army Air Forces during World War II, inspects the tow-line of a CG-4A glider. These 300-foot tow-lines were one of the primary reasons for the scarcity of women's nylon stockings during the World War II years – a single tow-line contained enough nylon to make 1,620 pairs of stockings. When cutting loose from his tug ship, the glider pilot would release the hook seen in the upper part of this photo. The line would then drag behind the tow-plane which, during training manoeuvres, would drop it in a designated area where it could be picked up and used again. In combat, the tow-plane pilots jettisoned the ropes. With General Arnold are Colonel Y. A. Pitts (left), and Colonel Reed Landis. *U.S. Air Force*

Torrey Pines, California, 1940. Soaring champion John Robinson and his Zanonia sailplane. During the war years, Robinson formulated the first instructional programmes for American military glider pilot students and taught glider flying at Elmira, New York, and Twenty-nine Palms, California. He is one of only two Americans ever to become a three-time winner of the National Soaring Competitions and was the first person in the world to complete the 'Diamond C', still the greatest soaring achievement worldwide. *John Robinson*

Vernon M. Guyman, the first and only chief of the U.S. Marine Corps' glider pilots. Like many Marine aviators, Guyman began his career as a ground soldier. During World War I, he was twice wounded while serving with the Marine Brigade in France. After winning his wings in 1926, he served in Nicaragua with the 2nd Marine Brigade. There he was awarded the Navy Cross for heroism for having repeatedly risked his life while flying wounded Marines to safety. Guyman retired in 1949 as a Brigadier General. *U.S. Marine Corps*

Paris Island, South Carolina, May 1941. U.S. Marine Corps student glider pilots preparing for a training flight in their Schweizer 2-place sailplanes. The U.S. Navy and Marine Corps designated this glider the LNS-1. In the U.S. Army it was known as a TG-2. *U.S. Marine Corps*

The U.S. Navy's 2-place (side-by-side seating) Pratt-Read LNE-1 training glider. Pratt-Read built 100 of these sleek sailplanes during World War II. Seventy-three of them were transferred to the U.S. Army where they were redesignated as TG-32 training gliders. *Vintage Sailplane Association*

February 1942, Wright Field, Ohio. Soldiers from Fort Benning's 29th Infantry debark from a CG-3A, the first large troop-carrying glider developed by the United States. This method of debarkation undoubtedly was very hard on the ankles of the passengers. Only 100 CG-3As had been built when the U.S. Army adopted the larger CG-4A glider which had side exit doors for passengers and pilots. *U.S. Army*

Faced with a critical shortage of training gliders in 1942, the U.S. Government converted hundreds of 2-place powered airplanes into 3-place gliders by replacing the engine with another pilot's seat and controls. Shown here is (top) the Aeronica Defender after its conversion into the TG-5 glider; (centre) a Taylorcraft Tandum Trainer that has been converted into the TG-6; and (bottom) a Piper Cub modified into a TG-8 glider. *Aeronica Aircraft Corp*

A CG-4A glider coming in for a test landing with a 10-foot nylon drag parachute serving as a giant air brake. Parachutes enabled gliders to land more quickly on small fields. They were used extensively during landings in Europe. This test glider is also equipped with a Griswold Nose. *U.S. Air Force*

Major Frederick R. Dent, Jr., the first chief of glider development and procurement for the U.S. Army Air Force, in the front cockpit of a Schweizer TG-2 training glider. *U.S. Air Force*

CG-4A gliders under construction. The fragile CG-4A glider had no protective armour as did all other combat aircraft, no machine guns for self-defence, and only a thin outer skin made of canvas. Yet they were used in great numbers in nearly every major Allied invasion during World War II. *U.S. Air Force*

Major Lewin B. Barringer. A prominent civilian soaring enthusiast before the outbreak of World War II, Barringer was called to active duty in September 1941 by General Henry H. Arnold to become the first chief of the U.S. Army's fledgling glider pilot programme. This photo was taken in 1943, shortly before the airplane carrying Barringer and others disappeared over the Caribbean Sea while on a return flight from Europe. *National Soaring Society of America*

Glider qualification badges of World War II. From top to bottom: American glider pilot's wings; American Glider Badge (worn by the glider troopers); British glider pilot's wings; British second pilot's wings, and German Luftwaffe glider pilot's badge. *The Dennis Davies Collection*

June 28, 1942, Washington D.C. The German-born film star, Marlene Dietrich, smiles at Sergeant William T. Sampson II from the cockpit of a glider. A few hours after this picture was taken, Sampson was presented the first pair of glider pilot wings ever to be awarded to a U.S. Army glider pilot. *William T. Sampson*

Giza, Egypt, February 13, 1943. American glider pilots and other officers pose with Egyptian tour guides before the 4,500-year-old pyramids and the Sphinx. The mounted officers are, from left to right, F.O. Howard Johnson; Lt. William White, U.S. Navy; Lt. Frank Natolouis; F.O. Samuel Fine; and Hamilton Props Technician H. R. Doughtie. Standing in centre of photo is F.O. William Sneed. Five months after this photo was taken, Johnson and Fine volunteered to fly with the British Glider Pilot regiment during the night airborne invasion of Sicily. *Samuel Fine*

Tunisia, July 1943. Troopers of the British 1st Airborne Division's 1st Air Landing Brigade practise unloading ammunition carts from the American CG-4A gliders they will ride into combat during the invasion of Sicily. *Imperial War Museum*

Syracuse, Sicily, July 10, 1943. This is one of the many Allied gliders that crash landed in the sea during the invasion of Sicily. *U.S. Air Force*

England, 1943. A Whitley V bomber landing at Brize Norton. Designed in 1936 as heavy bombers, the Whitleys, on March 19, 1940, dropped the first bombs to fall on Germany since 1918. For the next two years Whitleys took part in leaflet raids, minelaying sorties, and missions to bomb targets in Germany and northern Italy. From 1942 onward, however, the Whitleys served primarily as glider tugs and paratroop trainers. Each Whitley was powered by two 1,145 hp Rolls Royce Merlin X V-12 liquid-cooled engines. Wingspan was 84 feet; length was 70 feet 6 inches. *Imperial War Museum*

Flight Officer Samuel Fine, one of the American glider pilots who survived the disastrous night glider landing on Sicily. This picture was taken in England in 1944. Note that Fine is wearing (on his right side) British glider pilot wings awarded him by Colonel Chatterton, commander of the British Glider Pilot Regiment.
*Samuel Fine*

St. Louis, Missouri, August 1, 1943. This disastrous crash of a CG-4A glider killed the mayor of St. Louis and several other city and state officials. *St. Louis Globe-Democrat*

June 1942, Wright Field, Ohio. A Stinson 10-C airplane from Richard C. DuPont's All-American Aviation Company makes an experimental pick-up of a military glider. The method was used extensively during World War II by larger gliders and airplanes. This glider is a Schweizer XTG-3 piloted by Lieutenant Chester Decker. *U.S. Air Force*

Wright Field, Ohio, June 1942. Richard C. DuPont (right) president of the All-American Aviation Company and future chief of the U.S. Army's glider programme, poses with Lt. Chester Decker (seated in the front cockpit of this Schweizer XTG-3 glider). This photo was taken during the period in which DuPont was demonstrating the pick-up of a grounded glider by an airplane in flight. DuPont and Decker were old friends and soaring rivals. Both had won the U.S. National Soaring Competitions during the mid-1930s. *U.S. Air Force*

August 1943, South Plains Army Air Field, Lubbock, Texas. A flight of three CG-4A gliders (lower right) have just cut away from their Lockheed C-60 tow-planes to make a blitz landing during an exercise. This method of steep-dive landings was later changed by Major Mike Murphy. *U.S. Air Force*

A CG-10A, the second largest glider built by America during World War II. It was constructed entirely of wood, had a wingspan of 105 feet, and could carry 40 soldiers. America planned to build 1,000 of these for the invasion of Japan. *U.S. Air Force*

The MC-1, also known as XCG-16, had a wingspan of 91 feet 8 inches and could transport 40 troops in two compartments on either side of the elevated cockpit. Richard C. DuPont and three other men were killed during a demonstration flight of this glider. *U.S. Air Force*

Italy, September 12, 1943. With the Abbruzzi Mountains in the background, German paratroopers enjoy a rest break beside the Campo Imperatore Hotel on the Grand Sasso after having just rescued Mussolini. *Imperial War Museum*

June 1943, Saybrook, Connecticut. This is the only known photograph of the experimental nose section developed by the Ludington-Griswold Company for the U.S. Army's CG-4A gliders. Though this proposed new nose section would have vastly improved the flying characteristics of the CG-4A, American military authorities refused to accept it. They did, however, use this streamlined nose idea on the new and larger CG-13 gliders that began rolling off assembly lines in January 1944. Roger W. Griswold II, president and chief engineer of Ludington-Griswold, can be seen standing inside the fuselage of this CG-4A. *Roger W. Griswold II*

don the bridge. All survivors, said Lathbury, were to hold on until darkness fell and then drop back to where Lieutenant Colonel John D. Frost's 2nd Battalion was still holding out in its positions just south of the span.

It was not until July 16 – three days after Fustian had been launched – that the airborne troops recaptured the bridge with the assitance of delayed advance guard units from the Eighth Army. All told, the British 1st Airborne Division suffered an additional 419 officers and men killed, wounded, and missing in action during their seesaw battle for control of the Primosole Bridge.

Now that the bridge was in British hands again, German defences stiffened considerably before Catania. By July 17 all forward movement of the Eighth Army had been brought to a halt. The stubborn defence by German troops at Catania forced Montgomery to shift the main thrust of his advance from the coastal road to the interior of the island, where he planned to reach Messina by going around the west side of Mount Etna. This major change in Monty's battle plan gave Patton the excuse he was looking for to try beating the British into Messina. With a fierce sense of competitiveness, he led his Seventh Army in a series of leapfrog amphibious and frontal attacks along the island's northern shoreline. The boldness of his tactics resulted in American troops entering Messina a few hours ahead of Montgomery's leading units on August 17.

The Germans and Italians had been conducting a skilful evacuation of their forces to the Italian mainland. Over 60,000 Italian and nearly 40,000 German soldiers were safely evacuated by the time the Allies occupied Messina. The Italians left behind all but 200 of their vehicles. The Germans, on the other hand, brought out nearly 10,000 vehicles, 47 tanks, and 17,000 tons of supplies.

So ended the 38-day battle for Sicily, which cost the Allies nearly 20,000 casualties. German losses were placed at 12,000 killed or captured. Fewer than 3,000 Italian soldiers were killed during the battle, but over 100,000 were taken prisoner. For the troopers of the British 1st Airborne who fought so gallantly at the Ponte Grande and Primosole bridges, the Sicilian campaign was but a foretaste of a far greater and bloodier struggle that awaited their division at another bridge, located at Arnhem, Holland.

The most significant outcome of the Sicilian campaign for the Allied side was the complete collapse of Italian resistance for the rest of the war. On July 25, while the battle still raged on Sicily, Italy's

King Victor Emmanuel removed the much hated dictator, Mussolini, and replaced him with Marshal Pietro Badoglio. As soon as he was appointed, Badoglio entered into secret negotiations with the Allies. On September 3, he accepted the Allied terms for Italy's uncon- ditional surrender. Six days later, American and British amphibious troops landed on the Italian mainland at Salerno.

The Dutch ship that had picked up Flight Officer Michael Samek eventually deposited him on the island of Malta. Going ashore dressed in a white shirt, white trousers, and a pair of white sneakers given to him by his hosts, Samek made his way to a headquarters building staffed by U.S. Army officers. There he explained to the colonel that he was a recently rescued glider pilot who was now making his way back to his outfit in Africa. Samek asked the colonel if he would help him obtain an American uniform. To Samek's surprise the officer replied curtly, 'No, we don't have any spare uniforms here – this is a headquarters building, not a quartermaster warehouse!'

Samek nearly hit the colonel. Knowing that it would only get him a court-martial, he restrained himself and stormed out of the building. Later that day, still wearing his white shirt, white trousers, and white sneakers, he caught a ride on a plane bound for Africa.

Upon their return to Africa, the surviving American glider pilots who had made the initial glider assault landing with the British were awarded the Air Medal by the U.S. Army Air Force. More honours were later bestowed on the Americans by Colonel Chatterton, the commanding officer of the British glider pilots. Chatterton made them honorary members of his regiment and presented their adju- tants with formal orders authorizing them to wear British glider pilot wings on their uniforms. Those few surviving American glider pilots were the only ones so honoured during the war.

Several British soldiers who had witnessed the heroics of Flight Officer Samuel Fine during the bitter fight at the Ponte Grande Bridge, and the subsequent escape from Italian guards, submitted written recommendations to his commanding officer, Colonel Harvey A. Berger, that he be awarded the Silver Star Medal. Colonel Berger agreed with the recommendations and forwarded them to Brigadier General H. L. Clark, commander of the 52nd Troop Carrier Wing, but Clark returned the recommendations with a terse typewritten response: 'Not favorably considered.' Clark did, however, allow Fine to be awarded the Purple Heart Medal for the three wounds he had suffered on Sicily.

The unexplained disapproval of Fine's Silver Star recommendation was the first in a long series of such events for many other glider pilots during the war. For some undisclosed reason there seemed to be a belief in most higher headquarters that glider pilots were incapable of personal heroics on the battlefield. Even though many ground soldier eyewitnesses submitted recommendations for glider pilots to be awarded similar combat decorations, they were seldom approved for presentation.

# Chapter 5

# *Aftermath of Sicily*

IN MANY RESPECTS THE Allied glider and parachute operations on Sicily were similar to the German experience on Crete. In both cases the attackers thought that the terrible casualties suffered by their airborne troops far outweighed results they had achieved. And, coincidentally, the defending commanders of both islands felt that the invading airborne troops had performed their missions in an extraordinarily successful manner. Each island proved to be a major turning point for parachute and glider forces. For the Germans, Crete marked the end of their large-scale airborne operations. Sicily, conversely, marked the beginning of Allied airborne operations on an even greater scale – but not until after considerable soul searching in Washington.

All of the top German and Italian commanders on Sicily made glowing statements on the performance of Allied airborne troops who drove them from the island. Unfortunately for the Allied side, those statements were not heard until after the war was over.

At his command post in Algiers, a very disappointed General Eisenhower came to the conclusion that there should be no division-size airborne units in the United States Army. In his after-action report on Sicily to General Marshall, the Army Chief of Staff in Washington, Ike wrote:

> I do not believe in the airborne division. I believe that airborne troops should be reorganized in self-contained units, comprising infantry, artillery, and special services, all of about the strength of a regimental combat team. Even if one had all the air transport he could possibly use, the fact is at any given time and in any given spot only a reasonable number of air transports can be operated because of technical difficulties. To employ at any time and place a whole division would require a dropping over such an extended area that I seriously doubt that a division commander could regain control and

[110]

operate the scattered forces as one unit. In any event, if these troops were organized in smaller, self-contained units, a senior commander, with a small staff and radio communications, could always be dropped in the area to insure necessary coordination.[1]

Eisenhower's letter to Marshall placed the entire glider pilot training programme in jeopardy and very nearly broke up the five American airborne divisions (11th, 13th, 17th, 82nd, and 101st) then in existence. As each of those divisions had two glider infantry regiments and one glider artillery battalion, plus other glider-transported support units, their deactivation would have meant a near total abandonment of the still faltering glider pilot training programme and a sharp curtailment in the many glider construction projects that were just then getting into full production. Before taking such extreme steps, General Marshall ordered a select board of officers convened to determine methods of improving glider and parachute troop operating procedures. This board became known as the Swing Board because it was chaired by General Swing, recently returned from his brief service in North Africa as Ike's airborne adviser. At the same time, Marshall directed the Army Air forces to conduct extensive manoeuvres with glider troops and technical tests of the CG-4A glider at the newly completed Laurinburg-Maxton Army Air Base in North Carolina.

The Swing Board was just preparing for its first meeting at Camp Mackall, North Carolina, when, as the result of a serious incident that occurred in St. Louis, Missouri, the attention of the American public became focused on the still virtually unknown CG-4A glider.

Earlier in April, Brigadier General Bennet E. Meyers, Deputy Chief of Staff of the Material Division in Washington, had submitted a report on glider manufacturers to Lieutenant General William S. Knudson, the Director of Production in the office of the Undersecretary of War. In that report, Meyers requested a decision on the desirability of cancelling contracts of those manufacturers whose work had been marginal or whose unit prices of CG-4A gliders were considered abnormally high. In passing the report along to his boss, Undersecretary Robert P. Patterson, General Knudson recommended that contracts with four manufacturers be terminated. One of those manufacturers was the Robertson Aircraft Corporation in St. Louis. On May 1, Undersecretary Patterson informed General Meyers that he believed it would be cheaper for the government to continue all CG-4A contracts than to cancel those of substandard

[111]

producers. Robertson Aircraft was therefore allowed to continue production, and, by the end of July, had delivered 64 gliders to the Air Force.

It was a sweltering hot Sunday, August 1, 1943, when the 65th CG-4A manufactured by Robertson Aircraft was delivered to the Lambert Field airport in St. Louis. Waiting there was an impressive assemblege of dignitaries, all of whom had volunteered to go for a ride in the glider to express their patriotic support of the workers employed in St. Louis' four glider manufacturing firms (Robertson Aircraft, Laister-Kauffman Aircraft, St. Louis Aircraft, and Christopher Aircraft). This bevy of dignitaries was headed by the popular cigar-smoking mayor of St. Louis, William Dee Decker. Others in the party were Henry L. Muller, presiding judge of the St. Louis County Court; Thomas N. Dysart, president of the Chamber of Commerce; Charles L. Cunningham, the city's deputy comptroller; Max H. Doyle, the director of public utilities; William B. Robertson, president of Robertson Aircraft; Harold A. Krueger, vice president of Robertson Aircraft; and Lieutenant Colonel Paul Hazelton of the Army Air Force Material Command. With a curious crowd of several thousand looking on and a police band blaring out a martial tune, the dignitaries began boarding the glider. The last man on was his honour, Mayor Decker.

Always anxious to promote the sale of war bonds, Decker had ordered that a banner bearing the words 'Buy War Bonds Now' be fixed to the glider's tail. But in all the confusion of preparation the car bringing the banner to the airport had got hopelessly stuck in traffic. The mayor, taking one last look around for the car and not seeing it, was furious. And so was his wife, Louise – for a different reason. Several days earlier she had received a personal invitation from William B. Robertson, president of Robertson Aircraft, to go along on the glider flight with her husband. She had arrived at the airport that morning looking forward to the flight, only to be told by military authorities that Air Force regulations did not permit civilian women to fly in military aircraft.

The police band was temporarily drowned out by the roar of airplane engines as a C-47 took off with the glider in tow. In the pilot's seat of the CG-4A was Captain Milton C. Klugh. In the copilot's seat beside him was Private First Class J. M. Davis, a glider mechanic who had been given permission to go along for the ride. After climbing to 3,000 feet, the airplane and its trailing glider circled back and made one pass over the airport where the crowd shouted and waved to the accompaniment of the police band. Just after passing over the airport, Captain Klugh hit the glider release lever above his head and watched the tow-line fall away. The glider rose gracefully a few feet in the air and then began to descend. Just as it did, there was a loud cracking noise, like a clap of thunder. The right wing shot violently upward, separating itself from the glider as if it had been sliced off by a knife. The band stopped playing and the horrified crowd stared in disbelief at the falling glider. Someone shouted, 'Oh my God, they'll all be killed!' Indeed, when the glider hit the ground not even a groan came from the wreckage; everyone aboard had been killed instantly.

Investigators from the Air Force and the FBI were rushed to St. Louis that same day. Nearly everyone in town was convinced that sabotage by enemy agents was responsible for the wing tearing itself away from the glider, but a detailed examination of the wreckage revealed that the disaster had in fact been caused by the failure of a wing lift strut-to-fuselage fitting that had been manufactured by the Gardner Metal Products Company in St. Louis, one of the many subcontractors supplying parts to Robertson Aircraft. Ironically, the Gardner Company had formerly been a manufacturer of coffins. Certified blueprints of the fitting showed that it was a 10-inch piece of cylindrical steel, hollowed out at one end to allow the wing strut to be inserted and welded into place. Once the strut had been welded into the fitting, it had been impossible to check the thickness of the part. The specified thickness of the fitting's steel wall after boring was three-eighths of an inch. However, the one taken from the wreckage by investigators had been overmachined to one-sixteenth of an inch, only one-sixth as thick as required by military specifications.

Investigators visited the Robertson Aircraft factory where they discovered that 25 per cent of the fittings in the stockroom had also been overmachined to dangerously thin tolerances. Two Robertson employees, Charles C. Letty, the quality control inspector in charge, and William A. Williams, the chief receiving inspector, were suspended but not held responsible for the crash. The civilian grand jury that investigated the crash stated in its report that 'It was considered odd that the defective part should have been the one and only item on the blueprint specifications that was never able to be properly inspected because there were no instruments or methods suitable for the purpose.'[2]

[113]

Although they did not hold the two inspectors at Robertson responsible for passing defective parts purchased from subcontractors, the military investigation board reported that quality control personnel at the factory were generally inexperienced and had inadequate inspection tools. Colonel Leonard M. Johnson, president of the investigative board, stated in his report on the crash that he was 'firmly convinced that the conditions which were in existence at St. Louis prior to this accident are prevalent throughout the country.'[3] As a result of the accident, the War Department began to set up centralized schools for quality control inspectors, and later developed a standardized set of tools for the measurement of glider fittings. In the meantime, Robertson Aircraft was permitted to continue building CG-4A gliders. By October of 1944 they had delivered a total of 147 gliders at a cost of $39,000 each.

On August 4, 1943 – only three days after the St. Louis glider disaster – all of the Air Corps' top brass, from General Arnold on down, arrived at the Laurinburg-Maxton Army Air Base in North Carolina to witness demonstrations of the flying and landing characteristics of CG-4A gliders. As General Arnold climbed out of his airplane, he looked worried. His pet glider programme was in deep trouble. Earlier in June many civilian and military officials in Washington had been shaken up by the news that Major General William C. Lee, the well-known father of the American airborne troops and now commander of the 101st Airborne Division, had been aboard a CG-4A that had crashed during field manoeuvres in Tennessee. Lee survived that crash with four broken ribs, but two other passengers had been killed. On top of that bad news came word of the calamitous July night airborne landings on Sicily, where so many CG-4As had been ditched in the Mediterranean Sea and scattered on the island. And as if those four unfortunate happenings were not bad enough, the St. Louis crash had all of Washington in an uproar.

Arnold's chief guide during the day-long visit to Laurinburg-Maxton was Major Michael C. Murphy, a man who was to become the best-known American glider pilot of World War II. For the last several days Murphy and a hand-picked group of glider pilots had been rehearsing the demonstrations Arnold and the others had come to see. Having graduated from the Twentynine Palms Air Academy only a year before, Murphy was still a newcomer to glider flying, but he was no stranger to aviation. In 1928, at the age of 21, with a solo in a Waco 10 airplane, he began a remarkable flying career. During the early years of the great depression he was hired to manage the airport in Kokomo, Indiana. To supplement his income he frequently barnstormed throughout the Midwest on weekends with friends in his two-seater Canuck airplane, giving short rides to whoever could afford them and performing wing-walking exhibitions and parachute jumps with other aircraft in the aerial troupe.

By 1936, Murphy was an accomplished aerobatic flyer and had developed a number of crowd-thrilling stunts. He was the first pilot in the world to take off and land an airplane on a moving automobile. His repertoire also included landing a seaplane – equipped only with pontoons – in a cornfield. And, in a truly unusual airplane that he designed and built himself – with landing gear mounted on its top and bottom – he became the first aviator to both take off and land upside down.[4]

Not wanting to waste General Arnold's time, Murphy guided him and the other VIPs directly to the flightline, where they saw CG-4As being towed by an assortment of airplanes that included C-46 and C-47 troop transports, a B-25 bomber, and a P-38 fighter. Next there was a successful demonstration of an aerial retrieval system, invented in 1938 by Dr. L. S. Adams of Morgantown, West Virginia, which enabled an airplane in flight to pick up a fully loaded glider that was resting on the ground. Adams had originally conceived his invention as an aid to faster mail pick-up in rural areas throughout the United States. The first system looked and functioned very much like a huge fishing rod and reel. A light airplane was outfitted with an exterior boom which acted as the rod, and an internally mounted steel drum which acted as the reel. Within the drum was a length of steel cable with a large hook on its trailing end. As the airplane passed low over the pick-up station, an operator riding in its after end would act as the fisherman, snagging mail sacks that had been rigged with a tow-line suspended between two thin wooden poles. Once the sack's tow-line had been hooked, the operator could haul it aboard with the motor-driven steel cable.

On May 12, 1939, the U.S. Postal Service had inaugurated this unique airmail pick-up service in rural sections of West Virginia and Pennsylvania. Working with the Postal Service was the All-American Aviation Company, which was headed by Richard D. DuPont, the future head of the military glider programme. Eventually the service was extended into Delaware (DuPont's home state), New York and Ohio. By April of 1942, All-American Aviation had made 93,934 airmail pick-ups without a single accident. Later that summer, DuPont had given a very convincing demonstration to military authorities at Wright Field in which a low-flying Stinson monoplane successfully picked up a 2-place Schweiser XTG-3 glider piloted by Lieutenant Chester Decker. DuPont and Decker were old friends and soaring rivals. In 1936, when DuPont was trying for this third consecutive win of the U.S. National Soaring Competitions, he had been beaten by that year's champion, Chet Decker. DuPont managed to become national champion the next year, but he never did manage to win the championship three times consecutively. That honour rests today with only two individuals: John Robinson and Richard H. Johnson.

By the time that General Arnold saw the glider pick-up demonstration in August of 1943, the system was still in the final phases of adaptation to heavier military airplanes and gliders. Under the watchful eyes of Colonel Ellsworth P. Curry, the base commander at Laurinburg-Maxton, and Major Richard A. Flood, the supervisor of power pilot training at the base, the model M-80 Glider Pick-up Mechanism (as it was officially designated) was eventually perfected. Most of the credit for its successful development belongs to Captain Chester Decker, who first tested its military application and who taught its use at Laurinburg-Maxton to hundreds of power pilots. As the war progressed, pick-up teams retrieved downed gliders from battlefields in France, Holland, and Burma. Medical units also used the mechanism to evacuate CG-4As loaded with stretcher patients from forward battle areas around the globe.

Though basically a sound retrieval system, the glider pick-up operation itself was filled with danger for the crews of both the glider and the pick-up airplane. Prior to the arrival of the tow-plane, two poles had to be positioned some 50 yards ahead and slightly to the right of the parked glider to allow the tow-plane plenty of clearance as it swooped in for the pick-up. Next, one end of the tow-line would be fixed to the glider's nose and the other end draped over the tops of the poles in a closed loop configuration. To prevent a premature pick-up while ground crews were setting this up, a yellow cloth panel would be laid on the ground in front of the poles to show aircraft in the area that the glider was not yet ready for pick-up. When all was in readiness, the panel would be moved to a perpendicular position between the two poles.

[116]

In making its approach to snag the tow-line, the airplane had to drop to an altitude of only 20 feet. Once the line had been snagged by the airplane's trailing hook, a length of cable would rapidly pay out of the drum. Tension would then be gently applied to the cable, drawing the tow-line taut almost at once. Coordination between pilots of both aircraft had to be complete, because in a matter of seconds the glider would be whisked off the ground at about the same speed as an accelerating city bus.

For his part, the glider pilot had to keep the glider from swinging too far to the right during take-off. Failure to maintain a steady position during this critical phase of the operation could cause either the steel cable or the tow-line, or both, to slap into the underside of the tow-ship's elevators, forcing them upward and causing the airplane to stall out and crash.

When the series of demonstrations had been completed for General Arnold and other VIPs, at the flightline, Major Murphy escorted everyone to a wooded area at the edge of the base, where a CG-4A equipped with special flotation devices made a perfect landing in a large pond. The entire company then drove to a large forested area where several CG-4As performed new landing techniques pioneered by Murphy.

Prior to this demonstration, the policy had been for the CG-4As to make what were called 'blitz' landings – a very low approach to the landing zone by the towing plane, a quick release of the tow-line, and then a dive nearly straight down to a landing at speeds upward of 100 miles per hour. The idea, of course, was to get on the ground as quickly as possible to avoid being a target for enemy gunners. The new technique Murphy demonstrated to the VIPs involved a high approach to the landing zone, followed by a cutaway and then a 90 degree turn which served to eat up some of the glider's airspeed, thus permitting a slower landing and a fairly quick stop on the ground.

The VIPs adjourned to the base officers' club for technical briefings and an early dinner. The setting sun was casting a beautiful array of colours across the sky when the VIPs left the officers' club and climbed on board a waiting military bus. With General Arnold's staff car in the lead, they headed out to a remote section of the base for a final presentation of night glider flying techniques – a very touchy subject because of what had happened over on Sicily only a few weeks before. All of the VIPs expected that this final class would simply consist of a short lecture, during which a briefing officer

[117]

would recite statistics about mandatory separation distances for gliders flying at night. In fact, Major Murphy had cooked up an incredible night-landing demonstration, well remembered today as the 'Pea Patch Show' because the landing zone had been a genuine pea patch before being cleared by army engineers for the show.

The bus delivered the VIPs to a large, open area just as the sun set. Except for a small row of bleachers and a thick stand of pine trees off to one side, not much else was visible for miles. When it was completely dark, Murphy started the show by ordering all lights and cigarettes extinguished. He then began talking to the VIPs over a loudspeaker about the virtues of CG-4A gliders. Unable to see Murphy, or anything else in the darkness, the VIPs had no choice but to sit and listen to him.

Murphy was nearing the end of his pitch when, in the dark sky several miles away, 10 CG-4As cut themselves loose from their tug ships at 30 second intervals and headed down toward a dim light concealed behind a barricade at the far end of the landing zone. Murphy's voice booming out over the loudspeaker system kept General Arnold and the other VIPs from hearing the muffled thumps and rumble of landing gear of the gliders touching down directly in front of them.

As he heard the last glider slide to a stop, Murphy yelled, 'Lights!' and turned night into day with a hidden battery of floodlights. The spectators were stunned. Less than half an hour ago the lights had gone out on an empty field. Now there were 10 menacing combat gliders sitting practically in their laps.

Mike Murphy was a supreme showman as well as an expert aviator. His audience was still staring at the big gliders when a nine-piece military band paraded out of one of them playing the Air Corps' marching song. Hollywood could not have staged a more professional show.

Later that night General Arnold flew back to Washington, convinced that fully loaded combat gliders could in fact make accurate and safe landings in darkness. Murphy's night-landing demonstration had breathed new life into the faltering programme.

The U.S. Army Air Force felt the need for bigger gliders that would be able to accommodate upwards of 40 combat troops and, alternatively, serve as transporters of vehicles larger than jeeps and heavy artillery loads. By the end of the summer of 1943, three new gliders, the CG-10A, CG-13A, and the XCG-16, were in various stages of production to meet those needs.

The first of the bigger gliders to be ready for full production was the

CG-13A. It had been designed by Waco Aircraft, the same company that had produced the smaller CG-4A glider. Boasting a wingspan of 54 feet, the CG-13A could transport 30 combat troops. Like the CG-4A, this glider was flown by two pilots, and its nose section was hinged at the top. A pair of hydraulic actuating cylinders was used to raise the entire nose section, exposing a huge cargo compartment 7½ feet tall, 6 feet wide, and 24 feet deep – only 1½ feet shorter than that of England's giant tank-carrying Hamilcar glider. The depth of the cargo compartment, coupled with the strength of its reinforced floor, enabled the CG-13A to lift a 105 mm howitzer complete with a jeep, ammunition, and gun crew; or a 1½ ton 6 by 6 truck loaded with supplies; or 10,000 pounds of assorted supplies and ammunition. The first models of this glider came equipped with only one set of landing wheels; later production models had a third wheel added in the nose section. A total of 132 CG-13As were built during World War II, 85 by Ford Motor Company and 47 by the Northwestern Aeronautical Corporation. Several CG-13As were used in combat by American troops operating in the Pacific and European theatres.

When the CG-13A was approved for quantity production in August 1943, the Air Force asked the Laister-Kauffman Aircraft Corporation in St. Louis to develop the CG-10A, a high-wing, full cantilever monoplane glider that could carry 40 troops. Because it was made entirely out of wood and could conceal 40 armed men, the CG-10A was nicknamed the Trojan Horse by its manufacturer. This huge glider, with a wingspan of 105 feet and a length of 68½ feet, had a maximum airspeed of 180 mph. That airspeed could be drastically reduced for landing by manually operated spoilers positioned along the upper surfaces of both wings. As big as it was, the CG-10A could easily be towed by C-46, C-47, and C-54 airplanes.

The CG-10A was the second largest glider to be built by the Americans during the war years (the U.S. Navy's XLRN-1 was the largest), and the only one to be equipped with clamshell doors in the aft end of its fuselage. Through those doors could be loaded 10,850 pounds of cargo; or one 2½ ton truck (better known as a deuce-and-a-half by soldiers); or two 105 mm howitzers; or one 155 mm howitzer and its gun crew with a supply of ammunition. Intending to use fleets of CG-10As in the invasion of Japan, the government ordered 1,000 of them into production. But the war ended before any of them could be employed in combat. The plan had been for the gliders to be shipped aboard barges from the point of manufacture in

[119]

St. Louis down the Mississippi River to New Orleans. There they would have been loaded aboard waiting Liberty ships and transported through the Panama Canal to American-held islands near Japan to be prepared for the great invasion. At the time the contract was cancelled the glider's manufacturer, Laister-Kauffman, had built a total of 10 CG-10As at a cost of $1 million each.

On September 9, 1943, Richard DuPont and Colonel Percival E. Gabel flew out to California from their Washington offices for a test ride in the experimental 42-place MC-1 (M for military, C for cargo) glider. Originally designed in 1942 by Hawley Bowlus, one of America's best-known glider enthusiasts during the 1930s, the MC-1 was a twin-boom, flying-wing glider that measured 48 feet 3 inches long and had a wingspan of 91 feet 8 inches. The unique feature of the futuristic-looking glider was its airfoil-shaped fuselage which had a large bulbous nose section and tapered off aft.

The fuselage of the MC-1 had two separate cargo compartments, separated by a wooden wall. Entrance to the compartments was gained through the front of the wing which opened like a giant human jaw. When the cargo compartments were fully opened the top sections of the wing were locked in an upward position, much like the nose of a CG-4A glider, while the bottom section of the fuselage rested on the ground to act as a loading ramp. Utilizing both of its 15-foot-deep cargo compartments, the MC-1 could carry two 105 mm howitzers; or a jeep and one howitzer; or a total of 10,080 pounds of other cargo.

Two pilots, sitting in tandem, flew the MC-1 from a cockpit on top of the fuselage. Maximum airspeed for this glider was 220 miles per hour. It landed on the same fully retractable tricycle landing gear mounted in P-38 fighter aircraft.

At the time Richard DuPont and Colonel Gabel flew out to California, the MC-1 was the property of the Airborne Transport Company, headquartered in Los Angeles. The chief officers of that company were Hawley Bowlus and Albert Critz. Anxious to secure a government contract to build production models of their experimental glider, Bowlus and Critz had invited DuPont and Gabel to California for a demonstration flight. DuPont was already an old friend and former student of Bowlus; nine years earlier, in 1934, DuPont had won the fifth annual American National Soaring Competitions at Elmira, New York, in the graceful 'Albatross II' which Bowlus had designed and built.

[120]

On September 10, with Bowlus at the controls and Colonel Gabel behind him in the copilot's seat, the MC-1 was towed aloft from March Field by a B-17 bomber for a practice demonstration flight. Gabel, an accomplished power pilot, was a complete novice at the art of glider flying, but with Bowlus as his teacher he quickly became familiar with the flight characteristics of the MC-1. Everything went like clockwork.

At 3:15 p.m. the following day, the MC-1 took to the air again, this time behind a Lockheed C-60 airplane piloted by Captain Paul Shoup. During this flight Hawley Bowlus remained on the ground and Colonel Gabel sat in the front pilot's seat. Howard Morrison, a civilian glider pilot in the employ of the Airborne Transport Company, was in the copilot's seat. Four passengers were also on board. Riding in the right cargo compartment were Richard DuPont and Curley Chandler, the civilian crew chief of the MC-1. Over in the left compartment were two employees of Airborne Transport, Harry N. Perl, a flight test engineer, and Paul Wells, an aircraft construction worker who had volunteered to go along for the ride. Both pilots and all passengers were wearing parachutes.

The tow-plane had reached an altitude of 3,500 feet when the glider began oscillating in pitch (up and down). During the second upward oscillation some of the 1,000 pounds of ballast that had been stowed in forward sections of the cargo compartments was thrown to the rear of the glider. On the third upward oscillation the tow-line release mechanism gave way. The MC-1 stalled out immediately and started falling toward the earth in a flat spin. Seeing that he could not bring the glider out of the ever-quickening spin, Colonel Gabel shouted, 'Hit the silk!' Hearing that dreaded command, Perl and DuPont quickly moved to the rear of their respective cargo compartments, threw open escape hatches above their heads, and began climbing out onto the wing. As he was climbing out of his side of the glider, Perl glanced over and saw DuPont doing the same thing on his side. Both men jumped free and grabbed their rip cord handles. Just as soon as Perl leaped into space Paul Wells followed him over the side. For some unexplained reason, Curley Chandler did not jump even after DuPont had cleared the falling ship.

Both Perl and DuPont were experienced glider pilots. As such they obediently followed standard emergency parachuting procedure, allowing themselves to fall well clear of the spinning glider before opening their chutes. But in so doing they fell through considerable altitude before their parachutes finally popped open. Meanwhile Paul Wells, a man of no aviation experience, had opened his parachute the instant his feet left the glider. Wells' lack of aviation experience was to save his life.

Having done everything by the book, and also having fallen a great distance in the meantime, Harry Perl was a mere 100 feet above the ground when his parachute finally opened. Dupont was not as fortunate. His chute was barely beginning to blossom when he hit, and he was killed instantly. Seconds later Paul Wells, the aviation novice, landed safely a few hundred yards away from DuPont and Perl.

As soon as he landed, Perl struggled to his feet and collapsed his billowing parachute. Quickly he peeled it off and ran as fast as he could to where DuPont lay motionless on the ground. Seeing that he was dead, Perl than ran over to the pile of wreckage that only a few moments ago had been a sleek MC-1 glider. There he found the bodies of Colonel Gabel and Curley Chandler, both of whom had died on impact. Morrison, the copilot, was still alive. An ambulance rushed him to the hospital, but he died later that day.

Despite the disastrous crash at March Field, the MC-1 subsequently proved itself to be an airworthy glider. Two months after the crash, the Army Air Force signed a contract with Airborne Transport Company for the delivery of two other MC-1s. In May of 1944 the company flew the first of those two gliders from Oxnard, California, to the Air Force's glider flight test centre at Clinton Army Air Field in Ohio. Given a new designation of XCG-16 by the Air Force, the glider was extensively tested by military pilots and aeronautical technicians at Clinton Army Air Field and at another military test centre in Orlando, Florida. At the conclusion of those tests, members of the review board ruled that the XCG-16 was not suitable for use as a military glider. In November of 1944 an Air Force airplane returned the XCG-16 to California and a contract termination letter was sent out from Washington.

On Sunday, September 12, 1943 – the day after the crash of the MC-1 glider in California – the Germans pulled off Operation Eiche (Oak), another of their spectacular wartime achievements involving the use of gliders. Since being removed by Italy's King Victor Emmanuel earlier in July, Benito Mussolini had been kept in confinement by Italian authorities. Fearing that the Germans or some Italian Fascist groups might try to liberate Mussolini, the Italian police periodically moved him to new hiding places. Hitler, meanwhile, ordered German intelligence agents operating in Italy to stay on Mussolini's trail until they found the place where he was being detained. Hitler's plan was to liberate Mussolini and restore him to power.

To ensure a successful rescue, Hitler dispatched to Italy his top unconventional warfare expert, Captain Otto Skorzeny, with a select group of 50 German paratroopers, many of whom spoke fluent Italian. Two weeks after arriving in Italy, Skorzeny learned that Mussolini was being held prisoner in the Campo Imperatore Hotel, located on the Grand Sasso. Resting on the tallest peak in the Abruzzi Mountains, some 65 miles northeast of Rome, the hotel could only be reached by cable car.

Skorzeny knew that there was a force of 250 Italian carabinieri (civilian police), all of whom were well known for their rock-solid allegiance to the crown, guarding Mussolini at the hotel, and that a platoon of Italian soldiers was in control of the cable car station at the base of the mountain. Working closely with General Kurt Student and his airborne staff in Rome, Skorzeny devised a plan for a lightning-fast rescue. It called for a special team of 120 paratroopers, led by himself, to land aboard 12 DFS 230 gliders in a small, grassy triangle just in front of the mountaintop hotel. On landing, this force was to storm the hotel, free Mussolini, and send him down to the base of the mountain in a cable car. There he would be met by a company of German paratroopers who would spirit him away to a nearby airport for evacuation to Rome aboard a Heinkel 111 bomber. Take-off time for the mission was set for 6:00 a.m. on September 12. Skorzeny estimated that one hour after take-off, he and his men would be landing on the mountaintop.

A bare 45 minutes before the gliders were due to take off, German intelligence agents delivered a very frightened Italian Carabinieri General, Antonio Soleti, to the Pratica di Mare airfield in Rome. There Soleti was told by Skorzeny that he would accompany the German troops on their glider raid for the purpose of ordering those carabinieri officers guarding Mussolini not to resist the rescue attempt.

On hearing Skorzeny's apparently mad scheme, Soleti drew his pistol and threatened to commit suicide. He was quickly disarmed, however, and Skorzeny told him forcefully that he would be going along on the raid.

Because of the late arrival of the gliders, which had to be towed in from France, and an Allied bombing raid that morning on the departure airfield, Skorzeny and his raiding party did not take off until 1:00 p.m., six hours later than planned. The first two airplane–glider combinations contained skilled navigators who were supposed to lead the way to the objective. Skorzeny and the Italian general rode in the third glider. When he got above the clouds, Skorzeny looked around for the two leading pathfinder tugs and gliders but could not find them. Unbeknownst to Skorzeny, both airplanes and gliders were still back at the airport, unable to lift off because their landing gear had been severely damaged by bomb craters at the end of the runway. Considerably perplexed, Skorzeny assumed the lead slot in the formation as it headed northeastward toward the Abruzzi Mountains.

Suddenly the Grand Sasso loomed into view. Tapping the glider pilot on the shoulder, Skorzeny signalled him to cut away from the tug ship and head down for the landing zone. With only a minute remaining to touchdown, the glider pilot released a drag parachute to reduce his airspeed. Using all the skill he could muster, the pilot thumped the glider down on its central belly skid to a perfect landing at the edge of the grass. Seconds later it came to a halt only 30 yards from the front door of the hotel. Holding his fire, Skorzeny ran into the entrance clutching the arm of the terror-stricken General Soleti, who kept screaming, 'Don't shoot, don't shoot, it is me, General Soleti!'

Without either side firing a shot, Skorzeny, who stood six feet four inches tall, pushed his way into the lobby, dashed up to the third floor, and burst into the room where Mussolini was being held captive. Outside the hotel, five other gliders were landing on the front lawn. The first four made it in without incident, but the fifth glider rammed a huge rock, killing all aboard. By the time the dust settled Skorzeny had, with the help of General Soleti, persuaded the commander of all police units on the mountain, General Mario Gueli, not to resist the rescue operation.

Now that Mussolini had been freed, there remained the problem of getting him off the mountain. A telephone call to the base of the mountain revealed that the getaway airplane had ruined its landing gear upon arrival at the local airport and would be unable to take off again. Skorzeny ordered the alternative escape plan into effect, and moments later a small, lightweight Fiesler Storch airplane that had been discreetly orbiting just east of the Grand Sasso area landed in the hotel's parking lot.[5] At its controls was General Student's personal pilot, Captain Hans Gerlach. With an apprehensive glance at the little airplane, Mussolini climbed aboard with Skorzeny while 12 German paratroopers held the tail and wings and Captain Gerlach revved the engine. When Gerlech dropped his upraised arm, the paratroopers released their grip and the little plane shot forward. After a couple of bounces, it skimmed over the edge of a cliff and levelled off. Benito Mussolini was free.

For having led this storybook rescue mission, Skorzeny was promoted to major and awarded the Knights Cross. Mussolini, after a sojourn at Hitler's field headquarters in East Prussia, was empowered to govern the northern part of Italy which was then still under control of German troops. There he served as Hitler's puppet until he and his mistress, Clara Petacci, were murdered in April 1945 by anti-Fascist Italian partisans.

Throughout the war, American flight engineers searched for ways to improve the crash survivcability of the CG-4A glider and to provide its pilots with greater protection during rough landings. The CG-4A's first major modification came in the form of a device called the Corey Skid. This was a wooden, ski-like device designed by Lieutenant Colonel Warner R. Corey, the chief glider maintenance officer assigned to Laurinburg-Maxton Army Air Field in North Carolina. Only four feet long and one foot wide, the Corey Skid was bolted to the bottom of the fuselage beneath the pilot's compartment. Mounted in that position it served to deflect most of the solid objects which formerly would have caved in the glider's nose and broken the legs of the pilots.

In October 1943, the Army Air Force took delivery of a larger and stronger crash protection device from the Ludington-Griswold Company of Saybrook, Connecticut. Several months earlier this company had submitted a proposal to the Aircraft Laboratory at Wright Field for a streamlined nose section it had designed for the boxcar-like CG-4A glider. Incorporated into the new nose section was an extremely rugged crash-protection structure which had been designed by Roger W. Griswold II, president and chief engineer at Ludington-Griswold. It consisted of a spiderweb-like series of curved rolled steel trusses, designed for progressive failure (gradual energy-absorbing collapse) and the deflection of obstacles, that would enable the glider to survive collisions with small trees, stakes, wire barriers, and other such objects with minimum loss of life or injury to pilots and passengers.

Officials at Wright Field liked the idea of added crash protection but protested against the sophisticated aerodynamics of the stream-lined nose section because it would require too much time and money. They told Ludington-Griswold to forget the new exterior nose section and to supply only the inner skeleton of the crash protection structure. On October 11, 1943, Captain Floyd J. Sweet, a design and development engineer at Wright Field, ferried the first CG-4A to be equipped with the new Griswold Nose (as it became known among glider pilots) from Hartford, Connecticut, back to Wright Field for testing. There it was accepted as designed and incorporated as a standard part of all newly manufactured CG-4As. Just prior to the Allied airborne invasion of Normandy, several hundred bolt-on nose kits were rushed to England and installed on CG-4A gliders. A great many glider pilots who survived the war owe their lives to the sturdy Griswold Nose.

By late October 1943, the U.S. Army had activated a total of eleven glider infantry regiments,[6] one separate glider infantry batta-lion,[7] and 10 glider artillery battalions.[8] One of the more amazing aspects of the rapidly growing American glider programme was the fact that duty in those glider combat units was not voluntary. Physi-cally fit soldiers were routinely assigned to glider duty just as other soldiers were sent to become members of infantry and tank divisions. Few men complained about being assigned to the glider troops; most felt it was their soldierly duty to go where the Army sent them. What galled the soldiers who rode in the motorless aircraft was that they received neither flight pay nor hazardous duty pay like the para-troopers. Nor were they given any special insignia and badges like those the paratroopers had. They were not even issued parachutes for emergency escapes, as were all crewmen aboard other military aircraft. Every glider flight was a do-or-die mission for them, and many of them were to die in the months ahead.

Homemade posters showing grisly photos of crashed and burned gliders were hung on barrack walls of the glider troop units. The captions read: 'Join the glider troops! No flight pay. No jump pay. But never a dull moment!' A song entitled 'The Glider Riders' was later written, describing the dangers of glider duty. Copies were mailed to several congressmen, who introduced legislation to award hazardous duty pay to the glider troops.

The inequitable pay situation was not rectified until July 1944, when glider troops were authorized the same hazardous duty pay as paratroopers: $50 a month for enlisted men, $100 a month for officers. At about the same time, the glider troops were awarded a special badge, similar in appearance to the paratrooper's silver jump wings. On the glider badge, the parachute had been replaced by a front-end view of a CG-4A glider.

Major General Ridgway, commander of the 82nd Airborne Division, wrote in his Sicily after-action report of November 6, 1943, that 'Both the 82nd Airborne Division and the North African Air Force Troop Carrier Command are today at airborne training levels below combat requirements.' A little further along in that report Ridgway commented on the night flying proficiency of American glider pilots: 'Up to the present, the Troop Carrier Command glider pilots have not had sufficient training to conduct a successful night glider operation. Several hundred well-trained glider pilots will be required for an actual operation. If this requirement is to be met, it is most important that an intensive night glider training program and combined training program be pursued without interruption.'[9]

Reacting to Ridgway's suggestion, the Air Force set up a triangular night glider flying course in North Carolina. The three corners were Camp Mackall, the Laurinburg-Maxton Army Field, and the city of Asheville. Almost every night, the drone of C-47 engines could be heard above those points as fully loaded gliders were towed around the triangle. Nearly all flights originated at Laurinburg-Maxton. After spending a few hours negotiating the triangle behind their tow-ships the gliders would be cut loose to land back at Laurinburg-Maxton, or occasionally at Camp Mackall.

Friday, November 19, 1943, was the third wedding anniversary of Captain Richard L. Hoyt of the 11th Airborne Division based at Camp Mackall. But Hoyt and his wife, Claire, were unable to celebrate together because he and his unit had been scheduled to participate in a night glider flying training mission that evening.

Knowing that he would be taking off at 8:50 p.m. from Laurinburg-Maxton and landing at the same field some two hours later, Hoyt made a plan that would salvage at least part of that special evening. During the flight he would wear his dress uniform and dress overcoat with a neatly folded overseas cap stowed in the left pocket. On top of all that formal attire he would wear his steel helmet, pistol belt, canvas leggings, and other required combat equipment. An hour after take-off his wife would drive the 40 miles down to the officers' club at Laurinburg-Maxton and meet him for a late night dinner and bottle of champagne.

It was cold and completely dark when, at 8:00 p.m., Hoyt and his men began loading their equipment through the upraised nose of a CG-4A on the airstrip at Laurinburg-Maxton. Two soldiers hauled aboard a wheeled M3A4 machine gun cart containing a large SCR-284 command radio. Positioning it behind the copilot's seat, they lashed it down firmly with half-inch sisal rope and a series of baker bowline knots.[10] When all equipment had been secured, the nose section was lowered and locked into place. Technician Fifth Class Harold Stephens and Privates Jerome Heltzel, Virgil Lash, Franklin Karrick and Marvin Beane filed into the glider through the side troop door and began strapping themselves into their seats along the left wall of the fuselage. They were followed aboard by Corporal Allen Henry and Private Andrew Russo, who seated themselves along the right wall in back of the cart containing the big radio.

Though all CG-4As had dual controls, they could be flown by a single pilot and very often were. On this flight Captain Hoyt and his men would have only one pilot, Flight Officer Michael J. Harty from the 82nd Squadron of the 433rd Troop Carrier Wing based at Laurinburg-Maxton. Since the copilot's seat was unoccupied, Hoyt slid into it and strapped himself down.

Only ten minutes into the flight Captain Hoyt noticed a bright white light flashing in the astrodome[11] of the C-47 tug-ship. 'How come that light is flashing?' he asked Flight Officer Harty. 'It means our tow-ship is in some sort of serious trouble,' Harty replied. 'We've got to cut ourselves loose immediately.' With that, Harty reached up and pushed the tow-line release lever. Descending through darkness, Hoyt and Harty craned their necks, looking for a clearing in which to make a safe emergency landing. But because it was a moonless night, the ground below looked like a large black blanket.

At 600 feet Hoyt spotted a light patch of earth and called Harty's attention to it. Harty, who had already seen the patch, was putting the glider into a 180 degree turn. With deft moves of his hands and feet, Harty calmly lined the glider up on the clearing, which now appeared to be large enough to accommodate several CG-4As.

Unfortunately, the safe-looking expanse turned out to be a loosely ploughed cornfield surrounded by tall trees. The treetops slapped the bottom of the glider as it passed through them in a steep nosedive. The instant the glider touched down, it dug its nose into the soft soil and was jerked to a halt with a tremendous crash. The violence of the sudden stop broke the safety straps holding Captain Hoyt in the copilot's seat, catapulted him through the windshield, and sent him spinning through rows of cornstalks.

Hoyt regained consciousness a short while later and stumbled back to the now silent pile of wreckage. Removing a few pieces of debris from the crumpled nose section, he found Flight Officer Harty wedged down between the foot controls. Harty was alive, but just barely; a large chunk of flesh had been cut out of his left leg by the rudder pedal. Harty, though only semiconscious, managed to pull the flare pistol from the broken wall beside him. Handing it to Hoyt, he told him to fire a flare so that other aircraft of their flight still passing overhead would see it and report their location to rescue crews back at the airbase.

Hoyt, his hands and arms throbbing with intense pain, was having trouble firing the flare pistol when Technician Fifth Class Henry came crawling out of the wreckage. Handing the pistol to Henry, Hoyt instructed him to fire it. Henry then walked a few steps away from the glider, aimed the pistol straight up into the sky, and pulled the trigger. The unexploded flare shell was still on its way up when Hoyt, gritting his teeth, set about removing the badly injured pilot from the nose section. Meanwhile, Henry climbed back into the dark troop compartment and begun unfastening the safety belts of the other passengers, all of whom were still unconscious.

Hoyt was so occupied with his struggle to remove Harty from the wreckage that he never saw the brightly burning red flare drifting back toward the glider. With horrifying accuracy, the flare landed on top of the glider's midsection and instantly set fire to its highly inflammable painted canvas skin. Fanned by a gentle breeze, the flames soon engulfed the entire glider. Seeing what had happened, Hoyt pulled as hard as he could on the trapped pilot, freed him, and dragged him off to safety. Then he dashed into the blazing troop compartment in search of other survivors. There he bumped into Henry, who was still unfastening seat straps of unconscious passengers. Private Lash, who had regained consciousness, was assisting Henry. Groping through the smoke-filled compartment, they found Private Russo, who appeared to be seriously injured. Russo's seat belt had been ripped out of its retaining sockets and he had been hurled out of his seat. They found him lying stuffed underneath the machine gun cart, which was still firmly lashed in place. As the cart containing the heavy radio was lifted off him, Russo regained consciousness and amazed everyone by running out of the glider.

The flames had burned clear down to the floorboards when Hoyt and Henry began dragging three unconscious men, Privates Beane, Heltzel and Karrick, out of the glider. Trying to determine the extent of their injuries, Hoyt discovered that Heltzel was dead. Beane eventually regained consciousness; Karrick died several hours later.

When all of his men and the pilot had been evacuated from the burning glider, Captain Hoyt began to feel sharp pains shooting through his entire body. Grabbing a bunch of cornstalks for support, he turned to Corporal Henry and told him to take another headcount to be certain that everyone was out of the wreck. Just then two civilians arrived, the farmer who owned the cornfield, and the farmer's wife. They had seen the crash from their farmhouse window. Speaking to Hoyt, the farmer said, 'I saw you when you shot out of that thing like a cannonball. You're mighty lucky to be still alive!'

Not having a telephone in his own home, the farmer volunteered to drive one of the least injured survivors to a farmhouse nearby that did have a phone. Captain Hoyt sent Corporal Henry. When Hoyt visited the farmer some time later, he was told that as soon as they pulled up in front of the neighbour's house, Corporal Henry jumped out of the car before it had stopped rolling, ran up the steps and through the door without knocking and demanded of the startled occupants, 'Where's your telephone?'!

The first medical help to reach the scene was a local doctor who arrived only half an hour after the crash. He had been standing on his porch, hoping to see the flight go by, when he saw the red flare. Because his brother was in the Air Corps and stationed at Laurinburg-Maxton, the doctor could guess that a glider had gone down. Pausing only long enough to grab his black bag, he had hopped into his car and gone scouting for the wreckage. One hour after the crash, military ambulances arrived to evacuate everyone back to the hospital at the airbase. There it was discovered that Flight Officer Harty had suffered a broken back, two broken legs, and cuts and bruises over most of his body. All of Hoyt's men had likewise suffered extensive cuts and bruises. The most seriously injured passengers were Private Russo, with a broken arm, and Private Beane who sustained a severe brain concussion. As for Captain Hoyt, X-rays revealed that he had suffered a bone fracture of the lower lumbar region of his back, a broken left leg and foot, and numerous cuts and bruises. There was no anniversary party at the officers' club that night.

Several weeks after the crash, Captain Hoyt was transferred by ambulance to the base hospital at Camp Mackall suffering from partial paralysis of both legs.[12] Flight Officer Harty, meanwhile, remained in a full body cast at Laurinburg-Maxton. It was not until 1980, some 37 years after the crash, that these two men re-established contact with one another through a letter, written by Hoyt, to the editor of *Silent Wings*, the quarterly newsletter of the National World War II Glider Pilots Association.

The special glider and parachute manoeuvres that Army Chief of Staff Marshall had ordered in the wake of the Sicilian invasion were held during the first week in December 1943. Because the objective of the manoeuvres was the Knollwood Airport in North Carolina, this key exercise became known in airborne history as the Knollwood Maneuver. The chief umpire and grader of the manoeuvre was Lieutenant General Leslie J. McNair, the hard-nosed commander of Army Ground Forces.[13] McNair had orginally been a strong friend of airborne troops, calling them 'high-spirited like the Rangers, but very fine soldiers'. But because of what he called their 'unsatisfactory performances' during earlier operations in North Africa and on Sicily, McNair's affection for the airborne troops had cooled considerably. Also observing the manoeuvre would be Undersecretary of War Robert P. Patterson; Major General Ridgway, temporarily back from Europe; and Brigadier Leo Donovan, the new commander of the Airborne Command at Camp Mackall.

The 'aggressor', troops for this manoeuvre were General Swing's 187th and 188th Glider Infantry regiments and his 511th Parachute Infantry Regiment, and the 101st Airborne Division's 501st Parachute Infantry Regiment. Defending troops were a composite team from the 17th Airborne Division and one battalion from the independent 541st Parachute Infantry Regiment.

On the opening day of the manoeuvre, General Swing launched a massive dawn glider and parachute assault from four separate airfields in North and South Carolina against several points held by the 'enemy'. Swing's troops knew that on their performance depended the very life of their division as well as the lives of other airborne divisions, and they put maximum effort into every task.

The manoeuvre was a huge success for the airborne. Six days after the initial glider and parachute assaults, the exercise ended with all glider pilots and participating troops herded onto army trucks for the long ride back to their bases through a freezing rainstorm. Huddled beneath ice-covered blankets aboard the bouncing trucks, the exhausted pilots and troopers got their first uninterrupted sleep in nearly a week.

On December 16, General McNair penned his verdict on the Knollwood Maneuver to General Swing:

> I congratulate you on the splendid performance of your division in the Knollwood Maneuver. After the airborne operations in Africa and Sicily, my staff and I had become convinced of the impracticality of handling large airborne units. I was prepared to recommend to the War Department that airborne divisions be abandoned in our scheme of organization and that the airborne effort be restricted to parachute units of battalion size or smaller. The successful performance of your division has convinced me that we were wrong, and I shall now recommend that we continue our present schedule of activating, training, and committing airborne divisions.[14]

The moribund airborne division concept had been revived. Future large-scale airborne combat action would demonstrate the wisdom of McNair's decision.

# Chapter 6

# *The Forgotten War in Burma*

JAPAN, IN PURSUIT OF HER goal to forcibly establish the 'Greater East Asia Co-Prosperity Sphere', struck quickly and devastatingly during December 1941 at the combined Pacific might of the United States, Great Britain and the Netherlands government in exile. Following a shrewdly calculated war plan which took full advantage of the fact that England was then locked in a death struggle with Germany and that the United States was unprepared for war, the Japanese armed forces launched simultaneous strikes at Pearl Harbor, Wake, Guam, Hong Kong, Thailand, Malaya and the Philippines. Japan's main goal in launching this centrifugal offensive was the rapid seizure of the rich southern resources area of Malaya and the Netherlands East Indies. Here were the raw materials she needed to continue her policy of conquest and domination: 85 per cent of the world's rubber, 65 per cent of its tin, and large quantities of oil, iron, gold, nickel, manganese and bauxite.

Moving with tremendous speed and audacity, Japanese army, navy and air force units, all of which had been thoroughly toughened by four years of combat in China, swiftly won their initial objectives. By February 15, 1942, Japan had destroyed the United States Pacific Fleet at Pearl Harbor; captured Wake, Guam, and Hong Kong; occupied Thailand and the Philippines, and forced over 70,000 British troops to surrender the so-called impregnable fortress of Singapore in Malaya. Pausing only long enough to resupply her extended forces, Japan next launched a ground and air assault into Burma, a jungle-covered country that occupies an area equal in size to the combined areas of France, Holland, Belgium, Luxembourg and Switzerland. Japan's immediate goals in Burma were to destroy all British forces there and to cut off the Burma Road, China's principal ground artery of supply.[1]

In Burma the Japanese were confronted by an assortment of

[133]

British units that had been hastily dispatched from India and Africa, and by two divisions of Chinese troops operating under the command of America's Major General Joseph W. 'Vinegar Joe' Stilwell. Despite the gallant efforts of those Allied forces, the Japanese promptly captured Rangoon, Burma's southern seaport capital, and began pushing north toward Mandalay. By the first week in May, Allied resistance throughout Burma had collapsed and there was a massive retreat into the relative safety of India. In only five months of campaigning, Japan had achieved all of her strategic objectives and had succeeded in completely isolating China except for one tenuous line of aerial resupply which extended from India over the 500-mile Himalayan Hump to China's Yunnan plateau.

Ending his retreat at the city of Imphal in India, Vinegar Joe Stilwell gave his brutally honest opinion of the first Burma campaign: 'I claim we got a hell of a beating. We got run out of Burma . . . I think we ought to find out what caused it, go back, and retake it.'[2]

Due to more pressing strategic requirements, the Allies would be unable to do much about retaking Burma until late in 1943. Before that time, however, a small brigade-sized guerrilla force of British, Burmese and Gurkha infantrymen was formed in India. After going through an intensive series of close combat drills at the Ramgarh training centre, this unit was given the mission of infiltrating into Burma, conducting raids against isolated Japanese positions, and then returning to India.

The commander of this brigade was Brigadier Orde Charles Wingate, one of England's finest but least understood combat leaders of World War II. Though only 40 years old, Wingate was already a well-known figure throughout the British army because of his extraordinary success as the commander of unconventional fighting forces in other parts of the world. He had first gained the attention of England's military brass in 1938 when, as a captain, he demonstrated his brilliance in Palestine. Axis-subsidized Arab terrorists had been puncturing the oil pipeline extending from Mosul to Haifa and terrorizing Jewish communities. To combat the terrorists, Wingate organized several small mobile units, called Special Night Squads, made up of British soldiers and Palestine Jews who were familiar with local terrain. Night after night his squads snared terrorist patrols attempting to damage the pipeline. Only six months after starting operations with his night fighters, Wingate had brought the terrorist problem under control. For that accomplishment he became known in Palestine as the 'Lawrence of Judea'.

Two years after his success in Palestine, Wingate, now a major, was dispatched to Italian-occupied Ethiopia where he commanded 'Gideon Force', an 1,800-man guerrilla unit composed of lightly armed Sudanese and Ethiopian soldiers. Operating in the fashion of the Old Testament Gideon, Wingate divided his force into three highly mobile marching columns and conducted his operations only at night. With his small army, Wingate waged fierce battles against Italian army units at several key points throughout Ethiopia. In May 1941 – only six months after arriving in Ethiopia – Wingate accompanied Emperor Haile Selassie as the Emperor triumphantly rode a white charger through the streets of Addis Ababa in a victory parade.

In September 1942 Wingate was called to India from England to organize and train the troops who were to conduct the long-range penetration and raiding missions into Burma. Wingate called his force Chindits, after the fierce-looking Chinthey, the mythological Hindu beast whose likenesses stand guard outside Burmese pagodas to fight off evil spirits. Early in February 1943, Wingate led his force of 3,000 Chindits on foot over the treacherous Chin Hills and down into north central Burma. There he and his Chindits launched night raids against Japanese occupation forces for three months, suffering a great many casualties. Throughout all of their operations inside Burma, the Chindits were supplied at night by parachute deliveries of ammunition and food from the Royal Air Force. When they exfiltrated into India during the middle of March, the Chindits had lost over one-third of their number to disease and the enemy. Because there was no way to evacuate them, nearly all of the seriously wounded Chindits had to be left behind in Burma.

The fighting on Sicily was just drawing to a close when, on August 14, 1943, President Roosevelt, Prime Minister Churchill and their Combined Chiefs of Staff gathered in Quebec, Canada. At the top of their agenda was the question of what the next Allied move should be in the China-Burma-India theatre. In attendance at these high-level meetings were a number of generals and admirals who were frequently called upon to present their views on points under discussion. One of the generals sitting in the wings awaiting his turn to speak was Hap Arnold, chief of the U.S. Air Force. Only 10 days before coming to Quebec, Arnold had been at the Laurinburg-Maxton Army Air Base in North Carolina for Major Mike Murphy's sensational night-time

Pea Patch Show and a series of other glider tactical flying demonstrations. Seated right across the aisle from Arnold was Britain's newly promoted Major General Orde Wingate, who had been summoned to Quebec from India by Prime Minister Churchill.

Churchill had come to Quebec well prepared to answer critics at home who were saying that Burma could not be retaken by the British army even with considerable help from the Americans. Churchill's star witness during the conference was General Wingate. With his usual display of showmanship, Churchill proudly introduced Wingate to the assembled dignitaries as England's newest successor to T. E. Lawrence ('Lawrence of Arabia').

Lecturing the assembled dignitaries on the tactics used during his recent raids in Burma, Wingate convinced them that his methods could be used on a far larger scale to assist General Stilwell and his Chinese divisions in reopening a land supply route from India across northern Burma into China. President Roosevelt was so impressed by Wingate's lecture that he instructed General Arnold to provide Wingate with a pocket-sized air force unit. The mission of that unit, said Roosevelt, would be to fly Chindits into battle, evacuate their wounded, supply them from the air, and provide direct air support in place of the artillery and tanks they lacked.

When the Quebec Conference ended on August 24, a number of important decisions had been made concerning the China-Burma-India theatre. A Southeast Asia Command was created, under England's Admiral Lord Louis Mountbatten. In the spirit of the Alliance, the man selected to be Mountbatten's deputy was the newly promoted Lieutenant General Stilwell. The tonnage of the Hump airlift to China would be increased and then, in the fall of 1943, an all-out ground and air offensive would be launched in Burma, utilizing whatever resources were available at the end of the monsoon season.[3]

Returning to his Washington headquarters from Quebec, General Arnold ordered the activation of the air unit that was to be sent to India to support General Wingate and his Chindits in Burma. Designated the 5318th Air Unit, this highly secret outfit was code-named Project Nine to conceal its identity and purpose. The officer appointed by Arnold to command Project Nine was Colonel Philip C. Cochran, a fighter pilot who had flown against the Luftwaffe in North Africa. At the time of his selection, Cochran was already famous; he was the real-life model for the swashbuckling character,

Colonel Flip Corkin, who appeared daily in Milton Caniff's comic strip, 'Terry and the Pirates'. General Arnold appointed Colonel John R. Alison, a fighter ace with seven Japanese planes to his credit, as Cochran's deputy. Cochran and Alison, close friends ever since they had attended flying school together, were naturals for the job.

Arnold gave Cochran carte blanche to obtain whatever aircraft, crews, and maintenance personnel he needed to give adequate supply and firepower to General Wingate and his Chindits. With a signed order from Arnold to back him up, Cochran visited the top personnel and logistics officers in Washington, acquiring an unusual assortment of aircraft: 12 B-25H medium bombers, 30 P-51A fighters, 13 C-47 and 12 C-54 transports, 100 L-1 and L-5 light airplanes, 100 CG-4A gliders, 75 TG-5 gliders, and 6 YR-4 helicopters. Cochran requisitioned 523 officers and men, all of whom were to be hand picked to operate and maintain these aircraft in combat. Such was the composition of the force that would gain fame as the 1st Air Commando Group, a military organization as unique and unorthodox as the Chindits themselves.

Cochran picked Major William H. Taylor, a soft-spoken Mississippian who had conducted experimental jungle landings with CG-4A gliders in Panama, to be the commander of his glider detachment. In late August of 1943, Cochran sent Taylor to the advanced glider pilot training base at Bowman Field, Kentucky, to interview in person 200 glider pilots who had volunteered for what had only been described to them as an extremely dangerous combat mission that would be carried out in an undisclosed overseas area. Since only 100 glider pilots were needed for the secret mission, Taylor could afford to be very selective.

At Bowman Field, Taylor reviewed the personnel records of all the volunteers before conducting his first interview. Those pilots who had the most flying time, and who were graduates of the glider mechanic course at Sheppard Field, Texas, were moved to the head of the interview list. During the interviews, Taylor told each of the volunteers frankly that they would return home from the top secret mission as either a dead glider pilot or a live hero. One week after arriving at Bowman Field, Taylor completed his selection process and organized the volunteers into four separate flights. Headquarter Flight was placed under the command of Captain Vincent Rose, First Flight under Lieutenant Donald E. Seese, Second Flight under Lieutenant James Siever, and Third Flight under Flight Officer Thomas Martin.

Among the volunteer glider pilots selected by Major Taylor was

Flight Officer John L. 'Jackie' Coogan, a former Hollywood child star and ex-husband of Betty Grable. Before his assignment to Bowman Field, Coogan had been a glider instructor at Twentynine Palms, California. Coogan, in addition to being an excellent pilot, was a talented musician and a powerful swimmer. As one of four glider pilots on the Bowman Field swimming team, he had helped to win several trophies during meets with local college teams.

By the second week in September, all 100 of the selected volunteer glider pilots had been moved by troop train from Bowman Field to Seymour Johnson Field at Goldsboro, North Carolina. There they were issued newly designed army paratroop uniforms and U.S. Marine Corps jungle boots. Thus attired, they were put through a gruelling six-week commando training programme that included hand-to-hand combat, 25-mile marches with full field gear, and qualification firing with all infantry weapons.

When that phase of their training had been completed, the pilots began intensive night glider flying and landing exercises at Chapel Hill, an auxiliary airstrip northeast of Seymour Johnson Field. Most of this programme was devoted to perfecting glider snatches by low-flying C-47 airplanes in total darkness. Even in daylight, this delicate manoeuvre was extremely dangerous. At night it was nearly suicidal, for the crews of both the glider and the snatch plane. The C-47 crews began their practice runs in total darkness, with only two small lights atop the glider tow-rope poles to guide them. The danger inherent in night operations was illustrated forcefully during the third practice run when a glider crashed only seconds after being snatched off the ground. Training could not be resumed that night until the body of the dead glider pilot and the wrecked glider were removed from the landing zone.

The heavy emphasis on night training and close combat at Seymour Johnson gave rise to rumours among the glider pilots about where their still-secret mission would be performed. With the memory of Colonel Doolittle's April 18, 1942 bombing raid on Tokyo still fresh in their minds, most glider pilots were betting that they were on their way to an objective in Japan.

From Seymour Johnson Field, the pilots were shipped to Miami, Florida, again by troop train. There, still not informed of their ultimate destination, they were placed aboard airplanes. Their first stop was in Puerto Rico. They then flew to South America, stopping first in British Guiana, then in Brazil. From there they proceeded to

Ascension Island, in the middle of the south Atlantic, and thence across Africa to Saudi Arabia. The last stop was Karachi, India. One of the glider pilots, learning that India was their final destination, remarked to his travelling companions, 'Well, you guys, it looks like we were wrong; we're not going to Japan after all . . . not for a little longer anyway.'

A small fleet of American Liberty cargo ships containing 100 crated CG-4A and 75 TG-5 gliders docked at India's southern seaport of Calcutta on December 3, 1943. Two days later Japanese bombers struck Calcutta, narrowly missing ships that were still unloading the huge crates onto the flatbed trains waiting at the dockside. Those trains hauled the crated gliders to the 28th Air Depot, an American Air Force installation at Pangarah, some thirty miles north of Calcutta, where a force of 100 glider mechanics and 100 glider pilots from the 1st Air Commando Group reassembled and test-flew them.

By the middle of December, Colonel Cochran had all of his 1st Air Commando team members, bombers, fighters and gliders assembled at several bases north of Calcutta. Shortly thereafter, he was approached by General Wingate who asked to be given a demonstration of what the motorless glider detachment could do. Wingate was curious, never having seen a large transport glider before, and although he did not tell Cochran so, he had serious doubts that gliders could really perform all the difficult missions the Americans had been bragging about to their British colleagues.

During their earlier excursion into Burma, Wingate's Chindits had used mules to carry ammunition and supplies. All of the pack animals taken in on that first mission had been requisitioned from Indian army artillery units. For the upcoming operations, larger and stronger mules had been imported from Argentina, South Africa and the United States. The newly arrived mules, averaging some 700 pounds in weight, had had their larynxes surgically removed so that they would be unable to give away their position while behind Japanese lines. At General Wingate's request, a CG-4A glider was rigged to carry three mules on a test flight. British soldiers built three padded stalls in the test glider and then, to everyone's surprise, were able to lead the animals aboard without a struggle. The glider pilot brought along a mechanic armed with an M-1 rifle. Just before take-off he instructed the mechanic: 'If any one of those three critters starts raising hell up in the sky you shoot him right between the eyes before he kicks our glider apart.'

The mules proved to be docile passengers throughout the flight, and that is the way the mules were eventually flown into combat in Burma: three at a time and with a soldier prepared to shoot them if they became violent. Records show that very few mules had to be shot. Their worst tendency was one of urinating and defecating profusely during unusually turbulent flights – hardly a capital offence.[4]

Having succeeded with the mule-flying experiments, Colonel Cochran staged an impressive troop-carrying and landing exercise for General Wingate, consisting simply of landing one fully loaded CG-4A in a partially cleared wooded area. While Wingate and Cochran observed from the edge of the landing zone, a squad of soldiers emerged from the glider and erected two tall poles. They then strung a tow-line across the tops of the poles and fastened it to their glider. That accomplished, the squad re-entered the CG-4A. Seconds after the last soldier had closed the troop compartment door, a C-47 came roaring across the field, snatched the glider, and disappeared with it. That convinced the doubting Wingate that the American bragging had a foundation in fact. Turning to Cochran, Wingate exclaimed, 'I say, that was a jolly good show.'

With Wingate a glider convert, there remained the task of convincing Admiral Lord Louis Mountbatten. Again, Cochran arranged a demonstration, but on a far larger scale then the one Wingate had watched. This time, 24 CG-4As loaded with infantrymen of the famous Black Watch Regiment would conduct a mock battle to seize and occupy a large airhead.

Using procedures that would later be employed during actual combat missions, Cochran began the manoeuvres by sending two CG-4As loaded with specially trained and equipped pathfinder personnel into the airhead one half-hour ahead of the main body of gliders. From a vantage point near the landing zone, Mountbatten and Wingate watched the two pathfinder gliders skid to a stop. Out of one of them came a squad of heavily armed Black Watch soldiers who spread themselves around the edges of the landing zone, forming a defensive cordon. Meanwhile, the soldiers that had arrived in the other glider were busy establishing a small radio station and placing a series of flares and a smoke pot to mark the sides and ends of the landing zone for the incoming main body of gliders. With almost parade field precision, the remaining 22 CG-4As landed, disgorging six mules and a battalion of Black Watch troops who conducted a simulated attack on a nearby objective. Later that night there was a second landing of 22 gliders in another landing zone. Mountbatten, his eyes straining in the darkness, thought it impossible that so many gliders could have landed with so little noise. Seeing signs of doubt on Mountbatten's face, Cochran summoned a jeep and personally drove him around the landing zone to count each of the CG-4As. Sure enough, all 22 of them were there. After counting the twenty-second glider, Mountbatten said to Cochran, 'I'm amazed, completely amazed, by what has happened here tonight.' With that impressive night landing exercise the gliders acquired their newest and highest-ranking convert in India.

When it had completed a series of landing demonstrations for just about every high-ranking Allied officer in the headquarters of the Southeast Asia Command, the 1st Air Commando glider detachment was deployed to the northeast Indian state of Assam. There it occupied Lalaghat and Hailakandi, two partially completed grass airstrips situated 12 miles apart in the Imphal Valley, not far from the border of Burma. At each of these new bases the glider pilots lived in primitive thatched roofed huts, called bashas, where they slept under netting to protect them from the malaria-carrying mosquitoes that annually infest that region of India. The daily routine at each base consisted of a few practice glider flights, after which the pilots and glider mechanics were required to assist the British engineer troops who were still working to complete the runways and revetment areas.

At Lalaghat, where Indian civilian labourers were using harnessed elephants to drag heavy logs away from the edges of the airstrip, the pilots experimented with a new tactic. A flight of 10 gliders had just landed on the runway, and following the prescribed parking procedure, all of the pilots sat patiently in their gliders waiting for a lone jeep to pull them, one by one, into a protected parking area at the far end of the base. With the blazing sun beating down, the temperature inside the gliders soon reached 100 degrees. The intense heat gave Flight Officer Jackie Coogan a bright idea. Rather than wait for the slow-moving jeep, Coogan struck a quick deal with one of the Indians – for a few American cigarettes, he would have the elephant pull the glider down to the parking area. In a matter of only a few minutes, the Indian backed his huge elephant up in front of Coogan's glider. He attached a rope to the nose of the glider, and a few sharp jabs of the guide's stick put the elephant into first gear with Coogan in tow. Fifty yards down the runway the elephant must have sensed that he was not hauling a heavy log. He stopped, turned his head, and panicked at the sight of a glider right behind his tail, probably thinking that it was about to smash into him. Breaking into a full gallop, the huge beast headed straight for the nearby forest, trying in vain to escape the pursuing glider. The elephant made good his escape only when the wings of the glider collided with some trees and the tow-line broke. In an area devoid of entertainment, this incident gave the glider pilots a much-needed laugh and taught them that elephants are unreliable tow-vehicles.

The long-awaited offensive to retake Burma was already under way by the time the 1st Air Commando glider detachment had arrived in Assam. Earlier in October, General Stilwell and his two Chinese divisions had marched out of India into the Hukwang Valley of northern Burma to begin their arduous task of wresting control of the Burma Road from the Japanese. Stilwell's troops were well into Burma by February of 1944, when they were reinforced by the all-American 5307th Provisional Unit, a specially trained infantry regiment commanded by Brigadier General Frank D. Merrill. Operating under the code-name of Galahad Force, this elite unit became popular in the American press as 'Merrill's Marauders'.[5]

At this juncture of the Burma offensive Admiral Mountbatten issued a joint operational order to General Wingate and Colonel Cochran, directing the Chindits to march and fly into Burma. Mountbatten's order specified that the Chindits establish themselves in a series of strongholds around the Burmese village of Indaw and from there operate under the command of Lieutenant General William J. Slim's British Fourteenth Army. Once inside Burma the Chindits were to carry out three main tasks: cut the lines of communication and supply of the Japanese 18th Division opposing the southward advance of General Stilwell's Chinese divisions, create a favourable tactical situation which would permit other Chinese divisions in the Yunnan Province of China to cross the Salween River and engage the Japanese in eastern Burma, and inflict the greatest possible casualties and confusion on the enemy in northern Burma.

The forces available to Wingate for this mission consisted of six infantry brigades comprised of British Gurkha, Indian and West African (Nigerian) troops, all of whom had been trained and indoctrinated in guerrilla warfare by Wingate himself. All of the brigades contained four infantry battalions, each of which was subdivided into two long-range patrol columns. Wingate had task-organized his force this way because he had learned from previous combat experience that small, manoeuvrable troop columns were better suited to guerrilla fighting and quick movement through jungle terrain than were conventional infantry battalions. Wingate knew that if a large-scale battle had to be fought he could quickly amalgamate his brigades and bring his massed firepower against the enemy.

Working in cooperation with Colonel Cochran and his American air staff, General Wingate formulated a complex but methodical three-part plan for carrying out Mountbatten's orders. Part one called for his 16th Brigade, commanded by Brigadier Bernard Fergussen, to make a strenuous foot march of 455 miles from the town of Ledo in India to a jungle stronghold located 27 miles northwest of the village of Indaw. During its southward march the 16th Brigade would be supplied entirely from the air by Cochran's 1st Air Commando Group, which was to make nightly parachute deliveries of food and ammunition. Wingate gave the code-name 'Aberdeen' to the 16th Brigade's base near Indaw, in honour of his wife's hometown in Scotland.

Part two of Wingate's plan would go into effect some four weeks after the 16th Brigade began marching into Burma. It required Brigadier Michael Calvert and his 77th Brigade to make a night landing with gliders and airplanes in two other strongholds near Indaw. In honour of the American airmen participating in the mission, Wingate gave the name 'Broadway' to the 77th Brigade's stronghold 35 miles northeast of Indaw. Not forgetting his own troops, Wingate gave the name 'Piccadilly' to the Brigade's other stronghold, 40 miles northeast of Indaw.

Part two also called for Brigadier Walter D. A. Lentaigne and his 111th Brigade to conduct a night airlanding operation into a third stronghold 35 miles due east of Indaw. In honour of the Indian troops serving under his command, Wingate named his third stronghold 'Chowringhee', after Calcutta's main street. All three strongholds had been personally selected by Wingate because they were deep in jungle areas that were inaccessible to all but lightly armed infantry units, and because each contained extremely large open areas suitable for glider and air-landing operations.

The last part of Wingate's plan called for the 14th Brigade, commanded by Brigadier Thomas Brodie, and the 3rd West African

(Nigerian) Brigade, commanded by Brigadier A. G. Gilmore, to be air landed aboard C-47s in the vicinity of Indaw, approximately four weeks after the 77th and 111th Brigades had arrived in that area.

No divisional headquarters or command centre higher than brigade level would accompany the troops in the field. Wingate planned to exercise command of his forces through occasional personal visits aboard small airplanes and through a network of radios. Signals beamed from powerful transmitters in India would be received in the field by large portable radios carried on the backs of mules.

Brigadier Fergusson and his 16th Brigade had been marching through the rugged terrain of northern Burma toward their Aberdeen stronghold for some two weeks when, in mid-February of 1944, the 1st Air Commando Group began a series of night glider landing manoeuvres to prepare for operations at Broadway and Piccadilly. The decision had been made for each airplane to pull two gliders into Broadway and Piccadilly, something that had been done successfully during training manoeuvres in the United States, but had never before been attempted in combat. During double two operations, the glider on the right was towed at the end of a line measuring 425 feet. In order to obtain that extreme length, two tow-ines (one measuring 350 feet and a second of 75 feet) had to be joined by means of a special steel connector link. The glider on the left was towed by a line measuring 350 feet. Each glider was 48 feet 3¾ inches long, so the one on the right rode well behind the other, and mid-air collisions were avoided. When the two gliders arrived at their landing zone, the one on the left (short tow) always cut off first.[6]

During one of the night double two practice missions at Lalaghat, one of the gliders somehow broke loose from its tug-ship and crashed, killing four British soldiers, two American glider pilots and a glider mechanic. The remaining members of the detachment were distressed by the crash: they knew that they had lost not only three close friends but probably also the confidence of the Chindits they were to fly into battle. The commander of the American glider detachment, Major Taylor, was therefore very pleased when, on the day following the accident, he received a note from the British commander of the Chindit unit whose men had died in the crash. The note read: 'Please be assured that we will go with your boys any place, any time, anywhere.'

D-Day for Operation Thursday, the code-name assigned to the

glider landings at Broadway and Piccadilly, was planned to fall during the period of the first full moon at the end of the monsoon rains. Confusingly enough, Thursday's D-Day was set for March 5, a Sunday. Early that morning, British Lieutenant General Slim, the commander of the Fourteenth Army under whose command the Chindits were to operate, flew from his headquarters in Comilla, India, to the American glider base at Hailakandi. In his book *Defeat Into Victory*, Slim described what he saw there as his aircraft was preparing to land: 'Below me, at the end of the wide brown air strip, was parked a great flock of squat, clumsy gliders, their square wing tips almost touching; around the edge of the field stood the more graceful Dakotas (American C-47 airplanes) that were to lift them into the sky. Men swarmed about the aircraft, loading them, laying out tow-ropes, leading mules, humping packs, and moving endlessly in dusty columns, for all the world like busy ants around captive moths.'[7]

At Hailakandi, General Slim met with General Wingate and Colonel Cochran in their grass shack headquarters. There he was briefed by Cochran on the plan for flying the Chindits some 165 miles behind Japanese lines to their strongholds at Broadway and Piccadilly. Pointing to a large map on the wall, Cochran told General Slim that a total of 80 gliders would take part in the mission, 40 of them to land at Broadway and the other 40 at Piccadilly. In anticipation of some gliders accidentally unhitching enroute to their landing zones, a flight route had been selected which led over areas where few Japanese units were known to be located. Take-off time was set for 20 minutes before six that evening, when the sky would be just about dark. Immediately after take-off all tow-planes were to orbit the base until they reached an altitude of 4,000 feet and had formed themselves into a single column. From that point, they were to head for Burma and climb to an altitude of 8,000 feet so as to safely clear the Chin Hills along the India-Burma border.

Motioning with his hands, Cochran explained to Slim that gliders ordinarily fly at a level slightly above their tow-ships. 'But,' said Cochran, 'because this night mission will be flown under total blackout conditions to avoid detection by the enemy, I have instructed the glider pilots to fly in the low tow position so that they will be able to make out the tug-ships by their silhouettes against the moonlit sky and the light blue flames of the engine exhausts under their wings.'

[146]

After Cochran's briefing, General Slim wandered around the airfield, chatting with clusters of Chindits making final preparations for the mission. Meanwhile, Cochran held a final conference with his deputy, Colonel Alison, who was to fly the lead glider going to Broadway. Originally Cochran had planned to pilot the lead glider into Broadway himself. But on orders from Wingate, he now had to remain behind at Hailakandi to control the launching of the entire mission.[8] While speaking with Alison, Cochran expressed his concern about the general shortage of glider pilots in the group. With 80 gliders committed to this mission, there simply were not enough pilots available for each aircraft to have a qualified copilot. Therefore, each glider would have to be taken in with only one pilot at the controls. 'God help us,' said Cochran, 'if any glider pilot gets wounded by Japanese ground fire between here and his LZ in Burma.'

From his conference with Alison, Cochran proceeded to a large clearing near the base operations centre, where all the glider pilots had been gathered for a final briefing and pep talk. In friendly yet blunt terms, Cochran spoke of the importance of the mission on which they were about to embark. He ended his short pep talk by saying: 'Nothing you've ever done, nothing you're ever going to do counts now. Only the next four hours. Tonight you are going to find your souls.'[9]

To preserve the complete secrecy of his impending moves into Broadway, Piccadilly and Chowringhee, General Wingate had issued strict orders that no airplanes were to fly anywhere near those three areas until the initial glider landings had been completed. But Cochran was very concerned about the safety of his glider pilots and, during the afternoon of D-Day, he took it upon himself to send a high-flying B-25 bomber equipped with aerial reconnaissance cameras on a secret flight into Burma to photograph the landing zones. One of the photos struck terror in the hearts of all the brass at Hailakandi: hundreds of teakwood logs were lying in rows across the landing zone at Piccadilly.

When he saw the photograph, Wingate became extremely angry, not so much because Cochran had disregarded his orders but because he believed that his plan had somehow been compromised and that the Japanese were waiting at Broadway and Chowringhee for his Chindits to arrive. The photos unnerved Wingate so much that he took them to his boss, Lieutenant General Slim, and recommended that the entire operation be cancelled. But Slim thought differently. It was his opinion that if the Japanese wanted to keep the Chindits out of those areas they would have blocked all three landing zones with logs. Slim also knew that General Stilwell and his Chinese divisions were badly in need of assistance from the Chindits. Following a brief staff conference with American and Royal Air Force officers gathered at Hailakandi, Slim gave his command decision on Wingate's recommendation, saying that the operation would proceed but that Piccadilly was not to be used; all gliders would have to land at Broadway.

At 12 minutes after six that evening, the leading C-47, with its two pathfinder gliders trailing behind, sped down the runway at Hailakandi. Seated at the controls of the glider in the left (short tow) position was Major Taylor, the commander of the 1st Air Commando glider detachment. The glider to his right was piloted by Lieutenant Neal J. Blush. In quick succession, four other C-47s pulling the remainder of the pathfinder team took off into the rapidly darkening sky. The first all-glider airborne invasion of the war was finally under way.

Half an hour after the pathfinders had been launched, the leading aircraft of the main body began taking off from Hailakandi and Lalaghat. Though all of the gliders were difficult to control and took a long time to lift off the runways, they eventually disappeared into the night, wobbling behind their tugs.

Earlier in the week, Major Taylor had authorized a maximum overweight pay-load of 4,500 pounds for each glider taking part in the mission. (The usual pay-load for the CG-4A glider was only 4,060 pounds). All glider loads had been meticulously planned to the last ounce by efficient British logisticians who calculated the weight of each Chindit and the equipment he was to take in on the mission. But the logisticians had not counted on the extra unauthorized ammunition that most Chindits had carried on board their gliders when nobody was looking. The Chindits certainly meant no harm in sneaking their extra ammo aboard; like all good infantrymen, they were making sure that they would not run short. But they added dangerous extra pounds to gliders that were already loaded beyond established safety limits.

The first sign of trouble that night came only half an hour after the main body had started taking off. Word was flashed back to Wingate's command post by ground observers that red flares, the

[148]

distress signal of downed gliders, could be seen in the sky near the India-Burma border. Shortly thereafter a tow-plane landed back at Hailakandi. Its chief pilot was Captain Richard Cole, who earlier in the war had been Doolittle's copilot during the celebrated Tokyo bombing raid. When questioned by Cochran about why he had returned to the base, Cole blurted out, 'I lost both of my gliders! The tow-lines snapped just as we were starting our climb over the Chin Hills.'

By eight o'clock two other tow-pilots had returned with the same story of broken tow-lines. This meant that a total of six gliders had already been lost before even entering Burma. Nevertheless, the decision was made by Colonel Cochran to keep on launching the remaining airplanes and gliders in double tow.

With radio silence in effect for the tow-planes, Cochran and the other commanders back in India were unaware of what was happening with the long skytrain heading for Burma. Just after it got over the Chin Hills and crossed the Chindwin River in Burma, the skytrain encountered turbulent air and a thick haze which obscured the tow-planes from the trailing glider pilots. Since there was nothing else they could do, the glider pilots continued to fight the controls of their overloaded gliders, bouncing along at the end of the tow-lines. Unfortunately for some of the overloaded gliders, their tow-lines eventually broke under the constant strain and they were forced to make emergency landings at various points along the route to Broadway.

The haze finally disappeared about half an hour out of Broadway, and Major Taylor, who was flying the lead pathfinder glider, was able to recognize his landing zone the instant it came into view in the moonlight. Taylor reached up, pushed the tow-line release lever, and guided his heavy glider down through the darkness. Moments later he could hear four-foot-high elephant grass slapping the bottom of the glider. Then Taylor felt a hard jolt and heard a familiar loud ripping noise that told him his wheels had been torn away. Minus both wheels, the glider touched down on its belly skids and came to a halt within 50 yards of the point selected by Taylor during the early planning stages of the mission.

Taylor and his passengers were busy unloading their equipment when the glider flown by Lieutenant Blush whistled past them in the darkness and came to a halt about 100 yards away. With Blush leading the way, the squad of troops from his glider moved rapidly around the perimeter of the LZ, setting out lighted smudge pots. When the last pot was in place, Blush marched with two guards to a point one mile down the enormous jungle clearing, where he emplaced a battery-powered signal light that would mark the point where incoming gliders were to cut loose from their tow-planes.

When Colonel Alison had learned that his mission to Piccadilly had been cancelled, he had volunteered to fly one of the pathfinder gliders into Broadway. Seeing Alison touch down, Taylor began running over to meet him. As he ran, he discovered that the surface of the LZ was covered with deep ruts and furrows that were sure to cause some rough landings when the main body arrived. Because they had been hidden by the tall grass covering the LZ, neither of these landing hazards had been detected in aerial photographs used in planning the mission.

Taylor found Alison beside his glider, helping some Chindits unload their heavy equipment, and was just starting to tell Alison about the ruts and logs when the glider loaded with the pathfinder team's radio equipment crashed into some trees along the side of the LZ. Nobody aboard the glider was seriously injured, but the radio set that was to have been used for communications back to India was damaged. Alison managed to take it all in his stride. Patting the shaken communications officer, Major Ernest Bonham, on the shoulder, Alison said, 'Ernie, see what you can do to get that set working as quickly as possible.' He then disappeared into the darkness to make a final check on preparations that had been made for the main body which was due to arrive in just a few minutes.

The faint humming of airplane engines in the distance grew to a roar as, one by one, the big glider tugs converged over Broadway. The first glider to touch down struck a hidden log just beyond the first row of smudge pots marking the leading edge of the LZ, tearing itself apart and coming to rest upside down. Seconds later another incoming glider collided with the wreck, welding the two gliders into a single ball of scrap.

Seeing what was happening, Alison shouted, 'We've got to move the release point light forward so the others will not hit this pile of wreckage when they come in!' Though the light was shifted forward, nearly all of the incoming gliders were severely damaged, tearing themselves apart on teak logs or flipping over on their backs when their wheels became snagged in deep ruts. Several times the release light was moved forward to compensate for the wreckage piling up on

[150]

the LZ. Everyone that was physically able to do so pitched in with the task of moving the smudge pots; rank mattered not at all. Even the British brigade's commanding officer, Brigadier Calvert, could be seen carrying a flaming smudge pot to the place where a corporal instructed him to put it down in line with the others. But in spite of the frantic shifting, the incoming gliders continued crashing into logs, ruts, and each other.

Flight Officer Thomas Height and his overloaded CG-4A glider had lifted off from India carrying several five-gallon gasoline cans, a generator and a set of electric lights to outline the airstrip that would be built at Broadway. Seated beside him in the copilot's seat was Sergeant Robert S. Bovey, a glider mechanic. Passing over the great Irrawaddy River in Burma, Height saw two gliders that had made emergency landings on a wide sandbar. Shortly thereafter, he arrived over Broadway where he cut loose from his tug and landed without incident. Height and Bovey were still climbing out of their glider when Lieutenant Virgil Scobey ran up to them and said, 'Quick, get the hell away from here! You're the only one that hasn't cracked up yet.' Taking Scobey's advice, Height and Bovey ran to the edge of the LZ amid the sounds of crashing gliders.

With a jeep tied down directly behind him in his glider, Flight Officer Edward G. Scott was apprehensive about the landing he would have to make on the dark LZ at Broadway. Like the other members of his group, Scott had heard horror stories of jeeps tearing loose from their tiedowns during rough landings and crushing pilots to death. That thought was uppermost in his mind when his tug arrived at Broadway and he received the signal to cut away. Scott hit the release lever, took a firm grip on the controls, and hoped for the best. As he touched down a few moments later, Scott had both wings of his glider torn off by two piles of black wreckage on the LZ. Still rushing downfield, his wingless glider struck a log which tore out a huge section of flooring in the cargo compartment. Finally the glider skidded to a gradual halt. Scott turned round and looked at the jeep. It had not moved an inch.

The luckiest pair of air commandos to land on Broadway that night were Flight Officer Gene A. Kelly and his acting copilot, Sergeant Joseph A. DeSalvo. Their glider, overshooting the LZ, whizzed between two trees spaced 10 feet apart, neatly shearing off both wings. The fuselage jerked to an abrupt halt, causing the 4,139-pound bulldozer it contained to shoot forward like a giant projectile from the mouth of a howitzer. By a stroke of luck, the moving dozer unhinged the glider's nose section, throwing it into the upraised position with the pilot and copilot still strapped in their seats. Then it hurtled out of the nose, turned over twice, and came to rest right side up. When they climbed down from the nose section a few moments later, Kelly and DeSalvo could not believe that they were still alive.

Elsewhere on the LZ, Colonel Alison was horrified at the continuing crashes that he was powerless to stop. Everything had gone so perfectly during the maneouvres conducted in India before the invasion. But his well-laid plans were almost literally coming apart at the seams in Burma.

Back at Hailakandi airfield in India, Generals Slim and Wingate and Colonel Cochran were beside themselves with worry. Six hours had elapsed since the first pathfinder gliders had been launched, and not a single radio message had been received from Broadway. Doubts turned to fear as all three men came to the conclusion that the glider force had been ambushed by the Japanese upon landing in Burma and been wiped out.

Wingate was nervously pacing around the command radio when, at 2:30 a.m., a message came crackling through from Broadway. It was from Brigadier Calvert and it consisted of only two words, 'Soya Link.' This was the prearranged code word phrase that was to be used to indicate failure and to stop all glider departures from India. So the Japanese had in fact ambushed Broadway!

With fire in his eyes, Wingate gave General Slim a long hard stare and then stormed away from the radio. Just then it crackled again with the sound of Calvert's voice. 'Many of our gliders are still missing. Most of those that did arrive have suffered considerable damage and casualties. But there are no, repeat no, enemy troops in this area. Will do the best we can with what we have at hand.'

Reacting swiftly to Calvert's Soya Link message, Cochran flashed word to the control towers at Hailakandi and Lalaghat to cease operations at once. Eight gliders already on their way to Broadway had to be recalled. They later landed without incident at Lalaghat.

At dawn, Colonel Cochran and his staff sat down to assess the situation. Patching together a series of radio reports received from the field and several sightings by tow-plane pilots, they were able to determine that only 31 of the 68 gliders launched had made it to Broadway. Virtually all of those gliders that reached Broadway had been so damaged that they were unsalvageable. Only three of them were later snatched out for use in other missions. Cochran discovered that nine of the 36 gliders that did not reach Broadway had gone down deep in enemy territory. Nine more had landed in friendly country short of the Burma frontier; two had disappeared without a trace. The remaining 16 gliders were recalled to their departure airfields after Broadway warned that no more could be safely landed at that end.

The worst news of the damage and casualty assessment meeting was the discovery that 31 men had been killed at Broadway, 30 more seriously injured, and 238 others badly shaken up though still able to perform light duty. Considering that not one enemy soldier had been on or near the Broadway LZ at the time of the landings, these casualty figures were indeed deplorable.

On the plus side of the ledger, Cochran's air staff announced that a total of 539 men, three mules and 65,972 pounds of cargo had been put down on Broadway. All three mules survived the rough landings without so much as a scratch.

Captain Patrick Casey, the U.S. Army engineer officer who was to have been in charge of clearing the glider LZ of debris and turning it it into a full-fledged powered airplane runway, had been killed when his glider crashed at Broadway. At first light, Colonel Alison sent for Casey's assistant, Lieutenant Robert Brackett. Pointing at the piles of wreckage littering the LZ, Alison inquired, 'Lieutenant, how long do you think it would take you and your engineers to clear up that mess out there and convert this place into a serviceable runway?'

Brackett squinted, glanced around the field, and casually replied, 'Oh, I'd say we could have the job done for you by late afternoon, sir.' True to his word, Brackett had the wrecks cleared away and the ruts filled in by four o'clock. Shortly thereafter, light airplanes from India landed to begin evacuating the most seriously injured Chindits to hospitals at Imphal.

By nightfall Lieutenant Brackett and his exhausted engineers had cleared and filled a dirt runway 300 feet wide and 5,000 feet long. Later that night more than 500 Chindits and several thousand pounds of ammunition and supplies were air-landed in C-47 airplanes, some of which had earlier towed gliders into Broadway.

While the transports were landing at Broadway, a flight of 12 gliders commanded by Lieutenant Colonel Clint Gatty, chief main-

[153]

tenance officer of the 1st Air Commando Group, was flying through the night sky behind their tow-ships, bound for Chowringhee. These gliders had taken off from Lalaghat loaded with an assortment of American engineer troops, a small bulldozer of the type used at Broadway, and three platoons of Gurkha infantrymen.

Flight Officer Jackie Coogan was piloting the lead pathfinder glider heading toward Chowringhee. As soon as he had landed in the dark field, Coogan directed his load of Gurkhas to the edges of the LZ where they began setting up a perimeter defence to protect the American engineers while they carved out a runway. Then Coogan began laying out a series of lighted smudge pots to guide in the remaining 11 gliders. Meanwhile, in one of the other gliders approaching Chowringhee, a Gurkha soldier needed to answer the call of nature. None of the American gliders were equipped with toilet facilities, so the Gurkha, wearing his regulation hobnailed boots, made his way back into the deepest part of the tail section, drew his bayonet, and sliced an opening in the canvas. The pilot, Lieutenant Charles B. Turner, was stunned to learn what the squatting Gurkha had managed to do without falling through the floor to his death. The only way that Turner could get other glider pilots to believe the story later was to show them the hobnailed footprints implanted on both sides of the improvised bomb bay.[10]

Turner's glider had been customized with another unique feature. Prior to taking off at Lalaghat, Turner had obtained a machine gun from the wreckage of a B-25 bomber that had crashed earlier in the week. With the aid of mechanics, he mounted the gun in the nose of his glider so that it could be fired by the Gurkha Lance Corporal who was his copilot on this mission. During World War II, all German gliders were equipped with one or more machine guns. But Turner's was the only American glider to enter combat during the war with a machine gun protruding from its nose.

Guided by the smudge pots set out by Coogan, the remaining 11 gliders in his flight began landing at Chowringhee. Two of them sustained severe damage while making rough landings. The one flown by Lieutenant Turner had both of its wings broken off as it shot past two others on the LZ. Turner, his Gurkha copilot, and their 12 Gurkha infantrymen managed to crawl out of the wreckage with only minor injuries.

Some five minutes after Turner's rough landing, a glider being flown by Lieutenant Robert Dowe began its descent over Chowringhee. Tied down inside Dowe's glider was a 2-ton bulldozer. Seated alongside it were three American engineer dozer operators whose job it was to carve a dirt runway down the middle of the glider LZ. Overshooting the LZ on the first pass, Lieutenant Dow put his heavily loaded glider through a graceful 180 degree turn and lined it up again on the smudge pots glimmering in the distance. But as it was approaching the far end of the LZ, Dowe's glider smashed head on into an unseen tree and was sent cartwheeling across the field. Dowe and all others aboard were killed in the crash, and during one of the glider's many tumbles the dozer tore through the nose and hit the ground with such force that it was demolished.

Without the vital dozer there was little Lieutenant Colonel Gatty and his small force could do that night to prepare a runway at Chowringhee. After radioing his desperate situation report to Colonel Alison some 50 miles away at Broadway, Gatty moved his troops far into the nearby jungle, so as to not create a target for prowling Japanese airplanes.

At sundown the next day, the Gurkhas at Chowringhee started cutting down the four-foot-high elephant grass with their razor-sharp kukri knives. They had just completed clearing 12 acres of runway area when, at 9:00 p.m., two gliders piloted by Flight Officers Vernon Noland and Billy Mohr landed with another bulldozer and a jeep filled with engineer equipment. On Colonel Cochran's orders, these gliders had been snatched out of Broadway by tow-planes sent from India. Two other gliders, both coming from India, landed at Chowringhee shortly thereafter with two more pieces of engineer equipment and a jeep.

Starting at 9:30 p.m., the American engineer detachment under Lieutenant Jerome Andrulonis cranked up the machinery and went to work. Exactly four hours later they completed a 3,000 foot dirt airstrip. And a bare quarter hour after the bulldozer rumbled off the end of the strip, the first C-47 bringing in the lead elements of Brigadier Lentaigne's 111th Brigade landed at Chowringhee.

Japanese bombers destroyed the airstrip at Chowringhee only three days after it had been built, but by that time Brigadier Lentaigne and his Chindits had moved out, heading for distant objectives assigned them by General Wingate. The Americans, too, were gone. Earlier that day they and all of their engineer equipment had been snatched out aboard the same gliders that had brought them there. All the Japanese had to show for their expensive bombing run was two wrecked gliders that had been left behind by the Americans.

Though Chowringhee had been closed down, Broadway was doing a booming business. By March 11, some 9,250 Chindits had been flown into the airstrip during darkness. Most of them were immediately sent out on missions around Indaw, where they ambushed Japanese supply truck convoys and blew up ammunition dumps. Other incoming Chindit units were kept at Broadway to protect the base against enemy attacks. During this period, nearly all of the glider pilots who had flown the initial batch of Chindits into Broadway remained at the base, performing tasks ranging from simple guard duty to manning radios in the makeshift control centre that had been established in a wrecked glider.

The lack of Japanese reaction to the landings at Broadway puzzled Admiral Mountbatten and his staff. The first enemy move against the base did not occur until March 13 – eight days after the initial landings – when 30 Japanese fighter planes launched a daylight attack. A flight of Spitfires of the 221st Royal Air Force Group happened to be parked on Broadway when the attack started. They quickly took to the air, shooting down half of the Japanese planes and driving off the remainder.

The tardiness of the Japanese High Command's reaction to Broadway's being established in its back yard enabled Brigadier Calvert to move his 77th Brigade undetected to Mawlu. There he quietly established a jungle stronghold that was christened 'White City'. On March 16, Calvert's troops emerged from their stronghold and dynamited four highway bridges and several miles of tracks on the Mandalay-Myitkyina railroad. Thus, in only 11 days, Wingate's Chindits had accomplished their first major objective of the operation: the cutting of road and railroad communications to the Japanese 18th Division fighting Stilwell's troops.

Stung by the rail-cutting operations near White City, the Japanese sent a force of 3,000 troops to drive the Chindits out. A brisk battle ensued near the small airstrip at White City. During a lull in the fighting, five 1st Air Commando gliders landed with a fresh supply of ammunition. Three of them had been snatched back out, fully loaded with wounded Chindits, when the Japanese mortared the field and destroyed the remaining two. Having lost their places of employment, the American pilots of the destroyed gliders, Captain Vincent Rose and Lieutenant James S. Bartlett, reverted to the role of infantry foot soldiers and joined the Chindits.

The tense quiet at White City was broken later that night when screaming, shooting Japanese soldiers made a banzai charge against the Chindit positions. Calvert's force held their ground and repelled the attack. At daylight, glider pilots Rose and Bartlett walked with the Chindits among the piles of dead enemy soldiers to collect souvenirs. Rose returned to the defensive position with two Japanese battle flags; Bartlett brought back a samurai sword that he had taken from the body of a fallen officer.[11] Rose and Bartlett remained with the Chindits at White City for 10 days before being evacuated to India by airplane.

Just one day after the Japanese supply lines had been severed at White City, Brigadier Fergusson's marching 16th Brigade arrived at Aberdeen and began setting up a base of operations. In slightly more than six weeks this hardy brigade of Chindits had walked over 450 miles through some of the most treacherous terrain on earth, all while under constant threat of attack by superior Japanese forces – truly a feat of endurance.

While the 16th Brigade had still been on the march toward Aberdeen, its commander, Colonel Fergusson, had sent a radio message back to India requesting some form of assistance in getting his troops across the broad and swiftly flowing Irrawaddy River. At midnight on March 16, a single glider piloted by Flight Officer Allen Hall, Jr. landed on the sandy banks of the Irrawaddy carrying four collapsible engineer boats. Waiting Chindits removed the boats, unfolded them, and began ferrying their equipment across the river. This operation was still in progress when a brawny British sergeant walked up to the glider with four Burmese civilian prisoners known to have provided assistance to Japanese occupation forces. With lightning-fast punches, the sergeant knocked all four of his prisoners unconscious. Then he dragged them aboard the glider and tied them to the vehicle tie-down rings positioned in the floor. At three o'clock in the morning the tow-plane returned to the riverbank, snatched up the glider and flew it back to India, where the prisoners were interrogated by British intelligence officers.

Protected by Chindits already in position on Aberdeen, six gliders carrying engineering equipment and bulldozers landed there on March 21. A dirt runway was completed one day later, enabling C-47s to begin delivering supplies of ammunition and fresh food. The first six airplanes to land at Aberdeen were used to tow the gliders back to India.

All glider pilots at Broadway were returned to their bases in India by the middle of March. With the Burma offensive now in full swing, the pilots received very little rest. Almost daily, many of them flew gliders heavily loaded with supplies to Chindits still operating behind Japanese lines. So as not to give away locations of the Chindit patrol bases, the majority of those missions had to be flown at night.

In a typical resupply mission, the glider landed in a jungle clearing with a load of food and ammunition. While its contents were being unloaded, the tow-plane would leave the area for approximately half an hour. During that time, Chindits who were seriously wounded or ill with malaria or dysentery would be loaded aboard and strapped in place while the pilots were erecting a glider snatch apparatus. Two blue lights atop the pick-up poles would be turned on to signal to the returning tow-plane pilot that it was permissible for him to swoop down and snatch the supply glider, now transformed into a flying field ambulance. Using this evacuation procedure, the glider pilots were able, at great risk to their own lives, to save hundreds of seriously wounded and ill Chindits from certain death in the jungles of Burma.

Not all of these resupply and evacuation missions had happy endings for the glider pilots. Late in March 1944, Lieutenant Donald E. Seese, leader of the Air Commando's First Glider Flight, was given the job of selecting 16 pilots to fly eight gliders (two pilots per glider) into Burma on a night resupply mission. No sick or wounded Chindits were to be evacuated on this run. As worked out at Group Headquarters, the plan called for the eight gliders to land near the jungle hide-out of a Chindit column that was preparing to depart on an extensive raid deep behind Japanese lines. While the Chindits were unloading the supplies, the pilots were supposed to quickly prepare one glider for a snatch pick-up and then climb aboard it. On a light signal to be sent by one of the glider pilots, the last tow-plane would swoop down, grab the glider containing the 16 pilots, and return them to their base in India. The remaining seven gliders were to be abandoned in the jungle.

On the night the mission was flown, the first seven tow-planes unerringly found their way to the LZ located near the Chindit patrol base. All seven gliders they were towing cut loose and landed without incident. But the eighth plane – the one that was supposed to return and make the vital pick-up – lost its way in the dark.

Just after sunrise the missing tow-plane appeared with its glider still in tow. But to the bewilderment of the pilots on the ground, it flew directly over the LZ without releasing its glider and disappeared from view. That left the glider pilots on the LZ with two choices; they could remain at the hide-out after the Chindits had marched out on their mission and attempt to arrange some sort of snatch rescue mission by another tow-plane, or they could accompany the Chindits on their raiding mission and hope to be evacuated during some future night resupply and casualty evacuation mission.

With Japanese troops not far away from the Chindit patrol base, the thought of remaining there by themselves for a doubtful rescue did not appeal to the glider pilots. As the leader of the pilots, Lieutenant Seese took a vote. It was 13 to one to accompany the Chindits; Seese was the only one who voted to remain where they were and attempt a snatch rescue.

The leader of the Chindit force to which the pilots had attached themselves was British Major Philip Blaine, a tough, no-nonsense veteran of the commando raid at Dieppe, France, and the earlier Chindit operations in Burma. Blaine's troops feared and respected him. They knew he had proved himself on numerous occasions to be a courageous and efficient combat leader; they also knew that he was perhaps the most ruthless disciplinarian in the British army.

Some five days after marching away from the patrol base where the American glider pilots had joined them, the Chindits drew near an area known to be infested with Japanese patrols. Nerves were already on edge when someone in the long Chindit column accidentally discharged his rifle. An outraged Major Blaine ordered the troops to take cover, then motioned his officers and squad leaders to the head of the column to find out who the guilty party was.

As leader of the American pilots, Lieutenant Seese moved forward and joined the cluster of British officers and sergeants standing stiffly at attention in front of Major Blaine. The major demanded to know who fired the shot. Nobody answered. His face flushed with anger, Blaine paced silently up and down in front of the group for a few moments. Then he stopped in front of Lieutenant Seese, looked him in the eye and said in an accusatory tone, 'Gentlemen, I am warning you that if ever another shot is fired, I shall personally walk up and down this column until I find out who did it. And when I find him, I shall shoot him dead with my revolver.' No one, especially Lieutenant Seese, believed that the iron-handed major was bluffing.

After the patrol resumed its march, Seese established to his great relief that it was not one of his inexperienced soldier-pilots who had fired the shot. Speaking in a whisper, a British squad leader later confessed to Seese that the round had been accidentally fired by a Chindit who had tripped over a log in the jungle.

After two weeks of patrolling jungles with the Chindits and numerous skirmishes with Japanese patrols, Lieutenant Seese and his pilots were told that they were to be returned to India aboard a light airplane that was going to land in a nearby dry rice paddy to evacuate some wounded troops. The Chindits guided their wounded and the pilots to a secure hide-away near the paddy, then disappeared into the jungle to continue their mission. Less than an hour later a small airplane arrived and began the slow process of flying out one and two men at a time. As commander, Seese decided that he should be the last of the pilots to be evacuated. Waiting alone at the crude landing field for the plane to return for him, Seese wondered who would win the race to get him, the Japanese or the airplane. The airplane won.

In between the hazardous resupply and medical evacuation missions, the glider pilots volunteered to fly as copilots of C-54 transports hauling supplies over the Hump to China and in B-25s making bombing runs into Burma. Glider pilots knew that one advantage of flying in a B-25 bomber was that the pilot's and copilot's seats were protected by built-in bulletproof steel plates. The seats in their flimsy gliders had no protection devices whatever.

Flying as copilot of a B-25 making a low-level bombing attack on a train station in Burma, glider pilot Lieutenant Charles B. Turner could hear and feel his ship being hit by Japanese ground fire. A .50 calibre bullet suddenly tore through the nose of the bomber, struck the seat Turner was sitting in, and fell harmlessly on the floor by his feet. When the bullet cooled off, Turner picked it up, put it in his pocket, and said to himself, 'Thank God this didn't happen to me in my glider.'[12]

General Wingate flew into Broadway on March 24 to visit his troops and to issue them new marching orders. During the return flight to India later that day his airplane crashed, killing all aboard. News of Wingate's death flashed through the Southeast Asia Command and the Chindit force in the field like an electric shock. That Wingate should be killed when his forces were achieving their great success and proving his guerrilla tactics to be flawless seemed a cruel stroke of fate. Brigadier Lentaigne, the commander of the

111th Brigade of Chindits, was chosen by Admiral Mountbatten to replace Wingate.

Under Lentaigne's command, the Chindits in northern Burma continued with their guerrilla style hit-and-run operations against the Japanese throughout the months of April and May. During that time they were resupplied continuously by night parachute drops and had their increasing casualties evacuated by gliders and light airplanes of the 1st Air Commando Group. Taking advantage of the great number of Japanese troops tied down by the Chindits, other units of General Slim's British Fourteenth Army entered western Burma from India and began pushing southward toward the capital, Rangoon, a city whose name means 'end of strife'.

Meanwhile, in northern Burma, General Stilwell was closing in on his final objective of Myitkyina. During the previous six months his depleted forces had marched over 500 miles into Burma and won major engagements against seven tough Japanese regiments, one of which had helped to capture the seemingly impregnable bastions of Singapore. On May 17, Stilwell's Chinese 150th Infantry Regiment seized an airfield only 1,500 yards west of the main Japanese defensive positions around the city of Myitkyina. As soon as the airstrip had been secured, a pre-arranged coded signal, 'Merchant of Venice', was flashed back to the Burmese town of Shingbwiyang where 10 gliders loaded with troops and equipment of the American 879th Engineering Aviation Battalion were waiting for deployment to the front. All 10 gliders landed that afternoon at the newly won airfield, depositing the engineers who immediately set to work preparing it to receive follow-up C-47s loaded with troops and supplies coming from India. Although they controlled the airfield, it took Stilwell's forces until August 3 to overcome the tenacious Japanese defenders of Myitkyina.

Fighting had still been in progress at Myitkyina when, earlier in May, Colonel Alison, the deputy commander of the 1st Air Commando Group, along with Major Taylor, the glider detachment commander, and ten selected glider pilots, were returned to the United States. Alison and Taylor were allowed only a few days of leave with their families before being shipped to England. There they were assigned as advisers to General Eisenhower's staff and took part in planning the glider landings that were made in France, Holland and Germany. Other pilots who had returned home with them were given teaching assignments in the United States.

Shortly after the fall of Myitkyina, the physically exhausted Chindits, their numbers now considerably reduced by wounds and illness, were withdrawn from Burma for a well-deserved rest in India. During its support of the Chindits, the 1st Air Commando Group's glider detachment had flown a total of 96 sorties. Nearly all of them had been flown at night into LZs surrounded by enemy troops and extremely dangerous landing hazards. It is most unfortunate that this courageous performance by a determined group of glider pilots who not only flew supplies to the Chindits, but also evacuated their wounded and often fought alongside them as infantrymen, has gone virtually unmentioned in published histories of the war in Burma.

Operation Thursday officially came to a close when the last Chindit brigade was pulled out of Burma in August 1944. At the time of their return to India, the Chindits had accomplished all of the missions assigned them by Admiral Mountbatten. They were also credited with pinning down two divisions of Japanese troops which had been kept constantly on the move trying to catch them. Because of its brilliant planning by the late General Wingate and its great success in combat, Operation Thursday became a model of how to wage effective three-dimensional warfare deep behind enemy lines.

The fall of Myitkyina, coupled with the extremely successful operations of the Chindits, created a very favourable tactical situation for the Allied forces in Burma. By the end of August, the Japanese had been obliged to relinquish their grip on northern Burma, and their army was in full retreat to more secure positions in the southern regions of the country.

Capitalizing on recent events in northern Burma, British Lieutenant General Slim and his Fourteenth Army raced after the Japanese. During their southward thrusts, Slim's troops were supported by gliders of the 1st Air Commando Group and the newly arrived 2nd Air Commando Group. The latter, organized in the same fashion as the 1st Air Commando, was commanded by Colonel Arthur J. DeBolt.

Fighting with their traditional valour, the Japanese soldiers made the British Fourteenth Army's advance a slow and costly one. Mandalay, the city made famous by Rudyard Kipling, fell on March 21, 1945, but it was not until May 3 that the capital, Rangoon, was liberated by a combined Allied amphibious–airborne force, and the war in Burma could be deemed over.

It had been a long and hard fight in Burma. Only four days after the liberation of Rangoon, German General Alfred Jodl arrived at General Eisenhower's headquarters in faraway France to sign the instrument of surrender for all the German armed forces.

## Chapter 7

# Cross-Channel Attack

No CAMPAIGN IN THE HISTORY of warfare has ever been planned with such thoroughness as Operation Overlord, the Allied invasion of German-occupied France in June 1944. As early as March 1943, British Lieutenant General Sir Frederick E. Morgan was appointed chief of staff to the as yet unnamed supreme Allied Commander and given instructions to begin planning the cross-channel invasion of Normandy.

Assisted by a staff of British and American air, ground and naval officers, Morgan immediately set to work at Norfolk House in London, where he had earlier formulated plans for the Allied invasion of Northwest Africa. In September of 1943, one British and two American airborne planners were added to Morgan's staff. The British officer was Lieutenant General Frederick Browning, the father of England's airborne forces, who had been one of the chief planners of the airborne assault on Sicily. The first of Browning's two American counterparts was Major General William C. Lee, commander of the newly arrived 101st Airborne Division. The second was newly promoted Brigadier General James M. Gavin, deputy commander of the 82nd Airborne Division, which was then still fighting on the Italian mainland.

Also serving on Morgan's staff was an American airman, Brigadier General Paul L. Williams, commander of the newly activated IX Troop Carrier Command based in England. Williams had directed the troop carrier and glider tug airplanes during almost all of the earlier Allied airborne operations in the Mediterranean theatre. At the time Williams joined Morgan's staff, the IX Troop Carrier Command consisted of only one troop carrier group, the 434th, and a small detachment of the 315th Group with three C-47 airplanes.[1] All other groups that would take part in Overlord were then either back in the United States undergoing training or still fighting in the Mediterranean theatre.

Fresh from a series of victories in Africa, Sicily and Italy, America's General Dwight D. Eisenhower was chosen in December of 1943 to become the Supreme Commander of the Allied Expeditionary Force that was massing in England for the invasion. Ike was blessed with a magnificent staff and a host of dynamic combat commanders to assist him in the herculean mission of breaking Hitler's iron grip on the Continent. Field Marshal Sir Bernard Montgomery, the man who had bested Rommel in Africa, was appointed to be Ike's commander of all Allied ground forces going to Normandy. Directly under Monty were the mild-mannered Lieutenant General Omar N. Bradley, who was to command the American half of the beachhead, and Lieutenant General Sir Miles Dempsey, who would command the British and Canadian forces who were to assault the other half. Bradley had never set foot on the Continent, but for Dempsey the coming invasion would be his third trip to France. During World War I he had fought there as a young infantry officer, and more recently he had commanded the 13th Brigade when it fought a brisk rearguard action covering the Dunkirk evacuation in May of 1940.

Overlord was to be executed in two phases. Phase One required Monty's ground troops to make an amphibious assault along some 60 miles of the Normandy shoreline, extending from Caen in the east to the base of the Cotentin Peninsula in the west.

Once he had established himself on the Continent and had built up sufficient combat power within his beachhead, Monty was to blast into Phase Two: a breakout from the beachhead and the launching of a massive ground drive aimed at the heart of Nazi Germany.

This was a bold and risky plan. More than anyone in his headquarters, Eisenhower knew that the margin for success was slim. As Ike saw clearly, the basic plan of Operation Overlord involved a frontal attack that was to be launched from the sea on one of the strongest armies in the world, which sat inside the most elaborately equipped defensive network ever established on earth.

Three combat-ready airborne divisions, one British and two American, were in England by January 1944. All three had been selected to play leading roles during Overlord's Phase One. Their task was to jump and glide into opposite ends of the wide Normandy beachhead to seize key terrain and disrupt German defences.

[165]

Because of the known heavy concentration of German anti-aircraft guns along the French coastline and the need for secrecy and surprise, the airborne assaults were set to start at one o'clock in the morning of D-Day – some five hours prior to the time that the amphibious assault troops would hit the beaches.

The British 6th Airborne Division, commanded by Major General Richard N. Gale, had been in existence since May of 1943 and was stationed on Salisbury Plain. Its major manoeuvre elements consisted of the 3rd and 5th Parachute Brigades and the 6th Air Landing (Glider) Brigade.[2] In Phase 1 of Overlord, Gale and his division were to carry out a number of missions that included knocking out the Merville Battery, whose large guns could fire down the entire length of the British assault beaches; securing bridges over the Orne River and Caen Canal; and blocking the movement of German units which were expected to launch major counterattacks from the east against the beaches.

Over on the western half of the Allied beachhead, General Bradley had the 82nd and 101st Airborne Divisions to assist him with his mission of securing a lodgement on the Continent. General Ridgway's 82nd Airborne had arrived in England just before Christmas of 1943, after heavy ground fighting in Italy, and after a brief training period in Northern Ireland it was quartered in the English Midlands near Leicester. General Bill Lee's 101st Airborne had come to England direct from U.S. training camps earlier in September, and was stationed further south, around Newbury and Exeter.

General Bradley planned to drop both American airborne divisions into an area six to ten miles inland from Utah Beach, over which the United States 4th Infantry Division was to make an amphibious landing on D-Day. There the airborne troops were to seize several communications centres and a number of roads leading inland from the beach.

Eisenhower's right-hand man in charge of all air operations associated with Overlord, Air Marshal Sir Trafford Leigh-Mallory, was strongly opposed to Bradley's intended use of American parachute and glider troops behind the heavily defended Utah Beach. Initially the air marshal had been in favour of Bradley's plan, but a number of alarming reports about additional anti-airborne defensive measures being employed there by the Germans convinced Leigh-Mallory that the two main parachute and glider landings would fail and that troops participating in them would suffer at least 50 and possibly 80 per cent casualties.

Leigh-Mallory was so certain that the American airborne assaults would end in disaster that he went to Eisenhower's headquarters and pleaded that they be cancelled. Following the air marshal's visit, Ike called in Bradley to hear his side of the argument. In his book, *A Soldier's Story*, Bradley had this to say about their discussion:

> I conceded that Leigh-Mallory's low-flying C-47s would run into ground fire almost from the moment they made landfall in France. And the Normandy hedgerows would undoubtedly make the glider landings difficult and costly. But those risks, I asserted, must be subordinated to the importance of Utah Beach and to the prompt capture of Cherbourg. Certainly I would not willingly risk the lives of 17,000 airborne troops if we could accomplish our mission without them. But I would willingly risk them to insure against failure of the invasion. This, in a nutshell, was the issue.[3]

From his statement one can see that Bradley was applying an old and grim military rule: the mission comes first; if precious lives must be spent to accomplish it, then so be it.

Ike now found himself in the difficult position of having to decide between opposing recommendations from two of his most senior subordinates. It was an especially painful decision to make, because the American airborne troops were certain to suffer high casualty rates if they were used as Bradley wanted. After several hours of wrestling with his conscience, Ike decided to approve Bradley's plan.

Before departing Italy for England with his 82nd Airborne Division late in November of 1943, General Ridgway had been required to leave behind a combat team to take part in ground fighting with the Fifth Army. The unit he selected to remain in Italy was the 504th Regimental Combat Team, comprised of Colonel Reuben Tucker's 504th Parachute Infantry Regiment, two artillery battalions, and an engineer company. Thus when the 82nd Airborne arrived in England to begin training for Normandy, its major manoeuvre elements consisted of only the 505th Parachute Infantry Regiment and the 325th Glider Infantry Regiment.

Tucker's 504th Parachute Combat team finally arrived in England early in May, but it was so badly depleted by battle casualties that it would be unable to participate in Overlord. To make up for this loss, Eisenhower temporarily attached two independent units, the 507th and 508th Parachute Infantry regiments, to the 82nd Airborne.

When General Bill Lee had brought his 101st Airborne Division to England earlier in September, it consisted of the 502nd and 506th

Parachute Infantry regiments and the 327th and 401st Glider Infantry regiments. In January of 1944, Lee's division was beefed up with the addition of the independent 501st Parachute Infantry Regiment, commanded by Colonel Howard R. Johnson, the most flamboyant parachute officer in the U.S. Army. When his regiment was going through its initial jump training at Fort Benning, Georgia, Johnson – who was already a qualified parachutist – would demonstrate the kind of courage he expected his men to display in battle by making three to five jumps each day, depending on the weather. Johnson carried this drive to display his fearlessness in combat, refusing to take cover when German artillery fell on his position. His bravery – or foolhardiness – would later cost him his life in Holland.

There were two major differences between the parachute and glider regiments: the glider regiments contained only two battalions, while the parachute units had three; and the glider troops still were not receiving hazardous duty pay, nor were they equipped with parachutes. The inequitable pay and safety situation galled the glider troops, who knew that the men in the airplanes towing them were drawing flight pay and wearing escape parachutes.

Some four months before D-Day, American airborne planners decided to add a third battalion to the 82nd Airborne's 325th Glider Infantry and to the 101st Airborne's 327th Glider Infantry. To accomplish this, Colonel Joseph W. Harper's 401st Glider Infantry Regiment had to be cut in half. Harper's 1st Battalion remained a part of the 101st Airborne; his 2nd Battalion was attached to the 82nd Airborne's 325th Glider Infantry. Harper, naturally enough, was displeased by the splitting of his regiment because it meant that he was out of a job. (Once the split was made he was attached to the 101st Airborne's G-3 section. Later, during ground fighting in France, he would be given command of the 327th Glider Infantry.)

Ever since General Lee had become the 'father' of American airborne troops in the summer of 1940, the 48-year-old commander of the 101st Airborne had been working 16-hour days to prepare himself and his troops for combat. The physical and mental strain of that self-imposed work schedule led to a near-fatal heart attack only four months away from combat in Normandy. With Lee hospitalized, all of the senior American airborne officers in England expected that command of the Screaming Eagles would pass to Brigadier General Donald F. Pratt, the assistant division

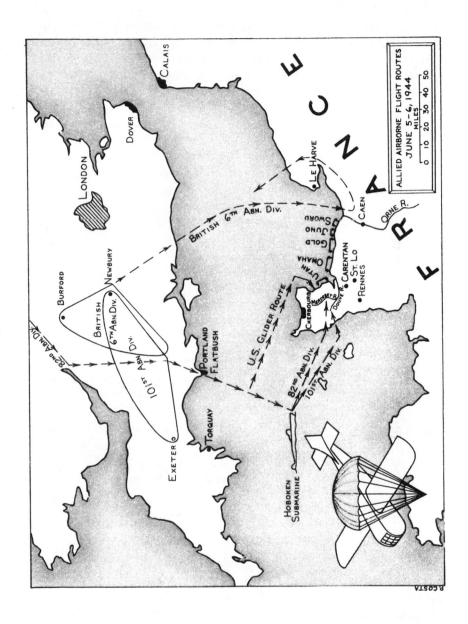

ALLIED AIRBORNE FLIGHT ROUTES
JUNE 5-6, 1944
MILES
0 10 20 30 40 50

commander. But neither Pratt nor Brigadier General Anthony C. McAuliffe, the 101st Airborne division artillery commander, had combat experience, and at General Ridgway's urging, General Bradley named Maxwell D. Taylor, the 82nd Airborne assistant division commander, to succeed Lee. This move surprised everyone, including Taylor, who was five years junior to Pratt and had graduated from West Point four years after McAuliffe. But what he lacked in seniority, Taylor more than made up for with his combat experience in Sicily, and his highly dangerous mission to Rome, in September 1943, when that city had still been behind German lines. During that daring mission, Taylor travelled from Allied occupied Sicily to the Italian mainland in the middle of the night aboard a small boat, then slipped into Rome hidden in the back of a Red Cross ambulance which was allowed to pass through German roadblocks. There he met with Mussolini's successor, Field Marshal Pietro Badoglio (who had already secretly surrendered his country and agreed to terminate its alliance with Germany), in what turned out to be a futile attempt to gain approval for a massive night parachute landing in Rome of the American 82nd Airborne Division coincident with the public announcement of Italy's surrender. It was Taylor's discovery of greatly increased German troop strength in and around Rome, and the inability of the Italian Army to provide assistance to the Americans, which led to cancellation of the airborne mission.

By February of 1944, a total of 2,100 crated Waco CG-4A gliders had been shipped to England from American factories. At General Hap Arnold's urging, the first of these gliders had arrived in May of 1943. American cargo ships delivered the crated Wacos to the port of Southampton. From there they were transported by trains and trucks to a storage area at Cookham Common, about 40 miles southwest of London. Though spacious and conveniently located, Cookham Common lacked facilities for the efficient assembly of gliders, and it was located in a part of England known for frequent wind and rainstorms.

During the summer of 1943, the Eighth Air Force headquarters in England had delegated the intricate job of assembling the gliders to untrained British civilians. With only one American sergeant and several sets of complicated written instructions to guide them, the well-intentioned civilians opened the huge crates and began assembling the gliders. The result of this poorly organized project was unsatisfactory – 51 of the first 62 gliders assembled were found to be unflyable – and in October the newly activated IX Air Force Service Command took over at Cookham Common. The inexperienced and ill-equipped Americans managed to assemble only 200 Wacos out of a quota of 600 before the end of 1943. Production figures were just starting to climb appreciably when, early in March, a violent windstorm blew across the assembly area, destroying 100 completed gliders. That storm shocked the Americans into realizing that they might not have enough gliders available for the coming invasion.

Additional manpower was rushed to Cookham Common in the form of glider mechanics recently arrived from the United States. Working a seven-day week and three shifts per day, they managed to put together 910 Wacos by the middle of April. With only five weeks remaining until D-Day, the glider shortage had barely been conquered in time.

Late in April, some of the gliders that were to take part in the invasion were equipped with recently developed modifications that included deceleration parachutes, landing lights, glider-plane intercommunication sets, and Griswold Nose crash-protection assemblies. When work was halted on the gliders a week before D-Day, only 288 Wacos had been fitted with Griswold Noses. Not until the first week of March 1944, were the airplanes and crews of the IX Troop Carrier Command that were to fly the American glider and parachute forces to Normandy in June fully assembled in England from previous duty stations in the United States, Italy and North Africa. By that time the command had its full complement of 14 groups and three wing headquarters.[4] All of those units were initially stationed at airfields in northeast England, where they would be relatively safe from German air raids and would not interfere with Allied bombers and fighters based in southeast England. The plan was to gradually move two full wings to bases in southern England, where they would be closer to their D-Day objectives in France. By April 1, the 50th and 53rd Troop Carrier Wings had been deployed southward where they become guest tenants on nine RAF airfields.[5]

Just as British glider pilots had flown American Wacos during the invasion of Sicily, some American glider pilots would be flying British Horsas during Overlord. This was at the request of the Americans, who needed the larger Horsas to deliver the large-calibre anti-tank guns and artillery pieces certain to be needed to beat off the German counterattacks in Normandy. During the first week in March, several instructional teams from the British Glider Pilot

Regiment had begun teaching the Americans how to fly the Horsas. The majority of the American glider pilots took an immediate shine to the Horsas, their only reservation being that the Horsa was constructed entirely of wood and therefore provided little crash protection. As fragile and small as the Waco CG-4As were, their steel tubing frames gave the American glider pilots at least some slight margin of survival during rough landings.

Earlier in February, General Williams of the IX Troop Carrier Command had been directed by Eisenhower's headquarters to get together with the two American airborne division commanders and prepare an intensive training programme that would culminate in May with a division-size parachute and glider manoeuvre. The goal was to raise the proficiency of the troop carrier pilots to a level at which they could deliver paratroops by night to within a mile of their DZ and fly glider missions by twilight or moonlight to a given LZ in formation and within one minute of schedule. By the end of February such a programme had been worked out. It called for intensive joint training with airborne troops to commence on March 15.

The 53rd Troop Carrier Wing managed to get a head start in the training programme by beginning its glider exercises during the first week in March. Two of its groups, the 434th and 437th, were selected to specialize in towing American Waco CG-4A and British Horsa gliders. The pilots of both groups were puzzled by the endless glider-towing exercises. What they did not know was that they had been chosen to fly the lead and follow-up glider assault missions on D-Day.

Glider training in the 53rd Wing rose to such intensity that during the month of April the 53rd logged 6,965 hours of towing time. Experimentation proved that the most satisfactory flying formation was the pair of pairs in echelon to the right.[6] The benefits of so much air-time were exhibited in an exercise on April 21, when the airplane pilots, most of whom had towed a Horsa for the first time less than seven weeks before, released 241 out of 245 of them at their proper LZs after a flight of nearly three hours. Equally large formations of Wacos were later released with similar results.

Though all of these large-scale landing exercises had been conducted inside the LZs less than 400 yards long and had resulted in minimal damage to the gliders, they were misleading in that they had been made during daylight. In combat, pilots would have to land in complete darkness – with enemy soldiers shooting at them.

[172]

Concurrent with their extensive flying duties, glider pilots of the IX Troop Carrier Command underwent a series of rugged ground combat training courses. Infantry fighting skills, hastily acquired before shipment overseas, had to be re-learned in detail. Those skills ranged from qualification firing of pistols, rifles, machine guns and mortars to bayonet and hand-to-hand combat drills. For some glider pilots, these courses were the first genuinely effective infantry training they had received.

Exercise Eagle, the full-dress rehearsal for the Normandy glider and parachute landings, was held during the night of May 11-12. The planners wanted the manoeuvre to be as close to the real thing as possible. In almost every case the departure airfields were the ones the troops would use on D-Day.

With the exception of a few parachute drops that went astray in the dark, Exercise Eagle was a success. The airborne phase of the exercise ended at dawn on May 12, when an assortment of Waco and Horsa gliders landed in the manoeuvre area without incident.

While Allied ground and air units were finalizing their invasion preparations in England, the Germans were busy on the other side of the English Channel. They knew that with the arrival of good summer weather the Allies would launch a decisive strike against the Continent. Two questions remained in the minds of the top German brass: exactly where would the attack be made? – and when?

The majority of German commanders and staff officers were convinced that the Allies would land in the Pas-de-Calais area of France, where only 20 miles of water separated England from France. The intuitive Hitler, however, held a different opinion. He alone reasoned that the Allies would land on the Cotentin peninsula and seize the deep water port of Cherbourg, through which they could feed fresh troops and supplies into their beachhead.

As far back as 1941, German labour battalions had been building what was called the Atlantic Wall around their stolen empire. A string of giant casemented coast artillery guns, underwater obstacles, and all manner of mines and booby traps extended from the seacoast of Holland along the entire English Channel to the border of Spain. As formidable as this wall was, it was only the first line of defence; just behind it was a series of mutually supporting pillboxes and gun emplacements positioned to deliver automatic weapons fire on all beachfronts. Further inland was a third line of artillery and mortars sited to provide indirect fire on the beaches and on all open fields where glider and parachute forces might land.

Sixty-nine-year-old Field Marshal Gerd von Rundstedt had been called out of retirement by Hitler to command all German forces in the west. Directly under Von Rundstedt, in command of Army Group B, was Germany's most celebrated field marshal, Erwin Rommel.[7]

It was interesting to note that Rommel, the brilliant tank commander who always favoured a mobile defence, was in full agreement with Hitler's determination to stop the Allied invasion forces while they were still on the beaches. A consummate tactician and staunch realist, Rommel recognized that the much-vaunted Atlantic Wall possessed the flaw basic to all cordon defences: complete uselessness once it had been breached. 'We must,' said Rommel, 'stop the assaulting forces in the water, not only delaying but also destroying all enemy equipment while still afloat.'[8] Rommel knew that if his troops could not stop the Allies at the water's edge, the defeat of Germany was inevitable.

Rommel anticipated that the Allies would be using glider and parachute units in large numbers. To deny his enemies suitable landing zones, Rommel directed the units positioned inland from the beaches to sow all open fields with what became known as Rommelspargel (Rommel's asparagus).

Rommelspargel actually consisted of wooden poles measuring eight to 12 feet in length and six to 12 inches in diameter. French civilians were forced by German troops to 'plant' these poles across miles of open fields in Normandy where Allied gliders might land.

In its final form the plan for employment of American airborne troops during Overlord required the 101st Airborne Division to lead the attack by jumping and gliding into three DZs and one LZ lettered A, C, D and E respectively. All four were located some six miles inland from Utah Beach, where the U.S. 4th Infantry Division was to make its amphibious landings and then advance inland over four separate causeways.

DZ A was assigned to Colonel George Mosely's 502nd Parachute Infantry Regiment. Mosely's mission was to secure two of four causeways, labelled Exit 3 and Exit 4, and to knock out the German coast artillery battery at Saint Martin-de-Varreville.

Into DZ C would go Colonel Robert F. Sink and his 506th Parachute Infantry, with the mission of securing the other two causeways – Exit 1 and Exit 2.

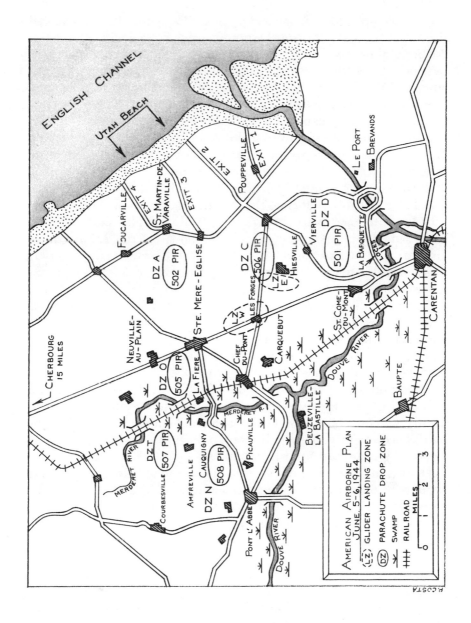

ENGLISH CHANNEL

UTAH BEACH

FOUCARVILLE
EXIT 4
ST. MARTIN-DE-VARAVILLE
EXIT 3
EXIT 2
POUPPEVILLE
EXIT 1

LE PORT
BREVANDS
LA BARQUETTE
LOCKS
CARENTAN

VIERVILLE
DZ D
501 PIR

DZ A
502 PIR

DZ C
506 PIR
LES FORGES
HIESVILLE
LZ E
LZ W
CARQUEBUT

STE. MERE-EGLISE

ST. COME-DU-MONT

NEUVILLE-AU-PLAIN

CHEF DU PONT

DOUVE RIVER

BEUZEVILLE-LA BASTILLE

BAUPTE

← CHERBOURG 15 MILES

DZ O
505 PIR
LA FIERE

MERDERET R.

PICAUVILLE

DZ T
507 PIR
COURBESVILLE
AMFREVILLE
DZ N
CAUQUIGNY
508 PIR

MERDERET RIVER

PONT L'ABBE

DOUVE RIVER

AMERICAN AIRBORNE PLAN
JUNE 5-6, 1944

(LZ) GLIDER LANDING ZONE
(DZ) PARACHUTE DROP ZONE
⊹ SWAMP
┼┼┼ RAILROAD

MILES
0   1   2   3

R. COSTA

[175]

Colonel Howard Johnson and his 501st Parachute Infantry would drop into DZ D, the southernmost drop zone inside the 101st Airborne Division airhead. Johnson was given a number of important objectives. Foremost was the capture of the large stone locks spanning the Douve River at La Barquette. The Allied planners believed that if those locks were not captured on D-Day, the Germans would blow them up. With the locks destroyed, the rising tide coming in from the sea would flood the swampy areas along the Douve and Merderet rivers, making any movement of parachute infantry virtually impossible further inland.

Two glider landing missions were to be flown in direct support of the 101st Airborne during the Normandy invasion. Both were scheduled to take place in LZ E on D-Day. The first mission, code-named Chicago, was loaded with troops of the 327th Glider Infantry and an assortment of anti-tank guns and ammunition. It was scheduled to land, under cover of darkness, at 4:00 a.m., some three hours after the paratroop landings. Brigadier General Pratt, the assistant division commander of the 101st Airborne, planned to personally lead the Chicago mission into battle aboard the first American glider to land in France.

The 101st Airborne's second glider mission was given the code-name of Keokuk, a small city located in Iowa. Gliders in the Keokuk mission would not begin landing until 9:00 p.m. on D-Day. Because of the British 'double summertime schedule' then in effect, all gliders in this mission would have the advantage of landing in full daylight and, concomitantly, the disadvantage of having to run the gauntlet of German anti-aircraft fire while doing so.

During its assault into Normandy, General Ridgway's 82nd Airborne would use three glider LZs lettered *E*, *O* and *W*, and three parachute DZs lettered *N*, *O* and *T*, all of which were located some ten miles inland from Utah Beach.

Drop zones N and T were completely isolated from the rest of the American airhead, in that they lay west of the Merderet River and therefore the deepest in enemy territory. DZ N was assigned to Colonel Roy E. Lindquist and his 508th 'Red Devils' Parachute Infantry and DZ T to Colonel George V. Millett's 507th Parachute Infantry. Both regiments had the job of setting up defences in those areas and of attacking westward in order to seal off the Cotentin Peninsula.

Drop Zone O was reserved for Colonel William E. Ekman and his

[176]

505th Parachute Infantry. Ekman's mission was to occupy the key communications centre of Sainte Mère-Église and to seize control of two stone bridges leading over the Merderet into areas occupied by division's other two parachute regiments.

Four separate glider landing operations were scheduled to be flown in support of the 82nd Airborne. Two of them were set to take place on D-Day, the others on D-Day plus one.

The first mission, code-named 'Detroit', was to start landing in LZ O before sunrise on D-Day, only 10 minutes after the first gliders had touched down over in the 101st Airborne's area.

Glider mission Elmira was comprised of two separate echelons, both of which were to land in LZ W. Its first echelon would arrive in Normandy a few minutes after the 101st Airborne's 9:00 p.m. landing. The second echelon would not land until 11:00 p.m., by which time with British double summertime in effect there would still be a vestige of twilight in the western sky. This second echelon of Elmira would mark the end of all D-Day glider missions.

The two final glider combat missions of the Normandy invasion, code-named 'Galveston' and 'Hackensack', were scheduled for execution during the first few hours of daylight on D plus 1. Their purpose was to deliver Colonel Harry L. Lewis and his reinforced 325th Glider Infantry Regiment into the American airhead. Upon its arrival in Normandy the 325th was to become the reserve fighting force of the 82nd Airborne Division and would have to be prepared to take on any combat mission assigned to General Ridgway.

Galveston was scheduled to be executed first. It consisted of 150 gliders divided into two serials, both of which were to land in LZ E.[9] Its first serial of 82 Wacos and 18 Horsas was to land shortly after daybreak. In those gliders would be 717 troops comprising the 1st Battalion of the 325th Glider Infantry, part of a glider engineer company, and several jeeps and artillery pieces. The second serial of Galveston was made up of 50 Wacos carrying an additional 251 glidermen from the headquarters of the 325th Glider Infantry, the 82nd Airborne's Reconnaissance Platoon, and a number of additional glider artillerymen along with their howitzers and a supply of ammo.

Hackensack was made up of 100 gliders divided into two serials that would be landing in LZ W starting at a few minutes before nine o'clock on the morning of D plus 1. Its lead serial of 50 gliders (20 Wacos and 30 Horsas) would land 982 troops comprising the 2nd

[177]

Battalion, 325th Glider Infantry and most of the 2nd Battalion, 401st Glider Infantry, which was attached to the 325th and acted as its third Battalion.

The other serial of Hackensack contained 50 Wacos carrying 363 glidermen, most of whom were service troops of the 325th and 401st, a large number of jeeps and trailers carrying 81mm mortars, and several more tons of ammunition.

Some of the 82nd Airborne's glider troops and the majority of the 101st Airborne's glider units would be going to Normandy aboard naval vessels. Colonel Edson D. Raff, the former commander of the famous independent 509th Parachute Infantry Battalion that had fought in Africa, was placed in command of a special attack force composed of 90 glidermen from the 325th Glider Infantry, elements from the 82nd Airborne's glider field artillery battalions, and a company of tanks from the attached 746th Tank Battalion. Raff's mission on D-Day was to make an amphibious landing on Utah Beach with his forces and then attack inland to link up with General Ridgway at the division command post near Sainte Mère-Église.

There were two primary reasons for transporting the bulk of the 101st Airborne's glider units to Normandy by boat. The first was Air Marshal Leigh-Mallory's objection to massive glider landing on Normandy's hedgerow-covered terrain. The second that there still existed in England a severe shortage of American glider pilots. One of the biggest problems faced by the airborne planners of Overlord was getting enough pilots to fly the gliders to Normandy. Because of the shortage, many gliders were to be flown with a glider trooper or paratrooper sitting in the copilot's seat. The flight training of these inexperienced soldiers consisted only of a few short lectures by the glider pilots they were to ride with on D-Day. Most pilots began their lectures by saying, 'Now if I get shot or killed on the way over to France, here's what you're going to have to do in order to land this crate all in one piece . . .' Many of the 'copilots' did in fact have to take over the controls when their pilots became casualties. As General Gavin would later say, 'Having to land a glider for the first time in combat is a chastening experience; it gives a man religion.'

In the original plan, D-Day for Overlord had been set for Monday, the 5th of June. But English weather, renowned for its unpredictability, nearly upset the entire invasion. On June 3, weather experts on General Eisenhower's staff gave him an exceedingly bad forecast for June 5. They were predicting winds in excess of 22 knots, thick clouds below 500 feet, and a four-foot surf on the Normandy beaches. From his painful experiences during the earlier invasion of Sicily, Ike knew all too well that such winds were too great for the paratroop drops, and that the low visibility would make the towing and landing of gliders next to impossible. Worst of all, Ike knew that the amphibious landings were sure to be disastrous in the high surf. Two anxious meetings with his Allied commanders persuaded Ike to postpone the invasion for 24 hours.

Across the Channel in France, German weather experts were also forecasting bad weather for the next few days. For the German field commanders this was good news; it meant the Allies would not chance a landing during stormy weather.

On June 4 – the day on which Ike had issued his order to hold everything for 24 hours – Field Marshal Rommel left France by car for Germany to be with his wife on her birthday. Lucie-Marie Rommel's birthday was June 6.

Rommel's staff car was heading through rain squalls toward Germany when, at 9:30 on the evening of June 4, Ike convened a meeting of his top commanders and staff officers in the library of his headquarters at Southwick House in Portsmouth. The meeting opened with some good news from Group Captain James M. Stagg, Ike's senior meteorologist. Stagg announced to the assembled generals, admirals, and air marshals that a sudden shift in the weather pattern gave promise of relatively good weather for the next two days. Beyond that the outlook was questionable. This meant, Stagg said, that the choppy sea would subside long enough for the invasion fleet to sail, and that the cloudy sky would become clear enough to permit both pre-invasion bombings and the critical parachute and glider landings.

Ike thanked Stagg for his briefings and began to discuss it with his commanders and staff. Ike's Chief of Staff, General Bedell Smith, suggested the attack be launched on the 6th, but Air Marshals Leigh-Mallory and Tedder were pessimistic. Both thought it would be risky to attempt a landing during weather that might hamper maximum use of air power. Field Marshal Montgomery was the most emphatic. He looked straight at Ike and said, 'I would say – go!'

Eisenhower knew that it was now up to him to make a decision. The room fell silent. Seldom has one man been charged with the responsibility for such a weighty decision, one which would affect the lives of three million troops under his command, and would largely determine the outcome of the war in Europe.

[179]

After a few minutes of agonizing thought, the Supreme Commander announced his decision: 'I'm positive we must give the order. . . . I don't like it, but there it is . . . I don't see how we can possibly do anything else.' Thus the invasion was set to take place on June 6. Its advance guard, the paratroops, would strike out from England on the night of June 5.

Allied intelligence officers knew that the entire eastern coastline of Cotentin Peninsula was invested with German radar stations and heavy anti-aircraft guns. To protect its paratroop planes, the IX Troop Carrier Command plotted a paratroop flight plan which entered the Cotentin through the back door. The plan called for all air units to fly from their departure airfields through an imaginary aerial funnel which emptied out into the English Channel at checkpoint Flatbush – the town of Portland. Upon reaching Flatbush, all units were to proceed south along a 10-mile-wide corridor at an altitude of 500 feet until they reached checkpoint Hoboken. At Hoboken a British marker submarine would signal them to make a 90 degree left turn and fly a 54-mile leg between the islands of Guernsey and Alderney, keeping out of range of German anti-aircraft guns on both islands. After passing the islands, all planes were to climb up to 1,500 feet to avoid enemy shore batteries on the mainland, keep that altitude until they passed the coastline of France, and then drop back down to 500 feet for the final run to the drop zones. Once the parachute drops had been made, all aircraft were to return to England by proceeding out over the east coast of the Peninsula to the St. Marcouf Islands (checkpoint Paducah). There they were to begin a sweeping left hand turn which intersected at checkpoint Gallup with the route by which they had come.

Staff officers from both the 82nd and 101st Airborne divisions agreed that their initial Detroit and Chicago glider missions should follow the same route taken by the paratroopers. Since both missions were to arrive in the objective area at four o'clock in the morning of D-Day, they could rely on darkness to give them a degree of protection from German anti-aircraft guns as they flew across the Contentin peninsula. The airborne staff officers also decided that all subsequent glider missions, rather than fly across the fully alerted Contentin in broad daylight, were to approach their LZs from the eastern side of the Peninsula, following the same route by which the paratroop planes had returned. They would return home the same way.

With the memory of the Sicily disaster still fresh, representatives of the IX Troop Carrier Command had met with British Admiral Sir

Bertram Ramsey, the top Allied naval commander, early in May to discuss the subject of flight routes. Because of the great importance attached to the paratroop and glider missions, Ramsey agreed to accept the flight routes and to impose an absolute prohibition on all naval anti-aircraft fire at those times when airborne missions were scheduled to pass over his fleet.

To ensure that Allied naval and land gunners could not possibly mistake its aircraft for German planes, the IX Troop Carrier Command decided to apply a distinctive painted marking to all paratroop planes and gliders. The pattern chosen for those aircraft consisted of three white and two black strips, each two feet wide, around the fuselage back of the door, and from front to back on both wings.

To familiarize the naval forces with the special markings, an exercise was held on June 1 in which only three striped airplanes were flown over the invasion fleet. However, for security's sake, the order for the painting of the remaining airplanes and gliders that were to take part in the invasion was not given until June 4. Throughout that entire day, and well into the night, hundreds of glider mechanics, pilots and troop carrier personnel worked feverishly to apply the large white and black stripes to their aircraft.

The order for the painting of the stripes came as a complete surprise to the IX Troop Carrier Command personnel. While on his way to evening chow at the Exeter airbase on June 4, glider mechanic Joe Hann met his group's glider engineering officer, Lieutenant Alfred J. Barnowski, who instructed him to report back to the flight line right after he had finished eating. No reason was given for the order. When Hann returned to the flight line about an hour later, he joined a small crowd of glider and airplane mechanics who were given a briefing on how the stripes were to be painted on the aircraft. At the end of the briefing Hann and his associates were issued with chalked strings with which to mark outlines of the stripes, wide brushes, and five-gallon cans of black and white paint. Application of the stripes was slowest on the fuselage, where care had to be taken not to get any paint on the large stencilled star insignia that identified all American airplanes. Though the wing areas were much larger, those stripes went on more quickly.

One and a half hours before midnight on June 5, the whole of central and southern England began to reverberate with the sound of aircraft engines. One thousand and eighty-six paratroop airplane

[181]

engines were warming up for the assault on Hitler's Fortress Europe.

At 11:00 p.m. sharp, six serials of three planes each, loaded with American pathfinder teams who were to mark the drop and landing zones with radars and lights, began rolling down the runways.[10] Behind the pathfinders, right on schedule, the first elements of the main body of paratroops began taking off at 12:21 a.m.

Guided by skilled navigators, the pathfinder aircraft flew across the cloud-covered west coast of the Cotentin Peninsula without being detected by German radar. But the same clouds that hid the airplanes from enemy gunners also obscured vital ground navigation points; most of the pathfinder aircraft failed to find their DZs. In the 82nd Airborne Division area, only the 505th Parachute Infantry's pathfinders going into DZ C were dropped with any accuracy.

Because the pathfinders had been misdropped, the main body of approaching parachute assault troops had, with few exceptions, nothing to home in on. By the time jumpmasters of the main body leaped out the doors of their airplanes, anything resembling an organized drop was purest coincidence.

The leading 101st Airborne Division was able to sneak past most of the German anti-aircraft batteries, but by the time the 82nd Airborne Division approached the coast of France virtually all of the sleeping Germans had been rousted out of bed and were manning their guns, the 82nd suffering the most from bad drops. Only one of its three regiments – the 505th – landed on or fairly close to its DZ.

The commander of the 82nd, General Ridgway, landed in a grassy field. Before the air spilled out of his chute the general drew his pistol and crouched down, ready to shoot the first German soldier who came near him. A few moments of silence convinced Ridgway that it was safe enough for him to get out of his harness, but as he did, he dropped his pistol. Stooping to grope in the grass for it, he caught sight of a figure moving toward him. On his knees now, and still fumbling for the pistol, the general challenged, 'Flash,' and waited for the countersign of 'Thunder'. When no answer came and he still could not find his pistol, Ridgway grew very nervous. His fears were calmed, however, when the figure, coming closer, proved to be a cow.

General Taylor, the commander of the 101st Airborne Division, had also landed in a cow pasture. After freeing himself of his chute, he began trying to locate the other men who had jumped from his plane. Just when he was beginning to wonder if he was ever going to

[182]

locate one of his troops, Taylor came across a lone private. Overjoyed at having found another friendly soul, the two men hugged each other. Right after this unusual private-to-general greeting, a few more paratroopers began appearing out of the darkness. All of them clustered around Taylor and went with him as he continued trying to locate his staff.

Throughout the huge American airhead, hundreds of misdropped paratroopers were assembling themselves into cohesive fighting units. The initial dispersion caused by bad drops was severely aggravated by hedgerows – earthen walls averaging some four feet in height and covered with thick hedges – that made assembly of the paratroops almost impossible. Extending throughout the entire battle area, the hedgerows boxed in large open fields belonging to various farmers. There was no standard size to the fields: some were square, others triangular, trapezoidal, or oblong. Some were larger than a football field, but most were much smaller. And virtually all of the fields were ringed by poplar trees averaging thirty feet in height.

The paratroopers in France were still skirmishing with German patrols and trying to assemble themselves when, at 1:19 a.m. in England, a flight of 52 planes of the 434th Troop Carrier Group, each towing a Waco, began taking off from Aldermaston airbase. Aboard these gliders were troops and equipment of the 101st Airborne Division's Chicago mission, all of which were heading for LZ E. The lead tow-plane was piloted by Colonel William B. Whittaker, commander of the 434th Group, and Major Alvin E. Robinson. Brigadier General Maurice M. Beach, commander of the 53rd Troop Carrier Wing, was with them.

The glider being towed by Colonel Whittaker's airplane was nicknamed 'The Fighting Falcon'. Its pilot was newly promoted Lieutenant Colonel Mike Murphy. Officially, Murphy had no business taking part in the invasion. His formal duty station at this time was Stout Field, Indiana, and he had only recently been sent to England to supervise the final training of American glider pilots by IX Troop Carrier Command. However, he had talked his way into piloting the invasion's leading glider. In the copilot's seat beside Murphy was Lieutenant John M. Butler. Strapped into seat number one, directly behind Murphy, was Brigadier General Donald F. Pratt, the assistant division commander of the 101st Airborne. Pratt was supposed to have travelled to Normandy by boat with the first batch of infantry reinforcements, but he had arranged to ride in the lead glider so that he could get into the fight sooner. Pratt's aide-de-camp, Lieutenant John L. May, was across the aisle from him in seat number two, clutching a briefcase that bulged with top secret maps. A few feet further back in the glider was Pratt's command jeep, heavily loaded with radios and extra five-gallon cans of gasoline.

Murphy's glider, the Fighting Falcon, was a very special aircraft, not so much because of its high-ranking tow-pilots and passengers, but because of the way in which it had come into military service. The Fighting Falcon had been constructed a year earlier in the small town of Greenville, Michigan, by the Gibson Refrigerator Company.[11] Gibson was one of the several companies with no previous aviation experience that was manufacturing war gliders. For many years before the war, the company had manufactured only wooden ice boxes, the forerunners of modern electric refrigerators. William J. Delp, a former assistant master mechanic at Gibson, recalls the day on which Gibson became involved in the production of gliders: 'When blueprints came in, the works manager threw a huge pile of them on the desk and said, "You asked for the job, now get going!" What a mess! What I didn't know about aircraft drawings would fill several books. But I had plenty of company because no one else did either. Only one or two people in the whole company had been near an airplane. But true grit and determination prevailed, and we built a lot of the damned things.'[12] Gibson's senior craftsmen, who had hand-built its high-quality ice boxes in the 1930s, made the wooden parts of the gliders that were assembled in four converted warehouses.

Early in 1943, the students at Greenville High School had decided to buy one of the Gibson gliders and donate it to the U.S. Army Air Corps. They set out to raise the needed $17,000 through the sale of war bonds. Students from kindergarten through high school pitched in spare pennies, nickels and dimes from their lunch money. Students in the junior and senior high school classes approached distant relatives for contributions. When the drive ended, the students had sold $72,000 in bonds, enough for four Gibson gliders.

Mayor Oscar A. Rasmussen declared Wednesday, May 19, Glider Day in Greenville. Schools and stores were closed, and a parade was held through the city's streets. Marching behind the high school band, which led the parade, were eight students, each of whom had sold $1,000 or more worth of bonds. Those eight – Phyllis Tower, Nancy Whitelaw, Richard Kennedy, Max Larson, Carolyn Packard,

Nina Johnson, Rosellen Raymor, and Frederick F. Brace, Jr. – were all high schoolers except for Brace, who was nine years old. At the time the drive started he had been recuperating at home from a severe eye injury caused by a carelessly thrown snowball. Though blinded in one eye, young Fred Brace managed to visit friends and relatives who helped him raise well over a thousand dollars.

Greenville's Glider Day parade ended at the high school athletic stadium, where the Gibson Company had delivered one of the four gliders purchased by the students. There the students were presented with the U.S. Treasury Department's Distinguished Service Certificate, the first such award made to a group of students in the United States during the war. Following a round of speeches, the Gibson glider was christened the Fighting Falcon by Sally Church, a member of the junior class. Two weeks after this ceremony, the Fighting Falcon was shipped to England. In recognition of the students' patriotic effort, Ninth Air Force Headquarters ordered that the Fighting Falcon should be the first glider to land in Normandy.

By the light of a bright moon, the airplanes and gliders of the Chicago mission made a smooth take-off from Aldermaston and quickly assembled into columns of four in echelon to the right. Everything was moving like clockwork when one of the gliders suddenly broke loose from its tug, landing four miles from the base. Unfortunately for General Taylor, the glider contained the powerful SCR-449 command radio by which his 101st Airborne Division was to have communicated with the higher headquarters from France.

The remainder of the Chicago mission reached Normandy without incident, but while crossing the Peninsula it encountered sporadic enemy ground fire. One plane and glider were shot down near the village of Pont l'Abbé; seven tow-planes and 22 other gliders sustained hits during the final run into the LZ area. The growing intensity of ground fire forced the formation to disperse somewhat. One tow-ship became completely separated from the flock, releasing its glider near the town of Carentan, some eight miles south of the LZ. The other 49 combinations entered the release area accurately. To avoid congestion in the LZ they divided themselves into two columns. From an altitude of 450 feet, the lead glider in each column began cutting away from their tow-planes at 3:54 a.m., six minutes ahead of schedule.

With only the dim light of the setting moon to guide him, Lieuten-

[185]

ant Colonel Mike Murphy began his descent into the murky, hedgerow-covered Norman countryside. Though the fields that were beginning to take shape below him appeared to be very small and rimmed with trees, Murphy was confident that he could land his glider in one of them. Hundreds of practice landings had taught him that even an overloaded Waco could be brought to a full stop within two hundred feet from the point of touch down. What Murphy did not know was that the cow pasture below him was covered with tall, wet grass that would not provide him with the friction needed for a quick stop.

Like the master aviator he was, Murphy deftly slid his glider over the tops of some trees outlining the large field, made a perfect landing well short of its midpoint, and stepped hard on the brakes. But even though the Fighting Falcon's wheels were locked, it continued sliding across the field and smashed into a tree-studded hedgerow.

To his amazement, Murphy was not knocked unconscious in the crash. Even more surprising, his safety belt was still holding the upper half of his body inside the glider while the lower half of his torso was protruding through a hole in the left side of the nose. Both of his legs were tangled up in the glider frame's steel tubing and, from the look and feel of them, they were badly broken.

Glancing over his copilot, Lieutenant Butler, Murphy saw at once that he was dead. Murphy then called back into the passenger compartment to check on General Pratt and his aide: nothing but silence. He was just about to call to them again when he heard loud clanking outside. Murphy froze with fear. There, just behind the trees he had crashed into, were three passing German tanks. Fortunately for Murphy, the tank commanders seemed to think there could be no survivors aboard his terribly smashed glider. After a few seconds' pause, the tanks continued on their way, leaving Murphy to his misery.

The second glider of the Chicago mission landed one hundred yards to the left and slightly behind the Fighting Falcon. Its senior passenger was Captain Charles O. Van Gorder, a doctor assigned to the 326th Airborne Medical Company. Van Gorder had just stepped out onto the ground when another glider came hurtling out of the darkness and collided with his. Luckily, no one in either glider was injured. The men from both gliders were still unloading their equipment when they were forced to jump into a ditch to keep from being seen by the three German tanks that had just left Murphy's wrecked glider. After watching the tanks drive past them on the other side of the hedgerow, the Americans returned to the gliders and continued with their unloading operations. Meanwhile, Doctor van Gorder began making his way along the hedgerow toward Murphy's glider to see if any of its passengers needed medical assistance.

Van Gorder found Murphy on the ground beside the Fighting Falcon. Having done what he could to make Murphy comfortable, the doctor climbed inside the wreckage. There he found General Pratt sitting in the front seat of the jeep, his body slumped over the steering wheel. Apparently, the weight of his steel helmet had broken his neck when his head shot forward at the moment the glider hit the hedgerow trees. Lieutenant May, the general's aide, was on the floor, unconscious but alive. The old Army saying that rank has its privileges did not apply on D-Day. General Pratt was the highest-ranking American to be killed during the invasion.[13]

Flight Officer Hance A. Lunday and his copilot, Flight Officer Marvin Bryant, had a jeep and two soldiers aboard their glider. During the final approach to what they thought was the LZ, Bryant unlocked the glider's nose latch to facilitate a rapid exit by the jeep after landing. As they were about to touch down, Lunday saw that he was not on the proper LZ. He had been told that his LZ would be a large well-marked field, but this one was completely dark and studded with a thick crop of Rommel's asparagus poles. Suddenly he saw a wrecked glider dead ahead. Lunday tried to avoid it but misjudged his altitude and snagged a wing on the ground, throwing his glider into a cartwheel. The second part of the glider to strike the ground was its Griswold Nose. With an agony of ripping and tearing noises, the glider continued cartwheeling across the field. The unlocked nose section popped open and hurled copilot Bryant into the darkness. Then the jeep tore loose from its tiedowns in the wooden floor and crushed the skull of a passenger who had removed his steel helmet just before the glider touched down. Finally the big machine came to a halt.

With blood from a head-wound trickling down the side of his face, Lunday crawled into the cargo compartment and made a quick check of his one surviving passenger. Then he began searching in the darkness for his copilot. Following the trail of large chunks that had broken off his glider, Lunday finally located Bryant lying on the ground and complaining of great pain in his right leg. A medic arrived and, finding a large object protruding from Bryant's leg, diagnosed his injury as a compound fracture. With many other patients to attend to, the medic administered first aid to Bryant and then disappeared into the night. Lunday, meanwhile, returned to his glider to see what could be salvaged from the damaged jeep still inside the wreckage. A short while later he returned to Bryant's side to stand guard over him until medical evacuation teams could take him to a field hospital.

Much like the paratroopers who had earlier been scattered wide of the DZs, the majority of gliders in this Chicago mission had missed LZ E. After-action reports would later show that only six of them found the LZ in the darkness. Fifteen others managed to land within a half mile of it. Ten more landed in a neat cluster, far to the west, near the village of Les Forges and well inside LZ W. The remaining 18 were scattered east and southeast of LZ E, all but one landing within two miles of it. Nearly all of the Wacos managed to safely clear the tall trees surrounding the many fields they had landed in, but most had touched down well beyond the midpoint of the fields and had rammed into trees or ditches at the far end of them. Amazingly, despite the numerous crash landings, there were very few deaths. Five airborne troopers, including General Pratt, were killed, 17 were severely injured, and seven others were missing and presumed captured.

Detroit, the 82nd Airborne Division's initial glider mission, was flown from Ramsbury by the 437th Troop Carrier Group. The invasion plan called for it to arrive over LZ O at 4:10 a.m., exactly 10 minutes after the 101st Airborne's Chicago mission had landed. Upon reaching the coast of France, the leading aircraft ran into a thick cloud bank where seven gliders became separated from their tow-ships. When the tow-planes dropped down to 500 feet for the final run into the release area the clouds became thinner, but visibility was still poor enough to cause the premature release of seven additional gliders on the western side of the flooded Merderet River where General Gavin and a great many other paratroopers had been misdropped.

Once the Detroit mission emerged from the clouds, it began receiving heavy anti-aircraft fire. One tow-plane went down in flames, and several gliders sustained hits. Though badly disorganized, part of the formation managed a concentrated release in two columns near LZ O. Instead of smoothly spiralling into their designated fields, the gliders came down in ones and twos with each pilot following whatever pattern looked safest to him. Nevertheless, between 17 and 23 gliders managed to land on or near LZ O. Most of them were total wrecks but personnel losses were light. Only three airborne troopers were killed and 23 seriously injured.

Eleven jeeps were destroyed, but the artillery pieces proved to be more durable. All of the eight howitzers that landed within two miles of the LZ were in good working order, though two of them could not be put into action right away because they were stranded in gliders that had landed in waist-deep marshlands bordering the Merderet River.

Shortly after daylight, General Gavin was informed that a half-submerged glider had been located about a quarter of a mile away from his position on the western bank of the Merederet. Thinking that it might contain an anti-tank gun that was crucial to the division's survival, the general sent a patrol, led by Lieutenant Thomas Grayham, to retrieve it. As Grayham got within sight of his objective, German shells began falling all around him and the glider, forcing him to withdraw from the area. Reporting back to General Gavin, Grayham said that it would take an organized attack to reach the glider, and even that if it were reached, the heavy gun that was thought to be inside it would probably be impossible to remove because of the depth of the water and the river's slippery embankment. Reluctantly, Gavin decided to leave the glider and its cargo where it lay and to get on with the more important task of getting himself and the 150 or so troopers he had rounded up to the eastern side of the Merderet.

By mid-afternoon on D-Day, some order began to emerge from the scattered parachute drops and glider landings. Down on the southern portion of the airhead, General Taylor's 101st Airborne was still widely scattered but controlled most of glider LZ E and its other D-Day objectives. Elsewhere, General Ridgway's 82nd Airborne occupied the key communications centre of Ste. Mère-Église and had cut the main highway extending from Cherbourg to Carentan. However, most of the LZ W in the 82nd's zone of action was still occupied by German troops. Ridgway knew that his division's next glider landings were scheduled to be made in LZ W at dusk, and was greatly worried by the fact that his troops might not be able to clear the LZ of German patrols completely before the gliders arrived from England. But because all of his command radios had been misdropped into the Merderet River, Ridgway had no way of advising his superior, Lieutenant General J. Lawton Collins at VII Corps Headquarters aboard the U.S.S. *Bayfield*, that most of LZ W was still held by enemy troops.

Back in England, things were proceeding as planned for the early evening launch of the Keokuk and Elmira glider missions. To minimize their exposure to German anti-aircraft batteries, all airplanes and gliders were ordered to approach the Cotentin Peninsula from the east coast, where they would pass directly over the American-occupied Utah beachhead.

Keokuk consisted of 32 airplanes of the 434th Troop Carrier Group, each towing a Horsa glider. At 6:30 p.m. on D-Day they took off from Aldermaston, bound for the 101st Airborne Division's LZ E. Flying across the Channel by daylight and in good weather, everyone kept on course and in formation, comforted by the sight of numerous American fighter planes above them.

German infantrymen still in position at Turqueville, two miles north of LZ E, and at St. Come, two miles south of the zone, held their fire as the tow-planes passed over the beachhead at 8:53 p.m., but as soon as the gliders separated themselves from the tow-ships, they began shooting with rifles and pistols.

Passing over the coastline of France, Flight Officer Eddie Anderson remembered that during the pre-flight briefing his group commander, Colonel Whittaker, had advised all glider pilots to make a 360 degree approach to the LZ so that they would have sufficient time to select a good landing field. When the LZ came into view, Anderson picked out a large field and called 'cut' to his copilot, Flight Officer Jack Tucker.

In free flight now, Anderson guided the Horsa to the far end of the LZ area, trying to lose altitude. There he made a 90 degree turn to the left, then another 90 degree turn into the downwind leg. With copilot Tucker calling off the airspeed and altitude, Anderson started to put the Horsa through its final turn when Tucker bellowed, 'Watch out!' Looking to his left, Anderson saw another Horsa starting to cross his flight path. Jerking the controls back, Anderson pulled his glider up almost into a stall as the other Horsa shot under him with only inches to spare. Anderson then shoved the controls forward to regain his airspeed but saw that he no longer had enough altitude to complete his turn onto final. Spotting an alternative field dead ahead, he called to Tucker for full flaps. Seconds later they touched down and rolled to a stop, all in one piece.

Other pilots were less fortunate than Anderson and Tucker. Lieutenant Hayden G. Haynes and Flight Officer Ernest Prewitt narrowly missed a galloping cow as they landed in the middle of a large field. As they skidded toward several poplar trees and a stone covered embankment, Prewitt kept repeating, 'I'll take the trees instead of the bank!' Haynes kicked full left rudder, and the big ship swung around about 10 degrees and slammed into the trees.

When he regained consciousness a few minutes later, Haynes heard gunfire and could feel someone lying on top of him. It was Prewitt, moving his arms and legs to see what was still working. Haynes realized that he and Prewitt had been catapulted out of the glider and were lying under a pile of wreckage. Someone started clearing the debris away from them and a voice said, 'Get those medics down here!' Haynes was glad to hear that voice – he was beginning to ache all over, and Prewitt was suffering greatly from a broken leg.

Soon the pile of plywood had been lifted away and a couple of medics went to work on Prewitt. Meanwhile, to his surprise, Haynes was able to get up and move about without assistance. Walking back to the remains of his glider, he found that his three passengers had survived the crash without injury and were at work trying to remove the tail section so they could drive the jeep away to their unit's assembly area. Just then a squad of paratroopers arrived. The sergeant in charge surveyed the pile of plywood that had been the glider's nose section and inquired, 'Where are the bodies of the pilots?' Haynes replied, 'I'm the pilot. My copilot is right over there with a broken leg.' The sergeant shook his head as he said, 'Man, you guys gotta be crazy to fly these damn things.'

Haynes and his passengers were having difficulty removing the two steel bolts that held the Horsa's tail section in place. The paratroop sergeant solved their problem by climbing into the glider and blasting the bolts off with two short bursts from his tommy gun. With the tail section removed, the three glider soldiers hopped into their jeep and drove off in search of their unit.

Lieutenant Jerome F. LeVasseur had the misfortune to land his Horsa near the southern end of LZ E, where the Germans were still very much in control. As his glider came to a halt, the Germans subjected it to intense mortar and machine gun fire, forcing LeVasseur and all of his passengers to grab their weapons and take cover in a ditch. The two sides had been exchanging shots for nearly an hour

[191]

when the Germans launched a powerful frontal attack and overran the American position. A short while later Le Vasseur and all the surviving Americans were led into a nearby village for questioning by German Luftwaffe interrogators.

An after-action analysis of this Keokuk mission revealed that most of the gliders had released at least a mile short of LZ E. Several of them were landed with no more than moderate damage, but enemy fire and accidents had combined to kill 14 men and to cause 30 serious injuries. Ten more men were missing and presumed to be prisoners of the Germans. Keokuk, the Allies' first tactical glider operation in daylight, had proved that gliders could in fact be landed then without excessive losses.

The purpose of Elmira, the other glider mission flown on the evening of D-Day, was to reinforce the 82nd Airborne Division. To limit its flying columns to a defensible length and to minimize congestion during landings, the Elmira mission was split into two echelons. The first, consisting of 76 gliders, was to begin landing 10 minutes after the 101st Airborne's Keokuk mission. The second echelon, consisting of 100 gliders, would follow two hours later.

The destination of all gliders in the Elmira mission was LZ W, an oval area measuring 2,800 yards north to south, and 2,000 yards wide. Within that oval there were numerous small fields bordered by hedgerows and tall poplars.

Elmira's first echelon had two serials carrying a total of 428 troops, 64 jeeps, 13 anti-tank guns and 24 tons of supplies. The first serial was to be flown from Ramsbury by the 437th Troop Carrier Group. It consisted of 26 airplanes towing 18 Horsas and eight Wacos, all of which were to start taking off at 6:48 p.m. The second serial was made up of 50 planes from the 438th Group, which were to take off at 7:07 p.m. from Greenham Common, towing 36 Horsas and 14 Wacos.

By 7:21 p.m. on D-Day all airplanes and gliders of Elmira's first echelon were in the air and on their way to Normandy. Climbing with the heavily laden Horsas was a difficult job, but all tow-planes succeeded in assembling and setting out in an orderly formation. Out over the Channel, the two serials were joined by lavish fighter escort. As the big skytrain proceeded southward some of the fighter escort pilots played tag with the gliders, zooming in close so that their wingtips nearly touched, then, with a friendly wave of his hand and a thumbs-up good luck gesture, the fighter pilot would return to his position in the formation.

Unbeknownst to the pilots heading toward Normandy, the northern half of LZ W was still being traversed by German patrols, was full of snipers, and was under observed fire from mortars and 88-mm guns in position on the German-held heights marked on Allied maps as Hill 20, near Fauville. Earlier in the day two battalions from the amphibiously landed 8th U.S. Infantry Regiment had managed to clear the southern half of the LZ, but their advance had been stopped cold by the Germans.

Late in the afternoon Colonel Edson D. Raff of the 82nd Airborne had tried attacking through the stalled 8th Infantry in an attempt to link up with General Ridgway at Ste. Mère Église. Raff's force consisted of several Sherman tanks and nearly 200 glider infantrymen who had come ashore over Utah Beach. Raff had personally led two separate charges against the German positions, but on both occasions he and his troops were beaten to the ground.

At his command post near Ste. Mère Église, General Ridgway could hear his amphibious troops trying to break through to him from the beaches. He could also still hear German gunfire in the northern section of LZ W. But without his vital command radios the general was unable to warn the approaching tow-planes and gliders about the presence of German forces there.

With neither darkness nor the element of surprise to protect itself, the first echelon of Elmira flew over Utah Beach and headed for LZ W, only six miles inland. As the lead tow-planes and gliders passed over the LZ they began receiving moderate ground fire in the form of machine gun bullets and 20 mm flak. Two tow-planes went down in flames after releasing their gliders, but succeeding tow-planes kept roaring over the LZ, where the unsuspecting glider pilots cut loose and headed down to a warm reception.

Lieutenant Melville W. Sands and Flight Officer Haskell Hazelwood had a jeep, a 57 mm gun, and two sergeants from the 82nd Airborne aboard their Horsa. After passing through a hail of small arms fire, they managed to set the glider down safely in a large field but were unable to bring it to a halt before it crashed into a hedgerow at 50 miles per hour. The only one injured in the crash was Lieutenant Sands, who suffered a broken neck and a badly mangled right foot but was still alive. Exactly 12 minutes after touchdown the two airborne sergeants had the jeep and gun out of the glider and were firing at some Germans in an adjoining field.

[193]

Copilot Hazelwood, meanwhile, eased Sands out of the glider's smashed nose section and onto the ground, out of the line of fire.

Flight Officers Oliver C. Farris and John R. Jackson were piloting a Horsa loaded with eight men, a jeep, and three wooden crates filled with 105 mm artillery shells. Before taking off from England they had agreed that Farris was to fly the Horsa during the final run over the LZ while Jackson would closely observe the LZ, pick out a good field, and then land the glider in it.

Just as Jackson cut away from the tow-ship, the Horsa took a direct hit from a flak shell but kept on flying. Down now to an altitude of 150 feet, Jackson lined the glider up on a field he had earlier chosen to land in, but a burst of machine gun fire coming from that field forced him hastily to select another one that was ringed with poplars. Skimming over the treetops, Farris yelled, 'You'd better pancake it in!' The glider touched down hard, wiping away its landing gear and skidding headlong into some trees at the end of the field. With a great crunching sound one of the trees passed right between Farris and Jackson and brought the front end of their glider to an abrupt halt.

Meanwhile the rest of the glider continued forward, telescoping into the trees. When the noise finally stopped, Farris yelled back into the cargo compartment, 'You guys okay?' But there was no need for Farris to shout: all eight of his passengers were only a few feet behind him. Miraculously no one was seriously injured in the crash.

Elsewhere over LZ W the sky was still full of gliders in free flight. Under such dangerous circumstances, the pilots did fairly well. Only two gliders in the first serial landed inside LZ W. Twelve others came within a mile, and all but one or two others were within two miles of it. The second serial also landed in moderately good shape. Later casualty figures would reveal that five glider pilots had been killed, 17 wounded or injured, and four more were missing and presumed captured.

Elmira's second echelon was made up of two serials carrying a total of 418 troops, 31 jeeps, twelve 75 mm howitzers, 26 tons of ammunition and 25 tons of other supplies. The first serial consisted of 50 airplanes from the 436th Group at Membury towing 48 Horsas and two Wacos. The second serial was comprised of another 50 airplanes from the 435th Group at Weldford towing 38 Horsas and 12 Wacos. The great capacity of the Horsas (which could haul 7,380 pounds versus the Waco's 4,060 pounds) enabled these two serials to carry far more than the earlier D-Day mission.

The sun set a few minutes before the first serial flew over Utah Beach, and the LZ was filled with long shadows of trees and hedgerows. To their surprise, the men in the leading aircraft of both serials began to encounter ground fire at a distance of only three miles inland. Once the gliders were in free flight, the Germans concentrated their fire on them. In some areas the fire was extremely heavy, and many men were wounded and killed during the one or two minutes it took for their gliders to reach the ground.

Unfortunately for the second echelon of Elmira, many gliders landed in the northern half of LZ W and well within the German positions. As had happened during the earlier landings, many of these troops were fighting for their lives the instant the gliders rolled to a halt. Casualties in men and equipment ran high. Ten glider pilots were dead, 29 more were wounded or injured, and seven were taken prisoner. Passenger losses amounted to 28 killed and 107 wounded or injured.

As for the gliders, only 13 of 84 Horsas managed to survive the landings intact: 56 of them had been completely destroyed. Prior to this mission, the majority of American glider pilots had felt that the Wacos, with their gentler glide and more durable frames of steel tubing, would survive the tough landings in better shape than the Horsas. But that theory was disproved completely. Not one Waco survived the landings intact; eight were destroyed completely.

The fierce battle for control of the American airhead, which had started at 1:00 a.m. on D-Day with the dropping of paratroopers, was still in full swing at midnight. There was pandemonium throughout the many walled-in fields within the American airhead, where scattered bands of confused parachute and glider troops were fighting private wars with small groups of equally confused Germans. The airborne planners of Overlord had expected a high degree of confusion and mixing of personnel simply because of the large number of troops that had to be delivered into the huge airhead by parachute and glider. But never had they envisaged how chaotic the situation would actually be on D-Day.

Casualties were running high for both of the American airborne divisions, but not as high as Air Marshal Leigh-Mallory had predicted. At the close of D-Day, the 82nd Airborne listed 1,259 of its troops either killed, wounded, or missing in action. By coincidence the 101st Airborne casualty figures were nearly identical: 1,240. These personnel losses were only a part of the difficult situation

[195]

facing Generals Ridgway and Taylor. Well over 60 per cent of the supplies that had been delivered by parachute and glider were destroyed, damaged, or in the hands of German troops.

How much did the American glider and parachute attacks contribute to the success of the Normandy D-Day landings? This can best be answered by an examination of casualties sustained and results achieved by the troops who had to make the amphibious assault landings on Omaha and Utah beaches. At H-Hour (the time the leading infantry troops hit the beaches) there was no opposition to the landings in Utah Beach except for a few long-range artillery rounds. At the end of the day 20,000 soldiers and 1,700 vehicles were safely ashore. Casualties were astonishingly low. Only 12 men killed and 46 others were reported as wounded or injured. Another 60 troops were lost at sea when their vessels were sunk by mines.

On Omaha Beach, where no glider or parachute troops were deployed, the situation was far different. There the amphibious assault troops began taking casualties from the moment the landing ramps were lowered at the shoreline. Hundreds of infantrymen were killed before they stepped into the water. Those who got ashore had to fight for every inch of sand. Because of the intensity of the German defensive fire, no anti-tank or artillery units could land in Omaha. By the end of D-Day the amphibious forces had penetrated only a mile and a half inland. Just before midnight VII Corps Headquarters completed totalling the casualty list for Omaha. It amounted to 2,374 men killed, wounded, or missing in action.

Starting at two o'clock in the morning of Wednesday, D plus 1, troopers of the 82nd Airborne's 325th Glider Infantry Regiment, plus all of the division's remaining glider artillery and engineer units, were awakened at four separate airfields in England to begin preparations for their flight to Normandy. By 4:00 a.m. all of the troops had eaten a hearty breakfast and been marched out onto the darkened airfields where ground crews were preparing row upon row of dew-covered airplanes and gliders for take-off.

Because of the intense ground fire over LZ W on D-Day, the 53rd Wing made certain changes in Galveston, the first glider mission scheduled for D plus 1. Tow-plane pilots were instructed to approach the airhead four miles south of Utah Beach. Instead of using LZ W, all tow-planes were to deliver their gliders to LZ E and give the release signal one mile west of Ste. Marie-du-Mont.

These changes were supposed to keep all aircraft out of range of the German guns north of Ste. Mère-Église.

Galveston consisted of two serials, both of which were designed to provide more troop reinforcements and heavy weapons to the 82nd Airborne. Its first serial would be flown from Ramsbury by the 437th Group and was made up of 50 airplanes towing 18 Horsas and 32 Wacos. In those gliders were Lieutenant Colonel Richard K. Boyd and his 1st Battalion of the 325th Glider Infantry, plus two platoons of engineers, a total of 717 troops. Also on board the gliders were 17 jeeps, 9 howitzers and 20 tons of equipment.

The second serial would be flown from Aldermaston by the 434th Group. It was comprised of 50 airplanes and 50 Wacos. Those gliders were to carry Colonel Harry L. Lewis, commander of the 325th Glider Infantry, the Reconnaissance Platoon of the 82nd Airborne, plus several platoons of engineers and artillerymen, 251 men in all, along with 24 jeeps, 11 howitzers and 5 tons of ammunition.

Take-offs at Ramsbury and Aldermaston began at 4:39 a.m. and 4:32 a.m., respectively, in conditions of gusty wind, rain and very poor visibility. One greatly overloaded Horsa at Ramsbury wouldn't budge off the ground and had to be left behind. Another broke loose during assembly, but its tow-plane quickly landed and took off with it. Yet another Horsa broke loose as the serials were passing over Portland. It glided to a safe landing in a pasture.

Over the channel, the weather improved considerably. The rain stopped and, with the morning sun creeping above the horizon, visibility became excellent. At 6:55 a.m., five minutes ahead of schedule, the leading aircraft flew over the Normandy coastline where they immediately encountered small arms fire of medium intensity. Unfortunately for the glider pilots, all airplanes in this first serial were flying at exceptionally low altitudes ranging from a high of 300 feet to a low of 100 feet. Release at those altitudes meant they could not glide much farther than half a mile or stay in the air more than 30 seconds.

All but six of the gliders received the release signal too soon and were forced to land between the two southern causeways leading inland from Utah Beach toward LZ E. The gliders landing east of LZ E had only occasional mortar and sniper fire to contend with when they touched down, but they suffered numerous landing accidents.

[197]

Lieutenant Alexis M. Neel had aboard his Waco 15 passengers, one of whom was Lieutenant Colonel Boyd, the commanding officer of the 325th Glider Infantry's 1st Battalion. Minutes after zooming across the shoreline, Neel cut loose from his tug-ship. Nosing the glider downward, he searched frantically for a field large enough to land in. Through the big windshield he saw and rejected several fields that were studded with Rommel's asparagus. Then, seeing another glider land straight ahead of him in a cleared field, he decided to land behind it. As he watched, it raced along for several feet, struck a mine and was blown up. Just about out of altitude now, Neel tried to fly over a group of trees at the far end of that field, but he didn't make it. Travelling 70 miles per hour, his Waco crashed into the tops of the trees, bending them backwards. On impact, a case of mortar ammo that had been tied to the floor between Neel and his copilot, Flight Officer John Larenzo, was thrust into the pilot's compartment where it broke two of Neel's ribs and smashed the control panel. With its nose protruding between two recoiling trees and its smashed wings wrapped around several others, the Waco yielded to gravity and dropped like an out-of-control elevator. When the glider finally came to a halt on the ground its nose section and wings were still some six feet up in the trees.

Several passengers had been thrown out of the glider. One of them, Lieutenant Colonel Boyd, was knocked unconscious as he hit the ground. When he awoke a few moments later, Boyd saw that he was lying against the glider's twisted fuselage. With a splitting headache and his body racked with pain, he looked himself over to see what condition he was in. Terror gripped him when he saw that his right leg was missing. Just then a team of medics arrived on the scene. With their assistance, Boyd discovered that his 'missing' leg was still very much a part of him. It had simply been hidden from his view, pinned underneath the wreckage.

Personnel and glider losses for the Galveston mission were heavy. In the gliders, 17 troops had been killed and 85 more badly injured. A total of 10 Horsas were destroyed and seven were damaged. The Wacos suffered nine destroyed and 15 damaged.

Neptune, the last American glider assault landing of the Normandy invasion, was flown into LZ W two hours after Galveston. Its first serial, consisting of 50 planes towing 30 Horsas and 20 Wacos, was flown out of Up Ottery by the 439th Group. This serial carried the 2nd Battalion, 325th Glider Infantry and the 2nd Battalion,

[198]

401st Glider Infantry, which was attached to the 325th and served as its 3rd Battalion. There were 968 troops on board, with the Horsas carrying over 800 of them. The second serial was comprised of 50 planes and 50 Wacos of the 441st Group at Merryfield. They had 363 troops aboard, most of them service troops of the 325th and 401st, plus 20 jeeps, twelve 81 mm mortars and six tons of ammo.

At 8:51 a.m., nine minutes ahead of schedule, the lead serial began flying over Utah Beach. It was followed eight minutes later by the second serial. With no markings on the LZ to guide them, the glider pilots headed down wherever they saw a promising spot. Many of the gliders landed a mile west of the zone, in fields that had not been used by gliders during the previous day's landings. Twelve gliders from one squadron released a few seconds late and were forced to land in the northern half of the zone, where German troops were still present.

Small fields, tall trees, Rommel's asparagus, and debris from wrecked gliders combined to cause numerous landing accidents. Sixteen Horsas were destroyed and 10 were damaged, with 15 soldiers aboard them killed and 59 injured. Of the Wacos, only four were destroyed and 10 damaged. Two glider pilots were killed in those crashes and 11 others were seriously injured. Once again, the cargo aboard the gliders proved more durable than the passengers; all but two jeeps came through unscathed.

Terrible crashes and numerous skirmishes with German troops on the landing fields notwithstanding, the 325th Glider Infantry had assembled itself into an effective fighting force by 10:15 a.m. Some 57 of its troops were missing, all but one of those being from the 1st Battalion. About 90 per cent of the regiment was ready for action.

So ended the American glider assault landings in Normandy. Things had gone as well as most experts expected, and much better than some had predicted. The missions flown on D plus 1 proved conclusively that infantry units could be landed in daylight within range of enemy artillery and still have 90 per cent of their troops assembled and ready for combat within two hours.

The glider pilots constituted 20 per cent of the nearly 5,000 Americans delivered into the airhead aboard Horsas and Wacos. Plans called for them to assist in the unloading of the gliders and the clearing of enemy troops from the landing fields. Once that had been accomplished they were to assemble under the senior glider pilot in their vicinity and report to the nearest airborne division headquarters to assume the duties of guarding command post areas and German prisoners of war.

Some glider pilots, especially those who landed in the northern half of LZ W, continued to fight alongside the glider troops for a day or two following D-Day. During those skirmishes several more pilots were killed, wounded, and captured. But the majority of them managed to assemble in the vicinity of the 82nd and 101st Airborne command posts within a few hours of their arrival in the airhead. Some 270 of them were evacuated to the beaches on the afternoon of D plus 1. At noon on June 8, another 170 pilots who had been guarding the headquarters of the 82nd Airborne marched to the beaches while guarding 326 prisoners. Waiting LSTs ferried the pilots and prisoners to England later that afternoon.

Perhaps the most unusual role performed by a glider pilot during the Normandy invasion was that of a clergyman. On D-Day, a number of glider pilots had formed a defensive perimeter around the 101st Airborne Division hospital in the village of Heisville. All during the day and throughout the night, wounded and dead airborne troopers were brought to a walled-in courtyard adjacent to the hospital. There the wounded were carried to one side of the courtyard to await treatment. The dead, meanwhile, were laid in neat rows at the other end of the courtyard.

By the morning of D plus 1 it became obvious that something had to be done as quickly as possible with the dead, many of whom were now being stacked on top of one another to make room for the living. Seeing how desperate the situation had become, Flight Officer Eddie Anderson held a hasty meeting with Major James Lynch of the 101st Airborne, during which he volunteered the services of himself and his fellow glider pilots to perform the burial detail. A field just across the road from the hospital was quickly selected to become the first American cemetery in France. With Anderson and eight other pilots standing guard over them, a group of 20 German prisoners began digging graves. When the graves were completed the pilots and their prisoners returned to the courtyard, where, with the help of some paratroop medics, the pilots carefully wrapped each body in a parachute. The Germans were then made to carry the bodies across the road and gently lower them into the earth.

When it came time to start filling in the graves, all of the pilots and prisoners removed their helmets and assembled at the front of the cemetery. With all of the division's chaplains occupied across the street administering words of comfort and the last rites to seriously wounded airborne troopers awaiting surgery, one of the glider pilots at graveside said, 'How about someone saying a few words?' There followed a moment of awkward silence, at the end of which Flight Officer Anderson felt a gentle nudge and heard a voice behind him say, 'Go ahead, Andy.'

Anderson nervously cleared his throat and began to mutter something about soldiers dying for their country. Suddenly he remembered that he had a card in his pocket with the 23rd Psalm printed on it. As he read aloud, Anderson noticed that some of the prisoners had recognized the prayer and were reciting the psalm along with him in German. At the end of the reading there was another moment of silence. Anderson gave the order to fill in the graves.

While the American 82nd and 101st Airborne divisions had been landing in confusion on the Cotentin Peninsula, Major General Richard N. Gale's 6th British Airborne Division was, with great skill and accuracy, getting on with its mission of seizing some 24 square miles of enemy territory east of Caen.

General Gale and his airborne troops had three vital tasks to accomplish on D-Day: the seizure of two iron bridges spanning the Caen Canal and the Orne River, to be used by British amphibious troops scheduled to advance to the east from Sword Beach on D-Day; the neutralization of the powerful German coast artillery battery at Merville; and the destruction of five bridges over the Dives River, which marked the extreme eastern edge of the Normandy beachhead where the main German counterattack was expected to be launched. With those bridges destroyed, the Germans would be unable to effectively employ tanks during their counterattack.

General Gale's plan for this many-sided mission called for four separate glider landing operations, all on D-Day. Parts one and three of Gale's plan were reminiscent of the earlier German glider attacks on Fort Eban Emael in Belgium and the Corinth Canal bridge in Greece, but the British plans far exceeded the boldness and complexity of those German attacks. The Germans had launched both of their missions during daylight hours. In Normandy, the British would be launching two of theirs in total darkness against pinpoint targets.

Part one of Gale's plan called for two *coup-de-main* parties to take off from England on the night of June 5, immediately behind the initial pathfinder detachments, and to silently land beside two iron

[201]

bridges leading over the Caen Canal and the Orne River. While the paratroop pathfinders were landing elsewhere on their DZs, the British glider troops were to scramble out of their Horsas and seize control of the bridges before the Germans could get out of bed to stop them. Two small fields, labelled LZ Y and LZ Z, would be used for this mission. Both were situated immediately beside the targeted bridges. Because the fields were so small, the Germans had not bothered to place landing obstacles in either of them.

Though less dramatic than part one, part two was no less hazardous. It involved a 3:00 a.m. landing of 68 Horsas and four giant Hamilcar gliders carrying General Gale, the division staff, and part of the 6th Air Landing Brigade, on a section of LZ N west of Ranville. LZ N was a large area measuring roughly two miles long and one and a half miles wide. Unlike the postage stamp-sized fields in the American airhead, LZ N consisted of a single open field that was virtually free of hedgerows and trees. Instead, it contained hundreds of wooden Rommel's asparagus poles and several brick walls. Parachute engineers who were to drop into this same area with the 5th Parachute Brigade had the mission of blowing the poles and walls down with TNT.

Part three was to take place in total darkness, at 4:20 a.m. Its target was the Merville Battery, whose guns were protected by concrete casemates, barbed wire fences and minefields. A force of 58 volunteers in three Horsa gliders was to crash land on top of the battery at the exact moment that a previously dropped parachute battalion launched a ground attack against it. To enhance the chances for the success of this desperate scheme, all three Horsas had to rely on the battery's concrete casemates to tear off their wings and halt the forward progress of the fuselages.

Part four of Gale's plan contained a pair of historic firsts: it would be the largest mass landing of gliders thus far in the war, and it would mark the first time that a tank force was flown directly into a battlefield.[14] Scheduled for 4:30 p.m. on D-Day, this mission was comprised of 256 gliders (230 Horsas and 26 Hamilcars), all of which were to land northeast of Ranville in LZ N. Troops from previously landed gliders were to clear four separate lanes through the remaining Rommel's asparagus on LZ N to receive all 256 of these gliders during a 30-minute period.

Like their American counterparts, the British glider pilots had been through a series of landing exercises in England in preparation

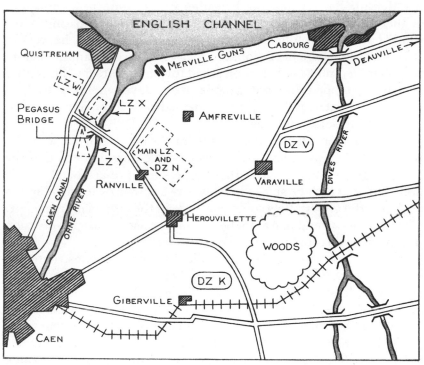

ENGLISH CHANNEL

QUISTREHAM

MERVILLE GUNS

CABOURG

DEAUVILLE

LZ W

PEGASUS BRIDGE

LZ X

AMFREVILLE

DZ V

MAIN LZ AND DZ N

LZ Y

RANVILLE

VARAVILLE

DIVES RIVER

CAEN CANAL

ORNE RIVER

HEROUVILLETTE

WOODS

DZ K

GIBERVILLE

CAEN

P. COSTA

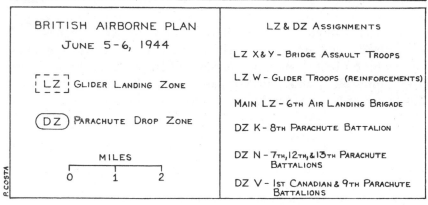

BRITISH AIRBORNE PLAN
JUNE 5-6, 1944

LZ & DZ ASSIGNMENTS

LZ X & Y - BRIDGE ASSAULT TROOPS

LZ W - GLIDER TROOPS (REINFORCEMENTS)

MAIN LZ - 6TH AIR LANDING BRIGADE

DZ K - 8TH PARACHUTE BATTALION

DZ N - 7TH, 12TH, & 13TH PARACHUTE BATTALIONS

DZ V - 1ST CANADIAN & 9TH PARACHUTE BATTALIONS

LZ  GLIDER LANDING ZONE

DZ  PARACHUTE DROP ZONE

MILES
0    1    2

for their D-Day mission. Because of the extraordinarily high risk of the Merville Battery mission, Brigadier Chatterton, the commander of the Glider Pilot Regiment, decided that all participating pilots would have to be volunteers. One month prior to D-Day, he went to Brize Norton where his B Squadron was stationed. Standing before the assembled pilots, Chatterton asked for six volunteers. The entire squadron stepped forward as one man. Overwhelmed by this response, Chatterton had to ask the squadron's commander, Major Ian Toler, to select the crews.

The most important requirements for the success of the Merville Battery, Caen Canal, and Orne River bridge missions was that the tow-planes accurately deliver their gliders to a pre-arranged release point and that they be able to quickly give a course over the intercom on which the glider pilots could continue to the targets in free flight. The courses would have to be given precisely, so pre-invasion training was directed toward that end.

A full-scale model of the Merville Battery was constructed at Newbury so that the paratroopers could rehearse their ground attack and the gliders could fly over and observe it. Elsewhere at Netheravon airfield several full-scale dress rehearsals of the Caen Canal and Orne River landings were carried out in complete darkness on small fields similar to those in Normandy. At both Newbury and Netheravon, British airborne engineers practised blasting down wooden poles that were of the same dimensions as the Rommel's asparagus photographed in Normandy by RAF reconnaissance airplanes.

At 11:03 p.m. on June 5, six converted Albemarle bombers containing 60 British pathfinders took off from Harwell bound for Drop Zones K, N and V in Normandy. Moments later, six Horsas took to the air behind their Halifax tow-ships from Tarrant Rushton. Three were heading for the bridge over the Caen Canal, the other three for the bridge over the Orne River. Aboard the gliders were two *coup-de-main* parties each comprised of three platoons from the 2nd Battalion, the Oxfordshire and Buckinghamshire Light Infantry (the 52nd Foot, as those troops liked to be called). Both parties were under the command of Major John Howard.

Staff Sergeants J. H. Wallwork and J. Ainsworth were flying the leading glider. Cruising behind their tug at an altitude of 5,000 feet, they could see moonlight reflecting off the channel. Soon the dark mass of the Normandy coastline came into view, and Wallwork could hear the navigator of the Halifax giving him the airspeed and minutes remaining to touchdown. He synchronized his stopwatch with the navigator's. Then came the voice of the Halifax captain through the intercom: 'We are now five miles out from your objective. Good luck.' Five seconds later the first Horsa was in free flight.

As the glider began to lose airspeed, Wallwork kept his eyes on the control panel's gyrocompass and Ainsworth began calling off their altitude and airspeed. From their many rehearsals back in England, both pilots knew it would take them exactly three and one half minutes to land beside their objective, the bridge crossing the Caen Canal. Passing over the canal at 3,000 feet, Wallwork ordered half flaps and put the Horsa through a 90 degree turn onto the crosswind leg. As he did so, the bridges appeared clearly below in the moonlight. Down now to 1,000 feet, Wallwork deployed the arrester parachute. When the big ship touched down, Wallwork released the chute and applied the brakes. There was a great screeching noise and a shower of sparks as the Horsa came to a halt with its nose actually protruding through the bridge's barbed wire fence.

The glider was still quivering from the sudden stop when its passengers pushed open the door, jumped to the ground, and raced across the bridge with their Sten guns blazing. Two loud thumps could be heard directly behind them as the other two gliders landed. Seconds later troops from those gliders joined in the assault.

Alert German sentinels on the bridge killed one British officer and wounded another before they themselves were killed by a fusillade of Sten gun bullets. A short five minutes after the first glider had touched down, the bridge was in British hands.

Three other gliders were landing only a few hundred yards to the east to attack the Orne River bridge. The leading glider of this party mistakenly landed some five miles off target near the Dives River. The other two landed a few hundred yards short of the bridge. Troops from those two gliders launched a vigorous assault on the bridge, only to find that its defenders were asleep. With both bridges now secured, Major Howard deployed his troops around them to repel the expected counterattacks from local German units.

It was now one o'clock in the morning, and the night was alive with the sounds of gunfire and the roar of airplanes dropping paratroopers into DZs K, N, and V. The earlier arrival of the gliders and path-finders had alerted the German defences, and when the drops were made into a brisk wind the sky was filled with tracer bullets and bursting flak shells.

Over on DZ N, two companies of engineers that had jumped with Brigadier Nigel Poett's 5th Parachute Brigade quickly assembled themselves and began blowing down the wooden poles obstructing the four 1,000-yard long lanes in which 68 Horsas and four Hamilcars were to land at 3:00 a.m. Three of these lanes had to be 60 yards wide for the Horsas; and the fourth had to be 90 yards wide to accommodate the large Hamilcars.

By the time the leading glider arrived off the coast of France with General Gale aboard, the engineers had all four lanes cleared and their boundaries partially marked with flaming smudge pots. Heavy flak greeted the British as they passed over the shoreline, wounding many men on board the airplanes and gliders. From an altitude of 2,500 feet, the glider pilots began cutting away from their tugs. Most of those fortunate enough to land first had little difficulty, but some of the succeeding gliders were forced to land outside the cleared lanes to avoid collisions with four Horsas that had crashed, littering the fields. Soon the sounds of gliders being smashed to pieces by wooden poles rose above the noise of gunfire on the flanks of the LZ.

One hour after the landings, General Gale received a disturbing report that only 49 of the 72 gliders that had taken off from England on this mission had arrived in France. It was later discovered that five of the missing gliders made emergency landings in England, three had crashed into the channel, and 14 more had somehow vanished without a trace.

The extraordinarily difficult mission of knocking out the deadly Merville Battery had been assigned to the intrepid Lieutenant Colonel Terrance Otway and his 9th Parachute Battalion. The plan for the battery's destruction called for Otway and his 600 paratroopers to jump on DZ V at 1:00 a.m. on D-Day. Next, the paratroopers were to meet four Horsas that would land near their DZ to unload heavy guns, mine detectors and flamethrowers. From those gliders, Otway was to move his battalion to a point one mile east of the objective and take cover while 100 Lancaster bombers plastered the battery. In the wake of the shock caused by the bombers, Otway and his men were to storm the battery. The last part of the plan was suicidal: at the same time Otway was making his final assault, the aforementioned three Horsas loaded with troops would crash land among the German guns to join in the final shoot-out.

Otway expected that parts of this plan might not work; several things had gone wrong during rehearsals in England. But he had not imagined just how badly things would go during the mission. Caught in strong winds over DZ V, his battalion became badly scattered in the dark. Of the 600 men that jumped with him, Otway could round up only 150 of them in the battalion's assembly area. Though he would have to make the attack with only a quarter of his battalion, Otway was still optimistic; he knew the Lancasters would soon arrive to bomb the battery. Unfortunately, the Lancasters missed the battery and devastated the sleeping village of Merville. And as if this was not enough bad luck for one night, the 11 Horsa gliders carrying the special assault group's equipment were unable to locate their LZ, which was obscured by smoke and dust caused by the misdropped Lancaster bombs. The Horsas were forced to make emergency landings south of Amfreville in a field cluttered with Rommel's asparagus. During these landings, seven glider pilots were killed and all of the gliders were so badly damaged that their cargoes of flame-throwers, jeeps and small artillery pieces could not be immediately unloaded for use in the assault on the German battery.

Crouched in a ditch behind the fully alerted battery with his well-laid plan in ruins, Otway decided to launch the attack anyway. After sending several men forward to cut paths through the battery's barbed wire, Otway looked up into the dark sky for some sign of the three Horsas that were to crash into the battery at the moment he made the assault. But even this part of the plan had gone wrong. A broken tow-rope had prevented one glider from leaving England. The remaining two were hit by flak, and troops aboard both were wounded. As those two gliders descended above the battery, their pilots were unable to see it because of the thick blanket of smoke coming from the burning village of Merville. In an amazing display of dead-reckoning airmanship, one pair of pilots managed to land their glider successfully only 50 yards from the battery. The other glider landed 700 yards away. Though not close enough to take part in the initial assault, troops from these gliders later managed to keep German reinforcements from reaching the battery.

In what is probably the most outstanding act of leadership and courage exhibited anywhere in Normandy during the pre-dawn darkness of D-Day, Colonel Otway stood straight up and shouted to his troops above the roar of German machine guns, 'Everybody in! We're going to take this bloody battery!' And with that he charged into the barbed wire.

Stunned by the sheer madness and ferocity of this British attack,

[207]

the German defences folded. Within minutes Otway and his troops were inside the battery and had spiked all four guns. It was a costly victory; no fewer than 70 British troopers had been killed or wounded. Of the original 132 Germans who had been manning the battery, only 22 were taken prisoner.

By dawn of D-Day, June 6, the 6th British Airborne Division had accomplished every one of its missions in Normandy. Throughout the day those glider pilots who were physically able were kept busy fighting alongside paratroopers who were beating back German counterattacks around the outer edges of LZ N.

The ground tactical situation had improved slightly for the British by the time their vast armada of 246 gliders crossed the coastline at 4:30 p.m. on D-Day. Aboard those gliders were nearly 7,000 troops of Brigadier the Honourable Hugh Kindersley's 6th Air Landing Brigade, 16 Tetrarch tanks, two artillery batteries, and eight anti-tank guns. In another amazing display of airmanship, every one of the Hamilcars and all but two of the Horsas landed well within the limits of LZ N, where they began disgorging their passengers and equipment under intense shelling. One of the Hamilcars buried its nose in the soil, jamming the main exit door. Seconds later it was struck by a German shell and set afire. Flames were racing along the length of the fuselage when the Tetrarch tank which had been trapped inside the glider could be seen chewing its way out of the nose section. Once clear of the burning wreckage the tank commander opened his turret hatch, spotted the German gun that had destroyed the Hamilcar, and charged straight toward it in a cloud of dust with all guns firing.

On June 8, all British glider pilots were withdrawn from the front lines to Sword Beach. There they boarded a ship which took them to England. A total of 34 British glider pilots were killed in Normandy.

American glider pilot casualties totalled 25 dead, 31 wounded and 91 seriously injured. Thirty-three other pilots were listed as prisoners of war. One of those prisoners, Captain William J. Adams, returned to Allied control on June 8 in a most unusual way. Adams had been captured on D-Day along with two other survivors of the British Horsa he piloted into Normandy. While inside a German prison the following day he observed that his captors were jabbering among themselves and pointing to the small American flag that was sewn on the sleeve of his jacket. With the aid of an American paratrooper prisoner who could speak Polish, Adams learned that virtually all of the guards were Poles, Czechs and Russians who had been pressed into frontline service by the Germans.

Through his paratroop interpreter, Adams told the guard commander that he and his men were hopelessly surrounded by thousands of airborne troops and that they should surrender to him before they were killed by the advancing Americans. Just then a mortar shell exploded in the distance, lending credibility to Adams's bluff. The guard commander left Adams and returned a short while later, saying he and the rest of the prison garrison wanted to surrender but his three German officers were unwilling to do so. Adams then instructed him to order the Germans to surrender or be shot. At gunpoint, the three German officers were forced to accept the ultimatum. Later that day, Adams marched into the American lines with 156 of his captors and 10 liberated American airborne troops. As quickly as June 9, the GI newspaper, *Stars and Stripes*, published a feature story about the exploits of Captain Adams, calling him 'The Sergeant York of Oratory'.

Seven American glider pilots returned to Normandy on June 10 and again on June 13 at the controls of Horsas and Wacos loaded with artillery shells and other forms of ammunition and supplies. By that time the Germans had been cleared out of the American airhead and the landings were made without incident on cleared fields within LZ E, near Heisville.

On June 21, Captain Roy Sousley and 10 other glider pilots from the 437th Troop Carrier Wing were sent to Normandy to begin preparations for the retrieval of the gliders used in the invasion. Sousley had orders from Ninth Air Force to conduct a survey of the entire American airhead area and then send back to England a report on how many gliders could be retrieved by using the aerial snatch method. The results of this survey were far worse than anticipated. Every one of the Horsas and all but 13 of the Wacos were found to be either located in heavily treed fields inaccessible to the snatch plane, or damaged beyond repair by rough landings, German shelling and vandals who roamed the airhead at night in search of souvenirs and firewood. The 13 flyable Wacos were snatched out of Normandy on June 25 and returned to England. The remaining Wacos, each of which cost a minimum of $15,400, were left to rot where they had landed.

General Williams, commander of the IX Troop Carrier Command, signed an order on July 5 authorizing the award of the Air Medal to each

[209]

of the glider pilots who participated in the Normandy assault landings. The citation accompanying the order was worded as follows:

> The magnificent spirit and enthusiasm displayed by these officers, combined with skill, courage and devotion to duty is reflected in their brilliant operation of unarmed gliders of light construction at minimum altitudes and air speeds, in unfavorable weather conditions, over water, and in the face of vigorous enemy opposition, with no possibility of employing evasive action, and in their successful negotiation of hazardous landings in hostile territory, to spearhead the Allied invasion of the continent. Their respective duty assignments were performed in such an admirable manner as to produce exceptional results in the greatest and most successful airborne operation in the history of world aviation.[15]

The glider pilots did not receive their medals until the latter part of July. By that time most of them had already recorded numerous additional hours in their flight logs as copilots of C-47 airplanes hauling supplies to British and American troops in Normandy.

# Chapter 8

# *Operation Dragoon*

OPERATION DRAGOON – THE INVASION of southern France – was one of the most controversial military actions undertaken by the Allied Nations during World War II. The issue was not in the way in which it was carried out – everyone, including the opposing German generals, has admitted that Dragoon was perfectly executed – but whether an alternative operation, one which might have beaten the Russians into the Balkans, should not have been substituted, as Sir Winston Churchill so strongly desired.

According to the original Allied timetable for the liberation of Europe, Dragoon was to have been launched in the spring of 1944 by a mixed force of American, British and French combat divisions drawn out of Italy and North Africa. Once the German Army became entangled in a major battle along the Riviera in the south of France, the Allies would land their main hammer blow – Operation Overlord – in the north along the sandy Normandy coastline. However, as the ground war in Italy dragged on into the spring of 1944, the chances of Dragoon being carried out before Overlord grew slim. Finally, in April, with most of the troops who were to make the amphibious assault landings along the Riviera still hemmed inside the Anzio beachhead in Italy, and apparently unable to penetrate German defences around Cassino, the Allies reluctantly decided to put Operation Dragoon on the shelf. Overlord, ruled the top Allied brass, would have to be launched in June without the benefit of an earlier diversionary landing in the south of France.

The British, who had responsibility for Allied combat operations in the Mediterranean theatre, were pleased to hear that Dragoon had been cancelled. For well over a year they had contended that the Allied forces in Italy should keep pushing northward until the Po River had been reached. From there, said the British, the Allies should push northeastward over the Italian Alps into Austria, Yugoslavia and Hungary to reach the Balkans ahead of the Russians and keep that region out of Communist hands after the war.

Dragoon was suddenly revived some two weeks after the Normandy invasion when representatives of Britain's Field Marshal Sir Henry Maitland Wilson, the Supreme Allied Commander of the Mediterranean theatre, arrived in London to discuss future operations with General Eisenhower. The Combined Chiefs of Staff presided over the discussions. At the outset of the meetings, British officers strongly recommended to the Combined chiefs that they give serious consideration to their previous arguments in favour of a mighty land thrust leading out of northern Italy into the Balkans. When it came time for him to present his case, Eisenhower opened by pointing out that Allied troops in Normandy had not yet broken out of their beachhead. He went on to argue in favour of reviving Operation Dragoon, pointing out that forcing the Germans to fight simultaneously on two widely separated fronts in France would seriously weaken them. Ike reminded the chiefs that Dragoon would give the Allied side the prize port of Marseilles, Europe's second-best seaport, through which cargo ships could easily supply his main thrust into Germany. It was imperative, Ike concluded, that Operation Dragoon be launched at the earliest possible date.

The Combined Chiefs sided with Ike. On July 2, they sent top secret orders to Field Marshal Wilson to execute Operation Dragoon 'as soon as possible'.

D-Day for Dragoon was set for Tuesday, August 15. Field Marshal Wilson selected the U.S. Seventh Army, commanded by Lieutenant General Alexander M. Patch, and comprising the U.S. VI Corps and the French I and II corps, to make the amphibious landings. Fortunately for General Patch, the majority of troops made available to him by Wilson were veterans of other battles in the Mediterranean theatre. Thus, despite the short time remaining until D-Day, Patch had little difficulty assembling an experienced force.

As worked out by the Allied planners, Dragoon was to be a scaled-down version of the amphibious and airborne landings in Normandy. During the initial D-Day landings in Normandy, the Allies had employed three airborne and five infantry divisions. For the forthcoming landings along the Riviera, they planned to commit only one airborne and three infantry divisions.

The airborne phase of Dragoon was to be carried out by a new division-sized unit, the 1st Airborne Task Force. Hurriedly activated near Rome on July 11, the Task force was a conglomeration of all the Allied glider and parachute units in the Mediterranean theatre.

England's 2nd Independent Parachute Brigade Group, commanded by Brigadier C.H.V. Pritchard, was the first major manoeuvre element to be assigned to the Task Force. Pritchard and his paratroopers had earlier seen considerable combat in North Africa and on the Italian mainland.[1] Shortly after his unit's mid-July arrival west of Rome, Pritchard was given operational control of the British Glider Pilot Regiment's 3rd Squadron which was then based on Sicily. By the end of the month, the British glider pilots, along with all of their Horsa gliders, had been deployed to the mainland of Italy to prepare for Dragoon.

The remainder of the 1st Airborne Task Force was made up of American units, some of which had never before heard a shot fired in anger. The most combat-experienced and versatile American unit in the Task Force was the famous independent 509th Parachute Infantry Battalion which was commanded by Lieutenant Colonel William P. Yarborough, one of the early pioneers of the U.S. Army's initial parachute troop experiments. During its North African service the 509th had made two combat jumps in Algeria and had fought as a regular infantry battalion against Rommel's Afrika Korps in Tunisia. Later, on the night before the Allied landings at Salerno, Italy, this same battalion was sent on a vital parachute mission to seize the mountaintop town of Avellino. Their airplane pilots became disorientated during the flight to the drop zone, resulting in the battalion being scattered over a wide area and most of its members getting captured or killed. After that disastrous mission, the battalion was brought up to full strength with new replacements and sent to fight as mountain infantry troops near Venafro. From the mountains, the paratroopers were sent to a rest area near Rome from which, in January 1944, they made an amphibious assault landing at Anzio. After 73 days of savage combat inside the Anzio meatgrinder, the 509th was withdrawn to another rest area where it was again filled with new replacements and assigned a new combat mission. That mission was Operation Dragoon.

Considerably less experienced than Yarborough's 509th Battalion was the 517th Parachute Combat Team commanded by Colonel Rupert D. Graves. Having just arrived from the United States, the 517th had only two weeks of front line service in Italy under its belt when it was withdrawn to Rome to prepare for Dragoon. With less than three weeks until D-Day, the 517th was reinforced by Company D, 83rd Chemical Battalion (a 4.2 inch mortar unit), and the Anti-tank Company of the 442nd Japanese–American Infantry Regiment. Since neither of these two outfits was parachute or glider trained, both were required to undergo a quick course of instruction in glider riding at an airborne base near Rome.

The 550th Glider Infantry Battalion was one of two units assigned to the 1st Airborne Task Force that did not have any combat experience. Commanded by Lieutenant Colonel Edward Sachs, the 550th had arrived in Italy direct from the training grounds of Laurinburg-Maxton Army Airfield in North Carolina. The 550th joined the Task Force in Rome during the first week in July, just after completing a series of intensive glider landing manoeuvres at the airborne training centre on Sicily.[2]

The other part of the Task Force without combat experience was the 551st Parachute Infantry Battalion, commanded by Lieutenant Colonel Wood G. Joerg. This unit had arrived in Italy in April and, like the 550th Glider Infantry, had just completed a number of tactical manoeuvres on Sicily when it was assigned to the Task Force.

Command of the newly formed Task Force was given to Major General Robert T. Frederick who, at the age of 37, was the youngest general in the U.S. Army. Before being named to command the Task Force, Frederick had been in charge of the 1st Special Service Force, an elite unit made up of American and Canadian volunteers who were highly skilled and experienced in night fighting and mountain warfare. While leading his troops in the mountains of central Italy, Frederick had been wounded no less than eight times.

On July 13, Brigadier General Paul L. Williams, commander of the IX Troop Carrier Command based in England, arrived in Rome to assume control of another newly created unit, the Provisional Troop Carrier Air Division. Activated for the sole purpose of delivering the airborne troops to southern France on D-Day, the Air Division was made up of the 51st Troop Carrier Wing from the Mediterranean theatre, and the 50th and 53rd Troop Carrier wings, plus the IX Troop Carrier Command's Pathfinder unit, from England. Only two days after Williams assumed command of the Air Division his troop carrier units based in England began their piecemeal deployment to Italy. So as not to arouse the attention of German intelligence, all of the troop carrier airplanes were flown to their new bases in Italy during hours of darkness and by way of North Africa. In a further attempt to deceive German agents known to be operating in England, Williams ordered that no gliders be transported to Italy. Some 450 Wacos had already been assembled there in great secrecy for use in Dragoon. Most of them would be flown during the invasion by glider pilots quietly brought in from England.

This formidable array of Allied airborne might was to be opposed on D-Day by the German 19th Army. Commanded by General Friedrich Weise, the 19th Army consisted of seven infantry divisions and one panzer division deployed along the south coast of France. All of Weise's infantry divisions were greatly understrength and contained some 35 per cent non-Germans, most of whom were from Russian and the Balkan countries. German coastal defences along the Riviera were similar to those encountered in Normandy but not nearly as extensive or well manned.

General Patch, the 7th Army commander, announced the plan for Operation Dragoon on July 29 to his assembled commanders and staff. He began by saying he would first isolate the flanks of the invasion beaches on D-Day with two French commando detachments who were to sneak ashore during the night of August 14-15 to cut coastal highways leading to Cannes and Toulon. Concurrent with those commando strikes, the American 1st Special Service Force would land on the offshore islands of Levant and Port Cros to knock out enemy batteries that could fire on the invasion beaches at H-Hour. (H-Hour is the precise time that the main assault force is to begin its attack.)

Just prior to dawn on D-Day, continued Patch, General Frederick and the bulk of the parachute elements from his Task Force would jump into the area around Le Muy, some 10 miles inland from the invasion beaches. There Frederick and his paratroopers were to prevent all counterattacking German forces from reaching the beachhead line and clear two main LZs in which glider and parachute reinforcements were to land later in the day. Then at H-hour (8:00 a.m.), the amphibious troops were to start landing over six main beaches extending 30 miles between Cavalaire in the west to Saint Raphael in the east. Once ashore, the amphibious troops were to seize control of several airfields in the Argens River Valley and be prepared to continue the attack northwestward on order. After American forces had secured the beachhead, the follow-up forces, consisting of General de Lattre de Tassigny's French I and II corps, would come ashore and attack westward along the coastline to liberate the port cities of Toulon and Marseilles.

As soon as he received his attack orders, General Frederick sat down with General Williams to hammer out a plan for accurately delivering the entire 1st Airborne Task Force to its D-Day objectives. The final air movement plan that they jointly formulated contained three main parts: 1) a pre-dawn parachute assault landing, 2) a daylight glider assault landing at H-Hour, and 3) a combined parachute-glider reinforcement landing mission during the early evening hours of D-Day.

Details of the plan called for three teams of American and British pathfinders to parachute into the Argens River Valley at 3:30 a.m. on D-Day. The pathfinders would have exactly one hour to set up their Eureka guidance devices for at 4:30 a.m., the 509th Parachute Infantry Battalion and the 517th Parachute Combat Team were to jump, in that order, into DZ A two miles west of Le Muy. Forty minutes after that time, the British 2nd Independent Parachute Brigade Group was to jump three miles north of Le Muy into DZ O.

The first glider mission, code-named Bluebird, was scheduled to take place at H-Hour while the amphibious troops were coming ashore over the beaches. Bluebird was comprised of two serials, each of which was to deliver troops, guns, and ammunition of the 64th Light Artillery Battery of the Royal Artillery to British paratroopers who would be waiting for them to land on LZ O. Serial number one was to arrive aboard 35 Horsas that would be piloted by British glider pilots and towed by the American 435th Troop Carrier Group based at Tarquinia. Serial number two consisted of 40 Wacos to be flown in double tow by American pilots of the same group. Not since their initial combat operations in Burma had the Allies flown gliders in double tow into a battle area.

The final phase of the airborne plan had been deliberately held off until the early evening hours of D-Day by General Williams, who wanted to make sure that the ground troops would have time to clear the Rommel's asparagus and other obstacles from the glider landing zones. At 6:00 p.m., the 551st Parachute Infantry Battalion was to jump into DZ C and assume the role of Task Force reserve. Right behind the 551st would come 'Dove' the biggest and last glider

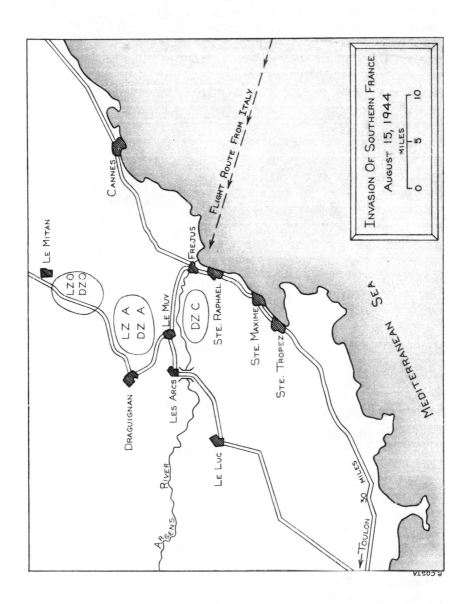

INVASION OF SOUTHERN FRANCE
AUGUST 15, 1944

MILES
0    5    10

FLIGHT ROUTE FROM ITALY

CANNES

LE MITAN

LZ O
DZ O

LZ A
DZ A

LE MUY

DZ C

FREJUS

STE. RAPHAEL

STE. MAXIME

STE. TROPEZ

DRAGUIGNAN

LES ARCS

LE LUC

ARGENS RIVER

TOULON 30 MILES

MEDITERRANEAN SEA

mission. Dove was to consist of 348 Waco gliders loaded with 2,250 troops of the 550th Glider Infantry Battalion, the 442nd Infantry's Anti-tank Company, the 596th Airborne Engineer Company, and Company D, 834th Chemical Battalion.

For quite some time German intelligence officers in the Mediterranean theatre had been predicting that the Allies were about to conduct a large amphibious landing somewhere along either the southern coast of France or in northern Italy. As proof of their predictions, the Germans cited the numerous reports that had been received from agents in Africa and Italy where virtually every major port was crowded with Allied warships and landing craft. Based on the pattern of Allied amphibious landings along the west coast of the Italian peninsula – first at Salerno, and again at Anzio – the Germans were strongly predicting that the next landing would be made not in France, but at Genoa in northern Italy.

By late evening of August 14, all of the parachute and glider units of the 1st Airborne Task Force had been briefed on their D-Day missions and were standing by their aircraft at 10 separate airfields north of Rome. To the glider pilot veterans of the Normandy invasion, when all participating units had been sealed in guarded marshalling areas some 10 days before D-Day, Operation Dragoon seemed like it was going to be a relaxed Sunday outing. Very few guards were present around the airfields in Italy, and virtually everyone was permitted to come and go as they pleased right up until their departure time. Far out at sea, meanwhile, a vast Allied naval armada consisting of over 2,500 vessels carrying some 145,000 troops of the 7th Army was night-steaming at top speed toward the lush beaches of the French Riviera.

The first checkpoint that all paratroop and glider aircraft would have to make on their way to France was the island of Elba, where Napoleon Bonaparte had been forced into exile in 1814. From Elba, the aircraft were to proceed to the northern tip of Corsica, across the Ligurian Sea, then head straight for a point east of Cannes on the southern coast of France. By a quirk of history, this aerial route followed the one that Napoleon had sailed in 1815 toward his undoing on the distant fields of Waterloo.

At exactly 1:00 a.m. on D-Day, three airplanes loaded with pathfinders of the 1st Airborne Task Force took off from Marcigliana airport. Some two and a half hours later they arrived over the darkened coast of France and found it completely covered by dense

This is a staged publicity training photo, the purpose of which was to instil pride in the armed forces and to demonstrate modern fighting techniques. The scene shows a C-47 airplane towing two CG-4A gliders about to land in a field that has been secured by the paratroopers who can be seen attacking in the foreground. For dramatic effect a white phosphorous grenade was exploded in the background just as the photo was snapped. *U.S. Army*

The two trucks parked under its wing illustrate the immense size of this 30-passenger CG-13A glider. Despite its size and weight, a parked CG-13A could easily be picked up by a flying tow-plane using the glider snatch technique developed by Richard C. DuPont. A total of 132 CG-13As were manufactured during World War II. *George Aspinwall*

Calcutta, India, December 1943. England's Brigadier Orde
Charles Wingate (left) chats with Colonel Philip C. Cochran,
commander of the American 1st Air Commando Group. *U.S. Air
Force*

India, December 1943. American and British soldiers examine a
1st Air Commando glider that has just been damaged during a
training exercise. The diagonal white stripes on the tail of this
CG-4A were the distinctive markings of the 1st Air Commando
and British air units operating in India and Burma, painted on all
combat aircraft to make them easily identifiable to Allied ground
gunners. Just prior to Operation Thursday, the stripes were
extended around the entire fuselage. Allied Air Force officers in
Europe copied this stripe identification idea during the giant
invasion of Normandy in June 1944. *Thomas Hight*

Assam, India, February 1944. Glider pilots and mechanics of the 1st Air Commando Group pose during a training break at Hailakandi Airfield. Standing (left to right) F.O. Bruce Williams (holding submachine gun), F.O. Robert Wagner, Lt. James Bartlett, Sgt. William O'Brien, Sgt. Kinner, Sgt. Donald Johnson, F.O. Leo Zuk, Lt. James Siever, and Lt. Steve Uhmanski. Kneeling: F.O. Samuel Steinmaker, Lt. H. J. Delaney, Lt. Richard Kuenstler, Capt. Vincent Rose, Lt. Neal J. Blush, Maj. William Taylor, Lt. J. J. Shinkle, F.O. Patrick Hadsell, and F.O. Jackie Cooper. *U.S. Air Force*

Lalaghat Airfield Assam, India, March 5, 1944. A squad of British Chindit soldiers board an American glider preparing to take off for LZ Broadway which is located 165 miles behind Japanese lines in Burma. *Imperial War Museum*

March 6, 1944. Glider pilots of the 1st Air Commando Group take a break during salvage operation on LZ Broadway 165 miles behind Japanese lines in Burma. The two gliders in the background had crashed together during landings made in total darkness the preceding night. *U.S. Air Force*

Burma, March 6, 1944. A wrecked CG-4A at Broadway. This glider's nose section has been smashed in by a teakwood log that was on the LZ. *Neal J. Blush*

April 1944, Lalaghat Airfield, India. Glider pilots Capt. Vincent Rose (left) and Lt. Joseph Delaney display souvenirs captured from Japanese infantrymen who attacked their position at White City in Burma. *James S. Bartlett*

Behind Japanese lines in Burma, May 1944. Soldiers of the 3rd West African (Nigerian) Brigade of Chindits lower the nose section of a CG-4A that will soon be picked up and returned to India. Several wounded Nigerians have just been placed aboard the glider. The medic at right can be seen folding a stretcher that was used to carry wounded out of the jungle. *Thomas Hight*

Folkingham, England, April 1944. F.O. George F. Aspinwall (left),
a glider pilot in the 313th Troop Carrier Group, with his younger
brother, Lt. John E. Aspinwall of the 101st Airborne Division's
401st Glider Infantry. John was killed in action in Normandy on
June 16, 1944, 35 days after his daughter Lydia – whom he never
saw – was born at home. *George F. Aspinwall*

Aldermaston, England, 1944. Lt. Col. Michael C. Murphy (left)
chats with Lt. Robert M. Butler shortly before D-Day. Both officers
piloted *The Fighting Falcon* glider into Normandy in the first
wave. During that mission Butler was killed and Murphy
seriously injured. *Hance A. Lunday*

England, May 1944. Lt. William K. Snyder and the glider that he will have to land in Normandy at 4:00 a.m. on D-Day. Snyder's CG-4A is one of the 228 gliders that were modified just prior to D-Day with a life-saving Griswold Nose device and Corey Skid. Note standard landing skid (lower right) affixed to bottom of glider. *Hance A. Lunday*

Sergeant Joseph H. Hann, a glider mechanic assigned to the 440th Troop Carrier Group based at Exeter, England. During the evening of June 4, Hann was puzzled when his group glider officer instructed him to report to the flight line immediately after chow. When he reported as directed, Hann received a detailed briefing of how to paint the heretofore secret invasion stripes, which would make all Allied aircraft easily recognizable as such, on the wings and fuselage of gliders and airplanes. *Joseph H. Hann*

Tarrant Rushton Airfield, England. A glider fleet consisting of two Horsas and 30 immense Hamilcars stands marshaled on the centre runway for D-Day in Normandy. Parked on both flanks of the gliders are their 4-engined Halifax bomber tow-planes. A lone Halifax sits on the main runway well forward of the leading Horsa gliders. *Imperial War Museum*

England, May 25, 1944; *The Fighting Falcon*. Manufactured in 1943 by the Gibson Refrigeration Company of Greenville, Michigan, this glider (and three others) was purchased by students in the Greenville school system and donated to the U.S. Army. Standing (left to right) Lt. John L. May (aide to Gen. Pratt), General Pratt, (Deputy Commander, 101st Airborne Division), Lt. Col. Michael C. Murphy (chief pilot), and Lt. Robert M. Butler (copilot). Only Murphy and May survived the crash of *The Fighting Falcon* in Normandy. *U.S. Air Force*

F.O. Eddie Anderson. On June 7, one day after he had landed his glider in Normandy, Anderson found himself performing the duties of an Army chaplain. *Eddie Anderson*

Below: Normandy, June 6, 1944. American troops push a British Horsa to the side of the road to make room for field ambulances evacuating wounded down to the beaches. A second Horsa can be seen farther down the road. *U.S. Army*

Normandy, France. Because these glider pilots were unable to make their individual ways back to Allied lines until June 14 (D plus 8), each of their families received a missing-in-action telegram from Washington. A few of them had been wounded, but not seriously. The small American flags on the right arms of the men's jackets were standard issue to all American airborne troops taking part in combat missions. Top row: (left to right) Flight Officers James P. Townsend, Robert R. Cross, Floyd W. Hand, Earl Evans, John Chartier, and Lawrence W. Kubale. Kneeling: Flight Officers Reimer Pedersen, Thomas H. Leathem, Harry Einstein, and George H. Johnson. *Lawrence W. Kubale*

A French farmer's cows graze beneath a British Horsa that had been used by American troops. Note tall trees in background. American intelligence officers had mistakenly informed all glider pilots that the trees in Normandy were no more than 10 feet tall. *U.S. Air Force*

June 8, 1944, Normandy, France. The Orne River Bridge on the eastern edge of the British airhead line. It was captured intact during total darkness at 1:00 a.m. on D-Day by a glider *coup-de-main* force of two rifle platoons from the 2nd Battalion, the Oxfordshire and Buckinghamshire Light Infantry. The extreme accuracy of the British landings is demonstrated by the proximity of the two Horsas to the right of the bridge. The French government renamed this span Pegasus Bridge in honour of the British airborne troops who captured it. *Imperial War Museum*

Grosetto, Italy, August 14, 1944. F.O. Jack R. Merrick (centre) with two members of the famed 442nd (Japanese-American) Infantry Regiment that were his passengers on D-Day of Operation Dragoon. *Jack R. Merrick*

Tarquinia Airport, Italy, August 14, 1944. A glider pilot (standing at extreme right) and the troops that he will fly to southern France. The troops are wearing Mae West life jackets. Those jackets were inflatable by means of two carbon dioxide cartridges, or they could be blown up manually if cartridges failed or were lost. Though the glider pilots and troops were always issued with life jackets, they were never given parachutes. *William S. Fritcher*

Below: Nice, France, August 18, 1944. American glider pilots relax while waiting to board U.S. Navy ships that will return them to Italy. *George J. Mouton*

*Overleaf:* LeMuy, France, August 15, 1944. British paratroopers and American members of the 509th Parachute Battalion resting beside a French farmhouse. *U.S. Army*

August 16, 1955. An American glider pilot, F.O. Stanley Juroski, shown in front of wrecked British Horsa glider on LZ O. Both British pilots were killed in the crash. *John H. Smith*

August 14, 1944, Guidonia Airfield, Rome, Italy. Ground crewmen prepare to tow this CG-4A glider out to the flight line for its participation in Operation Dragoon. Note that glider has been equipped with both the newly developed Ludington-Griswold crash protection device mounted on its nose, and the large ski-like Corey Skid which can be seen at the lower centre of the nose. *George J. Mouton*

August, 15, 1944. Flight Officer Richard D. Wade (centre, seated on captured motor cycle), and other glider pilots, assemble in a French village. House in background has been converted into a hospital by the Allied airborne troops. Note abandoned German staff car parked by the roadside. *Richard D. Wade*

August 16, 1944. Jeep-mounted American glider pilots escort captured German soldiers to prison compounds. *Richard D. Wade*

Field Marshal Walter Model, commander of the German troops opposing the Allies during Operation Market-Garden. As a veteran of extensive combat in Russia, Model was eminently qualified for the difficult fighting in Holland. *U.S. Army*

Near Le Muy, France, August 15, 1944. A single stalk of Rommel's Asparagus. At Field Marshal Rommel's direction German troops erected thousands of these tall wooden poles in the open fields of Normandy and southern France so as to deny their use to Allied airborne forces. *Richard D. Wade*

*Opposite:* British Lieutenant General Frederick Browning, commander of all Allied airborne troops during Operation Market-Garden. A highly experienced airborne officer, Browning was both a parachutist and rated glider pilot. *Imperial War Museum*

Paratrooper Technician 4th Class Andrew E. Rassmussen, 101st Airborne Division. Due to the extreme shortage of trained American glider pilots in September 1944, many paratroopers were pressed into service as copilots during the invasion of Holland. Despite the fact that he had no flying experience and was recovering from wounds sustained on the Normandy night jump, Rassmussen served as copilot of a glider bound for LZ W near the city of Zon. *Andrew E. Rassmussen*

England, September 15, 1944. American CG-4A gliders and their tow-planes marshaled for Operation Market-Garden. *U.S. Air Force*

This excellent photo was taken by a glider pilot just as his tow-plane was starting across the North Sea to Holland. Note the telephone cable wrapped around the tow-line for communication between pilots. The slack in the non-stretchable telephone cables allowed for the expansion of the tow-line during flight. *Hance A. Lunday*

September 17, 1944, LZ S. Lt. Col. W. F. K. Thompson (left) of the
Royal Artillery helps unload equipment from the Horsa in which
he and his troops have just landed four miles west of Arnhem.
*Imperial War Museum*

September 17, 1944. Four Horsa gliders have just landed on LZ Z, four and one half miles east of Arnhem. Large white and black invasion stripes were painted on to identify these unfamiliar aircraft to Allied sea and ground gunners. *Imperial War Museum*

Holland, September 18, 1944. Heavily loaded American CG-4A
gliders bound for LZ W in the 101st Airborne Division's area.
*Imperial War Museum*

*Left:* LZ W, September 17, 1944. A group of young Dutch boys wearing wooden shoes marvel at the small bulldozer that has just been unloaded from this glider. These minidozers were especially developed for the American airborne divisions. Markings on this dozer show that it is the property of the 101st Airborne's 326th Engineer Battalion. *Hance A. Lunday*

*Below:* September 17, 1944, Eindhoven, Holland. American glider troops assemble after having just arrived from England. The motorcycle was captured from the Germans. In its sidecar rides the German soldier who had been driving the motorcycle when the Americans landed. *Joseph Mendes*

LZ W, Holland, September 18, 1944. Troopers of the 101st Airborne using axes and other implements to rescue a badly injured glider pilot (seen at bottom centre of photo) pinned in wreckage of his CG-4A. *U.S. Army*

Zon, Holland, September 19, 1944. A convoy of British trucks is halted by German artillery fire while still in the 101st Airborne Division's area. Medics in foreground have moved their patients into a ditch from ambulances until shelling subsides. *U.S. Army*

September 20, 1944. Oosterbeek, Holland. Though this picture
was taken in the midst of a ferocious battle, Major General Robert
E. Urquhart, commanding general of the gallant 1st British
Airborne Division, managed a smile for the camera. Urquhart is
standing behind the Hartenstein Hotel, his command post during
Operation Market-Garden. The hotel, ruined during the battle,
was fully restored after the war. Today it is a museum where
visitors can view equipment used by British and Polish airborne
troops. Visitors to the museum can also walk through the cellar
where, by candlelight at 6:05 a.m. on September 25, 1944,
General Urquhart received the order to withdraw his battered
division from the battle area. *Imperial War Museum*

ground fog. Unable to see any landmarks on their first pass over the DZ area, all three aircraft circled back out to sea without dropping the pathfinders. German flak batteries fired several warning shots while the planes made their second and third passes over the DZ area without spotting the critical landmarks. On their fifth pass the pilots flipped on the green-light jump signal over what they thought was the correct drop point. In fact, the DZs were some 15 miles farther to the east.

Misdropped pathfinder teams were still trying to collect themselves up in the hills of the Argens River Valley when, at 4:30 a.m., the lead airplanes of the main parachute assault force arrived over the coastline of southern France. Even though they had no ground guidance devices to home in on, the jump planes flew unerringly to the correct DZ and made the most accurate night drop of the entire war. Nearly 85 per cent of all jumpers landed well within the limits of their DZ.

There were, unfortunately, three serious errors made during the drops. Just a few minutes before jump time, a lone aircraft loaded with troops of the 509th Parachute Battalion became separated from the flock. Thoroughly confused by ground fog and apparently thinking he was over land, the pilot of that plane turned on the jump signal while he was still several miles out at sea. Not one of the 15 paratroopers who jumped from that airplane was ever seen again.

Three other planeloads of troops from the 509th Parachute Battalion, along with two planeloads of the 463rd Parachute Field Artillery, were given the green light when they were just crossing the coastline. All five planeloads landed on the outskirts of Saint Tropez. There they banded together, linked up with Free French forces, and quickly liberated that posh resort town.

The final serious error made during the drop involved the 3rd Battalion of the 517th Parachute Infantry. That entire outfit was mistakenly dropped in three batches, each four miles apart, near the village of Callien, nearly 20 miles east of its DZ near Le Muy. Shortly after dawn the battalion commander, Lieutenant Colonel Melvin Zais, rounded up his scattered troopers and started speed-marching with them toward their assembly area at Sainte Rosseline. It would take Zais's battalion until 4:00 p.m. to safely reach Sainte Rosseline.

Zais and his marching paratroopers had just got into high gear when, at 7:30 a.m., a great fleet of American, British, French, Polish, and Greek warships began a ferocious bombardment of the

[219]

German coastal defences. Simultaneously, some 12,000 American assault troops of the Seventh Army started moving toward their assigned beaches aboard crowded landing craft. The leading troops stormed ashore at 8:00 a.m. – right at H-Hour. Enemy resistance was generally light; only in the 45th Division's area, east of Saint Tropez, were the Germans able to put up a good fight.

The third wave of amphibious assault troops were still pouring across the beaches when the faint sound of airplane engines heralded the approach of the Bluebird mission. Some three hours earlier, when it had begun taking off in a sandstorm from Tarquinia's packed-dirt runways, Bluebird had consisted of one serial of Horsa gliders and one serial of Wacos. All aircraft got off the ground without difficulty, but, after clearing the coast of Italy, one of the airplanes had to turn back with the two Wacos it was towing because its engines were overheating.

The commander of the leading Horsa serial was just passing over the island of Corsica when he received a radio message from General Williams instructing him to return all aircraft to Italy because the landing zone in France was obscured by ground fog. Williams's experiences during the recent Normandy landings led him to fear that the heavily laden Horsas would suffer excessive losses if they were to land in the fog-covered Argens River Valley. While the Horsa serial was turning around off Corsica, two of its tow-planes developed engine trouble that forced an emergency release of their Horsas, both of which made a safe landing on Corsica.

Though he had recalled his Horsa serial for reasons of safety, General Williams allowed the Wacos to continue to France. As they were passing Corsica, one of them was forced to leave the formation when its tow-line snapped in two. Having planned what they would do in such an emergency, the glider pilots peeled away from the serial, circled downward, and made a perfect water landing. Fortunately this mishap had taken place above one of the many Allied naval ships pre-positioned along the flight route. In a matter of minutes, the vessel had rescued all hands.

From where he sat at the controls of his C-47 airplane at the rear of the Waco serial, Lieutenant Gene Roberts had a perfect view of the gliders skimming along in pairs behind their tugs. Everything was proceeding so smoothly that Roberts was beginning to get sleepy, but suddenly he witnessed a horrifying event that he would remember for the rest of his life. The right wing suddenly fell off the glider in front of him, and in a flash, the stricken Waco heaved violently over on its side and broke loose from its tow-line. The glider disintegrated as it fell, spilling its passengers into the sea. At that great height there was no hope that anyone could survive the fall. The remainder of the serial continued on its way toward France.

When the Wacos arrived over the Argens Valley they found it still blanketed by an impenetrable layer of ground fog. The flight leader decided that rather than chance landing the Wacos in such hazardous conditions he would orbit the LZ to see if the fog would clear. His patience paid off; after nearly an hour of orbiting above Le Mitan the fog dissipated sufficiently for the glider pilots to recognize terrain features within their LZs. At 9:26 a.m., the tow-planes swooped down through the layer of light haze still hanging over the valley floor, and the Wacos began cutting loose.

Thanks to the aggressive actions of British paratroopers who had earlier jumped at Le Mitan, all German troops and most of the deadly Rommel's asparagus poles had been cleared from the LZ. Consequently, this was one of the most casualty-free glider landing operations made by the Allies during the war. Although eight pilots were seriously injured when their gliders flipped over in vineyards along the flanks of the LZ, not one passenger or pilot was killed.

By noon on D-Day, all major combat units of the Seventh Army had fought their way inland and were in firm control of their initial objectives. At 1:00 p.m., the French I and II corps stormed ashore on the left flank of the beachhead and, without breaking stride, launched a vigorous attack westward along the coastline toward Toulon and Marseilles. Far up in the hills beyond the beachhead, meanwhile, the scattered parachute units of the 1st Allied Airborne Task Force had assembled and had occupied nearly all of their objectives. Colonel Graves's 517th Parachute Combat Team (minus its misdropped 3rd Battalion), was holding two key towns in the northwestern sector of the airhead. The 1st Battalion had a grip on Les Arcs, but so did the Germans. Four miles north of Les Arcs, the 2nd Battalion was in full control of La Motte and had tied in with the British paratroopers on its right flank.

The British paratroopers had set up their command post in the liberated village of Le Mitan. Just south of Le Mitan, the 509th Parachute Battalion (less its Company A and some artillerymen), was busy consolidating itself and preparing to attack Le Muy.

Back at Tarquinia airfield in Italy, meanwhile, British glider pilots

[221]

and ground crews of the American 435th Troop Carrier Wing, who had been ordered to return there earlier in the day just as they were flying past Corsica, were feverishly working to realign the Horsas and tow-planes. At 2.30 p.m., the last tow-plane was refuelled and the last Horsa rolled into position behind it. Thirty-four minutes later, the entire serial was in the air and once more on its way to France.

Hard on the tail of the Horsa serial flew another serial, consisting of 41 airplanes loaded with the 551st Parachute Battalion bound for DZ C. Both serials arrived over the coast of France at 5:45 p.m. Without any fanfare, and no enemy opposition, the Horsas went on to land in LZ O and the paratroopers jumped in one large, neat cluster in DZ C.

The paratroopers were just clearing off their DZ when they heard the thunderous roar of airplane engines approaching from the eastern end of the Argens River valley. This was the giant Dove glider mission consisting of seven serials towing Wacos that had been scheduled to release above Le Muy and then land in LZs A and O.

All airplanes and gliders of the Dove mission had taken off from seven airfields along the east coast of Italy. According to a methodical master flight plan worked out by General Williams, each of the seven serials was to bypass the island of Corsica at rigidly set 10-minute intervals and maintain that spacing all the way into the objective area to permit an orderly landing of all gliders. With the exception of one glider in the 440th Group that had to make an emergency landing at Ombrone, the take-off and assembly phase of the mission went like clockwork.

The first sign of the serious trouble that was to plague the Dove mission appeared just as the 332nd Group left the Italian mainland near Point Ala. There the tow-planes had to drop below their specified airspeed to avoid other airplanes loaded with the 551st Parachute Battalion that were cutting across their flight path. As a result of that reduction in air speed, the four serials flying behind the 332nd Group were also obliged to slow down to keep from overrunning one another.

Far more serious was the mishap caused by Dove's leading serial, which was being towed by the 442nd Group. Just after passing Corsica the pilot of the leading glider informed his tow-plane pilot that he was going to have to make an emergency landing because the tail section of his Waco was starting to vibrate badly and he feared it

[222]

might tear itself away from the aircraft. Rather than cut the glider loose to make an emergency landing in the sea, the serial leader banked his airplane to the right and headed back for Corsica where the stricken Waco could at least touch down on dry land. This was a noble gesture on the part of the serial leader, but he forgot to tell the rest of the trailing tow-planes what he was doing. True to their training, and apparently believing the mission had been cancelled, the entire serial obediently followed its leader into the turn. As the glider cut off to make its landing on Corsica, the serial leader looked back and saw all of the other tow-planes following him. Realizing his error, the serial leader then headed back into the mainstream of traffic, taking up a position not at the head of the formation, but in its already crowded midsection.

These uncoordinated moves by tow-planes and gliders put an end to the critical time interval between serials. In a matter of 30 minutes, the skytrain became a hazardous jumble. Many tow-planes slowed to keep from overrunning serials ahead of them. Others increased their speed to catch up with their serials, but in doing so created a very dangerous situation for the Wacos, which were likely to come apart if towed in excess of 150 miles per hour. During these hectic manoeuvres, four Wacos became separated from their tow-ships and crashed into the sea. Rescue ships were able to save only 12 men.

One of the serials taking part in the Dove mission was comprised of gliders from the 91st Squadron of the 439th Group. Earlier, on December 23, 1943, while the squadron was at Fort Bragg, North Carolina, two of its pilots had been ordered to switch duty assignments just prior to a night formation flying training mission. The two pilots, Lieutenants Milton Dank and Robert Hamilton, had been good friends for several months. Hamilton was to be married on Christmas Day, only two days away; Dank would be his best man.

For the training flight, Dank was instructed to give his position of flight leader to Hamilton and to take over the latter's job of ground officer. None of the gliders taking part in the training mission had a copilot. Later that night, as the gliders were preparing to land at Fort Bragg's blacked-out airport, the control tower operator mistakenly gave permission for a C-47 airplane to take off straight into their glider path. Dank was scanning the sky for some sign of the approaching gliders when he saw a bright flash of light. Seconds later he heard the dreaded crashing sound of a glider hitting the ground

[223]

near the edge of the runway. Upon reaching the crashed glider, Dank saw that everyone aboard it was dead and that its pilot was his friend, Bob Hamilton. The glider's right horizontal stabilizer had been neatly sliced off by the C-47 that had just taken off.

Because of the close friendship between these two glider pilots, Dank's squadron leader selected him to escort his comrade's body to the Hamilton family in Dallas, Texas. After the funeral services, Hamilton's mother requested of Dank that her son's name be carried into battle on the side of a glider.

In compliance with that request, Dank had chalked the words, 'Hamilton's Reply' on the right side of his glider's nose section just before taking off for southern France from Orbetello, Italy. Dank's copilot on this mission, Flight Officer B. K. 'Bud' Klimek, had used that same piece of chalk to print his wife's name, Regina, on the other side of the nose section. Riding aboard their glider were two Nisei anti-tank gunners from the 442nd Infantry Regiment.

Copilot Klimek was at the controls of *Hamilton's Reply* when the 91st Squadron arrived off the coast of France and began passing over some warships of Vice Admiral Henry K. Hewitt's Western Naval Task Force. One of the vessels resting at anchor below the gliders, providing some long-range gunfire support to the ground troops ashore, was the U.S.S. *Tuscaloosa*, a veteran of the Allied landings in North Africa and Normandy. As he gazed down at the great fleet of warships, Lieutenant Dank saw the *Tuscaloosa*'s anti-aircraft guns open fire. A split second later there was a loud bang in the rear of the glider and the entire aircraft shuddered as if its tail had been struck by lightning. Though neither of the pilots then realized it, history had just repeated itself: the glider named in honour of Lieutenant Robert Hamilton had just had its right horizontal stabilizer knocked off.

Lieutenant Dank took hold of the wheel as *Hamilton's Reply* fell off uncontrollably on its right wing and dived nearly 200 feet, still attached to its tow-plane. As both pilots fought to regain some control over the falling glider, the tow-line jerked its nose upward and checked the dive. The glider was still flying nose high and well beneath the tow-plane when the formation began passing over the heavily wooded 800-foot hills east of Saint Raphael. After barely skimming over the treetops, pilot Dank caught sight of his LZ dead ahead and cut loose from the tow-ship. Copilot Klimek pulled on full spoilers, and the spoiler plates rose vertically on top of the wings.

[224]

Dank then skilfully landed the crippled Waco at 90 miles per hour in a large open field. The glider was skidding straight for an earthen embankment at the far end of the field when Dank managed to force its nose down and bring it to a halt. Less than a moment later the two anti-tank gunner passengers, who had been sitting in their jeep puffing on cigarettes throughout this hair-raising landing, bid their pilots a cheery farewell and drove away in search of their platoon sergeant.

Meanwhile, the sky directly above the village of Le Muy was in chaos. No fewer than four serials of Wacos had released over the LZ at the same time, at altitudes ranging from a low of 600 feet to a high of 3,000 feet, and now there were several layers of gliders in free flight simultaneously. Their pilots had to worry about mid-air collisions as they tried frantically to select a safe landing field.

In an amazing display of airmanship the majority of pilots managed to avoid one another as they spiralled to earth. But then accidents began to happen as several craft collided while attempting to land in vineyards already crowded with other gliders. There was only one mid-air collison. No one saw it, but Flight Officer Leon Luczak observed a result of the accident from his cockpit when a tumbling jeep fell past him as he was preparing to land his Waco on LZ O.

Earlier, during his pre-flight briefing at Grosseto, Italy, Flight Officer Theodore V. Sampson of the 440th Group had been shown an aerial photo of his landing zone in France. The briefing officer told Sampson that his LZ was 1,200 feet long, with six-foot bushes at the approach end. The signal to cut, continued the briefing officer, would be given at 600 feet with the tow-plane heading north. However, when Sampson arrived over the LZ at the controls of a Waco loaded with nine troops and four cases of artillery shells, he was given the signal to cut at 3,000 feet while heading south.

With the Waco in free flight now, Sampson's copilot kept him informed of the other gliders above, below, and on both sides of him while Sampson looked for a landing area that matched the briefing photos. At 400 feet he finally spotted the field, but the six-foot bushes turned out to be 60-foot trees, and the 1,200 feet had shrunk to 600 feet – with a cliff at the far end. On final approach, Sampson levelled out his Waco and cleared the trees with only a few feet to spare. Seconds later he set his glider down and, by deliberately running his left belly skid into an irrigation ditch, brought the glider to a full stop well short of the cliff.

Elsewhere in the crowded LZ many other gliders crash-landed at speeds upward of 90 miles per hour. Virtually all were total losses. In the rush of events following the invasion, the Wacos were left unguarded where they had come to earth; foul weather and souvenir hunters combined to ruin the few gliders that could have been salvaged. Not one of the American or British gliders used in the invasion of southern France was ever recovered.

In lives and human suffering, the cost of the Dove mission was high. Eleven pilots were killed and 32 others seriously injured in the landing crashes. The passengers, meanwhile, suffered six dead and 126 seriously injured. As usual, the cargoes of jeeps and artillery pieces, though difficult to extract from the wrecks, were nearly all in good working order.

Those glider pilots who survived the rough landings in good condition made their way off the landing fields and joined up with the nearest airborne unit headquarters. There they were put to work guarding German prisoners and paratroop battalion command centres.

By sunset on D-Day, the Allies could proudly claim that Operation Dragoon had been a complete success. General Patch's Seventh Army report summarized the D-Day activities as follows:

> At the close of D-Day all the combat elements of the VI Corps had landed, and the exploitation of a weak and confused enemy was in rapid progress; the corps casualties had been almost negligible. The enemy could offer only scattered resistance. The German Air Force had been weak and ineffective. Enemy reinforcements never arrived in the beach area, and no large-scale counterattacks were launched. The three divisions advanced inland according to plan, already ahead of their time schedule.

Early in the morning of D plus 1, a German battalion occupying the town of Le Muy was attacked by a mixed force of American glider pilots, British paratroopers, and a few platoons from the 509th Parachute Battalion. At a cost of one man killed and 15 wounded, the Allies liberated Le Muy before noon and captured over 700 prisoners. Later that afternoon teams of glider pilots marched the prisoners down to the beaches and turned them over to American military police units.

Before they had taken off on their mission to France, the glider pilots had been instructed to make their way down to the invasion beaches as soon as possible after landing and climb aboard any naval vessel returning to Corsica or Italy. Upon reaching Corsica or the Italian mainland, they were to report to the nearest airfield, where waiting airplanes would ferry them back to their bases. The majority of pilots followed those instructions and were back with their squadrons within a few days. But others exploited their situation by deliberately taking a roundabout route and enjoying themselves along the Riviera until their money ran out.

By noon on August 17, D plus 2, all three infantry divisions had penetrated far inland and established contact with the 1st Airborne Task Force. In the meantime over 86,000 troops, 12,000 vehicles, and 46,000 tons of supplies had been landed over the beaches, and 7,845 prisoners had been captured. Encouraged by his stunning success, General Patch, the Seventh Army commander, ordered his troops to pursue the retreating German divisions into the hills. It was tough going, but with the assistance of French Maquis units the Seventh Army made its way up the Rhone Valley and liberated Lyons – France's third largest city – on September 2. One week later a French armoured reconnaissance company operating west of Dijon joined forces with a patrol from General. Patton's Third Army, giving the Allies a continuous line from the Mediterranean to the Atlantic.

At the successful conclusion of the airborne phase of Operation Dragoon, the Provisional Troop Carrier Division was unceremoniously disbanded. As early as August 20, all airplanes and most glider pilots of the 50th and 53rd Wings had been returned to England. It was not until September 8 – nearly one full month after Dragoon's D-Day – that the last pair of glider pilots made their way back to Italy from the Riviera.

After only a few days of taking life easy in London, the American glider pilots who had taken part in the invasion of southern France were put back on a rugged schedule of day and night landing exercises. The almost immediate resumption of training served to remind the glider pilots that the war was far from over. It also gave rise to a new batch of rumours about another airborne mission on the Continent.

# Chapter 9

## *Costly Setback in Holland*

As the summer of 1944 drew to a close, the once vast areas of Europe controlled by Germany had dwindled considerably. Stalin's tank divisions were closing in on the Reich from the east at the rate of several miles per day, and Tito's Yugoslav partisans were carving up Wehrmacht units almost at will. To the south, in Italy, the American Fifth and the British Eighth Armies, though weakened by the loss of forces siphoned off for Dragoon, were manoeuvring through Tuscany toward the Po River. And in the west, Eisenhower had some 48 combat divisions advancing on a broad front toward the Rhine River, Germany's great natural defensive barrier.

Soldiers on the Allied side, in every rank from private to general, could now see clearly that victory over Germany was a matter of time. And with German defences rapidly disintegrating all across France, the Allied combat troops began saying confidently that they could 'end the war in forty-four'.

Field Marshal Montgomery had never been in complete agreement with Eisenhower's pre-Normandy strategy of attacking everywhere at once on a broad front. When he saw that the Nazi armies opposing him in France were collapsing even earlier than had been hoped, he suggested to General Bradley that a new strategy was needed. As Monty now saw things, his own Twenty-First Army Group and Bradley's Twelfth Army Group should be joined to form a single mass of 40 combat divisions. Once joined, said Monty, this enormous force should be launched on a lightning-fast northward drive that would take it through Belgium, where follow-up divisions could open the port of Antwerp. Then without stopping in Belgium, continued Monty, the attacking forces should dash around the right flank of the Siegfried Line, punch their way into Germany, and keep going at full speed until they had overrun the industrial Ruhr area and occupied Berlin.

[228]

On first hearing Monty's battle plan, Bradley was in favour of it; he knew that if it worked, it really could end the war in 1944. But after discussing it with his own staff and with his Third Army commander, General Patton, he changed his mind and went to see Montgomery with a plan of his own. Based primarily on the fact that Patton's rampaging tank divisions were then a full 100 miles out in front of Monty's forces, Bradley suggested that the main Allied thrust be made by his own Twelfth Army Group. If he were given the lion's share of gasoline and ammunition supplies, said Bradley, he would drive due east from his present positions, cross the Rhine south of Frankfurt, and lunge deep into Germany to deliver the fatal blow. Bradley's plan meant reducing Monty's Twenty-First Army Group to a secondary role in the north and, quite naturally, did not appeal to Montgomery in the slightest.

On August 23, these opposing recommendations for a change in strategy were presented to the Supreme Commander, General Eisenhower. Once again Ike found himself in the distasteful position of being forced to side with one of his two top commanders. On the one hand, Eisenhower was inclined to side with Bradley, because Patton's tanks were indeed very far out in front of the British. But he liked Monty's plan to drive into Belgium, because it would result in British troops opening the port of Antwerp and overrunning coastal launching sites of the V-1 missiles that were killing hundreds of civilians in and around London. In the end, Eisenhower announced a compromise decision. Monty's northward drive into Belgium would be given first priority in all combat supplies, and the American First Army, commanded by Lieutenant General Courtney H. Hodges, was to advance along with the British to protect their right flank and ensure the success of Monty's attack. But once Antwerp had been taken, the Allied land armies would revert to the pre-invasion plan of all forces having an equal share of supplies and advancing toward the Rhine 'on a broad front north and south of the Ardennes'.

Learning of Ike's decision to give Montgomery the lion's share of logistics, Patton flew into a rage. He knew it would result in an almost complete halt of his heretofore lightning advance on the Rhine. Patton was so upset that he burst into Bradley's headquarters 'bellowing like a bull' and roared, 'To Hell with Hodges and Monty. We'll win your goddam war if you'll keep Third Army going!'[1] But in spite of Patton's wrathful remark, the decision stuck. Patton later called it 'the most momentous error of the war'. In view of subsequent events on the Western Front, it would appear that Eisenhower's decision is deserving of that dubious honour.

Almost as soon as Ike gave the green light, Montgomery and his Twenty-First Army Group charged into Belgium and, on September 3, liberated the capital, Brussels. The very next day, Monty's forces raced 30 miles forward and seized the prize port of Antwerp intact. Pausing only long enough to resupply his extended spearhead columns and to bring his artillery forward, Monty resumed his offensive on the seventh and soon crossed the Albert Canal east of Antwerp. But in the week that followed, Monty advanced only 18 miles, to the Meuse-Escaut Canal along the Belgium-Holland border. There his attack was stopped by stubbornly defending German troops.

Sitting in England during these Allied ground gains on the Continent was the newly activated 1st Allied Airborne Army. Eisenhower had personally directed the formation of this organization because, in his opinion, parachute, glider and troop carrier units were theatre-of-operations forces, and all plans for their combined employment ought to be prepared by a central agency empowered to direct the coordinated actions of all land, sea and air forces in the area involved. According to Ike's operational directive, the principal functions of the 1st Allied Airborne Army were to supervise training; prepare battle plans for airborne missions, including the delivery of supplies by parachutes; and control such operations until ground forces linked up with the airborne troops.

When activated on August 2, 1944, the 1st Allied Airborne Army was given operational control over Major General Paul Williams's IX Troop Carrier Command; Major General Matthew Ridgway's XVIII Airborne Corps Headquarters; the U.S. 17th, 82nd and 101st Airborne divisions; all British airborne troops; and 'such Royal Air Force troop carrier formations that might be allocated from time to time'.

The British strongly felt that their airborne commander, Lieutenant General Frederick Browning, should head this new airborne command. The Americans, meanwhile, thought it proper that an American get the job since they were contributing most of the airplanes and a majority of the airborne troops. But they found it difficult to field a candidate who was a match for Browning. Finally, Eisenhower chose an American, Lieutenant General Lewis Hyde Brereton.

Although junior in rank to Browning by a few months,[2] Brereton had a variety and length of service unsurpassed in the Army Air Forces. Oddly enough, this 54-year-old flying general had begun his military career as a naval officer, but following his graduation from Annapolis in 1911 he transferred into the Army, where he became one of its first aviators. As a fighter pilot in World War I, Brereton managed to shoot down a German plane, getting himself wounded and winning a DSC in the process. After recovering from his wounds he was assigned to Colonel William 'Billy' Mitchell's staff. There he helped draw up plans for converting volunteers from the 1st Infantry Division into parachutists and using bombers to drop them behind German lines. The war ended before that daring enterprise could be carried out. During the 1920s, Brereton had played a prominent role in the development of military aviation; he and Billy Mitchell were jointly credited with inventing the technique of dive-bombing. Brereton had also served with Mitchell during Mitchell's public criticism of the low state of preparedness of the tiny Air Service and of the poor quality of its equipment. Mitchell used the press to fight his case; and when, in September 1925, the U.S. Navy's dirigible *Shenandoah* was destroyed in a storm with heavy loss of life, he handed reporters a scathing 9-page indictment which castigated the War and Navy departments for 'incompetence, criminal negligence and almost treasonable administration of the national defense'. President Coolidge ordered Mitchell court-martialled for insubordination. At his widely publicized trial, Mitchell's military defence lawyer was Major Brereton. Despite the best efforts of Brereton, Mitchell was found guilty and sentenced to five years' suspension from rank and pay. In February 1926, Mitchell resigned from the army and retired to his farm in Virginia where he continued to promote air power and warn against the dangers of America being outstripped by other nations, particularly Japan.

Thus far in World War II, Brereton had served with distinction in every major war zone. He had been a major general commanding the Far Eastern Air Force in the Philippines when the Japanese struck there the day after attacking Pearl Harbor. With the handful of B-17s that he was able to salvage there, Brereton retreated to Java, where he carried on the air war against the Japanese over the Java Sea and in Burma. In March 1942, he was ordered to India to organize the Tenth Air Force and establish an aerial supply route across the Himalayas to China. Three months later, he was transferred to Egypt as commander of Ninth Air Force, flying support for the

[231]

British Eighth Army fighting Rommel's Afrika Korps. While in Africa, Brereton planned the epic long-range air strikes against the pretroleum refining complex at Ploesti, Rumania, which was supplying fuel to Hitler's panzer divisions in Russia. The largest of those raids took place on August 1, 1943, when 177 American B-24 bombers taking off from bases in Libya flew high across the Mediterranean and over the mountains of Albania and Yugoslavia to the Danube River in Bulgaria, where they were met by successive waves of fighter attacks. Punching their way through the fighters, the bombers entered Rumania and dropped to 500 feet in accordance with Brereton's plan for a low level attack. Soon the refineries and oil tanks were covered with raging fires and billowing black smoke. The severity of fighting during the raid is illustrated by losses suffered by the attackers. Forty-one bombers were shot down, and 446 of the 1,733 men on the mission were killed. Another 108 airmen who parachuted from crippled bombers were taken prisoner. Five participants in that raid earned the Medal of Honor. Through his close association with the British, first in India, and later in Egypt and Libya, Brereton had come to admire their fighting qualities. When senior American officers made unfavourable comments about their British colleagues, Brereton would remind them: 'We have no right to pass judgement. We've shown nothing yet that stacks up to the Battle of Britain.'

Ike realized that even though Brereton had a remarkable record in two world wars, he was basically a flying officer and knew little about conducting land battles. So for a deputy Ike gave Brereton a soldier, Lieutenant General Browning, who was then commanding the British 1st Airborne Corps.

In the first six weeks of its existence, the 1st Allied Airborne Army prepared 18 plans for mass parachute and glider assaults in the paths of Allied ground troops advancing across the Continent. But one by one they were cancelled as proposed drop and landing zones were overrun by armoured spearheads of the ground forces.

At one point during the rapid Allied thrusts across France, Ike offered the services of Brereton's Airborne Army to General Bradley. But Bradley politely turned down the offer, saying he would rather see the jump airplanes flying gasoline to Patton's tank columns.

Ike next offered the Airborne Army to Montgomery on September 5, while his forces were advancing across Belgium toward the border of Holland. Four days later, Monty summoned Brereton's deputy, General Browning, to his field headquarters in Belgium for a secret briefing on an audacious plane code-named 'Operation Market-Garden', the first major daylight air assault to be attempted by any military power since the German attack on Crete more than three years before.

Market-Garden was to be a combined airborne-ground offensive deep into Holland. As envisioned by Monty, the operation would accomplish three main Allied goals: it would cut off all German forces in western Holland, then still bitterly defending along the Schelde Estuary and preventing the Allies from utilizing the port of Antwerp; it would outflank Germany's much-vaunted Siegfried Line; and the successful outcome of the operation would place sizeable British forces across the lower Rhine at Arnhem. Once across that formidable water barrier, they would be able to smash rapidly through the back door of Germany for a decisive drive to Berlin.

Montgomery briefed Browning in person in front of his operations map. He began by explaining that Market, the code-name for the airborne half of the operation, would require the Airborne Army to lay a carpet of glider and parachute troops over the 55 miles of highway stretching from Eindhoven northward to Arnhem. The Airborne Army's mission in Holland, said Montgomery, would be to seize control of five major bridges and all cities between Eindhoven and Arnhem. It would also have to provide flank protection along the entire length of the carpet to guarantee the success of Garden, the ground half of the operation.

Garden called for British General Brian Horrocks's XXX Corps, with the elite Guards Armoured Division leading the way, to rip a hole through German defences on the Dutch frontier. Following that ground penetration, continued Montgomery, Horrocks's corps was to dash down the path being secured by the airborne troops until it reached the Zuider Zee area, some 90 miles inside Holland. There Horrocks's tank units were to be given a brief rest period; then the full weight of British might would be loosed on the Ruhr area.

Monty emphasized to Browning the importance of five major bridges. Running his finger up the long wall map, tapping each bridge as he passed it, Monty told Browning, 'Your airborne carpet will be very long and narrow. It is of the utmost importance that you land as many men as possible to rapidly seize these bridges so badly needed by Horrocks's tanks.'

[233]

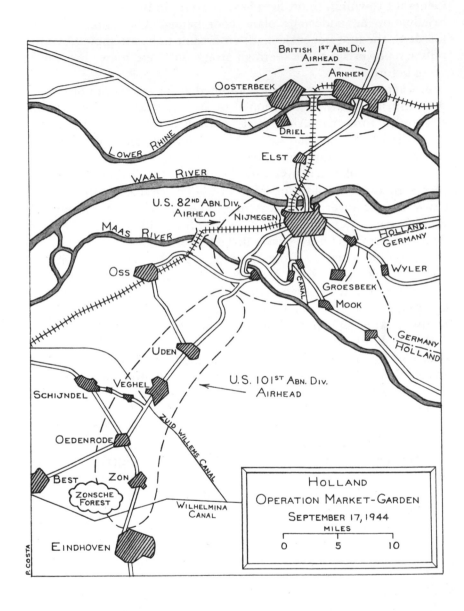

Even though he knew there were sufficient airborne troops back in England to complete the task just outlined by Monty, Browning was concerned about the depth of the airborne penetration into Holland. Pointing to the bridge at Arnhem, the one at the extreme end of the carpet, Browning inquired, 'How long will it take our tanks to reach us here?'

'Two days,' replied the Field Marshal.

Still staring at the map, Browning said, 'We can hold it for four.' Then, as an afterthought, Browning said, 'But I think, sir, we may be going a bridge too far.'

Montgomery was pleased with Browning's assurance that the airborne troops could hold open the route from Eindhoven to Arnhem long enough for the tanks to dash forward and effect the ground link-up. Full of enthusiasm for his Market-Garden plan, Monty met with Eisenhower the following day at the airport in Brussels to obtain final approval for mounting the operation. Ike was impressed with the plan, going so far as to call it the 'boldest and best move' the Allies could make at that point in the war. Browning flew back to England that day with orders from Monty to execute Market, the airborne half of the operation, on Sunday, September 17. D-Day was only seven days away.

At 6:00 p.m. on September 10, General Brereton hurriedly convened a conference of his troop carrier and airborne commanders and their staffs in the war room of his 1st Allied Airborne Army Headquarters in Sunninghill Park. Brereton began by asking Browning to outline Montgomery's conception of Market. All those present in the war room were profoundly impressed by the unprecedented magnitude of the operation and the great distance behind German lines at which the airborne troops were being deployed. Only three months earlier many of these officers had taken part in the Normandy mission, flying 100 miles across the Channel to D-Day objectives only six to 10 miles inland. But for its forthcoming Holland mission, Brereton's Airborne Army would transport and land nearly 35,000 troops – almost twice the number employed in Normandy – a distance of 300 miles to Holland, where most of them were to drop 64 miles behind the German front lines.

When Browning completed his briefing, Brereton took his place at the planning map and announced a number of command decisions. He was placing General Browning in command of all airborne troops taking part in the mission. Browning would maintain that command

[235]

until firm link-up was made with the ground forces. This decision pleased British officers, whose opinion it was that no one was better qualified to lead the Airborne Army into battle than Browning. As they were fond of pointing out, the 47-year-old Browning had more experience and command time with airborne troops than any other Allied officer. Browning had graduated from Sandhurst, England's military academy, in June of 1915 and, only a few months later, was fighting the Germans in France. During World War I he won the Distinguished Service Order and the French Croix de Guerre before his twentieth birthday. More recently, he had commanded Britain's 1st Airborne Division from November 1941 to May 1943, and had helped plan the airborne invasions of Sicily and Normandy. And in addition to that impressive list of credentials, Browning was both a qualified parachutist and a rated glider pilot, something no other Allied airborne officer could say.

Brereton next announced that the units he had selected to conduct the assault phase of Market would be the British 1st Airborne Division, the American 82nd and 101st Airborne divisions, and the Polish 1st Independent Parachute Brigade. All of those units, he said, were to make their parachute and glider landings in daylight to achieve a high degree of delivery accuracy, and to avoid a repetition of the confused night drops in Sicily, Normandy and southern France. Brereton remarked that he based his decision for a daylight operation on the twin assumptions that the Luftwaffe was too weak to offer effective resistance, and that Allied bombers would be able to beat down German flak batteries along the flight routes.

Another matter settled by Brereton was the question of the number and type of flight routes the jump and glider tug airplanes would follow to Holland from their bases in England. Preliminary terrain studies showed there were two basic routes, one a northern course which led directly across the North Sea to Holland, the other a southerly course that wandered down and across the Channel to Belgium, where it doglegged almost due north and passed over the German–British front lines on its final run into Holland. The more direct northern route would require the airplanes to traverse 80 miles of German territory in Holland before reaching their drop and landing zones, but it was an almost straight line and was believed to be relatively free from flak. The southern route had a good side and a bad side. It would enable the airplanes to fly over Allied-controlled Belgium before they made only a 30-mile dash into Holland to make their drops, but it required the airplanes and gliders to cross directly over the German–British front lines while entering Holland, a move the Allied brass was loath to make because of the numerous German flak batteries known to be positioned there.

In the interest of delivering as many parachute and glider troops as possible in the shortest time yet avoiding air-traffic congestion, Brereton had decided to use *both* routes on D-Day. A noteworthy innovation was the massing of serials in three parallel lanes spaced one and one-half miles apart. In addition, the British 38th and 46th Groups were to fly gliders over the northern route at a level 1,000 feet above the Americans, making the route a four-lane skyway.

The American parachute and glider tug airplanes were to fly at 1,500 feet on the way to Holland, descend to 500 feet to make their drops or releases, and return to 3,000 feet to avoid incoming traffic. After passing their zones, they were to turn 180 degrees left or right, depending on the position of their zone, and return the way they had come. All of the American glider formations would again fly into battle in columns made up of four gliders in echelon to the right, in serials comprised of some 40 gliders each. British tow-planes and gliders, meanwhile, would proceed in a loose column of pairs at 10 second intervals, flying at 2,500 feet on the way to their objectives, and returning at 5,000 to 7,000 feet.

It was approaching 11:00 p.m. when Brereton concluded his meeting at Sunninghill Park and released the assembled commanders and staffs to issue initial pre-combat warning orders to their units. On the morning of the eleventh, Major General Paul L. Williams, commander of all air operations associated with Market, delivered a discouraging bit of news to Brereton. There were not enough airplanes and gliders, he said, to deliver all three and one-half airborne divisions to Holland on D-Day. Using every airplane at his command, the best Williams could do would be to deliver half of Browning's required troop strength. Vital hardware, such as anti-tank guns, artillery and jeeps scheduled for the gliders could only be delivered to those units who were expected to be targets of the heavy counterattacks anticipated from German tanks and infantry.

Brereton had counted on being able to deliver over one-third of the Airborne Army to Holland aboard gliders on D-Day, sending in the remainder by parachute. Now the best he could do would be to make piecemeal commitments of his forces by flying the three and one-half divisions to their objectives over a period lasting three days.[3]

[237]

An avid student of military history and a talented tactician, Brereton disliked the idea of committing his forces to battle in this fashion. The inherent risks of a piecemeal commitment were numerous. Anti-aircraft fire from alerted enemy gunners would intensify with each passing day; counterattacking German forces might surround and defeat the isolated Allied airborne troops before ground link-up could be effected. And there was always the possibility of foul weather grounding airplanes before they could finish delivering all of their loads into the airheads. High winds, a prolonged rainstorm, thick ground fog – all very likely to occur in Europe in September – could bring the entire operation to a halt on any one of the three days it would take to complete it.

Later that day – September 11 – General Browning assembled his unit commanders to issue his attack order. To the British 1st Airborne Division he gave the difficult task of dropping at Arnhem, the city at the point deepest inside German-occupied Holland. The 1st Airborne's primary mission at Arnhem was to seize the 2,000-foot-long concrete and steel highway bridge spanning the Lower Rhine River which flows through that city. To increase the 1st Airborne's chances of holding onto the bridge, Browning tasked the 1st Polish Parachute Brigade to jump in beside it on D plus 2.

To 37-year-old Brigadier General Gavin, the newly appointed commander of the 82nd Airborne Division,[4] Browning gave the mission of dropping along the 10-mile stretch of road between Grave and Nijmegen. There, Gavin and his troopers were to seize the huge nine-span, 1,500-foot-long highway bridge over the Maas River at Grave, the 1,960-foot-long single-span highway bridge at Nijmegen, and at least one of the four smaller bridges spanning the Maas-Wall Canal between Grave and Nijmegen.

Another chore that Browning assigned to Gavin was the seizure of the Groesbeek Heights, a ridge some 300 feet high, located about two miles southeast of Nijmegen along the borders of Holland and Germany. This ridge was the only high ground in the area and it dominated the region.

The Reichswald, a large forested area in Germany only four miles east of the Groesbeek Heights, was of great concern to Browning and Gavin. Allied intelligence had estimated that strong German tank forces were concealed in the Reichswald and could quickly assemble and storm the Groesbeek Heights shortly after the parachute drops began on D-Day. With the Heights under their control, the Germans

[238]

would be capable of delivering aimed fire throughout the 82nd Airborne's parachute and glider landing zones. Because of the tactical value attached to the Groesbeek Heights, Browning directed Gavin not to assault the Nijmegen bridge until all of his other division missions had been accomplished and the high ground around Groesbeek was firmly in his hands.

To Major General Maxwell D. Taylor, the 46-year-old commander of the 101st Airborne Division, Browning gave the mission of jumping at the extreme southern end of the airborne carpet, only 10 miles from the British tanks that would race forward on D-Day from their positions along the border of Holland and Belgium. Taylor's troopers were to land between Eindhoven in the south and Veghel in the north, where they had to secure a 15-mile stretch of the main highway connecting those two cities. Major objectives assigned to the 101st Airborne were the bridges at Zon, Saint Oedenrode, the Veghel, plus the city of Eindhoven. If everything went well on D-Day, Eindhoven would be the first large Dutch city through which the advancing British tank columns would pass on their way up to Arnhem.

Serving as commander of the 1st British Airborne Division was 42-year-old Major General Robert 'Roy' Urquhart, a rugged Scot who stood six feet tall and weighed 200 pounds. Unlike the other two airborne division commanders going to Holland, Urquhart had never made a parachute jump and had never been inside a glider. He had, quite unexpectedly, been chosen for his airborne assignment when the previous division commander, General Eric Down, was transferred to India in January 1944 to organize new airborne units there. But although he was short on airborne service, Urquhart was long on combat experience. In many vicious battles across North Africa, on Sicily, and in Italy, he had proven himself an exceptionally competent combat leader with the 51st Highland Division.

Urquhart's 1st Airborne likewise had a wealth of combat experience, but none of it was recent. To the frustration of Urquhart and all of his troopers, the division had not been sent into Normandy. Because they had not seen any action for over 10 months, the men of the 1st Airborne were beginning to say jokingly that they were being kept in reserve to march in the victory parade that everyone now expected would take place in 1944.

Earlier in the war the 1st Airborne had suffered terribly during the disastrous Allied airborne attack on Sicily. There its 1st Air Landing (glider) Brigade had been widely scattered during the night attack in which many gliders had landed in the sea. And it was also on Sicily that the division's 1st Parachute Brigade had been fired upon by friendly naval units only seconds before it was to jump. From Sicily, the 1st Airborne had been sent by boat, on September 9, 1942, to fight as straight infantry on the Italian mainland. There its original commander, General G. F. Hopkinson, was killed during the division's advance on Castellaneta. In November 1943, the division had been returned to England to refit and prepare for its next combat mission. Holland was to be that mission.

As General Urquhart correctly saw it, the formidable highway bridge in Arnhem was his primary D-Day objective. But with no airborne combat experience to guide his thinking, and the RAF's complaining about the very real danger of numerous German flak batteries around Arnhem, Urquhart made the fatal error of plotting his DZs and LZs six to eight miles west of the highway bridge. In so doing, he sacrificed surprise – an absolute necessity for success in any initial airborne strike – and consigned his troops to marching for more than two hours across territory full of alerted enemy soldiers. During those two hours, even the worst German tactician in Arnhem would be able to guess the objective of the British airborne troops and would order the bridge either to be destroyed or to be strongly reinforced.

Handicapped by the shortage of airplanes, Urquhart was forced to plan on having his division and the attached 1st Polish Parachute Brigade delivered to Arnhem over a three-day period. In keeping with British airborne doctrine of sending in the glider troops before dropping paratroopers, Urquhart tasked Brigadier Philip 'Pip' Hicks and his reinforced 1st Air Landing Brigade to land at 1:00 p.m. on D-Day in two separate LZs, lettered S and Z, west of Arnhem. Hicks, a veteran of the night glider assault on Sicily, was pleased that the Holland mission would take place in daylight. Anything, he said, would be an improvement over the Sicily invasion where he had swum ashore from a glider that had landed in the ocean. For the D-Day trip to Holland, Hicks and his brigade would utilize a total of 284 Horsa and 13 Hamilcar gliders, towed by the RAF's 38th Group.

The second and final D-Day airborne operation for the British was scheduled to take place at 1:55 p.m., by which time it was expected that elements of the Air Landing Brigade would be in control of a wide, open area that Urquhart had named DZ X. There the 1st Parachute Brigade, commanded by Brigadier Gerald Lathbury, was to jump from airplanes of the American 52nd Troop Carrier Wing, quickly assemble itself, and strike out on foot for the Arnhem highway bridge seven and one-half miles to the east.

During their foot march to the bridge, the paratroopers were to be preceded by a reconnaissance squadron mounted in jeeps and on motorcycles brought in before them aboard the gliders. Meanwhile, the glider troops and glider pilots were to remain where they had landed to provide security for the parachute and glider troops due in on D plus 1.

The next part of Urquhart's plan called for Brigadier John 'Shan' Hackett's 4th Parachute Brigade to jump into DZ Y on Monday, D plus 1. Right behind Hackett's paratroopers would come the remainder of the 1st Air Landing Brigade, which was to land in LZs S and X and immediately move to occupy the high ground due north of Arnhem.

On the third day of the operation, the Polish 1st Parachute Brigade was to jump into DZ K, which was located on the south side of the Arnhem bridge. Urquhart believed that by the time the Poles made their jump the bridge would be his and the enemy flak batteries near it neutralized. But Major General Stanislaw Sosabowski, the 54-year-old commander of the Polish paratroopers, felt differently. It was the opinion of this former Polish War Academy professor that the entire Arnhem venture was certain to end in disaster for the Allied side. Sosabowski demanded that Urquhart give him his orders in writing so that his countrymen would not hold him responsible for what he felt was sure to be the senseless slaughter of free Poland's finest troops.

Brigadier General Gavin, commander of the 82nd Airborne Division that was to drop some 14 miles south of the British near the city of Nijmegen, tailored his ground tactical plan around the availability of airplanes and General Browning's directive not to attempt taking the Nijmegen bridge until the Groesbeek Heights had been secured. With those considerations in mind, Gavin planned that on D-Day he would drop his 505th and 508th Parachute Infantry regiments and his 376th Parachute Field Artillery Battalion, into two DZs – N and T – both of which were located between the Groesbeek Heights and the Reichswald Forest. The primary missions of those regiments were to occupy and defend the heights, to secure LZ N on which

[241]

gliders would land on D-Day, and to defeat any German counter-attack that emerged from the Reichswald Forest.

Having thus assured himself of sufficient strength with which to secure the Groesbeek Heights, Gavin then plotted a third jump area, DZ T, within his airhead. This one was situated on the other side of the heights where the highway connecting Nijmegen to Arnhem was located. His 504th Parachute Infantry would go there, with the mission of capturing the huge iron highway bridge over the Maas River north of Grave.

All three of the 82nd Airborne's parachute regiments were scheduled to make their jumps as the first British glider troops were landing at Arnhem.

Gavin also planned to send some of his glider units to Holland on D-Day. Starting at 1:47 p.m., only a half hour after the paratroop drops, some 50 Wacos, loaded with anti-tank guns, jeeps and some light artillery, were to land in LZ N on the Reichswald side of the Groesbeek Heights to provide firepower to the paratroopers defending the heights.

The final D-Day operation scheduled into the 82nd Airborne's airhead was to be performed by the RAF's 38th Group. The RAF was to deliver Lieutenant General Browning and the entire staff of his 1st Airborne Corps Headquarters to LZ N aboard 32 Horsa and six Waco gliders – the first time that any nation had flown a corps headquarters into combat by glider. Browning and his staff were scheduled to land at 2:00 p.m. on D-Day and then set up shop alongside General Gavin's command post just south of the city of Groesbeek, not quite two miles from the edge of the Reichswald.

In planning his D plus 1 air operations, Gavin decided to conduct a massive landing of 454 Wacos carrying the bulk of his divisional artillery into LZ N. On D plus 2 he would conclude his airborne missions by landing his 325th Glider Infantry Regiment, 80th Anti-aircraft Battalion, and an assortment of engineer, reconnaissance, and military police glider units. All of the D plus 2 troops were to be brought in aboard 406 Wacos that would land in LZ T, located next to LZ N.

Major General Maxwell Taylor's 101st Airborne Division was task organized for Holland exactly as it had been for Normandy. In keeping with General Browning's orders that he secure the 15 miles of highway connecting Eindhoven and Veghel, Taylor planned to drop all three of his parachute infantry regiments on D-Day. Because of his own terrible experiences in the Normandy night drop, where his division had been badly scattered and he had spent much of the night lost in the dark, Taylor planned to take full advantage of the daylight Holland invasion by dropping his paratroopers into just two principal areas, thus facilitating a rapid assembly of troops. The main concentration of paratroopers would be dropped into an area designated LZ W. This was a large, wide open triangle situated east of Hell's Highway whose vertices were the cities of Saint Oedenrode, Zon, and Best. Within this large area were DZs B and C.

Taylor planned to round out his D-Day air operations with two serials from the 437th Group containing 35 airplanes apiece, each towing a Waco glider. All gliders were to land in LZ W immediately behind the paratroop drops.

Taylor planned to land another 450 Wacos into the same area – LZ W – on D plus 1. Aboard those gliders would be two battalions of his 327th Glider Infantry Regiment, the 326th Airborne Engineer Battalion, and the 326th Airborne Medical Company.

The 101st Airborne's third and final airborne mission to Holland was planned for D plus 2. For that day, Taylor scheduled yet another 385 Wacos to land in LZ W to deliver the third battalion of his 327th Glider Infantry, three battalions of artillery, and his gliderborne anti-tank battalion.

Had Field Marshal Montgomery launched his Operation Market-Garden two weeks earlier than he did, it would have resulted in a resounding success for the Allies. Quite possibly, it could have resulted in the Allies winning the war in 1944. But because the operation was not launched early in September, the great mass of German units that had been withdrawing across France and Belgium were able to halt in Holland and significantly strengthen their positions there in time to blunt the coming Allied airborne assault.

Montgomery's very worthy opponent during Market-Garden would be German Field Marshal Walter Model, the commander of Army Group B. At 54, Model was the youngest Field Marshal in the Reich's short history. During World War I he had served as an infantry officer in France. In the current war he had distinguished himself during the 1939 invasion of Poland and the 1940 defeat of France, but he had really made a name for himself in Russia. There he had earned the nickname 'The Lion of Defence' because Hitler had switched him to the north, south and centre fronts in turn, attempting to stem the advancing Russian hordes. In late August 1944, when he was suddenly transferred to Holland, Model had been working miracles restoring the disintegrating front along the Vistula.

Second only to his record as the commander of large forces caught up in desperate tactical situations, the strongest card in Model's hand was his close relationship with Hitler. After the July 20 attempt on Hitler's life, he had been the first commander on the Eastern Front to send a telegram repledging his fidelity.

One of the first things Model had done on arriving in Holland was to send a blunt message to Hitler on September 3 describing the situation in the west as untenable. Pulling no punches, Model told the Führer that unless he received 25 fresh divisions at once, he would be unable to stop an Allied thrust through the back door of the Fatherland. Within hours of receiving Model's message at his field headquarters in East Prussia, Hitler telephoned General Kurt Student, chief of the German parachute troops, who was then in Berlin. Student was ordered to gather up every parachute unit undergoing training in Germany and rush them, and himself, to Holland to aid Model.

Scraping the bottom of his manpower barrel, Student came up with only 18,000 men – not quite the equivalent of one Allied infantry division. In a frenzied effort to obtain more men for Student, German authorities rounded up several more battalions comprised of sailors, civilian policemen, retired World War I veterans, and even 16-year-old schoolboys. This collection of soldiers and civilians was given the title of First Parachute Army and rushed by train to Holland under Student's command. It was with that hodgepodge of Germans that Student had stopped the advance of British troops along the Dutch–Belgian border during the first week in September.

In what proved to be the best combat order he ever issued, Field Marshal Model contacted his Fifth Army commander on September 3 and directed him to route the 9th and 10th SS Panzer divisions to Arnhem, Holland, for rehabilitation. At the time Model gave that order, those divisions were limping across France like two wounded lions, having suffered severe beatings at the hands of the Allies. Model unknowingly compounded his good luck on September 5 when he also ordered the 2nd Panzer Corps headquarters to Arnhem from France. This unit was commanded by Waffen SS General Willi Bittrich, who had recently fought in Russia under Model's command.

The sudden arrival of German tanks in Holland did not go unnoticed by the Dutch underground. As early as September 11, Dutch agents began sending warnings to England that a 'significant number' of panzers were arriving daily in the Arnhem area. By September 14, the Dutch confirmed that the tanks were from the 9th and 10th SS Panzer divisions.

Eisenhower's Chief of Staff, Lieutenant General Walter B. Smith, was alarmed by the reported tank build-up in Holland. With Ike's permission, he flew to Montgomery's headquarters in Belgium on September 15 – only two days before D-Day – and suggested that the equivalent of a second Allied airborne division be dropped in at Arnhem to deal with the enemy tanks and ensure an Allied victory at the end of the airborne carpet. But Monty, as Smith recalled after the war, 'ridiculed my idea and waved my objection airily aside.'[5] The airborne plan remained unchanged.

Early in the evening of Saturday, September 16, General Browning held a final conference of unit commanders in the war room at 1st Allied Airborne Army Headquarters. The meeting was brief. There were assurances by weather experts that good flying conditions would prevail the following day, and a report from all commanders that their units were primed and ready for action. Satisfied that his airplanes and troops were as ready as they were ever going to be, General Brereton gave the irrevocable decision to launch Market-Garden in the morning.

In preparation for the largest airborne assault in the history of warfare, members of the American 26th Mobile Repair and Reclamation Squadron based at Cookham Common had been working very hard to compensate for the loss of almost all the gliders used in Normandy in June. By July 1, they had managed to assemble 1,045 new Wacos received from United States factories, but that was only enough to lift the glider echelon of one airborne division. In anticipation of operations involving several divisions, a new assembly programme had been inaugurated at Cookham Common on August 8 to produce 40 completed Wacos a day. The Americans employed 26 officers and over 900 men working in three shifts, using automobile assembly line techniques. They proved capable of assembling 60 (and once even 100) gliders in a day. By the end of August, the IX Troop Carrier Command had 1,629 operational Wacos, and by September 15 that number had swelled to 2,160. Plans called for the employment of nearly 90 per cent of those gliders in Market.

Just over 1,900 American glider pilots were on hand at the end of

August in England. The arrival of 200 more from the United States gave IX Troop Carrier Command a grand total of only 2,060 on the eve of Market. Faced with this shortage, Generals Brereton and Williams were forced to forsake the use of copilots in the American gliders going to Holland. This command decision was a cause of great concern to the glider pilots. They knew that if they were incapacitated during the four-hour flight across the water to their objectives in Holland, there would be no one on board qualified to conduct a safe emergency landing. But by this time in their brief military careers, glider pilots were accustomed to command decisions not being in their favour.

The invasion of Holland actually began on the night of September 16, when 282 RAF bombers took off from England to eliminate as much as possible of the German anti-aircraft defences while concealing the fact that anything unusual was in the offing.

The Allies withdrew the blanket of secrecy from Operation Market-Garden early on the morning of D-Day when they launched a British force of 200 Lancaster and 23 Mosquito bombers to blast German flak batteries along the coastline of Holland. Right behind the British flew 852 American B-17 Flying Fortresses, with an escort of 153 fighters. Over the North Sea the B-17s split into two columns, one of which was to beat down German guns along the northern route while the other did the same along the southern route. Altogether, the B-17s dropped a staggering 3,140 tons of bombs on 117 known flak batteries. The cost to the Allied side was two B-17s, two Lancasters and three escort fighters.

The dust from these preparatory strikes had not quite settled when, at 10:25 a.m., 12 British and six American airplanes left England to drop pathfinders on DZs and LZs in Holland 20 minutes before H-Hour. Despite such obvious indications, the Germans in Holland failed to deduce what was about to happen. It was a beautiful, warm Sunday and Allied air raids had become commonplace in recent weeks.

At his headquarters in the Tafelberg Hotel in Oosterbeek, a few miles east of Arnhem, Field Marshal Model sipped a glass of wine before sitting down to his noon meal. Elsewhere in the many towns over which the airborne carpet would soon be laid, unsuspecting off-duty German occupation troops sat in the midday sun enjoying their beer and watching pretty Dutch girls walking home from morning church services.

[246]

Out over the North Sea and the English Channel, the greatest air armada ever assembled was thundering along parallel routes toward the coasts of Holland and Belgium carrying elements of three airborne divisions simultaneously into battle. Along the northern route flew the tugs and gliders of the British 1st Airborne Division, followed closely by paratroops of the 82nd Airborne. The southern route was completely taken up with the 101st Airborne.

For the average person today, who has never seen more than a few airplanes in the sky at one time, the magnitude of this airborne assault is difficult to visualize. On that day, Sunday, September 17, 1944, a titanic assemblage of 1,545 paratroop planes, 451 glider tugs and 451 gliders took off from 24 airfields in England and were all in the air at the same time, carrying the torch of liberty to Holland. Weaving a protective screen around those long streams of slow-moving unarmed transports and gliders were another 1,130 Allied fighter airplanes.

Along the northern route, where the British were leading the way, serious problems began at the moment of take-off and dogged the skytrain all the way to Holland. One Horsa was grounded by structural damage incurred while it was preparing for lift off, and 23 others broke loose from their tugs before clearing the coast of England. Over the North Sea, where they were flying at 2,500 feet, the British ran into patches of low clouds which the Americans, a thousand feet below them, had not encountered. In those clouds the British lost four more Horsas, all of which made successful emergency landings in the sea.

The skytrain eventually reached the Dutch coast at the ominously named island of Over Flakee, where it encountered some light flak from shore batteries and from a floating barge. Four more Horsas went down well short of Arnhem, all from broken tow-lines. On approaching their LZs east of Arnhem, the British glider pilots easily recognized the display of landing aids that the pathfinders had laid out for them. With excellent visibility and only a light wind to contend with, the remaining gliders landed on or very near their assigned fields. Several Horsas collided on the ground, tearing themselves to pieces, but there were no deaths or serious injuries in any of them. Two of the giant Hamilcars, each loaded with a 17-pounder (76.2 mm) anti-tank gun,[6] 100 shells for the gun, and 10 troops, touched down hard and began ploughing up waves of dirt. Suddenly both Hamilcars dug their noses deeply into the earth and flipped on

[247]

to their backs. There were no survivors in either glider. The remaining 11 Hamilcars avoided that obviously too-soft field and landed safely in neighbouring areas without incident. During the unloading the troops and gliders were subjected only to light rifle fire which did not prevent them from quickly establishing a defensive cordon around their two landing zones and DZ X.

At 1:53 p.m., two minutes early, Brigadier Lathbury and his 1st Parachute Brigade arrived aboard their American airplanes and made an extremely accurate drop into the middle of DZ X. To the amazement of all the Allied generals associated with Operation Market-Garden, not one of the airplanes that delivered the British to Arnhem had been shot down.

The 82nd Airborne, trailing immediately behind the British, was far less fortunate. Shortly after crossing the coastline of Holland all of the division's airplanes separated themselves from the skytrain by dropping down to an altitude of only 400 feet and making a right-hand turn on to a new course which led to Nijmegen. Skimming along at such a low altitude, many of the jump planes began taking hits from flak and even small arms fire. Though suffering badly from perforated wings and fuel tanks, the C-47 pilots bravely stuck to their controls so that the troopers could jump on assigned DZs. A direct hit caused one airplane to burst into flames and crash near Grave, killing all aboard. On final flight to their DZs, the airplanes ran into intense ground fire but remained on course and made bulls-eye drops on all DZs. As they passed over the Reichswald Forest, where they had to make a left-hand turn after completing their drops, six more C-47s were blasted out of the sky. (On the way back to England, two more were shot down over Holland, and one other had to ditch in the North Sea.)

The southern route to Holland – the one along which the 101st Airborne had to fly – was supposed to be safer than the northern one because much of it passed over territory occupied by friendly troops. But on D-Day the planes carrying the 101st Airborne's paratroopers began drawing intense flak at the instant they crossed into Holland. During the drops, 16 planes were shot down, 14 more were severely damaged but kept on flying, and 84 others sustained moderate damage.

Since the massive Allied invasion of Holland took place on a Sunday, it must have seemed like an act of God to those Dutch citizens still walking home from church. For over four years now these sturdy people had been praying for deliverance from the harsh rule of Adolf Hitler and his repressive occupation troops. Now with the heavens filled with hundreds of airplanes and gliders, it looked as if Holland's moment of salvation had come.

Despite the pre-invasion bombings and the roar of transports streaming across Holland, the Germans had been caught completely by surprise. General Student, the commander of the First Parachute Army, was at his desk in his headquarters in Vaught, a small village only seven miles from the 101st Airborne's main drop zone, when he heard the unmistakable drone of jump planes. As he was to tell interrogators after the war, Student rushed out on the balcony where he saw long columns of airplanes passing directly over his head. Staring up at planes that he knew must be filled with paratroopers ready to jump, Student remarked wistfully to his chief of staff, Colonel Ernst Reinhard, 'Oh, what I might have accomplished if only I had such a force at my disposal.'[7]

Student was back inside his command post and was issuing counterattack orders when at 1:48 p.m., some 42 minutes after the paratroopers jumped along the highway connecting Eindhoven and Veghel, the first gliders of the 101st Airborne arrived over LZ W. When towed into the sky from their bases in England, these two serials had been comprised of 70 Wacos loaded with 43 jeeps, 18 trailers and 311 men from the division's medical and signal companies, reconnaissance platoon and artillery headquarters. The absence of artillery pieces aboard these gliders was not a planning oversight: General Taylor had deliberately left his artillery in England on the assumption that the British ground troops would quickly link-up with him on D-Day and that he would be able to use their big guns if the need arose.

Even before they had cleared the English coast, Taylor's gliders began running into troubles that stayed with them all the way to Holland. Two of them broke loose from their tugs shortly after take-off and landed safely. A third, piloted by Flight Officer Gerald F. Kinnie of Grand Rapids, Michigan, was forced to cut away when the bolt holding its tail strut cable broke. Neither Kinnie nor his 14 passengers were wearing parachutes. As soon as the glider separated from the tug, its tail section folded and it went into a spin. It crashed a few seconds later, killing all aboard.

Out over the Channel another glider was forced to ditch when the canvas on its fuselage began peeling away like the skin of a banana.

Two more were forced to cut loose over Belgium under similar circumstances. All aboard those gliders were rescued.

Real trouble began shortly after the gliders were towed across the Belgium–Holland border. There, seven gliders were forced to make premature releases when their tugs were suddenly shot down by flak. Flight Officer Joseph D. Randolph could not believe his eyes when he saw his tug ship's left wing sheared off by flak. Randolph, who had a full load of medics from the 307th Medical Battalion on board his glider, gave the tow-line release knob a lightning-fast punch and watched helplessly as the plane that had been towing him spun over on its side and crashed, killing its entire crew. Moments later, Randolph made a safe emergency landing in an open field between Boxtel and Schijndel. There he and his passengers were met by Dutch patriots who hid them from the Germans for three days until American troops advanced into that vicinity. Five of the other gliders whose tugs had been downed managed to make safe emergency landings; all of their crews were rescued by Dutch farmers. The seventh glider plummeted into the ground behind its tug and exploded in a ball of fire.

The remaining gliders made it all the way to LZ W, where orderly cutaways took place. During the mass descent, two gliders that had survived a minor mid-air collision crash-landed on the zone, killing one pilot and injuring five passengers. All other gliders found ample room on the LZ and landed safely with 252 troops, 32 jeeps and 13 trailerloads of ammunition.

Further up the road, in the middle of the airborne carpet, the 82nd Airborne's gliders were making a simultaneously timed landing on LZ N. Their mission involved a single glider serial from the 439th Troop Carrier Group that had left England with 50 airplanes towing as many Wacos. On board those gliders were 216 troops, eight 57 mm anti-tank guns, nine jeeps and two trailers. While enroute to Holland, the serial had lost four of its gliders to broken tow-lines. A fifth glider was forced to cut loose when its tug was downed by flak over Schouwn Island. That glider landed safely in the sea but was shot to pieces immediately by flak guns on the island.

With those exceptions the trip to Holland was successful and comparatively uneventful. But on reaching the area of Groesbeek Heights the tug ships mistakenly gave their gliders the signal to release while still a few miles short of the LZ. Only six gliders, whose pilots stubbornly hung on after the release signal was given, managed to reach the LZ. All others landed at least a mile short of it. Two gliders were destroyed in landing and 14 were severely damaged, but there were no deaths.

Not quite a quarter of an hour later, a flight of 35 RAF airplanes towing General Browning and his staff flew over the Groesbeek Heights and released their gliders. Originally this mission had consisted of 32 Horsas, three of which had made emergency landings when their tow-lines broke, and six Wacos. Photos later established that 28 of the gliders landed on LZ N, and the balance within a half mile of it. Browning himself was safely landed aboard a Horsa piloted by Brigadier George Chatterton, commander of the British Glider Pilot Regiment, and Major Andy Andrews.

In his younger days, General Browning had been a champion athlete and had represented England in the high hurdles at the Olympic Games. Still keen on physical fitness, he could frequently be seen taking long morning runs near his headquarters at Moor Park on the outskirts of London. So it did not surprise anyone on the LZ when, shortly after climbing out of his glider, Browning sprinted over to the edge of the Reichswald. Upon his return a few moments later, he said to Brigadier Gordon Walch, his chief of staff, 'I wanted to be the first British officer to pee in Germany.'[8]

Meanwhile, in Oosterbeek, an affluent residential village only two miles from downtown Arnhem and some 14 miles north of where Browning and his staff were setting up their command post, Field Marshal Model was already living up to his reputation as the Lion of Defence. Like everyone else in his command, Model had been caught unawares by the massive Allied airborne assault. The first British pathfinders had jumped only two miles from his headquarters in Oosterbeek. Upon sighting the parachutists and gliders landing almost on his doorstep, Model calmly instructed his operations officer to send an order to General Bittrich, the 2nd SS Panzer Corps commander, to attack the British airborne troops at once. Next he sent an order to General Friedrich Christianson, commander of German occupation forces in Holland, to assist Bittrich by attacking immediately with whatever troops he could round up. His tactical orders completed, Model told everyone in his headquarters to grab what equipment they could and leave the area at once for Bittrich's headquarters at Doetinchem, 25 miles northeast of Arnhem.

In the five minutes that followed, Model ran upstairs to his room, where he threw important papers and some personal belongings into a suitcase. His chauffeur dashed off to get the field marshal's Mercedes staff car to the front door of the hotel. Model bolted out of the hotel. As he ran down the steps his suitcase popped open, spewing documents, family pictures, and underwear into the view of his waiting staff. Nobody dared to laugh. An orderly scooped up the spilled items and crammed them back into the suitcase. Moments later Model and his staff were racing toward the safety of Bittrich's headquarters.

Not knowing where Model was, Bittrich acted on his own in the absence of orders from above. To the 9th SS Panzer Division he gave instructions to get rolling toward the British landing areas. The 10th SS Panzer, meanwhile, was to drive south to Nijmegen where it was to defend the highway bridge over the Waal River; these were the troops that would prevent Gavin's 82nd Airborne from taking the Nijmegen bridge later that night.

Back in the British airhead, meanwhile, General Urquhart (who had landed aboard a Horsa glider) was busy consolidating in preparation for the first strikes to seize the high ground north of Arnhem and the all-important highway bridge over the Lower Rhine. But already he was being forced to alter his original plan of attack. On board the many gliders that had been lost enroute to Holland were the jeeps and motorcycles that were to have transported his reconnaissance troops into Arnhem so that they could quickly seize control of the bridge. Not until some four hours after the landing did Urquhart manage to dispatch three parachute battalions from Lathbury's brigade on foot toward Arnhem. Two of these ran into serious trouble when, only minutes after marching out of the airhead, they encountered the lead German tanks of the 9th SS Panzer Division, just then arriving from Arnhem.

During this initial scuffle with the Germans, the 2nd Parachute Battalion managed to sideslip them and continue on its way to Arnhem. Serving as commander of this battalion was the intrepid Lieutenant Colonel John D. Frost, already a living legend in the British airborne corps. In February 1942, as a captain, he had led the daring and successful night parachute commando raid at Bruneval, France, to hijack components of the superior German Wurzburg radar device for British scientists. Later, in July 1943, he successfully commanded a battalion during the night parachute assault on Sicily. While marching toward Arnhem, Frost's B and C companies became pinned down. Again, Frost scooted past the Germans, but this time only with his Company A. With that small force, he fought his way to the north abutment of the bridge and set up a defensive position to await the arrival of the remainder of the brigade. Only a few more paratroopers filtered in. After dark, Frost tried several times to move across the bridge to secure its southern end, but each attempt was beaten back. The night passed with Frost holding only the northern end, and the Germans holding the rest of the bridge.

Even though all three Allied airborne divisions had landed with far greater than expected accuracy, Operation Market-Garden was riddled with deeply serious problems at the end of D-Day. At the southern end of the airborne carpet General Taylor's 101st Airborne had been unable to take the key city of Eindhoven. In the middle of the carpet, Gavin's 82nd Airborne had been stopped cold only a stone's throw away from the Nijmegen Bridge. And at the carpet's northern end in Arnhem, General Urquhart's 1st Airborne had only been able to secure the north end of the vital Arnhem bridge. The rest of Urquhart's division was locked in combat trying to hold what little ground it had landed on near Oosterbeek. Equally discouraging was the fact that the hoped-for British tank thrust up the carpet had stalled after penetrating only four miles into Holland from Belgium.

On Monday, D plus 1, all three airborne divisions got on with their missions of improving their local tactical situations and of securing areas in which the initial glider and parachute reinforcements were scheduled to start landing at about 10:00 a.m.

Weather, the crucial element in every battle that even the highest-ranking generals and admirals are powerless to control, began to cause dire troubles for the Allied side on D plus 1. All across Holland the weather was beautiful, but in England all air bases were covered by a blanket of morning fog. Over the Channel, things were even worse; dense masses of low-lying clouds and rain showers had rendered the southern route to Holland unusable. General Brereton hastily ordered all missions to fly the northern route and postponed the landings in Holland to 2:00 p.m. in the hope that the English fog would burn off in time to fit that adjusted schedule.

The 101st Airborne was to be reinforced that day using 450 Waco gliders that would be towed to LZ W by airplanes of the 53rd Wing. Aboard the gliders would be 2,656 troops, 156 jeeps, 111 trailers and two bulldozers. The majority of those troops were members of the division's 327th Glider Infantry Regiment, now commanded by Colonel Joseph P. Harper.

Fortunately, the fog burned off in time to permit an 11:20 a.m.

[253]

take-off by the tow-planes and gliders bound for LZ W. The lead tow-plane in this mission was piloted by Colonel William B. Whittaker the popular commander of the 434th Troop Carrier Group. At the controls of the glider towed by Whittaker's aircraft was Lieutenant Victor B. Warriner. In the copilot's seat beside Warriner was Brigadier General Anthony C. McAuliffe, deputy commander of the 101st Airborne. Some two days prior to this mission, General McAuliffe had specifically requested that Colonel Whittaker be his tow-plane pilot and Warriner his glider pilot when he flew into Holland. During a meeting with those two pilots, McAuliffe had pointed to a small schoolhouse on a map of LZ W and told them that he wanted to land as close as possible to it. To acquaint himself with that schoolhouse, glider pilot Warriner had flown over to Holland along the southern route on D-Day as passenger in Whittaker's airplane during the initial paratroop drops on LZ W. Despite the distractions of flak and small arms fire during that flight, Warriner had managed to spot the schoolhouse and get its location fixed in his mind. But now that he would be flying to Holland along the northern route he was worried about being able to find it during an approach from a different angle.

Despite the improved weather conditions, 10 Wacos were unable to leave England because of tow-line breaks. Three more ditched in the sea and were quickly rescued. As the skytrain was nearing the Dutch coastline another Waco became uncontrollable. Cutting loose from its tug ship, the glider made an emergency landing on Schouwen Island where all aboard were taken prisoner by German flakgun crews.

A direct hit by enemy flak was something that all pilots lived in fear of. But before this mission was over, Flight Officer Roy C. Lovingood would be happy that his glider had been hit by flak. Since leaving England, Lovingood had been struggling to keep the inexplicably heavy left wing of his glider level. By the time the skytrain had reached the coast of Holland, Lovingood's arms were shaking from the constant strain of keeping the ship level. But still he held on to the control yoke. If he lost the tug of war, the glider would spin over and crash.

Unbeknownst to Lovingood, someone back in England had inadvertently failed to replace the inspection plate cover on the upper surface of the left wing during a recent safety check. Considerable water from the recent rainstorms had drained into the wing's cavity, and its weight was throwing the ship dangerously out of trim, Lovingood was nearing complete physical exhaustion when a flak shell tore through the troublesome wing without exploding. All of a sudden, water gushed out of the wing 'just like someone had flushed a toilet', and the glider righted itself. The remainder of the trip was uneventful for Lovingood and his nervous passengers.

While on final to LZ W, the skytrain began receiving light ground fire from flak batteries hidden in patches of trees. When he saw his tug take a direct hit and noticed its right engine in flames, Lieutenant Warriner picked up the intercom phone and called Colonel Whittaker, the tow-plane pilot, to inform him of the situation. Obviously annoyed by the phone call, the usually mild-mannered Whittaker snorted, 'Warriner, I know that goddamned engine's on fire. Now you just fly your glider and let me fly this airplane.'

Warriner turned to General McAuliffe to see how he was reacting to the severe emergency and found the commander sound asleep in the copilot's seat. With black smoke streaming out of his engine, Whittaker continued on to the LZ where he signalled the glider to cut away. By this time the general was awake and was casually looking out at the scenery below. Meanwhile, Warriner was anxiously looking for his landing spot. He could not find the little schoolhouse. After two left-hand turns, Warriner set the glider down in a large field. When it came to a halt he prepared himself to receive unkind words for having failed to land near the schoolhouse. But glancing to his left he saw it less than 50 yards away. Warriner did his best to look unsurprised when the general congratulated him on the accuracy of his landing.

One of the many untrained glider copilots flying to Holland on this mission was Technician 4th Class Andrew E. Rasmussen, a paratrooper from the 506th Parachute Infantry Regiment. At the time he had volunteered to serve as a copilot of this glider loaded with a trailer full of ammunition and a supply of maps, Rasmussen was still hobbled by an ankle broken during his night jump into Normandy earlier in June. During that mission he had been taken prisoner and rescued a few weeks later by advancing infantry troops. Rasmussen, like most paratroopers, had never been in a glider before. His flight training, such as it was, had consisted of a five-minute lecture by the pilot just prior to take-off on how to push the foot pedals and turn the steering wheel. It was during that flying lesson that Rasmussen noticed the odour of whisky on the pilot's breath. Yet by all outward appearances the pilot was cold sober.

[255]

The fact that his pilot had been drinking was a matter of some concern to Rasmussen, but what really aggravated him was that the pilot took both flak jackets from the pilot's compartment, laying one of them across his seat as a protective cushion and putting the other one on himself. Because this officer outranked him there was little Rasmussen could do but climb aboard and strap himself in.

Upon arriving over LZ W, the pilot told Rasmussen to hit the release knob. Then he immediately banked to the left where he very nearly collided with another glider. A few seconds later the glider was in level flight, heading straight for a wooden fence. After smashing through it the glider touched down and slid across an irrigation ditch which jarred its nose section slightly open. Still skidding along, the glider began to fill up with dirt like a great shovel. Then it suddenly lurched to a halt. 'Where do we go now?' asked the pilot. 'Right over to those woods, sir,' replied Rasmussen. 'You'll find some of our boys dug in over there.' As he made his way through the dust-filled cargo compartment, Rasmussen told himself it would be a cold day in hell before he ever climbed into another glider.

Elsewhere on LZ W, a total of 247 other gliders had landed, most without serious damage. When the returns were in, 2,579 troops had been mustered along with 151 serviceable jeeps and 109 trailers. Casualties amounted to 54 dead or missing and 23 injured. The mission had been about 95 per cent effective.

The 82nd Airborne's glider reinforcements were being towed to Holland by 454 airplanes from the 50th and 52nd Troop Carrier Wings. Packed into the gliders were 1,899 troops from the 319th, 320th and 456th Field Artillery battalions, along with Battery B of the 80th Anti-tank Battalion, and Headquarters Battery of Divisional Artillery. Also on board were 60 howitzers, 206 jeeps, 412 cans of gasoline, 133 trailerloads of ammo and a supply of gunpowder. Virtually every glider in this huge mission contained highly explosive and flammable materials. Where possible, precautions were taken to protect the glider pilots and their passengers from the terrifying possibilities. Seldom before had so many dangerous items been flown in a single massed formation.

The first glider-tug combination took off at 11:09 a.m., and it was nearly two hours before all aircraft were airborne. While still over England one glider was loosed by an hysterical soldier who suddenly ran from his seat and punched the release knob. Both landed safely. Over the North Sea the aircraft started running into patches of low clouds which caused some serious problems for the glider pilots who frequently lost sight of their tugs. Two gliders, caught in the prop-wash of several planes bunched together in the clouds, lurched suddenly and snapped their tow-lines.

As soon as he saw that his tow-line had broken, Flight Officer James J. DiPietro glanced at the altimeter and noticed that it read 200 feet. Then he looked over at the young artilleryman sitting in the copilot's seat. His face, remembers DiPietro, had 'turned white as a bedsheet'. 'What do we do now, sir?' asked the artilleryman. 'Pray,' replied DiPietro. The glider was still descending through thick masses of clouds when DiPietro turned his head and yelled to his 14 passengers: 'When we hit the water we will land tail first and you will feel two jolts. Release your seat belts after the second jolt. Then punch holes in the roof and get out on the wings. Whatever you do, do not open the doors. Keep your eyes peeled for a dinghy that will be dropped by our tow-plane.'

The water came into view and DiPietro set his glider down in it. Right after the second jolt the glider came to a standstill. When DiPietro turned to check on his passengers, all he saw were empty seats; they were already out of the glider and sitting on the wings. Even his 'copilot' was gone. DiPietro quickly released his seat belt, sloshed back into the fuselage, which was now knee-deep in water, and was pulled up on to the wing by two soldiers.

According to the pre-arranged emergency ditching procedure, DiPietro's tow-plane was supposed to circle back over the downed glider and drop an inflatable rubber raft. But on this mission he did not do so. After looking skyward for nearly an hour for some sign of his tow-plane, DiPietro heard a British Air-Sea rescue launch approaching. It pulled alongside the bobbing glider, hauled everyone aboard, and gave them hot tea, brandy, and a change of clothing.

Things began heating up for the glider skytrain after it made landfall over Holland. There, alerted German flak batteries began taking the Americans under fire. Three gliders broke loose when their tow-planes were struck and set afire. Two others had to cut away when their tugs were nailed by flak bursts which severed parts of wings and tail sections. Though they were getting an extremely hostile reception, the tug ships stayed on course toward the Groesbeek Heights area.

Dead ahead on LZs N and T, where these gliders were supposed to land, a bitter skirmish had erupted between elements of the 82nd

Airborne and a German force that had launched an attack out of the Reichswald. During this encounter, First Sergeant Leonard A. Funk of the 508th Parachute Infantry led a band of paratroopers in a charge across the LZs to meet the Germans. While crossing the open fields, Funk and his men killed 15 of the enemy, captured 40 others and knocked out seven anti-aircraft guns. For his heroics in this encounter, Funk was later awarded the Distinguished Service Cross.

The paratroopers succeeded in clearing the landing zones in the nick of time; the rifle fire had just stopped when the first glider serial arrived overhead. But deeper inside the Reichswald, other still active flak guns were beginning to shoot at the incoming aircraft.

The lead serial was comprised of gliders from the 313th Troop Carrier Group which had been overseas since before the invasion of Sicily, but had never been committed to combat. The initial releases of the 313th began at 2:31 p.m. at altitudes ranging from 400 to 800 feet, and landings were made into a gentle northeast wind. Seeing other German and American troops still fighting along the edges of their LZs, many of the glider pilots chose to come in fast while others landed at a relatively slow 50 to 60 miles per hour. In several cases, gliders were brought to a halt in as little as 50 feet by their arrester parachutes.

The approach flight to the area of the landing zones had been a nerve-racking experience for Flight Officer Melvin Burroughs. On board his glider were three artillerymen, a command jeep, nine rounds of ammo for the howitzer riding in his wingman's glider, and six cans of gasoline. His copilot was a sergeant who had brought along a sandbag to sit on as protection against German small arms fire. Shortly after passing over the coast of Holland in the low tow position behind his tug, Burroughs saw several German soldiers running for cover. Suddenly one of them stopped in his tracks, drew a pistol, and began shooting at Burroughs' glider. As the bullets cracked through the fuselage, the sergeant looked over at Burroughs and, pointing at the sandbag he was sitting on, shouted, 'Thank God I'm at least protected one end!'

Just after leaving the pistol-shooting German behind, Burroughs's glider was rocked by a flak shell which tore a hole in its side and burst one of the tyres on the jeep. Soon Burroughs got the signal to cast off from his tug. On the way down, a stream of machine gun bullets set his Waco on fire. Fortunately the fire was isolated in the tail section and he was able to crash-land his ship before it exploded.

As soon as he dived out of the flaming wreckage, Burroughs discovered that he had landed in a field full of turnips ready for harvest. Looking off to his left, he could see the glider of his wingman, Flight Officer Ray Rudolph, only 50 yards away. Both gliders were the targets of German gunners firing from a nearby woodline. Burroughs tried crawling over to Rudolph's position, but was wounded by shrapnel. The firing eventually died down, but every time one of the Americans made a move, it resumed with renewed intensity. It was during one of those renewed shellings that Burroughs was hit for the second time.

Burroughs had been lying in the turnip field 'for what seemed like a lifetime' when he felt something tapping his leg. Looking up, he saw a very young and very nervous German soldier pointing a rifle at him. The rifle, Burroughs observed, was actually shaking. Just then several other German soldiers appeared with the Americans from Rudolph's glider as their prisoners. That seemed to strengthen the resolve of the young German for he jabbed Burroughs with the barrel of his rifle and motioned him to start walking. Seeing this, Rudolph angrily said to the young enemy soldier, 'Leave him alone, can't you see he's wounded?' Though he appreciated his friend's concern, Burroughs cautioned him, 'Easy, Rudy, these guys are holding all the guns, so we better do as they say.' With that advice, the Americans were led off into captivity.

The eighth serial to arrive over LZ N was flown by the 61st Troop Carrier Group. As in all other serials, only its lead tow-plane was equipped with a radar navigation device. About a half hour out from the LZ, the lead airplane lost its glider when ground fire cut its tow-line. When that happened, the flight leader circled to watch the glider land and then went home. The next airplane to take the lead flew on dead reckoning and promptly got lost. Followed by eight other glider–tug combinations, he missed the zone and released his glider 12 miles inside Germany. Not one of those gliders, nor anyone aboard them, was ever seen again.

The following serial approached the LZ area with the radar device in its lead plane jammed by German radio interference. But the flight leader managed to locate the LZs after some minor navigation errors and the serial made its releases between three and five miles south of LZ T in the area of Gennep. There, most of the gliders were attacked by German infantry the minute they touched down. Survivors from those 40 gliders had to fight for their lives until darkness and then try to work their way into the 82nd Airborne's airhead. Twenty-two glider pilots, 160 artillerymen, 10 jeeps and two howitzers were saved that way. All other personnel in this serial were either killed or captured.

This attempt to reinforce the 82nd Airborne had been far less successful than the companion mission to the 101st Airborne. Of the 212 gliders that were supposed to have landed on LZ N, about 150 landed within a circle a half-mile in radius centred on the hamlet of Knapheide, a mile southwest of the zone. All but a few of the other gliders in those serials either landed within one and a half miles of Knapheide or stuck to their orders and landed on LZ N. The 242 Wacos intended for LZ T fared far worse. Approximately 90 of them did land on the zone and 52 others west of it but within one mile of panels and smoke that had been set out by pathfinders on its western edge. Another 20 were bunched slightly over a mile west of LZ T, and 19 more were scattered in German-held territory between one and four miles northeast of the zone.

While the 82nd Airborne had been having a bad time with its glider landings, the British up at the end of the carpet were experiencing worse troubles. Frost's paratroopers at the highway bridge in Arnhem were penned in by German infantry and panzers and were suffering badly. Valiant attempts by the 1st and 3rd Parachute battalions to break through to Frost from the DZ area only resulted in both those units getting whittled down to about 100 men apiece.

Back in the drop and landing zones, meanwhile, the British glider pilots and other troops were having a terrible time trying to hold their ground against repeated German tank and infantry attacks. At 2:06 p.m. (roughly a half hour prior to the 82nd and 101st Airborne's glider landings) American airplanes dropped 2,119 British paratroopers of Brigadier Hackett's 4th Parachute Brigade very accurately into DZ Y. British reports of this drop say that 'it was made in a shower of tracers', and that the American pilots dropped their troops 'slap in the right place'.

Right behind those paratroopers came 295 British airplanes towing Horsas loaded with the second echelon of the 1st Air Landing Brigade. Several were riddled by small arms fire as they were coming in on their final approach, but they all managed to land within the confines of LZs Y and Z.

With these reinforcements, the British tried to break through to help Frost at the bridge and to occupy the high ground north of

Arnhem. Both attempts failed. Gradually, the outnumbered and outgunned British were forced to withdraw into a tight perimeter around their initial landing areas. There, under constant attack from all quarters, they awaited help from the Polish Parachute Brigade, due to drop in on the following day.

D plus 1 closed on a sour note for the Allied side when a report came into the 82nd Airborne's message centre from Arnhem. The message had been transmitted by Dutch agents who still had use of restricted telephone lines. It was brief and to the point. The paratrooper clerk who received the message recorded it in his log this way: Dutch report Germans winning over British in Arnhem.

Later this same night, Flight Officer DiPietro, the glider pilot who had been forced to ditch in the North Sea and who waited in vain for a rescue dinghy to be dropped by his tow-plane, returned to his departure airbase in England. There he was greeted with surprise by several friends, all of whom had been told that he was dead. As DiPietro listened with fascination, his friends related that when his tow-plane returned from the mission earlier in the day its pilot reported that DiPietro's glider had hit the water nose-first and that there were no survivors. The pilot had been so sure there were no survivors that he decided against dropping the dinghy. After that mission the pilot strenuously avoided all personal contact with DiPietro. Whenever the two men had a chance meeting, he would always give DiPietro a sheepish smile and hurry past him without saying a word.

On D plus 2, September 19, the already bad weather in England got worse. Thick ground fog and heavy low-lying clouds forced General Brereton to order the cancellation of that day's Polish paratroop drop, so badly needed by the British, and the glider reinforcement mission of the 82nd Airborne's 325th Glider Infantry Regiment. However, he did give the okay for the 53rd Wing and the 442nd Troop Carrier Group to attempt a launch of their 385-glider mission containing the 101st Airborne's artillery units. Take-off time was set for 11:30 a.m.

Over in Holland, the weather was excellent. Earlier that morning, British tanks there broke through to the 101st Airborne's area. By 8:30 a.m. they had burst across the 10 miles of hostile territory north of Veghel and contacted General Gavin's understrength 82nd Airborne. This was the sort of dash that Montgomery had been dreaming of. However, this was as far north as the tanks would be

[261]

going for a while. The bridge over the Waal River in the 82nd Airborne's area was still in German hands.

Gavin knew he was working against the clock. With the British armoured column, which was already behind schedule, now sitting in his lap, he launched a combined British tank–American paratrooper attack against the bridge. When that attack failed to dislodge the Germans, Gavin drew up a daring plan to outflank them with a river crossing, to be made in the morning in borrowed British engineer boats.

Gavin was still finalizing his river crossing plan that day when gliders bringing reinforcements to the 101st Airborne arrived over Belgium after crossing by the southern route from England. When its leading combinations began taking off at 11:30 a.m., this ill-fated mission contained 385 Wacos arranged in 10 separately timed serials. On board were 2,310 troops of the division's 81st Anti-tank Battalion of the 327th and 907th Field Artillery battalions, and the 3rd Battalion of the 327th Glider Infantry. Also on board were 136 jeeps, 68 howitzers, 77 trailers of ammunition, and over 500 cans of gasoline.

The weather at take-off time had been horrible. Flight Officer Douglas E. Smith of the 436th Group jokingly recalls that 'the fog was so thick that the fireflies had to lead the crows around on the ground.' In its official history of this mission, the U.S. Air Force describes the weather as being 'barely passable with visibility poor and clouds closing in at about 1,200 feet. Beyond Hatfield conditions deteriorated rapidly, and before reaching the coast the serials ran into deep, dense clouds in which visibility was zero. Glider pilots unable to see their tugs had to guide their craft by the tilt of the tow-rope and by telephone conversation with the plane crew.'[9]

Many tow-planes managed to get below the clouds covering the Channel by dropping down to 100 feet above the water. But even then visibility was only half a mile. No fewer than 17 gliders were forced to ditch in the Channel. Over Belgium, 31 more broke loose or were released by their tugs, all presumably as a result of the extremely poor flying conditions. Confused by the dense clouds and ground mist, many tow-planes entered Holland west of the Allied-controlled road leading up to LZ W. There they were met by murderous blasts of German flak, machine gun and small arms fire. While running that gauntlet of enemy fire a total of 17 tow-planes burst into flames and crashed before their crews could parachute to safety. Five others had to be scrapped after making emergency landings in Belgium. An additional 170 tow-planes returned to England with extensive damage.

About half of the tug pilots whose planes were shot down managed to release their gliders on or close to LZ W. Several other gliders were shot loose, broke loose, or were prematurely released. One squadron in the next-to-last serial released 15 gliders by mistake nearly 10 miles west of LZ W. Another 26 Wacos disappeared without a trace somewhere over hostile territory inside Holland.

Unlike his two older brothers, both of whom had already been wounded while serving with other U.S. Army units fighting in Europe, Flight Officer George F. Brennan had not suffered so much as a scratch during his previous combat missions. On board Brennan's glider today were Sergeant Brasil Thompson – his acting copilot – and Privates John Anthony and Carmello Guglimino. Lashed down in the cargo compartment were a jeep, 20 rounds of artillery ammunition and five cans of gasoline. While crossing the Channel, Brennan's tug pilot, Lieutenant Trellis, dropped down to an altitude of only 15 feet above the water to see where he was going. At that altitude, Brennan saw several gliders that had earlier been forced to ditch, all of them with stranded survivors standing on their wings, waving for help. But there was no turning back to offer assistance. Everyone on this mission, including those men who were waving for help, knew that they would have to wait patiently for a rescue launch to save crews with the misfortune to become separated from their tug-ships.

Even at this low altitude, Brennan occasionally lost sight of his tug in patches of thick sea mist. Finally they made landfall and the tow-ship had to pull out to avoid ramming some buildings along the shoreline. The tug kept climbing until it reached 300 feet, where it levelled off and headed into Holland. At this point, Brennan noticed that the sky had cleared and his visibility was greatly improved. Unfortunately the first thing he saw in the wide-open sky was a black plume of smoke trailing from his tug's left engine. The Germans had just scored their first hit.

Brennan's problems began to multiply when his glider became the target of several German gunners. With loud snapping and ripping noises, numerous enemy bullets passed through the glider. Brennan was staring at his stricken tow-ship, hoping it could at least get him to the LZ area, when a 20 mm flak shell ripped through the floor, pierced his left foot, and exploded after it tore through the roof of his glider. Seconds later, another round came up through the floor. This one hit Brennan in his left hand, splitting it in two back to the heel of the palm. Still attached to his tug, Brennan asked his passengers if any of them had been hit. The two soldiers were uninjured but the acting copilot, Sergeant Thompson, reported that he had been hit by a bullet that passed completely through his thigh and into his scrotum. Fearing that he himself would soon pass out from loss of blood, Brennan yelled at Thompson to get his feet on the rudder pedals and his hands on the wheel. Then he looked down at his own injured foot for the first time and nearly vomited. One side of it was sticking out at a right angle to the rest of it.

Brennan's still-smoking tug was roaring on toward the LZ when another flak shell exploded near his glider. Fragments from it struck him in his left elbow, thigh, chest and buttocks. Copilot Thompson, now white with fear and loss of blood, asked Brennan if he would be able to hang on long enough to land the glider. Brennan nodded in the affirmative, thinking that the LZ would appear at any second. At this point a strong odour of gasoline became noticeable in the glider. An enemy bullet had ruptured a gas line in the jeep and gasoline was slowly mixing with the puddles of blood beneath Brennan's feet.

With a loud thump, the gasoline ignited as a tracer bullet tore through the floor, causing the canvas sides of the glider to billow outward. The force of the blast blew out most of the fire, but Brennan's face was singed and Thompson's trouser legs were in flames. Letting go of the wheel, Thompson beat the fire out with his hands.

Finally, the landing zone appeared ahead. Brennan hit the release knob and took over the controls, quickly putting the glider into a 180 degree left-hand turn. He was just about in level flight when another flak shell exploded near his glider. A fragment from it tore through the left side of his lower jaw and came out just below his right ear. The force of that blow was so great that it knocked him over into copilot Thompson. Crawling back up into his seat, Brennan managed, with his one good hand and foot, to set the glider down safely in an open field.

Aided by Privates Guglimino and Anthony, Brennan and Thompson headed for a ditch along the side of the field they had just landed in. Just short of the ditch, Thompson suddenly stopped, lowered his trousers and inspected himself to see what, if anything, was missing. When Brennan asked him why he had stopped, Thompson said with a smile, 'I just want to see if all this hurrying is worthwhile.' Once in the ditch, the two uninjured soldiers bandaged up Brennan and Thompson. Then, on orders from Brennan, they took off on foot toward Zon, several miles to the east.

A short while later, 12 German soldiers appeared and began looting Brennan's glider. They were talking so loudly among themselves that they could not hear Brennan and Thompson, only 50 yards away in the ditch, loading their submachine guns. The Germans never knew what hit them. In one long, continuous and sweeping blast, Brennan and Thompson emptied their entire magazines, killing all of the enemy soldiers. Knowing that their shots would attract more Germans, Brennan and Thompson hobbled away from the area and hid in a farmer's barn about a mile away from the glider. Totally exhausted by their harrowing experiences, and weakened by loss of blood, the two men flopped down on a pile of straw where they began to shiver violently. From their considerable first aid training, they knew that their bodies were entering an advanced state of shock. But because they were too weak to help themselves and unable to travel lest they be caught by enemy troops in the neighbourhood, they decided to remain where they had fallen. Shortly thereafter they both drifted into unconsciousness.

Elsewhere, Flight Officer George E. Buckley, along with the rest of his entire 74th Squadron, was towed straight into a heavy fog bank while crossing the Channel. But when he emerged on the other side of the fog, Buckley saw that his glider and tug-ship, piloted by Captain Theron Miller, were completely alone in the clear sky. After crossing the coast of Belgium, they circled over an area held by British troops, hoping that other tow-planes and gliders would join them so that they would not have to continue on alone. When no others arrived, they headed into Holland by themselves. Realizing that this was the last leg of his flight, Buckley asked himself what sort of a reception the Germans would provide for one lone tug and its glider. The answer was not long in coming.

Buckley's tug was hit by what appeared to be 20 mm cannon shells coming from a mobile flak wagon that he could see in a wooded area off to his left. The shells were ripping into the left side of the tug and exiting through the top right side, near the copilot's seat. The enemy fire was so intense that small pieces of the C-47 and spent fragments of flak were bouncing off the front of Buckley's glider. Even though his airplane was being riddled, Captain Miller never wavered or

[265]

wasted precious seconds with evasive action. Soon the firing stopped, and LZ W appeared dead ahead. Buckley cut away and quickly voiced a prayer that Miller and his crew would be able to re-run the gauntlet of German flak and make it back to England safely. After making a 360-degree turn to get the lay of the land, Buckley landed his glider in a potato patch, where its nose dug up a great mound of dirt before coming to a halt. It took 15 minutes of digging to get the glider's nose raised so that the jeep in the cargo compartment could be driven out.

Only five months before taking part in this mission to Holland, Flight Officer Lawrence W. Kubale had received the sad news that his older brother, Edward, had been killed while flying a B-24 bomber on a raid over Germany. Now the younger Lawrence, while on final to LZ W, was thrown right out of his seat by an exploding flak shell. Regaining consciousness a few moments later, he was unable to see; blood was pouring into his eyes from numerous lacerations on his forehead. Kubale assumed that his glider must still be flying. Wiping the blood away, he saw his inexperienced soldier copilot efficiently keeping the glider in level flight 'just like an old pro'. Although his vision was impaired, Kubale crawled back into his seat and gripped the wheel. It was then that he discovered that both his arms were also bleeding profusely.

'Don't worry,' Kubale yelled to his terrified copilot, 'I'll be able to get us down all in one piece.' Just then the LZ appeared and he cut loose from the tug. True to his word, Kubale set the glider down without causing injury to his passengers or cargo. Then he collapsed at the wheel. Paratrooper medics on the scene were able to prevent him from bleeding to death.

The increasingly dense layers of fog converging on the Channel caused General Brereton to order the recall of the whole last serial of the 101st Airborne after it had taken off. In that serial were gliders piloted by Lieutenant Asolph Riscky and Flight Officer Kenneth Hinkel. Each of their gliders was carrying three soldiers and a jeep. On the night before this mission, Riscky and Hinkel, both of whom had survived severe crash landings in Normandy and in southern France, tried to ease their nerves with a little Scotch whisky. But while they were drinking the two pilots started quarrelling, and a fist fight erupted. Friends broke up the scuffle when a submachine gun got into the act. In a rare moment of intense anger, the two pilots swore as they were being dragged apart that they would kill each other. The night ended with their friends seeing to it that they were kept in seperate rooms and their personal weapons under lock and key.

At Membury, where the returning gliders were to land, the ceiling had lifted to 700 feet but visibility was still poor. By the time the fifth glider-tug combination reached the release point, two gliders had accidentally collided while in free flight and could be seen burning in the landing area. In a bizarre twist of fate, Riscky and Hinkel had just killed each other and all of their passengers.

At the conclusion of the 101st Airborne's D plus 2 glider mission, only 1,341 of the 2,310 troops that had been dispatched from England could be rounded up on the LZ in Holland. Thanks to the spaciousness of LZ W, only 11 of those troops had been killed in glider crashes, and 11 others injured. The remainder had been returned to England, were afloat in the Channel awaiting rescue, or had landed somewhere well short of the zone. Only 40 out of the 68 howitzers reached the LZ. They proved their worth almost immediately, going into action and blunting a German tank attack force that was attempting to cut Hell's Highway.

Later that night, several members of the Dutch underground entered the barn where Flight Officer Brennan and Sergeant Thompson were lying unconscious. After concealing the two wounded Americans in a secret compartment of a farm wagon brimming with cow manure, the Dutch fighters delivered them to the Saint Lidwinia Maternity Hospital in the German-occupied city of Schijndel. This hospital was a unique establishment. It was in fact a genuine maternity hospital with a full staff of obstetricians and a large complement of Catholic nuns serving as nurses. It also had long been the headquarters of the local Dutch underground and a stopover point for downed Allied bomber pilots being smuggled back into friendly hands. But the hospital's entire ground floor was serving as the headquarters of a German infantry regiment.

Working well into the night, a team of Dutch surgeons closed Brennan's many wounds and patched up Thompson as best they could. Because Thompson was now conscious and ambulatory, they hid him in a locked storeroom where staff could look in on him without raising the suspicions of the German officers who frequently passed through the corridors. Brennan, meanwhile, was moved to a ward filled with pregnant women. There he was cleverly made up to look like an expectant farm wife who had been injured during the fighting going on all around the hospital. Pillows were used to build up his stomach to give him the appearance of imminent delivery, and several extra yards of gauze were wrapped around his head wounds to conceal his face. Thus disguised, Brennan remained a patient in the hospital until it was liberated nearly two months later by British infantrymen.

For the British glider and parachute troops who were still surrounded on their landing fields at the end of the airborne carpet, D plus 2 had been a day of utter disaster. All attempts to break out and attack through the streets of Arnhem to reinforce Frost's still-isolated unit at the bridge had ended in failure and very heavy casualties. Perhaps even worse than these reverses on the battleground in Holland was the fact that the 114 American airplanes that were to deliver the majority of the Polish Parachute Brigade reinforcements were still grounded by an impenetrable overcast at their airfields in England. Had the Poles arrived that morning in Holland as planned, they very possibly could have saved the Arnhem bridge, or they might have been able to evacuate what was left of Frost's battalion, which had got badly mauled that afternoon by German tanks that had begun a systematic destruction of his positions at the bridge.

The weather in England on D plus 3, September 20, brought more gloom and disgust for the Allied brass there. They had all been counting on three consecutive days of good weather to achieve success in Operation Market-Garden. But once again thick ground fog and overcast skies were to curtail their urgent glider reinforcement and parachute resupply delivery missions.

At his 1st Allied Airborne Army Headquarters, General Brereton stood looking out the window, slowly shaking his head. The general was very angry. He could not even see the flag pole 50 feet away. When at noontime he was handed a weather forecast promising continued ground fog, the usually unflappable Brereton snatched his hat off his desk and threw it across the room at the big wall map of England. Then he summoned his operations officer and ordered another 24-hour postponement of the crucial Polish paratroop drop and the glider delivery of the 82nd Airborne's 325th Glider Infantry Regiment.

Again, Holland was enjoying good weather. Throughout most of the day the 101st Airborne continued to deal effectively with moderate German activity along Hell's Highway. General Gavin and his

82nd Airborne, however, 'experienced the most difficult, and most successful, day in the division's combat history.'[10] The first major counterattack against the Allied corridor came at 11:00 a.m., by the German 6th Airborne Division[11] fighting as infantry and supported by tanks. The German plan was to rush out of the Reichswald Forest, roll over the Americans, and seize the Groesbeek Heights. Advancing behind heavy barrages from their artillery and mortars, the Germans penetrated 1,000 yards before being stopped short of the heights by the 505th and 508th Parachute Infantry regiments. In bitter fighting which raged into the night, the Germans were forced to withdraw back into the Reichswald. The situation became so critical that some 300 American glider pilots, who had been helping the 82nd Airborne to guard prisoners and command posts, were hastily thrown into the front lines that night on order of General Gavin. The actual piece of terrain that the pilots were assigned to defend lay between Companies A and B of the 505th Parachute Infantry Regiment, both of which were positioned beside the hamlet of Mook and facing the Reichswald Forest. Company C of the 505th, meanwhile, was shifted to the battalion reserve position, behind the pilots. This commitment of glider pilots marked the first time in American military history that an organized unit comprised entirely of flying officers served in the front lines as a combat infantry company. Though they did not know it when they were fed into the front lines, the pilots would remain there for the next three days and nights.

Earlier in the afternoon, while the Germans were still trying to seize the Groesbeek Heights, the 82nd Airborne's 504th Parachute Infantry Regiment began a daring and spectacular crossing of the Waal River in 26 small boats. Never having made a river crossing before, the paratroopers experienced great difficulty getting their flimsy canvas boats across the 400-yard-river, all the while under intense German fire from the far shore. Only 11 of the boats in the first wave returned to make the second trip. Not much more than a battalion of paratroopers got across, but they managed to attack and seize the north end of the vital highway bridge spanning the river.

Now that the Nijmegen bridge was in Allied hands, the American paratroopers expected to see long columns of British tanks racing across it for the final dash up to Arnhem, only 11 miles to the north. But the great herds of tanks did not materialize. The British were holding up the armoured thrust until their infantry units arrived to

[269]

provide the tanks with some form of flank protection. Darkness fell with no tanks in sight. At this point a wave of bitterness swept through the ranks of the 82nd Airborne's paratroopers who had made the desperate river crossing that day.

It was on the same day, September 20, that things became critical for the British airborne troops. Colonel Frost's gallant battalion, still clinging to the northern end of the Arnhem bridge, was down to a few bullets per trooper and physically exhausted from three continuous days and nights of close infantry combat. Two miles west of Frost's position, on the edge of Oosterbeek, the remainder of General Urquhart's 1st Airborne had been compressed into a perimeter measuring a half-mile wide and mile-and-a-half deep, where it was subjected to a rain of German artillery and mortar shells. But although his casualties were mounting and ammunition was running low, Urquhart still held out hope for a victory.

The desperate situation worsened for Frost's lone battalion at the bridge when German tanks began a steady drumbeat of point-blank fire into houses occupied by his troops. German infantry, meanwhile, closed in on his positions with automatic weapons and flame throwers.

Frost himself by this time had been severely wounded, and with conditions growing more hopeless by the minute and the battalion HQ burning fiercely, an arrangement was made with the Germans to evacuate the wounded from the blazing building. When this was completed, a few of Frost's surviving troopers set out to work their way back to the main division strongpoint near Oosterbeek. However, only a few succeeded. Frost, along with the other wounded members of his battalion, was taken prisoner that same day.

At the end of D plus 3, the Allied commanders believed success was still within their reach, provided their tanks could dash forward from the captured Nijmegen bridge and reach the British airborne troops at Arnhem the next day. But what they did not know was that Frost's battalion had already ceased to exist, and that the narrow road leading from Nijmegen up to Arnhem was heavily defended by German anti-tank guns.

Though the weather in England was again terrible on D plus 4, September 21, General Brereton gave permission for General Sosabowski and his Polish Parachute Brigade to be flown over to Holland. This decision was not entirely to Brereton's liking, but he knew that the desperate need of Urquhart's 1st Airborne Division for immediate help outweighed all risks associated with the mission. Sosabowski's brigade had the mission of seizing the southern terminus of the Heveadorp ferry near Driel. Once that had been done, the Poles were to cross over the river and reinforce Urquhart's beleaguered division in its small perimeter near Oosterbeek.

To the bitter disappointment of all the top Allied generals, this chancy and vitally important mission miscarried in Holland. Plagued by extremely poor flying conditions, many of the American airplanes carrying the Poles were forced to turn back while still over the Channel. Only 53 of the 110 planes managed to navigate their way through the cloud masses to Holland. There, at 6:00 p.m., they accurately dropped 753 paratroopers at Driel. General Sosabowski rapidly assembled his men and raced to the ferry site only to discover that the Germans were in control of the far shore and had sunk the ferry boat. Later that night 50 Polish paratroopers managed to get themselves, and a supply of ammunition, across the river. It was indeed a heroic action, but it was too little and too late.

The British tanks finally linked up with the Poles at Driel on D plus 5, September 22. However, with German troops in complete control of the Arnhem bridge now, there was no way for them to assist the airborne troops on the far shore. Across the river in Oosterbeek, meanwhile, General Urquhart and his stubborn defending troops continued to fight with bulldog tenacity in the belief that help would reach them at any minute.

The terrible weather conditions that had been plaguing the Allied side for so long finally took a turn for the better on D plus 6, September 23. In England, the day dawned bright and clear. Holland and Belgium, however, were reporting some early light rain and showers and ground fog. But late in the morning a cold front swept across the Low Countries, leaving behind clear skies and brisk, westerly winds. The path between England and Holland was now wide open at long last. On receiving this good news, General Brereton gave orders for the launching of the great array of gliders which had been standing marshalled on airfields of the 50th and 52nd Wings in the Midlands since September 19.

The mission alerted for departure consisted of 406 Wacos loaded with 3,385 troops, 104 jeeps, 25 howitzers and 59 trailerloads of ammunition. The bulk of these troops were from the 82nd Airborne's 325th Glider Infantry Regiment. However, 84 of the gliders were loaded with 395 artillerymen, plus some howitzers and ammo belonging to the 101st Airborne Division. All of those 101st troopers had been forced to turn back during previous attempts to reach Holland.

Plans called for this entire mission to fly the southern route. Those gliders going to the 101st Airborne were to drop out of the skytrain as it passed over LZ W. The remainder would continue on up the carpet and cut loose to land on LZ O in the 82nd Airborne's area. LZ O was an oval-shaped area measuring two miles across and three-and-one-half miles long lying northwest of Overasselt. It was into this general vicinity that the 504th Parachute Infantry had jumped on D-Day. By this time, all of LZ O was in friendly hands and out of range of German guns.

The lead tug-glider combination took off from England at 12:10 p.m. As usual when large numbers of gliders were involved, the launching and assembly of the skytrain was a tedious business and took nearly an hour to complete. Great blasts of prop-wash being generated by the tugs caused seven Wacos to break loose; they landed safely near their airfields. During this mission the intercom sets worked better than in past missions, but over 20 per cent of them still failed or functioned poorly. For most of the trip visibility was over five miles and cloud bases above 2,500 feet, though the column did pass through rain squalls at some points. For most pilots the flight across the Channel and Belgium went smoothly. Only one glider was forced to ditch in the Channel and one other dropped out over Belgium. Both were reached by friendly forces within minutes of touching down.

For some unexplained reason, the leading serial crossed the Dutch frontier outside of the Allied salient, and as a result was raked by German small arms fire west of Eindhoven. Five badly damaged gliders were released in that area. The skytrain pressed on and, on reaching the 101st Airborne's area in the middle of the carpet, released its Wacos as planned. With the exception of two gliders that made disastrous crash landings, all of the 101st Airborne's passengers safely reached the ground. There they were met by well-organized paratroop reception teams who assisted in the unloading of supplies and equipment.

As it continued up the carpet, the skytrain ran into serious trouble near Veghel, where there were large concentrations of German troops who had just been beaten back from an attempt to cut the highway. Quickly turning their guns skyward, the Germans managed to down nine tugs and damage 96 others. The first serial was especially hard hit. Two of the leading tugs were forced to cut their gliders loose, setting off a succession of premature releases from half its formation. The upshot was that 21 gliders in this serial landed between Veghel and Grave, well short of the 82nd Airborne's LZ O. The only good thing about this mishap was that all but four of those gliders landed close to the highway in friendly territory or so near to it that courageous Dutch civilians were able to rescue them from the Germans.

A similar incident occurred in the fourth serial when a squadron leader, whose airplane was about to crash, released the glider near Veghel. His trailing tug pilots faithfully followed his example, with the result that 16 Wacos in that formation came down six miles north of Veghel. Six of those gliders landed in hostile territory, and all aboard were either killed or captured.

At his pre-flight briefing earlier that morning, Flight Officer Theodore V. Sampson had been instructed that if the weather suddenly closed in while the skytrain was crossing the Channel, his tow-ship would return to England and release his glider over the first airfield it came to. If the skytrain made it to Belgium, said the briefing officer, but could not continue on to the objective, the emergency plan was for him to be released near Brussels. On board Sampson's glider were five medics and a jeep; the major in command of the medics was sitting in the copilot's seat.

Approaching Veghel, Sampson noticed that all the gliders in front of him were cutting loose from their tugs. Because his intercom phone was not working, he assumed that some change had been made in the original landing plan and that he should follow the example of the gliders ahead of him. The major agreed, so Sampson reached up and punched the release mechanism. Just after he made the cut, Sampson's glider was hit by a blast of machine gun bullets, some of which pierced the spare can of gasoline on the back of the jeep and started a fire. With only two or three minutes remaining until touchdown, Sampson forgot about the fire and concentrated on making a good landing.

When his blazing glider stopped rolling, Sampson saw a German 88 mm flak gun positioned only 75 yards to his left front. The sight of that big gun and the heat of the flames engulfing the glider, caused Sampson and his passengers to leap out on the ground and seek cover under the right wing. German bullets were cracking through the

[273]

glider when Sampson drew his pistol and started to return fire. Seeing his pistol, the major with him said, 'Put that damn thing away . . . we're supposed to be medics, not combat infantrymen!' Sampson obeyed, and soon the enemy firing stopped. Using the still-burning glider as a screen, the handful of Americans quickly crawled away from the scene to begin a harrowing journey that ended two days later with their safe return to the American front lines.

The remaining gliders in this mission began arriving over LZ O at 4:03 p.m. Three-quarters of them descended in formation after release somewhere between 800 and 1,200 feet, and took a 90 or 180 degree turn to the left (depending on their angle of approach) so that they would land into the wind. A minority of stragglers and nonconformists followed widely divergent patterns, turning to the right when the rest went left, or pulling away from their serial to avoid crowded fields. Most of the glider pilots landed at speeds between 55 and 75 miles per hour, frequently using arrester parachutes to great advantage.

Only eight gliders were destroyed, almost all by running into ditches and wooden fences after touching down. Another 102 received damage ranging from broken nose compartments and wings to smashed undercarriages. Of the over 2,900 troops that had landed, all but 10 were fit for duty. Not one glider pilot or passenger had been killed.

By 6:00 p.m. some 75 per cent of the 325th Glider Infantry Regiment, which was now commanded by Colonel Charles Billingslea, was assembled and marched to a defensive sector near the Groesbeek Heights. Most of the missing personnel from the gliders that had landed in error far short of the LZ O reported in during the next two days.

This final glider mission to Holland was a most welcome reinforcement. But the time when it could have any significant effect on the outcome of the battle was already long since past.

On Sunday, September 24, seven days after the start of Operation Market-Garden, all glider pilots that had been serving with the 82nd Airborne Division in the Nijmegen area were given permission to return to England as best they could. Shortly after noon that day the first contingent of 100 pilots was placed on 26 empty ammunition trucks heading back down the carpet to Belgium. The pilots were instructed that when they reached Belgium they were to thumb their way to the Brussels airport and hop rides on supply airplanes returning to England. From whatever airfield they landed on in England they were to hitch-hike to their respective home bases. The majority of pilots departing on this convoy bound for Belgium were from the four squadrons (29th, 47th, 48th and 49th) of the 313th Troop Carrier Group that had landed on D-Day.

Seated alongside the driver of the lead truck in the convoy was Captain Elgin D. Andross, Group Glider Officer of the 313th, who had been placed in command of the convoy and charged with the responsibility of seeing that all 100 of the pilots returned to England. Before becoming a glider pilot, Andross had served in the infantry, where he had developed a great respect for the firepower of Thompson submachine guns and the destructive capablilities of hand grenades. Knowing that both of those items were excellent tools for close combat, Andross had seen to it that all glider pilots in the 313th Group took a Thompson sub and six grenades to Holland. Before leaving the 82nd Airborne, Andross had all pilots in the convoy grab a fresh supply of ammo and grenades.

Everything went well for the convoy until it reached a point four miles south of Veghel in the 101st Airborne's airhead. There it was ambushed by elements of the 6th German Parachute Regiment which had been trying for the past several days to cut the highway. Commanded by Colonel Friedrich-August von der Heydte, a veteran of the Crete and Normandy campaigns, this regiment was one of the toughest and most combat-experienced units in the German armed forces.

As soon as they came under fire, the American truck drivers jammed on their brakes and fled into the roadside ditches. Seconds later they were joined by the glider pilots, most of whom had been dozing in the backs of the trucks. From the heavy volume of fire, Captain Andross became convinced that this encounter would end in either death or capture of all the Americans in the convoy unless they took some decisive counteraction. Without regard for his own safety, Andross ran out onto the highway in view of the Germans and began hollering at the pilots to return fire. When a sufficient volume of counterfire had been built up, Andross dashed back to the last truck in the convoy. There he directed one of the glider pilots crouching nearby to get in, put it in reverse, and back it down the highway out of range of the enemy guns. Throughout the next half hour, Andross continued up and down the column until 17 trucks and the bulk of the pilots were safely extricated from the killing zone of the ambush.

[275]

During that period the German paratroopers tried several times to overrun the pilots but were repeatedly beaten back and suffered heavy casualties.

At one point during the skirmishing, Andross saw Lieutenant Max Becker, the Glider Officer of the 49th Squadron, stand up and start to yell something to him. Just then a German sniper shot Becker in the face. Because Becker's mouth was open when the bullet struck him from the side, it tore a small round hole through each of his cheeks without causing further injuries. Seeing Becker knocked off his feet, Andross ran over to him. When he got to his side, Becker seemed none the worse for his wounds, so Andross simply patted both of his bleeding cheeks and said, 'Boy, what a hell of a way to get dimples!'

With a last-minute assist for some 101st Airborne troops and a Sherman tank, Andross and his pilots were able to disengage themselves completely from the ambush site and return to the 82nd Airborne's area. During this action ten glider pilots were wounded, three were killed, and another three were captured. A subsequent examination of the ambush site by 101st Airborne troops revealed that over 100 German paratroopers had been slain during their encounter with the glider pilots. For his heroics during the ambush, Andross was recommended for the Distinguished Service Cross by his fellow pilots. An awards and decorations board in England, comprised of headquarters staff officers, knocked the recommendation down to a Silver Star Medal.

Captain Andross and his pilots were still fighting for their lives in the ambush when, elsewhere, Field Marshal Montgomery and General Brereton came to the unpleasant realization that General Urquhart's 1st Airborne was about to be crushed out of existence and that there was just no hope of getting across the river to rescue it. Urquhart was therefore ordered to save what remained of his division by withdrawing back across to the south shore. Urquhart did not actually receive the withdrawal orders at his headquarters in the candlelit cellar of the Hartenstein Hotel in Oosterbeek until 6:05 a.m. on the twenty-fifth.

The weather, which had played so important a part in the defeat of the British airborne troops, saved them in the end from annihilation. At 9:45 on the night of the twenty-fifth, in a howling wind and rainstorm, the division stealthily made its way to the river, leaving behind its wounded to man the defences. Small groups of troopers found their way to the river's edge by following the directions of glider pilots who had been posted as guides along the evacuation route. There they were met by engineer boats that ferried them to the south bank. All night long the boats went back and forth across the river while British artillery positioned on the south bank kept up a steady series of barrages to cover the noise of the evacuation. At dawn all but 300 of the survivors had been evacuated. Many of those left behind managed to hide and later escape aboard homemade rafts provided by Dutch civilians.

When the evacuation was complete, General Urquhart took a head count of his division and the glider pilots who had fought with it on the far shore. The result of the tally was appalling. Of the 10,095 British paratroopers and glider pilots that had been sent in on this mission, no fewer than 7,212 were listed as killed, wounded or missing in action. Glider pilot casualties alone had amounted to 147 killed and 469 wounded or captured. Up to this point in the battle, the American casualties wer listed at 1,432 for the 82nd Airborne and 2,110 for the 101st Airborne.

Though they had suffered a severe beating in Holland, the British airborne troops and glider pilots returned to England with their heads held high. They had been sent to Holland with the mission of seizing a bridgehead at Arnhem and holding it for only two days until link-up by British tank columns. Against immensely superior German forces, they had accomplished their mission and held out for nine days, waiting for the help that never came. With their epic stand in Holland, the British airborne forces had added considerable battle honours to England's traditional 'thin red line' and provided a sterling example of courage that would inspire the Allied world in the many desperate battles that lay ahead.

That is how Operation Market-Garden, though close to being successful, ended in failure for the Allied side. Field Marshal Montgomery, pointing to the fact that most of southern Holland and over one and a half million of its citizens had been liberated, asserted that the operation had been 90 per cent successful, but the awful truth of the matter is that all objectives except the key bridge at the end of the airborne carpet had been won, and without that final bridge the rest were nothing. In return for so much courage, blood and sacrifice the Allies had won a 50-mile salient – leading nowhere. For the Allies, Normandy remained their greatest airborne victory, and Market their bitter airborne defeat.

Despite the complexity and vastness of the operation, there has been a remarkably high degree of agreement among Allied generals and historians on why Market-Garden did not succeed.

The primary reason was the extraordinary revival of German combat capacity generated by Field Marshal Model. Had the Allies' opponent been somewhat less experienced than Model, things might have ended differently. A second factor making for a German victory was the failure of the Allied intelligence analysts to give sufficient credence to accurate reports by Dutch underground agents about the presence of enemy tanks in and around Arnhem.

A third factor, the one which enabled the Germans to use those tanks to defeat the British at the Arnhem bridge and landing zones, was General Urquhart's error in plotting his parachute and glider zones between five and eight miles from his objectives. That decision was in conflict with all airborne doctrine, and Urquhart later admitted that it had been an unnecessary and fatal mistake. Next in order – though foremost, in Montgomery's opinion – was the bad weather which delayed the Poles' arrival from D plus 2 to D plus 4, and that of the 82nd Airborne's 325th Glider Infantry Regiment from D plus 2 to D plus 6. Montgomery believed, quite correctly, that if those two units had arrived on schedule, the Poles could have broken through to Frost's troops at the Arnhem bridge, and the 325th Glider Infantry might have provided the extra strength required to take the Nijmegen bridge and fight on through to Arnhem. Such an achievement by those two units could conceivably have resulted in an Allied victory.

But the real culprit was not Field Marshal Model, the weather, or faulty selection of landing zones. It was the master plan of the operation. The Allies had intended to make a great tank attack on the narrowest front ever attempted by a large army: a single road, both flanks of which contained soft soil on which it was impossible for the tanks to manoeuvre. The allies also planned to distribute the delivery of their airborne troops over a three-day period. That piecemeal delivery not only put the Allies at the mercy of the weather, but also forced the airborne divisions to waste too much of their strength guarding drop and landing zones for further missions that were constantly delayed. Either one of these factors could have led to an Allied defeat. Together they produced a disaster.

Although they were quick to give credit to the glider pilots as pilots, and to many as individual ground fighters in Holland, neither the 82nd nor the 101st Airborne division had any genuine praise for the pilots performing in ground tactical units.

General Gavin, commander of the 82nd Airborne, took time while still in Holland to send a lengthy personal letter to General Williams, commander of IX Troop Carrier Command, on the subject of air operations. In that letter, dated September 25, Gavin had this to say concerning the American glider pilots:

> In looking back over the past weeks' operations, one of the outstanding things, in my opinion, and one thing in most urgent need of correction, is the method of handling our glider pilots. I do not believe there is anyone in the combat area more eager and anxious to do the correct thing and yet so completely, individually and collectively, incapable of doing it, than glider pilots.
>
> Despite their individual willingness to help, I feel that they were definitely a liability to me. Many of them arrived without blankets, some without rations and water, and a few improperly armed and equipped. They lacked organization of their own because of, they stated, frequent transfer from one Troop Carrier Command unit to another. Despite the instructions that were issued to them to move via command channels to Division Headquarters, they frequently became involved in small unit actions to the extent that satisfied their passing curiosity, or simply left to visit nearby towns. In an airborne operation where, if properly planned, the first few hours are the quietest, this can be very harmful, since all units tend to lose control because of the many people wandering about aimlessly, improperly equipped, out of uniform, and without individual or unit responsibilities. When the enemy reaction builds up and his attack increases in violence and intensity, the necessity for every man to be on the job at the right place, doing his assigned task, is imperative. At this time glider pilots without unit assignment and improperly trained, aimlessly wandering about cause confusion and generally get in the way and have to be taken care of.
>
> In this division, glider pilots were used to control traffic, to recover supplies from LZs, guard prisoners, and finally were assigned a defensive role with one of the regiments at a time when they were badly needed.
>
> I feel very keenly that the glider pilot problem at the moment is one of our greatest unsolved problems. I believe now that they should be assigned to airborne units, take training with the units and have a certain number of hours allocated periodically for flight training. I am also convinced that our airborne unit copilots should have flight training so as to be capable of flying the glider if the pilot is hit.[12]

A conclusive answer to General Gavin's suggestion that glider pilots be assigned to the airborne divisions was rendered by General

Ridgway, commander of XVIII Airborne Corps Headquarters, on December 4, 1944. On that date, Ridgway ruled that since the primary duty of the glider pilots was to fly gliders, they belonged with the troop carrier units. And that, said Ridgway, was where they were going to remain.

The question of why the glider pilots did not, in the opinion of some senior commanders, perform better in Holland as a group should be examined in the context of the situation then existing. It had long been standard procedure to collect both British and American glider pilots at divisional command posts, use them for guard and supply duties, and evacuate them as soon as possible to fly additional missions. Instructions for Market stated that they were to be used at the front only as a last resort. An examination of after-action reports written by the troop carrier groups reveals that the equipment and briefing of the glider pilots for Market was, on the whole, unsatisfactory. Most of them were given no compasses; about half got no maps of their destinations, and few were informed of how and where the airborne divisions were to be deployed in the objective areas.

The pilots, once assembled, were indeed an unorganized mass because they had no staff present with them in Holland. The squadron and group staffs who ordinarily administered and commanded the glider pilots were back in England. The senior glider officer present in the 82nd Airborne's area, Major Hugh Nevins, did his best to exercise authority, but he had little to build on, as he had no formal command authority over pilots from all of the various squadrons that had flown in to Holland. To make matters worse, Nevins was from the 50th Wing, and most pilots in the Nijmegen-Groesbeek area with him were from the 52nd Wing, did not know him, and openly questioned his authority. (Even the most disciplined German and American infantry units frequently questioned orders from officers whom they did not know.)

Because of this lack of organization, and because the senior glider officers could not be everywhere at once, some pilots were sent out on unimportant ground missions by junior airborne officers who had no real authority to give such orders. This in turn gave observers the impression that the pilots were performing no useful function in the airhead. Furthermore, pilots in the airhead could easily get permission from someone, usually the ranking officer of his squadron, to set out for England in accordance with the long-standing policy of quick evacuation.

The fact remains, however, that over 90 per cent of the glider pilots did their utmost in a prolonged and difficult situation while serving faithfully on guard and supply gathering details, and even as front line infantry soldiers. While living in foxholes, under frequent shelling, soaked by repeated rains, and almost without food except for raw turnips and potatoes taken from the fields around them, they turned in a stellar performance in the unfamiliar role of a combat infantryman.

American glider pilots in Holland were operating under extreme handicaps imposed by their superiors which made them appear less disciplined and competent than they were. They did need more infantry training and a coherent ground organization of their own. But they also needed a more complete set of tools with which to fight and a more efficient assembly system. Had those vital needs been met, their performance undoubtedly would have satisfied even their harshest critics.

Reacting to pressure applied by General Hap Arnold, who had been greatly displeased with glider recovery operations in Normandy and in southern France, General Brereton undertook a vigorous effort to retrieve as many gliders as possible from Holland. Between September 25 and October 1, three repair teams of 150 glider mechanics each were flown to Holland to salvage the damaged American gliders that were scattered all over the liberated portions of that country. During these early operations the mechanics were frequently required to enter areas near the battle lines and often came under small arms fire. On three occasions they captured some German soldiers that were patrolling near their work sites.

The weather, a source of almost unending trouble during the glider missions, caused a severe setback to the recovery programme as well. On October 17, a storm blew across Holland, wrecking 115 gliders that had been completely repaired and readied for aerial snatch evacuation. By mid-December, when salvage operations ended, only 281 American gliders had been recovered. Rickety and badly weathered, they were all flown to airfields in France to await their next mission in Europe.

# Chapter 10

# *Battle of the Bulge*

UPON THEIR RETURN TO ENGLAND from combat in Holland, most of the American glider pilots were given a seven-day leave to relax and enjoy the pleasures of London and other English cities. Pilots not granted leave were kept busy as copilots of C-47 airplanes hauling supplies to units fighting in France and Holland.

Following its brief rest in England, the 50th Wing of the IX Troop Carrier Command was transferred late in September 1944 to several airfields southwest of Paris.[1] This move had been directed by General Brereton, commander of the 1st Allied Airborne Army. Brereton wanted at least part of his troop carrier force based on the Continent where it would be closer to the battle fronts and would not have to contend with the prevailing poor flying weather in England. Because so many of their Wacos had been lost in Holland, most of the glider pilots assigned to the 50th Wing had to make this trip to France as either passengers or copilots of C-47 airplanes. Within a week of their arrival on the Continent, however, the glider pilots began receiving new Wacos that were ferried across the Channel from the Cookham Common assembly facility. With the new gliders they began a series of training flights at their bases in mid-October.

The 82nd and 101st Airborne divisions were meanwhile kept under Field Marshal Montgomery's command in Holland to slug it out with German units that were trying to gain a foothold south of the Rhine area near Arnhem. After many requests by General Brereton for the return of his two American airborne divisions, Monty finally pulled the 82nd Airborne off the line on November 13, D plus 57. The last contingent of the 101st Airborne was not pulled off the line until November 27, D plus 71. Put aboard crowded trucks and trains, these two divisions were withdrawn to rest areas situated on opposite sides of the French cathedral city of Rheims.

In addition to being the site of General Eisenhower's SHAEF[2]

Headquarters, Rheims was also home base for Major General Ridgway's XVIII Airborne Corps Headquarters advance command post. Ridgway's rear CP was in England, where the newly arrived 17th Airborne Division was still undergoing training. Because of his split CP, Ridgway was required to spend much of his time in England working on secret airborne attack plans being formulated by the 1st Airborne Army. Operation Eclipse was one of the more intricate plans that Ridgway was labouring over. It was a massive glider and parachute operation the Allied High Command had anticipated carrying out in event that the collapse of Germany appeared imminent. Eclipse called for the seizure of Berlin by two American airborne divisions and one British airborne brigade. Another, even larger, plan Ridgway was just then considering called for one British and three American airborne divisions to make an assault landing in the vicinity of Kassel, Germany, in support of General Bradley's great thrust into the Ruhr industrial area.

Early in December 1944, Ridgway received instructions to send one of his airborne division commanders back to Washington to represent him in conferences regarding proposed changes in organization and equipment of American parachute and glider regiments. Ridgway chose General Taylor, commander of the 101st Airborne. On December 5, Taylor left France for the long trip home. With Taylor's departure, command of the 101st Airborne passed to his deputy, Brigadier General Gerald J. Higgins.

Taylor's return to the United States prompted a feeling among the airborne troops in France that no combat mission would come their way in the immediate future. This belief was strengthened considerably on December 10, when General Higgins, along with all of the 101st Airborne's regimental commanders, flew to England to present a series of lectures on their division's combat experiences in Holland. In Higgins' absence, command of the 101st Airborne passed to Brigadier General McAuliffe, the division artillery commander. Since General Ridgway was at his rear CP in England, command of the XVIII Airborne Corps rested with newly promoted Major General Gavin who was at the same time commanding the 82nd Airborne Division.

With nearly all of their top brass out of the country, the American airborne troops in France established a relaxed routine of light tactical training, an occasional practice glider ride or parachute jump, and plenty of passes to Paris. It was difficult for the men to put

[283]

their hearts into exercises; there was a widespread feeling that the Germans had been beaten and that it would only be a matter of time before they capitulated.

The 'beaten' Germans, however, were secretly assembling 29 combat divisions in the heavily forested Eifel region, 10 miles behind the Siegfried Line. There, concealed from Allied reconnaissance planes by trees and bad weather, the Germans made final preparations to strike out against the unsuspecting Allies in what would become known as the Battle of the Bulge.

The scheme for this enormous German counter-offensive had been spawned by Hitler himself. A quick thrust up to the port of Antwerp in Belgium, said Hitler, would cut off the British 21st Army Group from its main source of supply and isolate it from American units to its south. Once Antwerp had been taken, German combat units were to force the British to withdraw from the Continent as they had done at Dunkirk in 1940. Following his hoped-for quick victory over the British, Hitler planned to deliver a severe beating to other Allied ground troops remaining on the Continent. This accomplished, a small German force would be left on the Western Front to hold at bay what remained of the battered Allies, while the major German combat strength was transferred to the Eastern Front to confront the advancing Russians and snatch victory from the jaws of defeat.

Hitler personally selected Germany's most distinguished soldier, Field Marshal Gern Von Rundstedt, to lead the great counter-offensive. Von Rundstedt, then in his seventieth year, was serving as Commander-in-Chief West. Directly under him was Field Marshal Model, still serving as the commander of Army Group B. Both Von Rundstedt and Model considered Hitler's scheme far too ambitious. In private conferences with Hitler, the field marshals pointed out that Germany had neither the military strength nor the supplies necessary to carry out the battle plan. But even the convincing arguments of his two most trusted field commanders failed to deflect Hitler. 'The attack,' he said, 'will go as I have ordered.'

Hitler had chosen to launch his main thrust against the American troops occupying defensive positions along the Belgian and Luxembourg side of the Ardennes Forest. Perhaps he did this in the hope that history would repeat itself: it was along this same route in 1940 that his victorious armies had launched the dazzling blitzkrieg which resulted in the collapse of the Western Front in a matter of weeks.

[284]

The last thing the Allied side expected during this miserably cold winter of 1944 was a German counter-offensive. And the last place they expected action was in the forbidding, thickly wooded hills of the Ardennes. In keeping with the Allied view of the Ardennes as a trouble-free sector of his front, General Eisenhower had deliberately thinned out this area in order to have more troops available for offensive action elsewhere to the north and south. One by one, units were pulled out, and by December 16 Major General Troy H. Middleton's VIII Corps (consisting of the U.S. 28th, 99th and 106th Infantry divisions, plus the 14th Armoured Cavalry Regiment) was defending a front 85 miles wide – three times that prescribed by U.S. Army tactical doctrine for a defending force the size of Middleton's. It was through Middleton's depleted corps that the main German thrust was about to be made.

Two elements were essential for the success of Hitler's plan: quick seizure by German troops of Saint Vith and Bastogne, which were critical centres for road and rail traffic through the Ardennes Forest; and the rapid widening of the initial penetration through the American lines so that follow-up units could dash through for the quick kill.

At 5:30 a.m. on the morning of Thursday, December 16, Von Rundstedt opened his attack three hours before daylight with a thunderous barrage of artillery fire. Having achieved complete surprise, some 200,000 German troops comprising the veteran Sixth Panzer Army in the north, the Fifth Army in the centre, and the Seventh Army in the south, were hurled against an American front defended by 83,000 soldiers, many of whom had never been in combat. Under a curtain of ground fog, ploughing through mud and snow, the German panzer columns drove westward against light opposition. Overwhelmed by the crushing weight of the German onslaught, the American line buckled in the centre and then caved in. Von Rundstedt, sensing an early victory, poured his panzers through the 30-mile-wide gap, pushing the Americans to the west, north and south. Soon this massive rupture of the American line began to swell into an enormous bulge.

Because German artillery fire had knocked out most of the American communications systems at the battle front, realization of what was happening at Ardennes came very slowly to SHAEF Headquarters in France. At first General Patton, whose Third Army was then advancing against the Siegfried Line well to the south of the German

[285]

breakthough, thought the Germans were merely launching a limited spoiling attack to distract him from his goal. Eisenhower, too, did not know what to make of the sketchy reports coming from Belgium.

Early on the second day of the battle the magnitude of the German thrust became clear to the Allied side when Lieutenant General Hodges, whose shattered First Army had borne the full weight of the main German attack, appealed directly to Eisenhower for use of the Allied strategic reserve, which consisted of the depleted 82nd and 101st Airborne divisions. Although both divisions had come out of hard combat in Holland only three weeks before, Eisenhower approved Hodges's request. By eight o'clock in the evening of December 18, General Gavin had his 82nd Airborne Division deployed to the area of Werbomont, 28 miles due north of Bastogne, Belgium, along the northern shoulder of the German penetration. The 101st Airborne, meanwhile, had been dispatched to Bastogne.

As the 82nd and 101st Airborne divisions were being rushed to the front from France, Von Rundstedt's panzers were penetrating deeper into Belgium. Soon the vital crossroads at Saint Vith in the northern sector of the Germans' zone of attack was encircled. Bastogne was surrounded on the twentieth. Like two boulders in the path of a flash flood, Saint Vith and Bastogne, both of which were manned by vastly outnumbered American troops, forced the enemy attack to split, and in the process to grow weaker. The broad German thrust was now compressed into a sort of wedge, whose tip reached 30 miles into the Allied defensive zone in Belgium. Meanwhile, American infantry divisions defending along the shoulders of the mammoth breakthrough to the north and south of Saint Vith and Bastogne continued to hold against fierce attacks by the best troops Germany could throw against them.

On December 21, the American forces holding out at Saint Vith were overwhelmed by the German Sixth Panzer Army. This disastrous turn of events was precipitated by the wholesale surrender on December 19 by two complete regiments – 6,697 men in all – of the inexperienced 106th Infantry Division, which had been overseas for only one month and surrounded for only two days. The few American infantry and tank units that managed to survive the final battle to save Saint Vith retreated to the relative safety of new defensive positions then still being hastily constructed to their rear by the 30th Infantry and 82nd Airborne divisions.

The determination of the American forces digging in along the

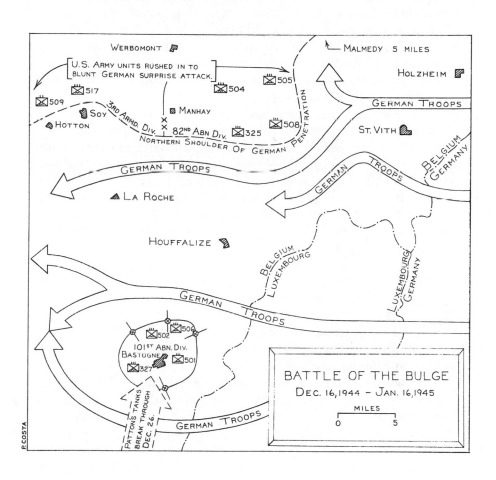

WERBOMONT

MALMEDY 5 MILES

HOLZHEIM

U.S. ARMY UNITS RUSHED IN TO
BLUNT GERMAN SURPRISE ATTACK.

505

504

517

509

GERMAN TROOPS

MANHAY

SOY

3RD ARMD. DIV.

82ND ABN. DIV.

325

508

ST. VITH

HOTTON

NORTHERN SHOULDER OF GERMAN PENETRATION

BELGIUM
GERMANY

GERMAN TROOPS

GERMAN TROOPS

LA ROCHE

HOUFFALIZE

BELGIUM
LUXEMBOURG

LUXEMBOURG
GERMANY

GERMAN TROOPS

502

506

101ST ABN. DIV.
BASTOGNE

501

327

BATTLE OF THE BULGE

DEC. 16,1944 - JAN. 16,1945

MILES

0          5

PATTON'S TANKS BREAK THROUGH DEC. 26.

GERMAN TROOPS

P.COSTA

[287]

northern shoulder of the widening bulge is illustrated by an incident that happened on December 22 near the small Belgian town of Manhay. A column of retreating tanks came upon a lone bazooka gunner who occupied a snow-covered bunker at a crossroads section. 'Hey, buddy,' asked the lead tank commander, 'where are the American lines?' Private First Class Thomas Martin of the 82nd Airborne's 325th Glider Infantry Regiment stood up and answered, 'You've just arrived at the American front lines, pal. Now you just pull your tank up behind me. I'm the 82nd Airborne Division, and this is as far as the bastards are going.'

Once Saint Vith had fallen, Bastogne became a lone island in a sea filled with freewheeling German panzer and infantry divisions. The extreme depth of the German penetration, which by now extended a frightening 60 miles into the Ardennes, caused considerable alarm among top Allied brass – except for General Patton, whose Third Army had been chasing the retreating Germans south of the breakthrough area. When Patton walked into General Bradley's headquarters in Luxembourg, he found a group of staff officers looking glumly at a map upon which was drawn the giant incursion by the Germans. As the officers turned to see who was entering, the outspoken Patton bellowed, 'What the hell is all the mourning about?' Walking over to his boss, General Bradley, who was standing in front of the map, Patton said, 'Brad, we've got him! We've wanted the German to come out in the open and now he's out there. He's got his head in a meat grinder.' With a grin on his face, Patton made a cranking motion with his fist, saying 'And I've got my hand on the handle!'[3]

Elsewhere inside the encircled town of Bastogne, General McAuliffe was commanding, in addition to his own 101st Airborne Division, an assortment of tank and artillery units from other divisions that had been driven back by the Germans during the past few days.[4] The non-airborne elements of McAuliffe's Bastogne command were nervous about being surrounded, but McAuliffe's glider and parachute troops, who were long accustomed to being behind enemy lines, were relatively calm about their plight. Of this dire tactical situation, the cocky airborne troopers would often say, 'The Germans have got us surrounded – the poor bastards!'

The German units surrounding Bastogne were part of the XLVII Panzer Corps commanded by 49-year-old General Heinrich von Luttwitz, a veteran of extensive combat in Russia. On the morning of December 22, von Luttwitz sent two of his staff officers under a flag of truce to the 101st Airborne. The German emissaries entered the American defensive perimeter through Company F of the 327th Glider Infantry Regiment and were met by a squad of glider troops who blindfolded them. The Germans were then led to the command post of the 2nd Battalion, 327th Glider Infantry where they told the battalion commander, Major Alvin Jones, that they wished to speak with the American commander of Bastogne. To their surprise, Jones denied their request and ordered them held under guard at his CP. Moments later, Jones left for the division CP, taking with him the surrender ultimatum which, it was later discovered, had been composed on a captured American typewriter.

When the message was delivered to General McAuliffe at the division CP, he asked Major Jones what it said. 'They want us to surrender,' Jones replied. At that, McAuliffe laughed and said, 'Aw nuts!' It actually seemed funny to him at the time. He felt he was giving the Germans 'one hell of a beating', and he knew his troops felt likewise. But he knew he must give the Germans some sort of a reply. He sat with pencil in hand for a few minutes but could think of nothing to say. 'I don't know what to tell them,' he remarked aloud. In frustration, he asked his staff what they felt he should write. Lieutenant Colonel Harry Kinnard, his G-3, replied, 'Well, sir, that first remark of yours would be hard to beat.'

McAuliffe didn't understand what Kinnard was referring to. Kinnard then reminded him, 'You said "Nuts" sir.' That drew a round of applause from the entire staff. With that McAuliffe scribbled on a piece of paper:

> *To the German Commander:*
> *Nuts!*

*The American Commander*

McAuliffe folded the paper containing his defiant response and handed it to Colonel Harper, commander of the 327th Glider Infantry Regiment. 'Will you see that this is delivered?'

Harper replied, 'It'll be a lot of fun.'

Reaching the area where the German messengers were being kept blindfolded and under guard, Harper said, 'I have the American commander's reply.' One of the German officers inquired, 'Is it written or verbal?'

[289]

'Written,' answered Harper.

A second question came from the German: 'Is the reply negative or affirmative? If the latter, I will negotiate further.'

Harper grew very angry. 'The reply is decidedly not affirmative,' he said. Then he added, 'If you continue this foolish attack your losses will be tremendous.' The German said nothing further at this point.

Harper escorted the German officers to his front lines, where he removed their blindfolds and said, 'If you don't know what "nuts" means, in plain English, it is the same as "go to hell." And I'll tell you something else – if you continue to attack we will kill every goddamn German that tries to break into the city.'

The Germans officers saluted Harper crisply, turned about, and walked back to their lines. Late that night the German Luftwaffe began a series of bombing attacks on Bastogne that lasted for the next four nights.

On the day the Germans issued their surrender ultimatum, General Patton's Third Army, which was then spread out between 50 and 75 miles south of Bastogne, was given a new set of orders by General Bradley. Bradley instructed Patton to halt his combat divisions, turn them 90 degrees to the left, and attack northward to cut off the German salient at its neck and at the same time open a safe corridor to Bastogne. Almost without breaking stride, Patton shifted his 133,000 tanks and trucks and all of his trailing supply columns and began charging due north. Patton's diversion of the Third Army from its extended positions in the Saar region to the snowcovered Ardennes battlefront became one of the most astonishing feats of generalship exhibited by the Allied side during World War II.

Meanwhile in Bastogne, the situation was growing more critical by the minute for the surrounded 101st Airborne Division. In an effort to cheer up his beleaguered troops, General McAuliffe issued a mimeographed message to them on Christmas Eve. It contained a copy of the German surrender demand and his response to it, plus a few personal remarks: 'The Allied troops are counter-attacking in force. . . . By holding Bastogne we insure the success of the Allied armies. We are giving our country and our loved ones a worthy Christmas present and, being privileged in taking part in this gallant feat of arms, are truly making for ourselves a Merry Christmas.'

That night Bastogne was bombed twice. During the first strike a bomb landed on a house that was serving as an aid station. It demolished the house, killing 20 patients and a Belgian woman who was caring for them. In the second raid another bomb struck the headquarters of Combat Command B, killing a dozen men and knocking down a Christmas tree in the message centre. The soldiers righted the tree, and in an elaborate ceremony a sergeant pinned the Purple Heart on a mangled doll that had somehow landed on the tree. Except for those bombings, Christmas Eve passed without unusual pressure from the Germans. The journal entries of the different regiments all used the word 'quiet' in describing the period.

Christmas Day started off with a bang at 2:45 a.m. when the Germans launched the first in a series of brisk tank–infantry assaults which continued until late afternoon. All were repulsed with light losses to the defenders. The day closed with the Americans sitting down to a delayed after-dark Christmas dinner of cold K Rations.

Earlier, on December 19, the Germans had captured the division's entire medical company and all of its surgeons during a sweeping attack north of the city where the field hospital had been established. And, almost as bad as the loss of medical personnel, the division was desperately low on artillery ammunition and gasoline. By Christmas Day, nearly 500 wounded parachute and glider troops had been delivered to the one small civilian hospital in Bastogne. Many of them died there while awaiting life-saving surgery by a struggling handful of Belgian doctors who worked around the clock.

In an attempt to remedy this desperate situation, General McAuliffe sent a message on Christmas Day to VII Corps Headquarters requesting an emergency glider delivery of combat surgeons, gasoline and artillery ammunition. His request was approved and was transmitted that day to the 50th Troop Carrier Wing in southwestern France for execution.

When he sent his radio message, McAuliffe stated that of all the things his division urgently needed, the combat surgeons should be given first priority for delivery. In accordance with that request a single Waco glider from the 96th Squadron of the 440th Troop Carrier Group based at Orleans was towed early the next morning, December 26, to a forward American fighter base at Etain near the famous World War I battlefield of Verdun. At the controls were Flight Officer Charlton W. Corwin, Jr. and his copilot, Flight Officer Benjamin F. Constantino, who had volunteered to fly a mercy mission to the surrounded Bastogne garrison. Upon their arrival at Etain, Corwin and Constantino were met by two combat surgical teams, 13 men in all, who had volunteered to fly into Bastogne with them.

Etain was only 60 air miles from Bastogne and the trip took less than an hour. During the flight the two glider pilots systematically checked off the passing landmarks on their map. Meanwhile, their passengers, none of whom had ever been in a glider, nervously stared out of the small circular windows of the fuselage at burning villages along the flight route.

Approaching Bastogne, copilot Constantino spotted a yellow smoke grenade below that had been thrown by Lieutenant Colonel Carl W. Kohls, chief supply officer for the 101st Airborne, to mark the spot where they had to land. Corwin hit the tow-line release knob and guided the glider to a remarkably smooth landing on the snow-covered field. A waiting truck whisked both surgical teams and their supplies to the hospital. Corwin and Constantino were meanwhile taken by jeep to the headquarters of the 101st Airborne. There they received hearty handshakes and personal thanks from General McAuliffe and the entire division staff.

While that first Waco had been making its way to Bastogne, another 20 volunteer glider pilots were being gathered back at Orleans to fly 10 more Wacos loaded with additional medical personnel, gasoline and artillery shells to the beleaguered 101st Airborne. It was approaching 3:00 p.m. that afternoon when all 10 of those gliders were hauled into the sky above Orleans for the 265-mile trip to Bastogne. The lateness of their take-off had the pilots worried. At that time of the year daylight was very short, and they did not want to be arriving at their destination in conditions of poor visibility. Sunrise that morning had occurred at 8:14, and sunset would be at 4:58 p.m.

The trip proved uneventful until the leading combinations crossed the Belgian frontier. There they began drawing fire from German ground units that had been alerted by the earlier single, and trouble-free, glider flight of Corwin and Constantino. Some 30 miles short of Bastogne the enemy fire began to grow in intensity. Four tug-ships took a number of hits, but all managed to keep on flying.

From his position in the number nine slot at the rear of the glider column, Flight Officer Harold W. Morgan could see the lead ships taking numerous hits from both small arms fire and flak. 'There's just no way we're going to get through that curtain of fire alive,' said Morgan to his copilot, Flight Officer Eppenheimer. 'I sure hope you're wrong,' replied Eppenheimer. Just then the shelling mysteriously subsided, just long enough for the tugs and gliders to get past the German guns without the loss of a single aircraft.

The landscape was already beginning to darken when Bastogne appeared dead ahead. As the leading glider, piloted by Lieutenant Wallace F. Hammargen, approached the outskirts of the city its tow-line was cut in two by a sudden burst of flak. Hammargen made the most of the bad situation by immediately putting his glider into a left-hand turn and diving to a smooth, fast landing. As he stepped out into the knee-deep snow he was met by an officer from the 101st Airborne who informed him that he had landed well within the division's perimeter.

Seeing Hammargen's glider diving, Flight Officer Morgan had punched his own tow-line release lever and followed Hammargen down. With 50 cans of gasoline in his glider, Morgan was anxious to get on the ground quickly before one of the tracers he saw knifing through the sky nicked one of those cans. His luck held and a few seconds later he pancaked into a field covered with deep snowdrifts that brought him to a gradual stop. There he was met by a paratrooper who ran out to his glider, banged on the window, and shouted, 'Quick, get the hell out and follow me . . . there's a bunch of Germans only a hundred and fifty yards from here!' That was all the prompting Morgan and his copilot needed. In seconds they cleared the glider and chased after the paratrooper. Later that night the gasoline cans were retrieved and brought into Bastogne.

Like several of the other glider pilots taking part in this mission, Lieutenant Robert H. Price was a veteran of the Normandy and Holland missions. During the pre-flight briefing back at Orleans, Price and his fellow pilots had been warned that Bastogne might be in German hands by the time their gliders reached the city. The intense volume of small arms fire and flak encountered during the final approach to the landing zone had convinced Price that the city had in fact fallen. But the signal to release had been given by his tug, so he hit the release knob.

As he descended through the darkening sky, Price could hear the unmistakable sound of bullets tearing through the cargo compartment and could smell the gasoline leaking out of the cans that must have been perforated. Any second now, he thought, a tracer bullet is going to ignite the 250 gallons of gasoline on board, and blow the glider to smithereens. Zooming in fast for a touchdown in the snow, Price could not avoid clipping a barbed wire fence that tore away the undercarriage – but without causing

[293]

a spark. The big gasoline-soaked machine kept flying for another 50 feet, ploughed into a snowbank and lurched to a stop beside a wooded area.

Price could not quite believe he was still alive. He and his copilot were surrounded by the smell of gasoline and counted 67 bullet holes in the fuselage. Miraculously, not one of the rounds had been a tracer.

A paratrooper suddenly appeared from out of the woods to inform the new arrivals that Bastogne was still operating under the protection of the 101st Airborne Division. On drawing close to Price, who still had a look of astonishment on his face, the paratrooper said, 'Lieutenant, you look like you could use a good stiff drink,' and pulled a bottle of 80-proof Belgian cognac from his pocket, offering it to Price. Ordinarily, even a two-fisted drinker can only stand a few sips at a time of that potent spirit. Price was 'not much of a drinking man,' but he grabbed the bottle, pressed it to his lips, pointed it at the sky whence he had just come, and guzzled down 'a good inch or more of the stuff'. Then he handed the bottle back to the paratrooper, who could not quite believe what he had just seen Price do without even squinting his eyes.

All other gliders in this mission landed within the 101st Airborne's perimeter. Most had been shot full of holes, but they managed to deliver 16 tons of desperately needed supplies. All 20 of the volunteer glider pilots survived the trip without so much as a scratch. But three surgeons and four medics they were carrying had been killed during the approach.

The last glider touched down at 4:30 p.m. on December 26. A bare 15 minutes later the first few tanks of Patton's armoured spearhead broke through to Bastogne on the southern side of the 101st Airborne's perimeter, thus ending the encirclement. The leading tanks in that spearhead were from the 4th Armoured Division's 37th Tank Battalion, whose commander was 32-year-old Lieutenant Colonel Creighton W. Abrams, Jr. Just five months previously, Abrams's battalion had led the Third Army's dramatic breakout from the Normandy beachhead.[5]

Although some of Patton's tanks had broken through to Bastogne, the tactical situation there was still precarious. The 101st Airborne still had a severe shortage of artillery ammunition and gasoline. Earlier in the week, on December 23, the division had received a parachute resupply drop of canned food and small arms ammunition.

Both food and bullets could be easily dropped by parachute: they were seldom damaged by rough landings. But only gliders could quickly bring in heavier or highly volatile items of supply such as artillery shells and gasoline. Another glider resupply run was laid on for the following day, December 27.

This second glider mission to Bastogne was to be considerably larger than the first one had been: a total of 50 Wacos would be used, most of them to be flown by pilots from squadrons of the 439th Troop Carrier Group based at Chateaudun, France. Despite the ample numbers of glider pilots available in France at this time, the officer conducting the pre-flight briefing announced that none of the Wacos in this mission would have a copilot. He also said that all pilots were to wear parachutes, something that none of them had done while flying a glider since their initial training days back in the United States.

All through the night of December 26-27, teams of glider mechanics, petroleum specialists and ammunition handlers worked to fill the 50 Bastogne-bound Wacos with bulky howitzer shells and five-gallon cans of gasoline. By dawn a total of 76 tons of cargo had been loaded and lashed in place.

Wednesday, December 27, dawned bright and bitter cold all across the Continent. The glider and tow-plane pilots at Chateaudun greeted the good flying weather with mixed feelings. They were pleased not to have to contend with the usual troublesome low clouds and ground haze while flying to Bastogne, but they knew also that good weather made them clear targets for German anti-aircraft gun crews.

The first tow-plane and glider combination from Chateaudun took to the air at 10:30 a.m. Within half an hour the aircraft were neatly formed up and the mission was on the first leg of its trip to Bastogne. Knowing that only one tenuous road had been opened into Bastogne, and that thousands of German troops were still operating around three of Bastogne's flanks as well as all along their flight route, the pilots expected to run into plenty of trouble.

The leading glider-tug combinations arrived in the vicinity of Bastogne strung out in a single column at 500 feet. Below them were burning farm houses and knocked-out tanks, all signs of the land battle that was still in full swing. The first few combinations managed to reach the LZ on the south side of the 101st Airborne perimeter, but their arrival alerted the German anti-aircraft gunners. Succeeding gliders found the clear blue sky suddenly filled with exploding flak shells and streams of machine gun bullets.

Flight Officer Thomas F. McGrath's glider was carrying a rather unusual mix of military supplies: a large quantity of 155 mm artillery shells designed to kill people, an equally large quantity of medicine and bandages intended to save lives. McGrath, one of the more fortunate pilots taking part in this mission, managed to get over the LZ area without taking a hit. The instant he saw the flashing green release signal given by his tow-plane, he punched the release knob and dived straight down to a smooth landing. Waiting paratroopers rushed out of a nearby woodline and began hastily unloading his glider. Further back in the long line of approaching gliders, meanwhile, fully alerted German anti-aircraft gunners were exacting a heavy toll. The whole sky seemed to be filled with flaming airplanes and gliders.

Flight Officer Pershing Y. Carlson was a veteran of the Normandy, southern France, and Holland combat missions. He had managed to come through the first two of them unscathed, but in Holland a German bullet had pierced his left hand just as he was landing a glider containing General Gavin's command jeep. Fully recovered from that wound now, Carlson was hoping that he could reach Bastogne without incurring another one. Before taking off, Carlson had hurriedly packed a travelling bag containing a woollen blanket, a few chocolate bars and a partially eaten fruitcake that his wife, Selma, had sent him for Christmas.

Carlson knew that he was in for an extremely rough time when he saw his tug hit by three flak shells simultaneously. The combined effect of those hits caused both of the tug's engines to burst into flames and sent it into a dive. He was just reaching up to disconnect the tow-line when his glider was rocked by an explosion that tore the bottom of its nose section completely out from under his feet and wounded him in the right ankle. With an icy blast of 120-mile-per-hour wind rushing into the glider, Carlson reached up again and completed the cutaway from his flaming tug. Just then another flak shell detonated above him. Fragments from it shattered the rolled steel cross bar positioned above his head, sending out slivers of metal into his neck, shoulders, and back. Then yet another bursting shell set his glider on fire. For a few seconds he thought of parachuting out through the gaping hole in the floor, but he was then only 200 feet above the ground, and he doubted that the chute would open in time. So he decided to 'ride her on in and hope for the best'.

Fortunately for Carlson, the rush of the wind during his steep dive to earth prevented the flames from reaching inside his glider and igniting the full load of 105 mm artillery shells he had on board. But as soon as he crash landed, the wooden floorboards caught fire and the entire fuselage began filling with smoke. Knowing that he had only about a minute remaining until the artillery shells began to cook off, Carlson snatched up his bag of goodies and dived into the snow. As he did so the parachute he was wearing popped open and spilled down around his feet. With a couple of quick moves he discarded the parachute harness, then started to run away from the smoky crash scene. He had run only about five yards toward a large tree when a voice inside him told him to drop down and crawl. Carlson believed the message 'must have come from heaven', for he had no sooner flopped down in the snow then his glider exploded mightily, sending a shower of shrapnel whizzing inches over his head. The force of the blast blew limbs off the trees that he had been trying to reach.

Carlson made his way into a thickly wooded area where he crouched down behind some bushes to inspect his wounds and take stock of the situation. Soon afterward, he heard an armoured halftrack pull into the area where he had landed. Cautiously peering out from under the bushes, he saw several German soldiers pointing at his scorched parachute, which was tangled up in the smouldering pile of wreckage that had once been his glider. Apparently convinced that the pilot had been blown to bits with his cargo, the Germans climbed back into their half-track and drove away.

The appearance of German soldiers driving freely around the countryside convinced Carlson that the area was fully under their control, so he picked up his few personal belongings and began walking deeper into the woods in search of a hideout. . . .

The result of this second glider mercy mission to Bastogne was that only 53 tons of supplies reached the 101st Airborne safely. The cost of their delivery had been exceedingly high. No fewer than 17 tow-planes and 15 gliders – nearly half of all the aircraft sent in on this mission – had been shot down. Fourteen other tow-planes suffered extensive damage and were grounded indefinitely for repairs. The 15 glider pilots who crash landed in enemy territory were listed as missing in action.

On Thursday, December 28, all of the glider pilots who had reached Bastogne successfully left for Luxembourg, the first stop along their return route to France. Most of them left aboard a truck convoy, where they served as armed guards along with a platoon of military policemen who were supervising the evacuation of some 700 German prisoners captured by the 101st Airborne. A few of the more fortunate pilots managed to hitch a more comfortable ride to Luxembourg on a train that had been penned up inside Bastogne since December 22, the day of the German encirclement.

The courageous stand of the 101st Airborne had thrilled the Allied world. After the breakthrough by Patton's tanks, congratulatory messages poured into Bastogne from all over the world. Newspapers in the Allied capitals gave full page-one coverage of the dramatic battle actions of both the airborne troopers and Patton's tanks. But in keeping with what seemed by now to have become an almost official policy of neglecting the many combat accomplishments of glider pilots, those same newspapers were singularly silent about their two daring flights into Bastogne.[6]

Flight Officer Carlson had been hiding for six days in a dense forest near his crash site. Unable to find a deserted hunting lodge or any other shelter from the elements, he had been forced to build himself a nest underneath the branches of some trees. Each day, Carlson would make his way to an observation post at the edge of the forest, hoping to see some sign of the American forces that he knew could not be far away. But all he ever saw were German troops sowing land mines in the roads, and panzer columns rolling back and forth across the frozen countryside. Having long since consumed the few chocolate bars and his wife's fruitcake, he decided to strike out on foot for the American lines, wherever they might be.

Weakened by his several minor wounds, Carlson was not able to carry his blanket or carbine, so he left his hideout on January 3, 1945, armed only with a pistol. On reaching the main road, which ran alongside the forest, he began walking at a brisk but cautious pace, watching for signs of the anti-tank mines he knew had been planted by the Germans. He had only been walking for half an hour when he was spotted by a German soldier guarding the entrance to a command post. In quick succession, the enemy sentry squeezed off two rifle shots, both of which just barely missed Carlson. For a split second he thought of running away, but the only place that was open to run was back down the road filled with mines. Knowing that he was trapped, and that the sentry had the drop on him, Carlson raised his hand.

To Carlson's relief, the jittery sentry did not fire a third shot. He simply advanced, relieved Carlson of his pistol, and marched him into a farmhouse where an American artilleryman was being held prisoner. There, after some questioning, his captors gave him some food, the first he had eaten in three days. Two days later, Carlson and his fellow prisoner began a long series of foot marches and train rides that eventually ended a month later at Stalag Luft I, a prisoner-of-war camp located 80 miles north of Berlin.

It was not until the end of January 1945 that the Battle of the Bulge officially came to a close. At its conclusion the German forces were pushed back to the original lines that had been pierced by the surprise attack on December 16. This had been accomplished by fierce ground and air attacks mounted by Montgomery's armies on the northern side of the bulge and by Bradley's on the southern side.

At its peak, the Battle of the Bulge involved more than a million soldiers and airmen. The weather turned terribly cold, and hundreds of wounded soldiers on both sides froze to death while awaiting medical evacuation. When the month-long struggle ended, it proved to have been the biggest and most confused battle the Allies fought on the Western Front in World War II.

As immense and important as it was, the Battle of the Bulge had not much changed the situation on the Western Front except for the grim fact that thousands of men had died. American casualties amounted to 81,000, of which 19,000 were killed and 15,000 captured. British units that fought briefly at the tip of the bulge suffered 1,400 casualties. About the only thing Hitler accomplished with his counter-offensive into the Ardennes was a six-week delay in the main Allied offensive north of that area. But it cost him 220,000 men (of whom 110,000 were listed as killed or wounded) and more than 1,400 tanks and assault guns.

The Third Reich was now stripped of the strategic reserve divisions it had needed to meet the coming Soviet offensive on the Eastern Front.

# Chapter 11

# Crossing the Rhine

AFTER THE BATTLE OF THE BULGE was concluded in January 1945, the Allied land armies were obliged to spend six weeks sorting themselves out and bringing up fresh supplies before they could resume their drive against Germany. General Eisenhower's plan for the resumption of his offensive was to attack on a broad front until the enemy had been pushed back across the Rhine River, the natural moat which for centuries had protected the western border of Germany from the rest of Europe. Once that had been accomplished he would conduct a huge river crossing operation in the area of Wesel and then drive into the heart of Hitler's war machine – the great Ruhr industrial area.

Eisenhower kicked off his offensive on February 23, fully expecting that once his troops reached the Rhine he would have to bring them to a halt temporarily while the combat engineers threw bridges across the enormous water barrier. On March 7, tanks of Patton's Third Army broke through German defensive positions in the Eifel (where Hitler had secretly massed troops for his counter-offensive into the Ardennes), and reached the Rhine south of Coblenz following a 60-mile push that took only three days. But there Patton was checked by the Germans, who had cleverly blown all bridges in that area as they retreated across the Rhine into the Fatherland. Two days later and some 35 miles further north along the river, elements of the First Army's 9th Armoured Division had the good fortune to seize the Ludendorff Bridge at Remagen, near Bonn, before the Germans could blow it up. Protected by covering fire delivered by their tanks, a detachment of American infantrymen rushed over to the east bank where they established the first Allied bridgehead across the Rhine.

Ten days after it was captured, the Ludendorff Bridge collapsed from extensive damage inflicted by repeated German artillery shelling and air attacks. However, by that time the First Army had formed an extensive bridgehead on the east bank and was pushing deeper into Germany. When Hitler learned what had happened at Remagen he flew into a rage and demanded to know why the Ludendorff Bridge had not been demolished in time to prevent the Americans from capturing it. He went so far as to arrange a special court-martial to prosecute the Wehrmacht officers who had been in charge of the bridge, and four of them were executed. He then fired the ageing Field Marshal von Rundstedt from his job as Commander-in-Chief West and replaced him with 59-year-old Field Marshal Albert Kesselring, a Luftwaffe officer who had formerly been in command of all German units operating in the Mediterranean area. In his previous assignment, Kesselring had gained a considerable reputation for his skilful and tenacious defence of Italy. Obviously, Hitler was hoping that Kesselring could repeat his performance on the disintegrating Western Front.

The sudden collapse of the big Ludendorff Bridge caused a number of problems for the Allies, who had been using it around the clock to haul supplies up to the front and evacuate wounded to hospitals in France. Temporary tactical bridges were built alongside the collapsed span, but they were unable to accommodate the heavy traffic of ammo trucks and ambulances passing to and from the battlefield.

In an attempt to speed up the evacuation of casualties piling up within the Remagen bridgehead, Lieutenant Colonel Robert Burquist, chief surgeon at IX Troop Carrier Command Headquarters, decided to imitate the evacuation procedure that other Allied combat units had been using successfully in southeast Asia for the past year. Burquist had just learned about the procedure, in which American gliders were being towed out of India to Burma, landing deep inside combat areas, taking on a load of wounded British soldiers, and being snatched back into flight for return to hospitals in India. If that method worked in Asia, said Burquist, it certainly ought to work in Europe. At his direction, the 304th Squadron of the 442nd Troop Carrier Wing based near Paris was instructed to convert two Waco gliders into flying ambulances and to stand by for a medical evacuation mission to an unspecified destination.

The work of converting the gliders was performed by Lieutenants Walter A. Barker, George E. Doyle, and Sergeant Orville Krause, all of the 304th Squadron. Using a set of blueprints prepared by

Lieutenant Doyle, these three men, who had no experience to guide them, experimented and improvised until they figured out how to equip the interior of a Waco glider so that it could transport twelve seriously wounded soldiers (with six casualties on each side of the fuselage), and then be rapidly reconverted to carry combat troops or cargo.[1] The result of their labours was a series of heavy duty nylon straps suspended from the glider's steel tubing roof and anchored in the wooden floor. The straps contained loop-holes into which the wooden handles of stretchers could be easily inserted, and were positioned so that as the patients were carried on board they could be stacked three deep with 18 inches of vertical clearance between stretchers. Preliminary testing of this Pullman car berthing arrangement proved that it would permit both the comfortable transportation of battle casualties and a quick reconversion.

Orders to fly the medevac mission were issued on March 22 by the IX Troop Carrier Command. The mission order directed the 402nd Squadron to tow its two modified gliders across the Rhine and release them for a landing beside the First Army's main medical clearing station, located on the east bank of the river near the city of Remagen. As soon as the gliders had been filled with wounded soldiers, the tow-planes were to return to the LZ, make an aerial pick-up, and deliver them to the 44th Evacuation Hospital, located 50 miles to the rear of the American front lines in France. There the gliders would be met by teams of medics who were to rush the wounded directly into surgery. If this worked it would be the first time that any of the combatants in Europe had used gliders to evacuate battle casualties.

It was nearing noon on the twenty-second when the two flying ambulances were hauled into the sky on the first leg of their flight to the Remagen bridgehead. The combinations flew in single file, one directly behind the other. The leading glider had Lieutenant Colonel Louis 'Skid' Magid and Lieutenant Howard Voorhees at its controls. The second glider's chief pilot was Lieutenant Walter A. Barker. His copilot was Major Howard H. Cloud, who had just recovered from a severe leg wound sustained five months earlier while landing a glider near the city of Groesbeek in Holland. Also on board the second glider was an army nurse, Lieutenant Suella V. Bernard, who had volunteered to go along on the mission to care in flight for the more seriously wounded soldiers. Bernard was a member of the 816th Medical Air Evacuation Squadron. She had flown a number of

[302]

similar missions aboard powered airplanes, but this was the first time she had ever been in a glider.

Less than an hour after departure the glider-tug combinations crossed the Rhine at an altitude of 600 feet. Barely visible in the distance were eight P-51 Mustang fighters escorting them. The leading glider cast off first and made a good landing beside waiting field ambulances which held 24 soldiers, most of whom had been seriously wounded that morning. Fifteen minutes after it touched down, the first glider was snatched out and on its way back to France.

The second glider came in, and teams of medics quickly loaded the remaining 12 patients on board while other soldiers assisted a ground crew that was preparing the glider for pick-up. During this loading period, Nurse Bernard discovered that the four most seriously wounded patients in her glider were German. Some of the American patients complained bitterly to Bernard about the presence of the Germans, saying that they should be left behind. She eventually quieted their protests, reminding them that the Geneva Convention obliged the U.S. Army to provide full and impartial medical treatment to both German and American battle casualties.

Four members of the ground crew lowered the glider's upraised nose section immediately after the last casualty had been loaded. Major Cloud and Lieutenant Barker then climbed aboard, strapped themselves into their seats, and went through a series of safety checks in preparation for the pick-up. A bare two minutes after the pilots made the final safety check, their tow-plane swooped down, snatched the glider, and lifted it smoothly into flight. One of the nylon straps supporting the litters was pulled loose from its tiedown, but Nurse Bernard, who happened to be near the strap when it gave way, repaired it before it could cause any further injury to the patients.

Some 30 minutes after they were snatched out of the Remagen bridgehead, both of the flying ambulances landed in a cleared field beside the 44th Evacuation Hospital in France. The evacuation had been a complete success. Both pilots and Nurse Bernard were awarded an Air Medal for the part they played in it.

Elsewhere in France and England the Allies had, for the past month, been massing parachute and glider troops that were to be employed in direct support of Field Marshal Montgomery's 21st Army Group during its crossing of the Rhine. With the textbook precision and thoroughness that were his trademark, Monty had assembled 25 infantry divisions and 1.4 million tons of ammunition and other supplies in preparation for his decisive attack.

D-Day for Montgomery's historic river crossing was set for Saturday, March 24. The site at which Monty planned to cross his main attack force was opposite Wesel, the hometown of Joachim von Ribbentrop, Foreign Minister of the Third Reich. Just 35 miles to the north, and on the same side of the Rhine as Wesel, is the Dutch city of Arnhem, the scene of Montgomery's defeat the previous September during the ground phase of Operation Market-Garden. Even at this late date Arnhem was still occupied by German troops commanded by Field Marshal Model.

Montgomery's grand plan for crossing the Rhine called for two separate operations. The first, code-named Operation Plunder, involved a pre-dawn amphibious assault across the river by elements of General Miles Dempsey's Second British Army. The second, Operation Varsity, envisioned the simultaneous dropping and landing of three Allied airborne divisions during daylight. Thus, in a complete turnabout of tactical doctrine, the Allied airborne troops were being scheduled to make their assault landings not prior to but *after* the start of the ground attack, and well within range of Royal Artillery guns poised on the west bank of the Rhine.

General Brereton, commander of the 1st Allied Airborne Army, had a total of six airborne divisions under his command at the time he was first informed about Operation Varsity. But three of them – the British 1st Airborne that had been shattered at Arnhem, and the American 82nd and 101st, both of which had recently sustained heavy casualties in the Bulge – would require several months to rifit and train for an airborne mission. Brereton therefore assigned the Varsity mission to his remaining three divisions: the British 6th and the American 13th and 17th. When it became clear that there were barely enough gliders and airplanes available to lift two divisions, Brereton ordered the 13th Airborne – which had just arrived in France from the United States – to stand down and become his strategic reserve division. Several missions involving the 13th Airborne were planned but never executed; making it the only American division in Europe that did not see combat in World War II.

Both the British 6th and American 17th Airborne divisions were combat-experienced. The troopers of the 6th Airborne were veterans of Normandy, and as recently as February 24, they had returned to their base camp on the Salisbury Plain of England from two months

[304]

of duty as straight infantry in the Battle of the Bulge and in Holland.[2] They were now at full strength and ready for combat. Their new commander, Major General Eric L. Bols, had led them at the Bulge and in Holland. The division's 6th Airlanding (glider) Brigade also had a new commander in Brigadier Hugh Bellamy. He was a replacement for Brigadier the Honourable Hugh Kindersley, who had been seriously wounded by friendly fire in Normandy. The 3rd and 5th Parachute brigades were still commanded by Brigadiers James Hill and Nigel Poett, respectively.

Major General William M. 'Bud' Miley and his American 17th Airborne Division had arrived at its base camp in Chisledon, England, from the United States in August 1944. The division's first combat came during the Battle of the Bulge, when it was airlifted at night to Rheims, France, and rushed up to the front aboard trucks. During that epic battle, the 17th Airborne conducted a fierce ground attack which cleared Bastogne's western flank of German units. It then turned eastward and attacked clear across Luxembourg to the Our River bordering Germany. There it skirmished with the German 5th Airborne Division, crossed into Germany, and began probing the Siegfried Line. On February 10, the 17th Airborne was relieved at the front and moved to Chalons-sur-Marne in France to prepare for Operation Varsity.

Late in February, at his base camp in Chalons-sur-Marne, General Miley received word that his 17th Airborne was being streamlined. The division's new table of organization, as decreed by a directive from Washington, called for it to have two parachute regiments and only one glider regiment. This resulted in the deactivation of the Division's 193rd Glider Infantry Regiment. Combat survivors of the 193rd were consolidated to form a new 3rd Battalion in Colonel James R. Pierce's 194th Glider Infantry Regiment. The division's 507th and 513th Parachute Infantry regiments, still commanded by Colonels Edson D. Raff and James W. Couts, respectively, also had their strength increased by the addition of a third squad to each rifle platoon.

Plans for the exercise of command and control of the Allied airborne troops during Operation Varsity were not completed until the end of February. By that time England's Lieutenant General Browning, who commanded the Allied airborne divisions in Holland, had been re-assigned as chief of staff to Admiral Mountbatten in India. During a staff conference in the new headquarters of his 1st

[305]

Allied Airborne Army at Maison Lafitte, on the outskirts of Paris, Lieutenant General Brereton announced that Major General Ridgway, commander of the XVII Airborne Corps, would be in charge of the airborne divisions during Varsity. Major General Gale, the former commander of the British 6th Airborne, was appointed Ridgway's deputy.

General Dempsey had orders for Montgomery to cross the Rhine between Wesel and Emmerich. Looking at his planning map, he saw that the most prominent terrain feature in his zone of attack was the Diersfordter Forest, which sat atop a six-mile-long stretch of high ground only three miles inland from the Rhine. Because the forest fronted the riverline, Dempsey correctly assumed that it contained German infantry and artillery units that could make his crossing extremely difficult. He therefore made the Diersfordter Forest the primary objective of the Allied airborne troops.

With the painful memory of costly errors made in Holland still fresh in his mind, General Brereton established some firm operational guidelines for the forthcoming airborne assault across the Rhine. During the initial planning conference with General Dempsey and representatives from Monty's headquarters and Eighth Air Force, Brereton insisted upon compliance with four points for the efficient combat employment of his 1st Allied Airborne Army. One was that all of the glider and parachute troops must be delivered into the airhead in a single lift on D-Day, thus avoiding a piecemeal commitment of forces which could be interrupted by bad flying weather. The second point was that both the British 6th and the American 17th Airborne divisions had to land directly on top of their assigned objectives. By doing so, he said, they would avoid repeating the fatal error committed in Arnhem where the British 1st Airborne was required to march some six miles to its most important objective. Thirdly, Brereton demanded that all known enemy flak positions be neutralized by ponderous air and artillery strikes before the start of the airborne landings. His final requirement was that gliders have two qualified pilots at their controls.

At the end of February General Williams's IX Troop Carrier Command had on hand 1,264 C-47 and 117 C-46 airplanes. Also available were 1,922 CG-4A gliders and 20 CG-13 gliders.[3] Roughly speaking, one C-46 airplane was equivalent in capacity to two C-47s, and one CG-13 glider equivalent to two Wacos. By this time all of the CG-13 gliders had been deployed to France from their base at

Folkingham, England. It was during their deployment to the Continent that one of the CG-13s was utilized to transport General Brereton's personal staff car – a 1940 Cadillac – to Orly, south of Paris. The chief pilot of that glider was Captain Elgin D. Andross from the 313th Troop Carrier Group.

General Williams decided against the big CG-13 gliders in Varsity because there were not enough of them to justify the complications their inclusion would produce in the flight plan. Because he had been instructed by Brereton to send three of his troop carrier groups to transport British paratroopers to their D-Day objectives, Williams announced that the American airborne division would be given a paratroop lift of 226 C-47s and 72 C-46s, the equivalent of 320 C-47s. The American glider troops, meanwhile, would ride into battle aboard 906 Wacos, many of which would be double-towed by 610 C-47s.

A complex Allied air-movement schedule required the 6th Airborne to take off from 11 airfields in England, and the 17th Airborne from 12 airfields in France. The forces were to converge over Brussels, Belgium, in three lanes spaced one and a half miles apart. From Brussels they were to turn northeast on to the final 103-mile-long leg of their massed flight to the airhead. Only the last six miles of the final leg were over enemy-occupied territory.

The left lane of the great Allied air armada was to be occupied entirely by the 6th Airborne. In fact there were to be two left lanes, flying at different altitudes. The American airplanes carrying British paratroopers were to fly at 1,500 feet while the all-British glider train flew above them at 2,500 feet.

The centre lane would be taken up completely by the 17th Airborne's glider serials. All of the American paratroop serials would fly in the right-hand lane.

Utilizing this massive formation, the Allies would be able to land all 21,680 glidermen and paratroopers of both divisions on D-Day in as little time as two hours and 36 minutes. The Varsity D-Day drop was to be the largest single airborne attack made by either side during the war – even larger than the one made in Holland on D-Day of Operation Market-Garden.[4]

The greatest problem facing Brigadier Chatterton, the commander of the British Glider Pilot Regiment, as he prepared for Varsity was that he did not have enough glider pilots available to fly the 6th Airborne's glider troops into battle. Combat losses at Arnhem had

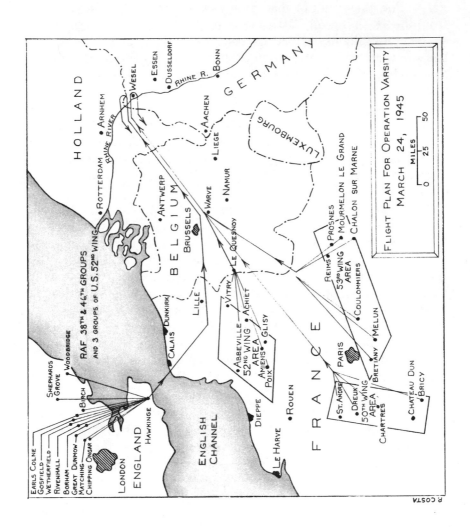

FLIGHT PLAN FOR OPERATION VARSITY
MARCH 24, 1945

MILES
0   25   50

P. COSTA

been so great for his regiment that Chatterton could only field 712 pilots for Varsity, yet his orders were to prepare a glider force large enough to fly 2,000 gliders across the Rhine. Chatterton knew he had to do something quickly. In desperation, he went to see Air Chief Marshal Sir Peter Drummond, the Director of Training for the RAF. Drummond agreed to transfer 1,500 power pilots into the Glider Pilot Regiment for Varsity. After a brief transition course in Hotspur training gliders, the power pilots were given a condensed programme of instruction in flying the larger Horsa gliders and using infantry weapons.

For some time now, the American troop carrier squadrons had been contending with a general shortage of glider pilots. With newly graduated glider pilots arriving each week from American schools, the situation was not as bad as it had been during the Holland mission, when most gliders had untrained airborne troopers for copilots. Nonetheless, the shortage was serious enough that the Americans, too, were forced to use power pilots as glider pilots in Varsity. Just about half of the copilots for the Wacos were volunteer and non-volunteer power pilots drawn from various fighter and bomber squadrons of the Eighth Air Force.

This unusual arrangement had been precipitated to a large extent by a requirement placed on the 1st Allied Airborne Army by Eisenhower's headquarters to keep a sufficient reserve of glider pilots available to fly 926 gliders in Operation Choker, a contingency airborne operation in support of the United States 7th Army's crossing the Rhine at Worms, some 160 miles south of Wesel. It was tentatively scheduled for March 29. As things turned out, there was no need to execute Choker. Nevertheless, a large pool of glider pilots had to be kept available up until the minute it was cancelled.

General Hap Arnold had taken the first step toward meeting the growing shortage of glider pilots in Europe while the Allied airborne divisions were still fighting in Holland. On October 8, 1944, he issued instructions to the headquarters of the Flying Training Command at Randolph Field, Texas, for a detachment of recent flying school graduates to undergo a brief course in glider flying. Two days later, 70 non-volunteer power pilots were on their way from Eagle Pass Army Air Field, Texas, to be enrolled as students in the South Plains Army Air Force Advanced Glider School in Lubbock, Texas.

Project Red was the code-name given to this first and only dual training programme administered to power pilots during the war. It lasted only two weeks, throughout which the power pilots complained loudly about being forced to fly gliders. At the end of the brief course they were all presented with glider pilot wings, which they wore below their power wings. Along with the glider wings came a set of reassignment orders to various troop carrier squadrons in Europe.

From the start of its existence the British Glider Pilot Regiment had been unique. It was a collection of glider pilots armed and equipped to fight as infantry upon their arrival in the airhead. Strict discipline and high standards of military bearing prevailed in the regiment. Initially it had been a part of the British Army, with the pilots organized into battalions, companies and platoons. But just prior to the Normandy invasion the regiment had been reassigned to the Royal Air Force, where its components were rechristened with the RAF's wing, squadron and other flight unit designations. Each flight contained four officers and 40 sergeants, all qualified glider pilots. A flight's armament consisted of four pistols, two tommy guns, two light machine guns and 32 rifles.

As a result of recommendations made after Holland by General Gavin of the 82nd Airborne and General Taylor of the 101st Airborne, special attention was given to the way in which the American glider pilots were task organized and the role they were to play in Varsity after the landings. Their status as members of the various Air Force troop carrier squadrons was not changed, but for combat purposes all of the glider pilots, and their converted power copilots, were organized into infantry companies similar to those found in the British Glider Regiment. During the ground phase of Varsity, command and control of those companies was to be administered by the wing glider officer and a small staff who would act as a battalion headquarters.

Significantly, the American glider pilots were to perform the same general tasks in Varsity as they had in previous combat operations. On landing they were to assist in the unloading of their gliders, then proceed to the same assembly area as the combat unit they had carried into the airhead. There they were to form their own tactical infantry units and be assigned to such tasks as guard duty, supply collection and, circumstances permitting, protection of usable gliders from vandalism. If the local tactical situation so demanded, the pilots were to be committed to fight as infantry, but only in a defensive role. Furthermore, they were to be evacuated from the battle area on the highest possible priority so as to be available for other airborne combat operations then on the drawing boards of 1st Allied Airborne Army.

The glider pilots themselves actually welcomed this long overdue move to organize them into fighting units. By this time most of them were not only experienced combat pilots but proficient ground soldiers as well. During their American training at Bowan Field, Kentucky, and at Laurinburg-Maxton Army Air Field in North Carolina, they had qualified with all infantry weapons from .45 calibre pistols to machine guns, mortars and bazookas, and had participated in tactical field manoeuvres, both day and night. In England and France their education continued with advanced courses in the use of hand grenades, .50 calibre machine guns, and small anti-tank guns. At long last the glider pilots were being equipped with a complete set of infantry combat tools.

In accordance with General Brereton's guidelines, staff officers at XVIII Airborne Corps devised a plan calling for the British 6th and the American 17th Airborne divisions to be dropped directly on top of their objectives so that they might swamp and overwhelm the German defenders. Despite the fact that a colossal preliminary bombardment and continuous artillery fire were promised them, this was a formidable order for the two airborne divisions to carry out.

The plan called for the British 6th Airborne to operate in the northern half of the corps's zone and the 17th Airborne in the southern half. Four paratroop DZs and six glider LZs were plotted in the airhead. Because of its small airhead area, Varsity was going to be the most congested airborne assault ever conducted by the Allies. All 10 zones were located in a relatively confined area measuring only five miles wide by six miles long. Almost all of the zones were on firm, level ground consisting of fields and meadows 200 to 300 yards in length. Aerial photos showed that there were numerous small wooden fences and several small drainage ditches in the glider LZs. That was the bad news. The good news was that no Rommel's asparagus had been sighted.

German Army Group H was sitting astride the path of General Dempsey's upcoming attack. Its commander was General Johannes von Blaskowitz, the former military governor of Bohemia. Blaskowitz had under his command some 85,000 troops, divided between

[311]

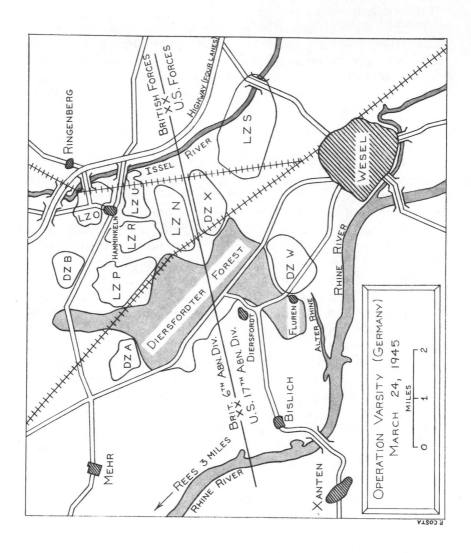

Operation Varsity (Germany)
March 24, 1945

P. COSTA

two mortally wounded armies, the Twenty-fifth and the First Parachute. Serving as commander of the latter was General Alfred Schlemm, who had been General Student's chief of staff during the battle for Crete in 1941. Directly under Schlemm was the veteran German 7th Airborne Division that had captured Crete.

As early as March 10, Blaskowitz notified all of his units in position along the Rhine to be fully prepared for an Allied airborne attack in their rear areas. The enormous gathering of Allied ground combat units and the increased training activities of the four (13th, 17th, 82nd and 101st) American airborne divisions then in France, had not gone unnoticed by German intelligence agents. The only thing the Germans could not predict accurately was the exact Allied crossing point along the Rhine. But on March 20, when British engineers set up smoke generators opposite Emmerich and began laying a continuous 60-mile-long smoke curtain across the riverbank, Blaskowitz put all units in that sector on red alert.

By rare good fortune for which all of the Allied brass were very grateful, Varsity had perfect flying weather throughout the three days of preparatory air operations and on into D-Day. In the three days before D-Day, 3,471 Allied bombers dropped 8,500 tons of delayed-fuse bombs on German highways, railroads and airfields surrounding the airhead while another 2,090 bombers released 6,600 tons of fragmentation bombs on flak batteries and troop positions. During these preparatory air strikes, known German flak guns in the airhead area were left alone so that they would not go into hiding. On D-Day, half an hour before the paratroop airplanes and the gliders were to land, RAF and American medium bombers were scheduled to pounce on those batteries and destroy them. Between the departure of the mediums and the arrival of the airborne troops, Royal Artillery guns firing from the west bank would hammer flak positions within the airhead.

At nine o'clock in the evening of March 23, several teams of British commandos began crossing the Rhine in small assault boats. They were still in mid-stream when, at 9:30 p.m., a flight of Lancaster bombers arrived and flattened Wesel, sending up a tremendous cloud of smoke and dust, which soon mixed with the huge smoke cloud drifting across the Rhine from Montgomery's smoke generators. The smoke would cause serious problems in the morning for Allied bomber pilots trying to pinpoint German flak positions in the airhead and the glider pilots seeking their designated landing zones.

[313]

At 10:00 p.m., General Dempsey's infantry divisions carried hundreds of assault boats to the riverline and began their crossing. By 4:00 a.m. they had established themselves in several small beachheads on the east bank, most of which were under heavy fire from the Diersfordter Forest to their front.

In England, meanwhile, troopers of the 6th Airborne Division were climbing into their gliders and parachutes. The first mission in Varsity to get under way was that of the 6th Air Landing Brigade. Its first glider-tug combinations took to the air at 6:00 a.m., an hour ahead of the initial paratroop serials. Early departure was necessary because it took almost a full hour to get the heavy Horsa and Hamilcar gliders into the air and still more time to haul them up to the prescribed 2,500-foot altitude.

The British readied 440 Horsas and 38 Hamilcars to transport the 6th Air Landing Brigade to its objectives. Take-off and assembly of their glider and paratroop serials went like clockwork on D-Day, but some gliders soon ran into serious trouble. Thirty-five Horsas broke loose from their tow-planes or had to be released while still over England. Two of them went down in the Channel, but all hands were saved by rescue launches. The remainder of the British skytrain made it all the way to Brussels without further incident. There it smoothly rendezvoused with the American skytrain coming from France and headed for Germany.

Colonel Raff's 507th Parachute Infantry Regiment was the lead assault unit of the 17th Airborne. With Prime Minister Churchill, General Eisenhower, and Field Marshal Montgomery all observing from the west bank of the Rhine, the planes carrying Raff and his troops roared overhead, bound for DZ W. Under ordinary circumstances DZ W would have been easy to locate from the air; it was situated right at the southern tip of the Diersfordter Forest, and a nearby finger-shaped lake pointed directly at it. Raff's pilot, Colonel Joel L. Crouch, knew that DZ W was precisely two and one half miles, or one and one half minutes' flying time, beyond the Rhine. But as Crouch crossed the river at the head of his serial, which contained 46 jump planes, he was shaken by the fact that he could see nothing in the airhead. All drop and landing zones were enveloped in the smoke and dust from the intensive bombing of Wesel, by the smoke screen generated by the British to conceal their river crossing operations, and by smoke from the artillery preparations that had set fire to the woods and buildings within the airhead itself. But even

Captain Elgin D. Andross. When his convoy of glider pilots was
ambushed near Veghel by elements of the German 6th Parachute
Regiment, Andross led them out of the trap. *Elgin D. Andross*

Brussels Airport, Belgium, October 14, 1944. After having just spent over three weeks in Holland with the 101st Airborne, glider pilot Joseph Mendes (right) shows a captured German flag to the power pilot who will fly him back to England. Mendes has a captured Schmeisser MP 38 submachine gun slung over his left shoulder, and a Walther P-38 pistol on his belt. *U.S. Army*

Shick General Hospital, Clinton, Iowa, 1945. Flight Officer George F. Brennan (right) one year after Market-Garden, still recovering from multiple wounds received in Holland. With Brennan is Lt. Bates Stinson of the 101st Airborne Division. *George F. Brennan*

May 8, 1982, Groesbeek, Netherlands. When the war ended in 1945 the Dutch government awarded its Order of William to the Allied airborne forces who took part in Operation Market-Garden. Due to an administrative oversight, the American glider pilots were left off the list. The Dutch government corrected the error in 1982, and the first group of veteran glider pilots to be honoured retroactively are shown here, 37 years after Market-Garden. They were personally decorated by Dr. G. H. J. M. Peijnenburg, Holland's Secretary General of the Defence. Standing (left to right) William Marks, Donald O. McKinley, Connie Nanartonis, William T. Richey, and Theodore V. Sampson. Dr. Peijnenburg is at far right. Kneeling: John R. Hauselt, Roy Barbata, William Edwards, and John D. Hill. *Connie Nanartonis*

*Opposite above:* September 20, 1944, Eindhoven, Holland. Citizens gather beside a house at 56 Johan Vesters Street to welcome American glider pilots who had landed at Zon two days before. Left to right: Mr. W. A. Tack (owner of home in background), F.O. John F. Boersig, an unidentified man holding Dutch flag, F.O. Jack R. Merrick, Mrs. Tack, and F.O. John J. Lang. *Jack R. Merrick*

*Opposite below:* Eindhoven, Holland, September 20, 1982. Former glider pilot Jack R. Merrick stands in front of the same house where 38 years before to the day, he and other American pilots were welcomed by Dutch citizens. *Jack R. Merrick*

Bastogne, Belgium, December 26, 1944. Soldiers from the all-black 969th Field Artillery Battalion and some 101st Airborne troopers unload 155-mm howitzer shells from a CG-4A glider that has just landed inside the surrounded American stronghold at Bastogne. *U.S. Army*

Flight Officer Pershing Y. Carlson and his wife, Selma. After
narrowly escaping death when his glider was shot down while
enroute to Bastogne, Carlson subsisted for four days on a small
fruit cake that his wife had sent him in a Christmas package.
*Pershing Y. Carlson*

Lieutenant Suella V. Bernard of the 816th Medical Air Evacuation
Squadron, U.S. Army Air Force. When she learned of the impending
glider flight into the Remagen bridgehead to evacuate casualties,
she volunteered to go along on the mission to care for the wounded.
She is the only nurse from any of the combatant nations to
participate in a glider mission during World War II. *Suella V.
(Bernard) Delp*

Remagen, Germany, March 22, 1945. This extremely rare photo, taken two days prior to
Operation Varsity, shows a CG-4A glider being loaded with American and German
wounded. Less than half an hour after this photo was taken, the glider was snatched into
flight by a C-47 and flown to a hospital in France. *U.S. Army*

March 24, 1945. From a vantage point on the west bank of the Rhine, Prime Minister Churchill (seated), General Eisenhower (centre) and Field Marshal Montgomery observe Allied glider and parachute assault landings taking place across the river near Wesel. *U.S. Army*

France, March 24, 1945. F.O. Earl W. Rishel just before boarding his glider for the historic Rhine crossing. Rishel is equipped with the standard fighting gear that most American glider pilots in Europe carried into combat. He is holding a .30 calibre semi-automatic M-1 carbine. Attached to its stock is an ammunition pouch containing two 15-round magazines. The small canvas bag on the muzzle has been put there to keep the bore clear of dirt. Strapped across his chest is a .45 calibre pistol and ammo pouch containing two 7-round clips. On his belt are two additional ammo pouches, one for the pistol, one for the carbine. A small bayonet is strapped to his right ankle so that if his chest and waist become entangled with debris after a crash, he will be able to reach at least one weapon. Anticipating a stay of one or more nights in the airhead, this pilot is carrying (strapped on his back) a wool blanket rolled in a rain poncho. *Earl W. Rishel*

March 24, 1945. British glider troops march past the twisted wreckage of a Horsa that was struck by German artillery fire on
LZ P. *Imperial War Museum*

Wesel, Germany, March 24, 1945. American troops unload a newly developed Mark II model of England's standard Horsa glider that has landed in their sector of the airhead. The hinged nose of the Mark II reduced unloading times of earlier Mark I models which had a single portside door. Horsa gliders were constructed almost entirely of wood. Aviation experts still call them the most wooden aircraft ever built. Mark I and II models were equipped with explosives that were sometimes used to blow off the tail section for quick unloading in combat. *Joe Quade*

March 24, 1945. The wreckage of two CG-4A gliders struck by point-blank German artillery fire on LZ N. Both gliders were full of troops when they were hit. There were no survivors. *U.S. Army*

Flight Officer Hance A. Lunday, who volunteered to provide covering fire for a group of infantrymen that were trying to break contact with German troops. After firing for a time he turned around to see how the infantrymen were doing only to discover they had abandoned him. The only man who remained with Lunday was his copilot. *Hance A. Lunday*

A glider pilot from the 77th Squadron sits atop the German tank disabled by Flight Officer Jella. Note the tank's burned bogey wheels, and the discarded German helmets on the ground. *Earl W. Rishel*

March 24, 1973, near Wesel, West Germany. On the twenty-ninth anniversary of Operation Varsity, retired British paratroop General Eric L. Bols (left centre in civilian clothes) stands stiffly to attention in a German military cemetery during memorial services for German troops who opposed his 6th Airborne Division during the 1945 drop across the Rhine. Beside Bols (in civilian clothes with hands clasped) is his former adversary, German General Kurt Student, the former commander and the father of the German airborne. *Joe Quade*

Flight Officer Elbert D. Jella, the dead-eye glider pilot who
disabled a German tank during the battle at Burp Gun Corner.
*Elbert D. Jella*

Wesel, Germany, March 26, 1945. American glider pilots resting during their long march back to the Rhine. Some transport equipment on 'liberated' bicycles and baby carriages. *Joseph F. Menard*

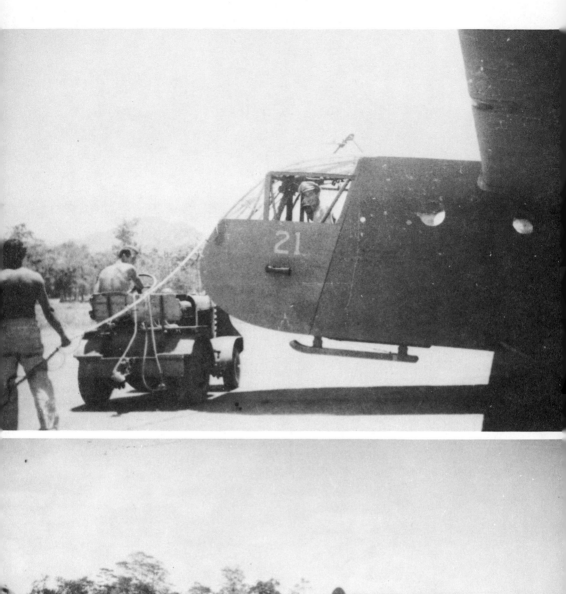

April 1945. Lt. Leo Cordier of the 78th Squadron, 485th Troop Carrier Group, and his CG-4A 'Connecticut Yankee' glider at Hildersheim, Germany. Cordier had landed as part of a two-glider sortie to establish an air traffic control centre to direct powered airplanes which were to land with supplies for General Patton's Third Army and then evacuate Allied POWs. The No. 5, and the five swastikas, painted on the glider denote Cordier's fifth combat mission. Only a handful of glider pilots lived long enough during World War II to complete five missions. Cordier's previous missions were to Normandy, southern France, Holland, and the Rhine River crossing. *Lt. Col. Leo Cordier*

*Opposite above:* October 1944, Nadzab Airfield, New Guinea. Lieutenants James Harlan and Donald Burke at the controls of their CG-4A, which is being towed into position for the flight to Hidden Valley. The aerial tow-line has an intercom wire wrapped loosely around it. The ground tow-vehicle is a Clark Clarktor, a rear-wheel drive industrial tractor used to move gliders and powered airplanes. *Earl F. Simson*

*Opposite below:* Nadzab Airfield, New Guinea, October 1944. Two of the four CG-4As that will take part in the hazardous mission to Hidden Valley are being lined up behind their tugs. *Earl F. Simson*

New Guinea, October 1944. Pay-day in Hidden Valley. A civilian
police officer distributes packets of salt to members of the
Kukukuka Tribe who are assisting the Americans to construct an
emergency landing field and radio station near their village in the
mountains. Tribesmen had agreed to work for one spoonful of
salt per day. *Earl F. Simson*

Biak Island, New Guinea, February 3, 1945. Three survivors of a glider ditching along the shores of New Guinea. Bearded and exhausted after their four-day walk through the jungles back to civilization are, left to right: Flight Officers Raymond Nutting, Harold N. Wallace, and David S. Kaufman. Four months after this photo was taken, F.O. Wallace was killed in a flying training accident. *David S. Kaufman*

Biak Island, New Guinea, December 1944. An aerial view of the
tent city inhabited by pilots of the 1st Provisional Glider Group.
The projection booth and benches of an open-air movie theatre
are at the lower left corner of this photo. *David S. Kaufman*

Biak Island, New Guinea. F.O. Robert J. Meer conducts briefing of glider mechanics and pilots on progress of Allied troops fighting in Europe and Pacific Theatres of War. Such briefings were presented once each week. *Robert J. Meer*

May 16, 1945. Crash survivors and 1st Reconnaissance Battalion troopers at Mike 1 camp near crash site. Left to right: Lt. McCollom (in T-shirt), T/Sgt. Decker, S/Sgt. Bulato, and Cpl. Ramirez. *Kenneth W. Decker*

*Opposite:* Lt. John S. McCollom (centre) with members of the Filipino-American 1st Reconnaissance Battalion who helped rescue him. Paratroopers display stone axe souvenirs purchased from natives. *Kenneth W. Decker*

June 15, 1945. Crash survivors, along with 1st Reconnaissance Battalion members and natives, rest during their arduous march down the mountain to Mike 2 camp-site. The survivors had spent 33 days on the mountain. Cpl. Margaret Hastings can be seen seated (left front) with hands clasped. Lt. John McCollom is seated at far right centre of photo. *Kenneth W. Decker*

A CG-15A landing during Operation Tarheel, training
manoeuvres held near Ft. Bragg, N.C., in 1949. The CG-15A was
similar in appearance to a CG-4A glider, but its wingspan was
21′4″ shorter, and it could carry 1,000 pounds more. *Arthur
Provost*

Lipa Airfield, Luzon, P.I., June 1945. This is the tent city in which
the American glider pilots lived during their stay on Luzon.
*Robert J. Meer*

*Opposite above:* This XCG-17 was a unique experiment in glider development. A standard
C-47 powered airplane was converted by removal of its engines. It was towed by a single
B-17 bomber, or by two C-47s in tandem. Only one XCG-17 was produced during the war.
*U.S. Air Force*

*Opposite below:* The most unusual experiments carried out with gliders in World War II
involved the conversion of some of them into powered airplanes. This former CG-4A,
equipped with two 125 hp Franklin engines, has been transformed into an XPG-1. No
powered gliders were ever used in combat. *U.S. Air Force*

Luzon, P.I., June 1945. A large cloud shadows part of the Japanese-built airfield at Lipa. The Gibraltar-like Mount Macolod, with its 2,700-foot peak, looms in the background. The 11th Airborne's 187th Glider Infantry Regiment fought on Mt. Macolod from March 23 to April 20, 1945, clearing it of tenacious Japanese defenders. The American glider assault at Appari was launched from this airfield. *U.S. Air Force*

June 23, 1945, near Appari, Luzon. This rare photo shows six of the seven gliders utilized by Gypsy Task Force during their landings on Camalaniugan Airstrip. Parachutes of earlier landed paratroopers can be seen littering the foreground. *U.S. Air Force*

though he could not see his DZ, Crouch believed he was on course because he had just passed directly over the marker panels displayed on the west bank. So at 9:50 a.m., exactly 90 seconds after crossing the river, he flipped on the green jump light.

General Miley, the 17th Airborne's commander, parachuted in on this initial drop accompanied by a few members of his staff. As soon as he landed, Miley knew he had been dropped on the wrong DZ. With enemy machine gun slugs cracking overhead, the general lay on the ground, looking for his staff. None of them had landed near him. He spotted three of his troopers about 20 yards away, hugging the ground for protection. Then the saw a parachute bundle marked to indicate that it contained a machine gun, and shouted to his troopers to meet him at the bundle. A few minutes later Miley and the three troopers had the gun firing at the Germans. The incident illustrates the old saying that when a paratroop general jumps into combat, he commands only those few troopers who land near him. Usually a few hours must pass before a general does the work of a general; before that he is just another soldier fighting to gain a foothold in enemy territory.

Like Miley, Colonel Raff recognized almost instantly that he, along with his entire 1st Battalion, had been misdropped near the village of Diersfordt, some two miles west of DZ W. Fortunately, the remainder of his regiment had landed squarely inside its DZ. After assembling the troopers who had landed with him, Raff led them through the woods to where the rest of his regiment was gathering. On the way he ran into a German artillery battery that was shooting at British troops down at the shoreline. He attacked the guns at once, killing the crews and taking some 350 prisoners. By two o'clock that afternoon, Raff had assembled all of his regiment on DZ W, and was able to report that all of his assigned objectives were secured.

The second part of the 17th Airborne to arrive in the airhead was the 513th Parachute Infantry Regiment. Confused by the same ground fog that had misled some of Raff's aircraft, all of the regiment's C-46 pilots missed DZ X, their designated drop area, and by mistake unloaded the regiment at 10:10 a.m. into the British glider LZs near Hamminkeln.

Colonel Coutts and his 513th Parachute Infantry landed not only in the wrong area but directly on top of a hornet's nest: Hamminkeln was strongly defended by German infantry and artillery troops. On landing, the Americans had to launch frontal attacks on dug-in artillery batteries that were all around them.

[315]

Amid all those skirmishes, British gliders started landing practically on top of the 513th Parachute Infantry. As their gliders skidded to a halt, members of the 6th Air Landing Brigade burst out of them with guns blazing, joined up with the Americans, and stormed Hamminkeln.

It was nearly 2:00 p.m. on D-Day when Colonel Coutts, suffering from wounds received near Hamminkeln, reported by radio to division headquarters that his 513th Parachute Infantry had secured all of its objectives. During its skirmishing the 513th had knocked out two tanks and two artillery batteries and had captured 1,152 prisoners.

Two glider landing zones, lettered S and N, were to be used by the 17th Airborne. The tactical plan called for the 194th Glider Infantry Regiment and all of its supporting units to land first in LZ S. That initial glider mission was to be followed one hour later by the landing of the division's engineer, signal and medical units in LZ N. Ten of the Wacos containing medical troops heading for LZ N had been rigged for quick conversion into flying ambulances. The plan was that if the Germans knocked out the bridges being thrown across the Rhine by British troops, all 10 of those gliders would be snatched out of the airhead and whisked away to surgical hospitals in France.

The first American glider contingent heading for LZ S consisted of 592 Wacos, all in double-tow, from the 435th, 436th, 437th and 439th Troop Carrier groups. On board those gliders were 3,594 troops and equipment of the 194th Glider Infantry, the 680th and 681st Field Artillery battalions, and the 155th Anti-aircraft Battalion.

Take-offs began at 7:34 a.m. Although the slowness with which the cumbersome double-tow combinations took to the air made observers hold their breath, there were no crashes. The task of holding the Wacos in level flight was so strenuous that many of the pilots and copilots had to alternate 15-minute periods at the controls. Two other serious problems facing the glider pilots was the too-slow prescribed 110 miles an hour, which caused some near stalls, and the fact that the intercom sets, as usual, did not work.

Formation flying along the route up to Brussels soon became even more difficult for the glider pilots because of extreme turbulence being generated by prop-wash of their tugs and cross winds. Disaster overtook a number of the bobbing gliders. Three pairs of Wacos in double-tow had the short-tow glider foul its mate's tow-line; two of the short-tow gliders lost wings and crashed. Improperly balanced loads and structural weaknesses forced an additional 18 gliders to make emergency landings. All others made it safely to Brussels, where they headed down the centre lane behind their tugs, bound for Germany.

On crossing the Rhine these initial glider formations encountered the same smoke and haze which had plagued the paratroop echelon. Visibility over parts of the run-in lane was as low as an eighth of a mile, and most of LZ S was obscured from view. During final approach to the LZ, German ground fire downed two tug planes, forcing their four gliders to land a mile short of their destination. The thickest enemy fire was right over the LZ. Of the 295 tug planes entering the battle area, 12 were shot down in flames. Another 140 were holed by flak but managed to keep flying.

As in previous airborne operations, most of the glider serials reached the airhead between five and 10 minutes ahead of schedule. The 436th Group actually arrived 14 minutes too early and began overtaking the rear formations of the 437th Group. As a result nearly half the pilots of the 436th's tug-ships had to climb up to let their gliders cut loose at altitudes of from 1,000 to 1,700 feet. The other serials maintained safe intervals so that the glider pilots could make their cutaways from heights of 400 to 800 feet.

The lead serial made its release at 10:36 a.m. As the gliders swooped down in their 270 degree turns, they became the targets of savage fire from flak cannons and machine guns. Over 50 per cent of the descending Wacos took flak, and a similar proportion were struck by small arms. Nevertheless, the incoming glider pilots kept cutting away from their tugs and diving into the hellhole that was LZ S.

Every building seemed to house a crew of snipers, and the zone was infested with entrenched German infantrymen who concentrated their fire on the gliders. There were several batteries of artillery which were firing on the British troops still crossing the Rhine. On seeing dozens of gliders suddenly skidding across their front, the German gun crews lowered their tubes for direct fire. The 194th Glider Infantry literally had to fight its way out of the Wacos. Within seconds of touching down, the widely scattered American glider troops and pilots were involved in at least 150 separate battles on their LZ. Under these circumstances, fighting came first and assembly second.

As they descended through the dense smoke, Flight Officer

[317]

George Julian and his copilot, Flight Officer Jack Neff, could hear the loud whack of German rifle bullets hitting the wings of his glider. At 200 feet the smoke thinned sufficiently for Julian to see that they were not going to reach their designated landing area. He dived down to the nearest field, crashed deliberately through two fences to reduce his airspeed, and hooked the port wing on a brick house. The glider slewed around and came to an abrupt halt.

Dust was still billowing around the glider when its plexiglass nose was shattered by machine gun fire. Both pilots and all passengers dashed outside and took cover in a nearby ditch that was half filled with water. With bullets kicking up clods of dirt all around them, one of the Americans in the ditch said, 'That fire is coming from the house we just hit with our glider!' At that, Julian instructed a bazooka gunner lying near him to pump a round into the house.

Using the bazooka fire for cover, Julian ran up to the front door of the house and threw a grenade inside. As soon as it exploded he dashed inside, expecting to see dead German soldiers. But all he found were several chickens and a goat, all of which had been killed by his grenade. Sure that some German soldiers were in the house, he ran through the hallway and tossed another grenade into the dining room. Again, no sign of the enemy. He eventually worked his way to the rear of the house where he found the back door wide open. He could see two German soldiers running away, and dashing out onto the back steps, he took aim, fired, and dropped them both in their tracks.

Julian walked back outside and rejoined his companions. Just then another serial of gliders began landing around them. One of the Wacos crashed into some tree stumps and tore itself to pieces. Julian and the others worked feverishly to extricate the injured from the wreckage but were hampered by a resurgence of German mortar fire.

Between mortar bursts, Julian removed one of the pilots whose left leg was almost completely severed at the knee. After applying a tourniquet and giving the pilot a shot of morphine, Julian examined the grisly wound. It was clear that the lower half of the pilot's leg would have to be removed to facilitate his evacuation from the battlefield. But there were no trained medics in the area, and Julian wondered who was going to perform the amputation. The growing intensity of German mortar fire convinced Julian that he would have to find a solution to the dilemma at once or the pilot would die before reaching a doctor. In desperation, Julian drew his M-3 bayonet, gritted his teeth, and sliced the leg off. Then he carried the pilot to a road along which he had seen jeeploads of troops racing to their assembly areas.

Standing by the roadside with the pilot lying at his feet, Julian waved frantically to the first jeep that came along. But the jeep driver, hellbent for the assembly area, refused to stop. Infuriated, Julian felt like shooting at the jeep, but he held his fire and stepped out into the middle of the road. When the next jeep came along he aimed his rifle straight at the driver's head and ordered him to stop. After loading the injured pilot into the back seat he instructed the frightened jeep driver to take him to the nearest aid station. With that, the driver stomped his foot on the gas pedal and roared away.[5]

Twenty-year-old flight Officer Richard F. Jaisonkowski was one of the rare individuals who could boast of being an alumnus of both the Air Force's power pilot training school and the Project Red glider flying course. For most of his life Jaisonkowski had been an avid aviation buff, building model airplanes and reading everything in print about the World War I air aces. Only seven months before, he had graduated from flight school with a burning desire to become a fighter ace in the skies over Europe. Now he lay in the dirt beside his just-landed glider with an infantryman's submachine gun in his hands and German bullets whizzing over his head. Just a few feet away from him lay one of his passengers, wounded during the descent into LZ S. It was a rude introduction to infantry combat for a school-trained fighter pilot.

Jaisonkowski and his party were the target of a group of German soldiers sniping at them from a barn only 50 yards from where they had landed. Three glider troopers tried silencing the Germans with rifle fire but were unable to do so. Seeing that heavier firepower was necessary for the task, Jaisonkowski left the cover of the glider and crawled off to one side, where he raised his submachine gun and hosed the barn down with a full magazine of .45 calibre slugs. That one courageous act put an end to the snipers and qualified Jaisonkowski the fighter pilot as a genuine combat infantry veteran.[6]

What little enemy fire remained in the area of Jaisonkowski's glider was completely silenced by the actions of an American jeep driver who had captured a German soldier. Though such treatment of prisoners is forbidden by the Geneva Convention, the jeep driver had forced the German at gunpoint to sit on the bonnet of his jeep. He then drove around the LZ with his human bonnet ornament in full view of the enemy gunners. Fearful of hitting one of their own troops, the Germans ceased firing. During that lull, many small glider units were able to tend their wounded and move to their assembly areas.

In a field one mile outside of LZ S, Flight Officers Hance A. Lunday and Dale Oliver slammed the belly of their Waco into the dirt at 90 miles per hour, skidded 100 feet with locked brakes, and came to a stop. About half an hour later they were rolling along in a two-jeep convoy that was making its way toward the LZ. Both pilots were passengers in the second jeep. Sitting on the bonnet of their vehicle was a young American glider trooper with his rifle at the ready.

Suddenly, as their jeep was turning a corner, it was fired on by German troops in the distance along the left side of the road. A shell exploded in front of the jeep, throwing the young glider trooper violently to the ground. At that, everyone dived into a ditch along the roadside. Their young trooper lay where he had fallen, silent and still. The unharmed jeep sat where it had been abandoned, its engine running in neutral.

During a brief lull in the firing Flight Officer Lunday volunteered to go and see if the glider trooper was dead or alive. He ran out on the road, knelt down beside him, and saw that he was conscious. 'Are you hit?' inquired Lunday.

'Yes sir,' replied the trooper, 'but I'm not sure where. I just hurt all over.'

As Lunday tried to figure out how to move the soldier, a blast of German machine gun bullets passed within inches of his head. He dropped to the pavement and slid around behind the jeep. With the enemy fire passing overhead, Lunday crawled back over to the wounded trooper and grasped both of his arms. Bracing his own feet against a jeep tyre for leverage, he flung the man into the ditch with his companions.

Returning to the ditch himself, Lunday examined the soldier. He discovered that his shoulder had been pierced by shrapnel and a large section of his back had been blown away. A conference was held, and the group decided to carry the wounded soldier over to the still idling jeep as quickly as they could and deliver him to a medical facility before he bled to death.

Because he had the most powerful weapon, a Thompson sub-machine gun, Lunday volunteered to provide covering fire for the getaway. His opening shots were to be the signal for everyone to start moving. Slapping a fresh 30-round magazine in his Thompson, Lunday began laying a heavy blast of fire into the German positions. When he turned around a few moments later all he saw was his copilot, Dale Oliver. Both jeeps, the wounded soldier, and everyone else was gone. 'What happened?' asked Lunday. 'Well, Hance, replied Oliver, 'it looks to me like they've gone off and left us.' Fortunately the German fire soon subsided, allowing Lunday and Oliver to withdraw and eventually to make their way to LZ S.

By noon the 194th Glider Infantry was 73 per cent assembled, and German resistance in LZ S was starting to crumble. When the shooting finally stopped at about 3:00 p.m., Pierce reported to division that his regiment had, with the assistance of numerous glider pilots, knocked out 42 artillery pieces and 10 tanks, and had captured 1,150 prisoners. Battle casualties for the 194th Glider Infantry amounted to 50 killed and 103 wounded. The glider pilots had suffered an additional 18 killed, 80 wounded, and 30 missing in action.

Fighting on LZ S was just starting to subside when, at 11:55 a.m., the leading serial of gliders bound for LZ N approached the Rhine squarely on course, within sighting distance of the yellow smoke marking the point at which they were to cross the river. A total of 313 Wacos from the 314th, 440th, 441st, and 442nd Troop Carrier groups were in this mission, all in single-tow. Only one glider had been forced to drop out during the long trip up the Rhine, making this the most successful massed combat approach flight ever performed by any nation during the war.

On board these gliders were 1,321 troops of the 139th Engineer Battalion and several small units of medical, signal and staff personnel. The planners of Varsity had counted on the 513th Parachute Infantry – which was to have been dropped on neighbouring DZ X at 10:10 a.m. – having LZ N almost completely cleared of German troops by the time these lightly armed specialists arrived there. But the 513th had been misdropped near Hamminkeln and was still engaged there when the glider pilots began their cutaways.

As had happened during the previous mission to LZ S, some tow-planes in the middle and at the end of the formations had, unfortunately, overrun the leading aircraft and were climbing to avoid collisions. Many of the gliders in the trailing 441st Troop Carrier Group had to make their cutaways at 2,500 feet, a record combat release altitude for the Americans.[7]

[321]

Intense fire, mainly from small arms, met the gliders as they coasted down. Because they could not see through the smoke, the Germans held their fire until the Wacos were below 500 feet. Unwilling to serve as targets any longer than necessary, most glider pilots dived down in tight spirals and made fast, rough landings. Over 50 per cent of the Wacos were damaged in accidents, but their loads came through intact. Some glider pilots managed to land among friendly troops north or south of LZ N, but the zone itself was strongly defended by German infantrymen. Every building and patch of woods seemed to hide at least a squad of enemy troops.

The glider piloted by Flight Officer Theodore Daugherty was packed full of dynamite belonging to the 139th Engineer Battalion. On the final leg of its 270-degree landing pattern it received a broadside blast of flak which ignited the dynamite and blew the ship to bits. The force of the explosion was so great that it rocked the wings of another Waco, flown by Flight Officer Harold W. Morgan, a veteran of the Bastogne glider mission. Morgan's glider carried crates of mortar shells and four passengers.

When Daugherty's glider had exploded, Morgan had been directly behind him and was diving to catch up to him. Morgan's airspeed indicator was reading 150 miles per hour when his copilot, a lieutenant power pilot who had been pressed into service as a copilot, exclaimed, 'We're going too damn fast, we'll tear the wings off this bird!' Morgan reacted by pulling the drag chute, but it failed to deploy completely. He then pulled on full spoilers and set her down hard, wiping out his undercarriage in the process.

Though Morgan and his companions did not suffer the same fate as Daugherty, they had the misfortune to slide to a halt only 100 yards away from a house packed with German soldiers. The four glider troopers managed to get out of the Waco without getting shot, but Morgan's copilot was wounded in the chest and throat just as he was dashing out the door. Morgan leaped out right behind him without getting hit.

With German rifle bullets thumping into the side of his glider, Morgan said to his small group, 'We're going to have to make a run for it before she blows.' Hearing this, the wounded copilot pleaded, 'Hey, you guys, don't leave me, I'm dying.' The German rifle fire was growing more accurate. Morgan raised his eyes toward heaven and implored, 'Please, God, get us out of here alive, and help me find a medic for my copilot.'

[322]

Morgan turned to the wounded copilot. 'Listen,' he said, 'I know you have been hit, but you're going to have to get on your feet and run with us to that pond over there or we are all going to die when this thing explodes any second now.'

'I can do it,' said the copilot. Morgan and his group scrambled to their feet and ran the 50 yards to the pond, firing at the enemy-occupied house as they went. Everyone made it.

Within one minute of their arrival at the pond, a glider filled with medical personnel skidded to a halt right beside them. Two of its passengers went to work on the copilot and saved his life. Morgan's prayer had been fully answered – and in near record time.

The intense enemy fire all across LZ N caused a number of gliders to be unloaded quickly, some within seconds of coming to a halt on the ground. Flight Officer Don F. Conover deliberately wiped out the landing gear of his Waco in an attempt to bring it to a quick stop. But he had landed on packed dirt, and his glider just kept sliding at a frightening pace. Finally the skids dug in, forcing the tail up into the air. A few seconds later the fuselage thumped down hard and the ship stopped moving. Concerned about the 14 soldiers he had on board, Conover quickly turned and yelled into the troop compartment, 'Everyone okay back there?' Conover heard a loud chorus of 'yes, sir', but he couldn't see a soul in the troop compartment. Turning around, he glanced out of the window, and saw all 14 of his passengers, who had already left the glider and were lying beneath the wings preparing to fight back at the Germans.

Many other glider crews never got the chance to begin unloading because of disasters which overtook them while they were still skidding across the landing fields. Flight Officer Theodore V. Sampson saw several of those unfortunate gliders as he made his way across LZ N. He passed one field in which eight badly burned British Horsas had landed after overshooting their assigned LZs. At its border was an unmanned German 88-mm flak gun with a big pile of empty shell casings beside it. Because all eight of the Horsas still contained the charred bodies of their pilots and crews, Sampson reckoned the German gunners must have hit them repeatedly with white phosphorous shells as they were slowly coming to a halt.

This was the fourth time that Lieutenant Robert H. Price had landed a glider in combat. Though he had been shot at on several occasions during his previous missions to southern France, Holland and Bastogne, Price had yet to come face to face with an armed

[323]

German on the ground. He therefore had never fired his weapon in combat nor harmed a German soldier.

Price and his copilot, Flight Officer Harry Orton, had a jeep and two passengers on board their glider. They were just preparing to set down in a large field when they spotted a German infantryman who had abandoned his foxhole on the LZ and was running across their glide path toward the relative safety of a stone house. Seeing the glider bearing down on him, the German panicked. He halted, snapped off a couple of shots at it and then changed course. Price kicked the rudder and pursued him. The German fired another few shots and changed course a second time. Price kicked the rudder again, realigning the big ship up on his prey. The deadly cat-and-mouse game ended a few seconds later, when the heavily loaded glider struck the German at 60 miles per hour. This is the only known instance during the war of an American pilot killing an enemy soldier with his unarmed glider.

It was not until 5:30 p.m. that the issue was decided in favour of the Americans on LZ N. The lion's share of the work in clearing the zone had been performed by the 139th Engineer Battalion fighting as infantry. Glider pilot casualties on LZ N amounted to 14 dead, 26 wounded, and 51 missing, a ratio indicating resistance almost as severe as that on LZ S.

In the British half of the compact airhead, no less than 70 of the American airplanes carrying Brigadier Hill's 3rd Parachute Brigade were hit by 20-mm shells or machine gun bullets during the run-in to DZ A. Nevertheless, the brigade was dropped accurately. A fierce battle erupted all across DZ A, but the British emerged victorious less than one hour after hitting the ground.

Some 2,000 men of Brigadier Poett's 5th Parachute Brigade began dropping on DZ B at 10:03 a.m. Their American jump planes fared even worse than those on DZ A. While turning to port after the drop, 10 were shot down east of the Rhine and seven more crash landed among British positions west of the river. Seventy others were hit but managed to keep on flying.

Poett's three parachute battalions encountered stiff resistance from German units on DZ B. But in an hour-long series of sharp skirmishes the British carved out a victory there and went on to storm Hamminkeln.

The 6th Air Landing Brigade's gliders were loaded with 3,383 troops, 271 jeeps, 66 artillery pieces, and several Tetrarch tanks. As he had done previously in Normandy and Holland, Lieutenant Colonel Iain Murray would again command the Glider Pilot Regiment on the ground in Varsity.

At 10:30 a.m. – precisely on schedule – the British gliders began spiralling down through the smoke into four LZs lettered O, P, R and U. All four were on the east side of the Diersfordter Forest and therefore at the deepest point inside German territory. While descending, the Horsas and Hamilcars were subjected to intense small arms fire and shelling from 20-mm flak guns. One flak gun scored a direct hit on a Hamilcar (which, when empty, weighs nine tons). The force of the explosion ripped the floor out of the giant glider, sending the tank it was carrying into a nose dive like an enormous bomb. In rapid succession nine more British gliders were blasted out of the sky, and 284 others were holed by small arms fire as they touched down.

Like all other units arriving in the airhead, these British glider troops had to start fighting the instant they touched down. About the only place where unloading could begin was LZ O, where much of the American 513th Parachute Infantry had been misdropped. Still, a number of glider troops landing there experienced some anxious moments.

Squadron Leader V. H. Reynolds, commander of the Glider Pilot Regiment's F Squadron, made his approach to the zone under a steady stream of fire from a four-barrelled 20-mm anti-aircraft gun. His ranking passenger was Lieutenant Colonel Mark Darrel-Brown, the commanding officer of the Oxfordshire and Buckinghamshire Light Infantry, who had requested to be landed near the railroad station in Hamminkeln. As they came down, Reynolds's copilot fired his Sten gun right through the front windshield, killing or wounding all of the troublesome 20-mm gun crew. A few seconds later they rolled to a stop beside the railway station. As they entered the station a disabled Horsa whistled over their heads and smashed itself to pieces on the railroad tracks, killing both pilots and all of its 16 passengers.

Earlier, during the Normandy invasion, special volunteers from the Oxfordshire and Buckinghamshire Light Infantry had landed aboard six Horsas in complete darkness. Their mission then had been to seize two key bridges over the Caen Canal and Orne River. Today, those troops once again had the mission of landing aboard six Horsas and grabbing a pair of key bridges, this time over the Issel River at Hamminkeln.

Moving with the same speed and courage they had displayed in

Normandy, the Oxford and Bucks crash landed on the outskirts of Hamminkeln and seized both bridges before the surprised Germans could destroy them. Elsewhere the 12th Devons and the Royal Ulster Rifles rooted out stubborn German defenders within Hamminkeln.

General Eric Bols, the commander of the 6th Airborne, landed aboard a Horsa on LZ P, only 100 yards from the Kopenhof Farm which he had selected from a map in England to be his division CP. Two Horsas were burning in an adjacent field and cases of ammunition inside them were cooking off, giving everyone the impression that a fierce firefight was in progress. As Bols leaped down on to the ground he was happily surprised to see troopers of the American 513th Parachute Infantry accepting the surrender of the last of the German troops who had been defending the farm.

At 11:15 a.m. General Bols had his entire headquarters staff assembled and functioning smoothly at the Kopenhof Farm. By that time all of his brigades had checked in on the division radio net, and contact was established with the Royal Artillery battalions on the west bank of the Rhine. During the early afternoon, Bols received the good news that his brigades had completed the capture of their final objectives and that ground link-up had been made by the infantry battalions advancing from the riverline.

When the shooting finally stopped later that afternoon, 38 officers and sergeants of the British Glider Pilot Regiment lay dead on the various landing zones. Another 77 had been wounded, and 135 more were missing. These were indeed heavy losses, heavier even than those suffered by the regiment during its first day at Arnhem or in Normandy.

Well before sunset on D-Day, Operation Varsity was declared a complete success. Link-up between the airborne troops and infantry units was actually made at 3:00 p.m., and the way was now clear for the ground troops to continue their drive deeper into Germany. D-day casualties for the two Allied airborne divisions were far greater than anticipated. The British 6th Airborne reported 347 of its men killed and another 731 wounded. The American 17th Airborne had 393 men killed and 834 wounded, and counted 282 as missing in action. Casualties among air crews of the American IX Troop Carrier Command, which conducted all of the parachute drops and towed the 17th Airborne's gliders, came to 41 killed, 153 wounded and 163 missing. The loss of 22 jump planes (all of them C-46s) and 12 glider-towing C-47s made this the war's most costly airborne operation.

By the time darkness began to settle over the battlefield on D-Day, the senior glider officer on LZ S had already dispatched 50 pilots to guard the CP of the 17th Airborne Division. He had also assigned two companies of pilots to occupy defensive positions along the railroad embankment at the west end of the zone, one company to guard prisoners, and one to defend a crossroads two miles northeast of Wesel.

General Ridgway and a few members of his staff from XVIII Airborne Corps had reached DZ W at 3:26 p.m. after crossing the Rhine aboard a British assault boat. From DZ W Ridgway proceeded into the town of Fluren and set up his headquarters beside the CP of the 17th Airborne Division. Around 8:00 p.m., the corps commander decided that he and General Miley should pay General Bols a visit at his CP on the Kopenhof Farm, only three miles due north through the Diersfordter Forest. Riding in one jeep, with a second armed jeep following, Ridgway and Miley drove through the forest at a snail's pace under total blackout conditions. Finally, at 11:00 p.m., they reached the 6th Airborne CP. For the next hour the three generals pored over tactical maps and made plans for the next day's operations.

Ridgway and Miley departed the Kopenhof Farm shortly after midnight on their return trip to Fluren. They had only been travelling a short while when Ridgway saw several darkened forms of men about 20 yards ahead of him on the road. 'Germans!' yelled someone in the rear jeep. With his trusty Springfield rifle in his hand, Ridgway leaped out of the jeep shooting. The lead German was knocked down screaming, with a bullet in him, and for the next few minutes, there was a wild exchange of gunfire between the two sides.

Having expended his first clip of ammo, Ridgway dropped to the ground beside his jeep to reload.[8] Just then a German hand grenade exploded under the jeep, sending steel fragments in all directions. Ridgway's life was saved by the jeep's right front wheel, but he did not escape the blast unharmed. A sliver of hot steel from the grenade had gone deep into his left shoulder.

Taking advantage of the confusion, the German patrol slipped away into the darkness. Ridgway's party crowded into the one good jeep and returned to Fluren without further incident. There a doctor patched up Ridgway's wound but was unable to remove the grenade fragment without performing major surgery. Rather than be incapacitated for several days while recovering from surgery, Ridgway told the doctor not to operate. He suffered through the rest of the war with that piece of German steel in his arm.[9]

The glider pilots from the 435th Troop Carrier Group had been

[327]

sent earlier in the afternoon of D-Day to defend the crossroads northeast of Wesel. The four squadrons that made up the group – the 75th, 76th, 77th and 78th – were deployed from left to right in an arc about the area with the 77th assigned to sit squarely on top of the crossroads. The strength of the 77th was 30 officers, some of whom had been injured and wounded earlier in the day out on the landing zones. Except for half a dozen brick houses at the crossroads, the entire area being defended by the 435th Group consisted of wide open farm fields. Several empty American gliders rested in those fields.

Sporadic rifle and machine gun fire rattled across the darkened airhead as airborne troopers rounded up small groups of Germans trying to infiltrate their front lines. Things were just starting to quiet down around the crossroads when, at 11:55 p.m., a stricken German Ju 88 bomber crash landed in a field right beside the crossroads and slid to a halt with its nose touching the wreckage of a Waco.

Flight Officer Oliver C. Faris, a glider pilot in the 75th Squadron, ran out to the bomber immediately, thinking it was a British aircraft. He found its two pilots alive and still sitting at the controls. Lying on the ground beside the fuselage were two crewmen, one dead, the other only semiconscious. Unable to see the bomber's markings in the darkness, Faris inquired of the two pilots, 'Are you British?'

'No,' said the one nearest him, in English. 'We are Germans, but this war is over for us.' Both pilots handed their pistols over to Faris.

Faris helped the pilot closest to him out of the wreckage and turned him over to the group of American glider troops who had joined him. He then motioned the other pilot to get out, but the German kept pointing to his leg, which was pinned under his seat by a propeller blade that had pierced the side of the cockpit. Faris had just about worked the pilot's leg free when, suddenly, all hell broke loose over in the crossroads. A barrage of enemy mortar shells set the roof of one house ablaze, and panzer engines could be heard growling in the distance. Recognizing the signs of an imminent German counterattack, Faris turned the enemy airmen over to the glider troopers and started running back toward his foxhole.

There was indeed a full-scale counterattack in progress, conducted by a German infantry battalion. Its main focal point was the crossroads being held by the pilots of the 77th Squadron.

Earlier in the afternoon those pilots had spent considerable time digging foxholes and gun emplacements alongside a large brick house that sat facing the main north-south street running through the crossroads. In an open field just across from the brick house was a .50 calibre machine gun nest occupied by three troopers of the 194th Glider Infantry Regiment. Most of the civilian occupants of the homes in that area had been evacuated to the rear while it was being prepared for defence by the pilots. However, the German family living in the big brick house was given permission by the glider pilots to remain in their home until further notice. In appreciation, its elderly occupants had invited some of the pilots in for a mid-afternoon plate of stew and boiled potatoes.

By the light of a few fires that had been started by incoming shells, the glider pilots caught sight of several German scouts advancing on their positions. Right behind the scouts came two platoons of infantrymen who suddenly opened up with their MP 38 Schmeisser submachine guns, a very rapid firing weapon which the Americans called a 'burp' gun. The pilots coolly held their fire until the Germans were just across the street, then cut loose with a murderous blast of rifle and machine gun fire which slowed the attack.

One of the Germans who had fallen in the crossroads kept calling out to his companions who had dropped back. When none of them came forward to rescue him, he pleaded in English to the pilots. 'Help, please, I am wounded. I have an uncle in Milwaukee.' He really sounded as if he was in great pain, but his plea cut no ice with the pilots, who were suspicious that the whole thing might be a trick to draw them out into the open. They let him lie where he was and reloaded their weapons.

A new barrage of mortar shells began falling in and around the crossroads. One shell struck a glider that had landed only 50 yards away from the crossroads and set it on fire. By the light of its bright blaze, the pilots saw two German tanks advancing on them. The leading tank had just entered the crossroads when it fired its main battle gun, knocking out the .50 calibre emplacement across the street from the brick house.

From his foxhole on the left side of the brick house, Flight Officer Joseph H. Menard could see several German soldiers mounted on the leading tank. He began firing at them with his M-1 rifle. The tank commander trained his turret around and began lowering the main battle gun at Menard. For a split second, Menard thought of climbing out of his foxhole and running, but he knew that if he ran he would certainly be killed by shrapnel of the German tank shell when

[329]

it exploded. In desperation, he shot a couple of bullets at the tank's gun in the hope that one of them would enter its muzzle, travel up the tube, and explode the shell being aimed at him.

At the moment that Menard was squeezing off his hasty shots at the tank, Flight Officer Elbert D. Jella was lining up the sights of his bazooka on the tank, from his position on the right side of the brick house. Jella fired, and not a moment too soon. His bazooka rocket struck the tank's right side, causing the German gunner to fire his main battle gun before its tube was properly aimed at Menard. The German shell hit a few feet in front of Menard's foxhole, ricocheted over his head, and struck the side of the house. Though he suffered an eye wound and could not hear very well, Menard was at least still alive.

With its right tread in flames, the lead German tank backed down the same path it had travelled into the crossroads. As it did, it ran over a small 20-mm anti-aircraft gun that it was towing. Shaking the demolished gun free, the tank limped backwards and took cover between two brick houses. The second tank followed suit, backing between two adjoining houses.

Having thus lost much of its shock effect and firepower, the German attack began to falter. Sensing that victory was within their grasp, the glider pilots fired everything they had until the attacking Germans withdrew, leaving only their wounded and two abandoned tanks on the field.

At daybreak the glider pilots counted 13 dead German infantrymen lying in the crossroads. Among the dead was the soldier whose uncle lived in Milwaukee. He appeared to be about 17 years of age. Seeing his body, an unsympathetic pilot remarked, 'Too bad, kid. You should have moved to Milwaukee with your uncle instead of letting Hitler get you in all this trouble.'

The pilots, along with some soldiers from the adjacent glider troop units, made a security sweep around their positions. They found 45 wounded German infantrymen lying about the crossroads, and they captured 80 others who had been cut off from their companions during the counterattack. At the completion of the sweep several pilots wandered over to take a close look at the Ju 88 that had crashed near them during the night. They discovered two bodies: one was the German crewman who had been thrown out during the crash, the other the pilot who had been trapped inside the wreckage. He was still sitting at the controls. Someone had shot him through the head.

So ended the struggle for the crossroads. It had cost the Americans three dead glider troopers, and two wounded glider pilots. Because the Germans had used so many Schmeisser 'burp guns', this battle is remembered by those pilots who took part in it as the Battle of Burp Gun Corner. On April 1, the *Stars and Stripes* newspaper carried a feature article about the brave band of glider pilots from the 77th Squadron who had repelled a vastly superior enemy force during Varsity. The writer titled his article 'The Battle of Burp Gun Corner' and heaped praise on the pilots for their outstanding achievement.

Though the 77th Squadron's pilots won acclaim in the press and throughout the ranks of the 17th Airborne, not one of them was ever awarded a decoration. The only medals handed out for that battle were two Purple Hearts, which went to the pilots who had been wounded.

At 9:00 a.m. that day, March 25, the Allied glider pilots were relieved from the line. In the 17th Airborne area, 583 American pilots marched all the way back to the Rhine as armed escorts for 2,456 German prisoners. After delivering the prisoners to military policemen the pilots were ferried across the Rhine to a British artillery base. Some British soldiers had erected a sign there in front of a few tents. It read, 'The Rhine Hotel – Glider Pilots a Speciality.' Below that was printed, '63 bedrooms – Constant cold water – No baths– DUKW hire service and trips across the Rhine.'

Waiting trucks transported the pilots to an airfield at Helmond. From Helmond, troop carrier planes ferried them back to their home stations in France. Despite some delays at Helmond, three-quarters of the American pilots were returned to France before the end of D plus 4, and almost all who were fit to travel were back within six days.

Glider salvage operations started on March 26. A small caretaker detachment arriving in the airhead that day found the gliders greatly damaged, and most of their clocks and compasses missing. Some 600 glider technicians arrived on April 4 and eventually repaired 148 Wacos which were then snatched out and returned to France for complete overhaul.

British glider technicians were only able to locate 24 Horsas worth saving. Because it was considered unfeasible to snatch the Horsas out, they were disassembled and hauled by truck to airfields in France. There they were reassembled and towed back to England.

The rest of the American and British gliders were cannibalized for spare parts. Salvaged material from the Wacos alone filled 47 trucks and 30 trailers.

[331]

From his previous combat experiences in North Africa, France and Holland, Field Marshal Montgomery had acquired respect for the German Army's ability to recover quickly from near mortal tactical defeats. He therefore denied his eager field commanders permission to advance deeper into Germany until he had moved 20 combat divisions and 1,500 tanks over to the east bank of the Rhine. Finally, on March 26 – two full days after Operation Varsity – Monty loosened the reins. Ridgway's XVIII Airborne Corps, with the British 6th Guards Brigade attached, led off the attack. With whole squads of airborne troopers clinging to them, the British tanks advanced eastward against light opposition. At the end of the day Ridgway's forces had advanced more than 3,000 yards deeper in Germany.

By March 28, Monty had considerably extended his beachhead line, to a depth of 20 miles across 30 miles of his front. During this eastward thrust, Ridgway's corps captured an additional 7,000 prisoners and occupied the critical defiles at Haltern and Dulman. Tanks from the American 2nd Armoured Division burst through those defiles on the twenty-ninth and began a great sweeping manoeuvre to the southeast. Far to the south, meanwhile, Patton's Third Army – which had crossed the Rhine unopposed at Oppenheim one day prior to Monty's crossing – began driving northward to connect with the 2nd Armoured. Like a pair of giant steel jaws, these two armoured formations rapidly penetrated far to the rear of the German units trying to halt Montgomery's frontal attack. The stage was now set for what became known as the great Ruhr encirclement. The fate of all German troops caught up at the Ruhr pocket, as this battle area was called, was sealed on March 31. The steel jaws snapped shut as the two American armoured forces met at Lippstadt to complete the encirclement.

Field Marshal Kesselring, Hitler's Commander-in-Chief West, managed to make a night-time escape from the Ruhr pocket by flying to Berchtesgaden aboard his private airplane. Though Kesselring had managed to elude capture temporarily, some 350,000 of his troops were taken prisoner in the Ruhr pocket. Included in that impressive count were 22 generals, one of whom was General Kurt Student, the father of the German airborne. For several days prior to his capture by British soldiers, Student had been hiding in the cellars of destroyed buildings. Another prominent officer captured by British troops was General Heinrich Luettwitz. It was Luettwitz who had demanded the surrender of the surrounded 101st Airborne Division three months before at Bastogne during the Battle of the Bulge.

Near the town of Stockhausen, a lieutenant in the 17th Airborne Division's 194th Glider Infantry captured Captain Franz von Papen, son and namesake of the famous German diplomat. Later that same day the glider troopers captured the elder von Papen. As a former Vice-Chancellor of Germany and envoy to both Turkey and the United States, Franz von Papen Senior was the most important political catch made in the Ruhr pocket.

Field Marshal Walter Model, the Lion of Defence, and the commander who had denied Arnhem to the Allies during Operation Market-Garden, was also caught up in the Ruhr Pocket, but he refused to surrender. General Ridgway's troops cornered Model in a large forested area along with thousands of his bedraggled Army Group B. In an attempt to avoid unnecessary bloodshed, Ridgway sent one of his aides, a captain fluent in German, to Model's headquarters under a flag of truce on April 19 with a written offer of an honourable surrender for Model and all his remaining forces. The aide returned a few hours later with a German colonel, Model's chief of staff. Speaking through the American captain, the colonel told Ridgway that Model was refusing to surrender because he had sworn a personal oath to Hitler to fight until death.

Without mincing any words, Ridgway then proceeded to tell the colonel that he was free to return to his own lines if he wished, but that if he did, he would surely be killed within a few days at most. Somewhat shaken by Ridgway's blunt statement, the colonel said that he wished to surrender himself at once. Two days later, as the Allied ring closed tighter around his headquarters near Dusseldorf, Model said to his aide, Colonel Klaus Pilling, 'My time has come. Follow me.' The Lion of Defence then walked briskly into a secluded part of the forest, halted and drew his pistol. Colonel Pilling begged repeatedly for Model not to commit suicide, but Model would not listen to his entreaties. In a voice heavy with despair, Model said, 'A field marshal does not become a prisoner. Such a thing is just not possible.' With that he pressed the pistol to his skull and killed himself.[10]

Despite the crushing defeat of his forces in the Ruhr, Hitler still held out hope for ultimate victory. When, on April 12, 1945, U.S. President Roosevelt died suddenly, Hitler's spirits lifted. He

[333]

believed that with Roosevelt's death the Grand Alliance between Western and Eastern powers would disintegrate and that each of the Allied nations would greedily pursue its own interests. But that, of course, did not happen. And when, on April 28, Hitler received the news that Mussolini had been arrested by Italian partisans while attempting to escape into Switzerland and had been executed along with his mistress, Clara Peracci, Hitler's morale reached a new low. On April 30, with vengeful Russian infantrymen only a few blocks from his Berlin command bunker, Hitler put the barrel of his pistol into his mouth and pulled the trigger.

Russian troops completed the capture of Berlin on May 2, but it was not until Monday, May 7, that Germany formally admitted defeat. At 2:41 a.m. General Alfred Jodl signed the official surrender document in a small schoolhouse in Rheims, France. The surrender ceremony was repeated the next day in Berlin for the benefit of the Russians, and U.S. President Harry S Truman declared that date, May 8, 1945, V-E Day, for Victory in Europe.

When news of the German surrender was announced it triggered wild celebrations throughout the Allied world. The news was received with far less fanfare by the Allied combat troops. To them it simply meant that there were no more foxholes to dig, no more glider landings or parachute jumps to sweat out, and another agonizingly long wait for their units to be shipped home.

The total destruction of the Nazi war and political machines placed an overwhelming burden on the small Allied military government units whose job it was to restore order in Germany. Millions of displaced persons, prisoners of war and ordinary German citizens had to be cared for by the conquering Allies. Another task, of more lasting significance than the food shortages and other emergencies found in all German cities, faced the Allied military government units: the vetting of individuals – preferably anti-Nazis – who were qualified to assume positions of leadership in a new municipal government structure.

When the Allied military government units began to buckle under the weight of their responsibilities, the top American and British brass issued orders to their now idle infantry and tank divisions to lend a hand. Whole battalions of combat soldiers who had fought to destroy the German army were now given the job of helping Germany get back on its feet. Armed now with shovels and bulldozers, they cleared rubble from city streets and restored broken water,

[334]

electrical, sewer and gas mains. The groundwork laid by those Allied combat battalions provided a firm foundation upon which the Federal Republic of Germany made an amazing economic and political recovery in the postwar years.

During this initial reconstruction period, the American glider pilots were employed as copilots aboard paratroop and glider tug airplanes that had been assigned to help relocate liberated prisoners of war and displaced persons to all parts of Europe.

While the copilot of a C-47 evacuating American prisoners of war out of Germany, Flight Officer Theodore V. Sampson spotted Flight Officer Roy Bailey, a former member of his own 97th Squadron. The last time the two men had seen each other other had been nine months before, in the middle of a firefight on a glider LZ in Holland. Though he was exceedingly thin, Bailey said he had not been mistreated by his captors. But when Sampson inquired about Flight Officer Eugene H. Meyers, who had also been captured in Holland, Bailey told him that Meyers and his whole crew had been shot by German troops immediately after they had surrendered on the LZ.

Meanwhile, in England, Brigadier George Chatterton and all surviving members of his British Glider Pilot Regiment were busy loading their personal combat equipment and crated Horsa and Hamilcar gliders aboard a small fleet of Royal Navy ships. Orders had been issued for the regiment's immediate redeployment to India, where it was to begin a rigid training programme with British Major General Eric E. Down's 44th Indian Airborne Division. Down's division was preparing to launch an attack into Japanese-occupied Malaya.

[335]

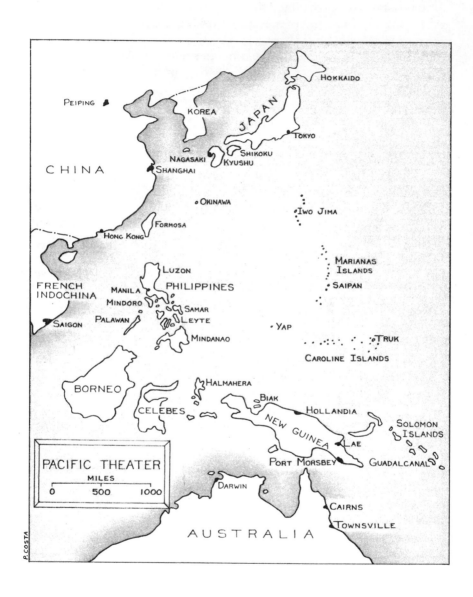

# Chapter 12

# *Deliverance From Shangri-la*

WHEN GENERAL MACARTHUR HAD first arrived in Australia from the Philippines in March of 1942 he was 62 years old and at the lowest point in his theretofore spectacular career.

Since graduating at the top of his West Point class in 1903, Douglas MacArthur had risen rapidly. He went overseas during World War I as a colonel in the 42nd 'Rainbow' Infantry Division. While serving with that division in France he was wounded twice, decorated for heroism, and promoted to Brigadier General in June 1918, at the age of 38. Not since the Civil War had so young an American been promoted to general officer rank. Following World War I, MacArthur further distinguished himself in such prestigious duty assignments as Superintendent of West Point and Chief of Staff of the U.S. Army.

But MacArthur's brilliant military record mattered not at all to the Japanese, who defeated him soundly in the Philippines and then forced his retreat to the island of Corregidor in Manila Bay. MacArthur had wanted to remain on Corregidor with his surrounded troops to the bitter end; President Roosevelt had to order him to escape to Australia. Like Germany's Field Marshal Rommel, who would be pulled out of North Africa just prior to the Axis collapse there, MacArthur was too valuable to be allowed to fall into enemy hands.

Within moments of his arrival in Adelaide, MacArthur made a brief but powerful speech, the last three words of which echoed around the world. 'The President of the United States ordered me to break through the Japanese lines and proceed to Australia for the purpose, as I understand it, of organizing the American offensive against Japan, a primary object of which is the relief of the Philippines. I came through and I shall return.'

Thousands of American infantry troops and tons of supplies were

[337]

pouring into Australia from the United States when, in July 1942, the Japanese decided to push deeper into the South Pacific to capture New Guinea and the Solomon Islands. The Japanese knew that control of those two strategically vital areas would enable them to sever the American supply line to Australia. That accomplished, they would launch a massive invasion of the Australian mainland.

When they made their move to capture New Guinea, the undefeated Japanese finally bit off more than they could chew. New Guinea, the fourth-largest island on earth, has a land area of 330,000 square miles – the size of France, Holland, Luxembourg, and West Germany combined. The elongated island, superimposed on a map of the United States, stretches from New York City to the Texas panhandle; or from London to Athens.

After landing first at Gona in eastern New Guinea, the Japanese stunned the top Allied brass by doing what everyone had thought was impossible: they marched up and over the Owen Stanley Mountains and closed on Port Moresby. Only 300 air miles from Port Moresby lay the exposed northern coast of Australia. Simultaneously they landed infantry and engineer troops on Guadalcanal in the Solomons. There they began constructing an airfield from which their bombers could attack American convoys bringing troops and war *matériel* to Australia.

Allied reaction to the twin Japanese attacks was quick and effective. Australian troops were rushed to New Guinea. Fighting with their usual tenacity, the Aussies halted the Japanese when they were only 30 miles from Port Moresby, and, on August 7, the American 1st Marine Division landed on Guadalcanal against light opposition. Within 24 hours the marines took the partially completed Japanese airfield, promptly renaming it Henderson Field in honour of Major Lofton R. Henderson, a marine dive-bomber pilot who had been killed while leading the air attack on Midway Island.

The Allies' counterattacks at long last checked the aggression of Japan at the southernmost fringes of its stolen empire, finally destroying the myth of Japan's invincibility.

Having been repulsed at Port Moresby, Buna and Gona, the Japanese next tried strengthening their shaky hold on New Guinea by reinforcing the garrisons at Lae and Salamaua. MacArthur reacted by ordering his troops on New Guinea to capture the area encompassing Lae, Salamaua, Finchaven and Madang. Most important of these four cities was Lae, gateway to the Huon peninsula. Ten thousand Japanese troops were defending the Lae-Salamaua area, all of them under Lieutenant General Hatazo Adachi, the 43-year-old commander of the 18th Army. With luck, the Allies could bag Adachi and all of his troops or, at the very least, run them out of the area.

MacArthur selected the heavily defended city of Lae as the main objective for the Allied forces on New Guinea. In order to deceive the Japanese defenders and cause them to diminish their strength at Lae, MacArthur directed his forces to attack Solamaua, which lies south of Lae, first. MacArthur knew that his opponent, General Adachi, would rush a considerable number of troops from Lae to meet his attack at Salamaua.

With Lae thus weakened, MacArthur planned to seize it with a daring manoeuvre employing parachute, glider, amphibious and air-landed troops. The plan called for the Australian 9th Infantry Division to conduct an amphibious end run up the coast of New Guinea, go ashore 20 miles east of Lae, and start attacking the city from that direction. The following day, in broad daylight, the American 503rd Parachute Infantry Regiment would jump 22 miles west of Lae to seize an abandoned airfield near the town of Nadzab. Right behind the paratroopers would come a landing of 25 American Waco gliders loaded with heavy engineer equipment.

Australian engineer troops from Tsili Tsili were to infiltrate through 45 miles of jungle to be near Nadzab on the day of the airborne mission and to meet the gliders bringing in the equipment. The paratroopers and engineers were to prepare the airstrip to receive American C-47s bringing in the Australian 7th Infantry Division from Port Moresby. Immediately after landing at Nadzab, the Australian infantrymen were to march through the paratroop positions and attack Lae from the west.

MacArthur's plan was designed to force General Adachi into making one of two bad moves – either stand and fight the superior Allied forces attacking him at Salamaua and Lae, or abandon both of those cities and retreat northward to new defensive positions with the hope of stopping the Allies there. D-Day for the airborne assault at Nadzab was set for Sunday, September 4, 1943.

The American glider pilots scheduled for the airborne mission to Nadzab were assigned to the 374th Troop Carrier Group, based at Townsville, Australia. All 28 had been members of the first all-enlisted class to graduate from glider training at Elmira, New York, in June 1942. From Elmira the pilots had been posted as instructors to the Army's new Elementary–Advanced Glider Flying School in Lockbourne, Ohio. Early in January 1943 they received urgent reassignment orders and were placed aboard a crowded troop train and shipped to California. There they boarded a converted B-24 bomber for Brisbane, Australia.

On arrival in Brisbane on January 18, the glider pilots discovered that nobody was expecting them. To add insult to injury, there were no gliders anywhere in sight. (The same situation would confront another group of American glider pilots due to dock at Port Tewf, Egypt, in just a couple of weeks.)

American military officials in Australia were not sure what to do with these glider pilots. As a temporary measure they assigned them to the 11th Air Corps Replacement Control Depot in Brisbane and supplied them with a borrowed Royal Australian Air Force 1929 vintage 'Gypsy Moth' biplane trainer so that they might maintain their flying proficiency.

The pilots had been in Australia only a few days when they heard that 30 CG-4A Waco gliders had been discovered at Eagle Farm, a military air depot located only a few miles south of Brisbane. Unfortunately, all of those Wacos were still in their large wooden shipping crates. None of the pilots had ever seen a crated glider before.

One of the pilots, Flight Officer William T. Sampson, II,[1] was summoned to Lieutenant General George Kenney's office. Kenney was the commanding general of the Fifth Air Force and MacArthur's chief air adviser, and Sampson was a bit nervous about being called before him. During his meeting with the general, which took place on a Monday, Sampson was stunned to hear Kenney say, 'I've never seen one of your gliders before, but I would like to learn all about them. I want you to put on a flying and landing demonstration with one of them for me this coming Saturday.' Then, as an afterthought, Kenney said, 'And don't worry, we've got plenty of Cubs to pull the gliders.' Sampson had just discovered that the ranking airman on MacArthur's staff knew nothing about gliders. But he was just a lowly flight officer facing a three star general. Sampson saluted, faced about, and marched out into the hallway.

There he complained to a major who was the general's aide, 'Major, I doubt that a Cub could take-off towing just the rope of my glider.' The major understood and got Sampson a C-47 for the demonstration.

Sampson and his cohorts worked day and night to assemble a glider for the command performance. Fortunately, the demonstration went smoothly and General Kenney was impressed – so much so that he planned to use gliders during the airborne assault at Nadzab.

On February 25, the glider pilots stationed in Brisbane, along with 39 newly arrived glider mechanics, were transferred to the 374th Troop Carrier Group in Townsville. With only two weeks remaining until D-day at Nadzab, the glider pilots ferried 25 of their Wacos some 400 miles across the shark-infested Coral Sea to the city of Port Moresby on New Guinea. A few days later the Wacos were loaded with engineer construction equipment, hooked up again to their tugs, and hauled over the treacherous Owen Stanley Mountains to their final staging base at Dobodura.

Moving according to plan, Major General G. F. Wooten's Australian 9th Infantry Division made an amphibious landing east of Lae on September 4 and began marching on the city. The following morning the American 503rd Parachute Infantry jumped at Nadzab, where they discovered the city to be free of enemy troops and the adjacent airfield in near perfect condition. Later that afternoon the Australian engineers, who had marched the 45 miles overland from Tsili Tsili, linked up with the paratroopers and began clearing the airfield to receive the C-47s that were due early the next morning.

When General Kenney was informed that there were no Japanese forces in the area of Nadzab, and that the airfield there was in good shape, he cancelled the planned glider landing mission. It would be too risky, he said, to fly the heavily loaded gliders all the way from Dobodura to Nadzab when the equipment they contained was not badly needed in the airhead. The glider pilots receiving this news were disappointed at missing out on a combat mission but relieved that they would not have to fly overloaded gliders some 320 miles over hostile jungle terrain.

It was nearing noon on September 6 when the leading elements of Major General Vasey's Australian 7th Infantry Division began landing at Nadzab aboard C-47s of the American 54th Troop Carrier Wing. As each flight landed, the Aussies disembarked rapidly and began marching toward Lae.

Lae fell to the two converging Australian divisions on September 16. Of the 10,000 Japanese troops that had been in the Lae-Salamaua area prior to the Allied assault, some one thousand of them were –

according to Japanese war records – killed during the first few days of fighting. All others were ordered by General Adachi to withdraw northward along dense jungle trails leading to Lio and Kiari. On their trek north, an additional 2,500 Japanese soldiers died of wounds suffered at Lae and Salamaua. Six hundred others perished on the trails from exhaustion and illness.

Having gained a firm hold on the Huon Peninsula, General MacArthur continued his westward advance on New Guinea. Because he had almost complete control of the sea and air, MacArthur's strategy for securing New Guinea involved a series of leapfrog amphibious assaults along the island's north coast, the object of which was to outflank and bypass strong Japanese units, leaving them cut off from their supply bases to die on the vine. This island-hopping strategy proved effective because it substantially reduced Allied casualties and permitted the same forces and equipment to be employed again and again, so that despite the very low priority given Pacific operations, they could be continued with unrelenting pressure. Aggressive air operations also served effectively to stop the flow of food and ammunition to the bypassed enemy units.

New Guinea's mountainous and jungle-covered northern shoreline precluded the use of gliders in support of the amphibious assaults. The Wacos that had been ferried over from Australia were therefore put into storage at Dobodura, and their pilots were reassigned to other flying duties. Half of the glider pilots were assigned to artillery battalions where they flew L-5 observation airplanes and directed fire on Japanese infantry units. The other half became copilots of C-47 airplanes hauling troops and supplies from Port Moresby up and over the Owen Stanley Mountains to newly captured Japanese airfields.

Throughout the remainder of 1943 and on into the new year, MacArthur's forces on New Guinea kept bounding along the northern shoreline. By April of 1944, the city of Hollandia, with its three excellent Japanese airfields and the nearby deep water port of Humboldt Bay, had been converted to Allied use. With their capture, MacArthur established his main headquarters at Hollandia. There he began mapping out his first moves for the liberation of the Philippine Islands still some 1,300 miles to the north of New Guinea.

Shortly after the capture of Hollandia, most of the glider pilots who had been sent to Australia in January 1943 and since diverted to other flying assignments were returned to the United States. After two weeks of leave with their families, they were required to report to Malden Army Air Field in Missouri, a base where newly graduated C-47 power pilots were being trained in the art of glider towing.

Though they had escaped death in New Guinea, some of these glider pilots were killed in their own country while being towed by inexperienced C-47 pilots. The routine at Malden Army Air Field required the glider pilots to participate in frequent night training missions. During one such exercise, two flights that were supposed to be at different altitudes crossed paths at the same altitude, and the glider pilots had to make emergency cutaways that scattered them far and wide on a moonless night. As one of the gliders crashed to earth it began skidding through a cornfield. Its right wing struck the porch supports of a large farmhouse, taking them down like bowling pins. The porch roof collapsed, tearing a gaping hole in the front of the house and terrorizing the occupants, who were in bed. When the glider pilot fired a green flare to signify no serious injuries, the farm family became even more frightened, thinking they were under enemy attack.

During the same training exercise, another glider made a pancake crash landing onto the roof of a barn. When the pilot stepped out of his glider to see where he had landed, he fell 15 feet into a pile of cow manure, saving his life but ruining his uniform.

It took ground crews from the base three weeks to retrieve all of the gliders that had been scattered across the Missouri countryside that night. The seriousness of this training accident sparked a minor rebellion among the glider pilots. For quite some time now, none of them had approved of the way training was being conducted at the base. When they were next instructed to prepare for a night mission, they refused to fly it until proper safety regulations were formulated and enforced. Even when threatened with court-martial, the glider pilots refused to budge from their barracks on the night the mission was scheduled to be flown. At this point the base commander became directly involved. After listening patiently to the many legitimate complaints of the glider pilots, he ordered that their safety suggestions be instituted immediately. That ended the rebellion. There were no courts-martial, and the programme was soon back on schedule.

Meanwhile, back in New Guinea, Major General Joe Swing and his 11th Airborne Division were pulling into Oro Bay aboard a fleet of troop ships that had sailed from California. The major manoeuvre elements of Swing's division were the 187th and 188th Glider Infantry and the 511th Parachute Infantry regiments. By the middle of June, 1944, those three regiments and all of the 11th Airborne's support units, were encamped at Dobodura. The division began a series of manoeuvres designed to prepare it for the forthcoming liberation of the Philippine Islands.

The only gliders available for use by the 11th Airborne at Dobodura were the 25 Wacos that had been left there the preceding September after the Nadzab landing had been cancelled. Unfortunately, the combined effects of New Guinea's humid climate, torrential rainstorms, and looters had rendered all of those gliders unflyable. To make matters worse for the 11th Airborne, there were now no glider pilots on New Guinea.

The Army Air Forces hurriedly dispatched the 1st Provisional Glider Group to New Guinea. This special unit, commanded by Major Edward C. Milau, was composed of 26 volunteer glider pilots and 26 glider mechanics gathered hastily from several training bases around the United States. On August 13, 1944, all of those personnel arrived at Nadzab, where they were assigned to the 54th Troop Carrier Wing.

The initial task assigned to the 1st Provisional Glider Group was that of assembling 25 brand new Wacos and four of the larger CG-13 gliders, which were still in their shipping crates on the docks at Finchaven. Despite oppressive heat which hovered at 100 degrees and primitive working conditions, the group had the gliders assembled in a week.

Using tug-ships from the 54th Wing to tow them down to Dobodura, the glider pilots worked around the clock training the 11th Airborne's glider units as well as its paratroop units. The glider training of General Swing's division continued unabated until the first week in October, when the 11th Airborne shipped out of New Guinea for the island of Leyte in the Philippines. By that time the assigned strength of the 1st Provisional Glider Group had swelled to over 100 glider pilots and a like number of glider mechanics shipped to New Guinea from American training centres.

The departure of the 11th Airborne prompted General Kenney, the Fifth Air Force commander, to order the 54th Wing to deploy all of its gliders based at Dobodura and Nadzab to Biak, a small island in western New Guinea's Geelvink Bay.

Along with that shift, Kenney ordered the establishment of a combined emergency landing strip and weather station high in the Owen Stanley Mountains. It was Kenney's opinion that too many pilots heading over the New Guinea hump were taking off to fly that stretch of wilderness with no idea of weather conditions there and no communications after they got out of radio range. It would be a good idea, Kenney said, for all pilots to have continuous radio contact and a place to make an emergency landing.

Aerial reconnaissance of the Owen Stanley Mountains revealed that the most promising spot for establishing an emergency landing strip was located at the extreme western flank of the range in a place called Hidden Valley. The floor of that wide-open valley sat at an altitude of 5,000 feet above sea level. Nestled in its middle was Ifitamin, an isolated village that appeared to be inhabited.

During the second week in October, four gliders, containing a platoon of U.S. Army engineer troops, a small bulldozer, a squad of civilian policemen, and a good supply of food, landed in Hidden Valley. No white person had been in the valley since 1938, and no natives had come out. Consequently, no one knew whether Japanese troops had infiltrated the area, or whether the inhabitants were armed. It was with considerable apprehension that the new arrivals walked toward the village.

The glider pilots expected to find the typical hill natives of New Guinea, who were noted for their large stature and advanced form of civilization. What they encountered were hundreds of pygmy-like people wearing only scanty loin-cloths. On seeing them, the interpreter accompanying the pilots swallowed hard and whispered, 'These people are Kukukukas!' – the fiercest cannibals in the interior of New Guinea.

There were a few anxious moments as the interpreter laboured to explain to the village chief that he and his companions had come in peace. Despite the dreadful reputation of his people, the chief smiled and welcomed the newcomers. He even offered to have some of his tribesmen help them build their airstrip.

Although the glider pilots had brought along such items as seashells, trinkets, mirrors and salt to trade, they found that the natives wanted almost nothing. Still living in the stone age, they used no metals of any kind and slept on the ground in the most rudimentary of huts. Their food was prepared simply by throwing it into a fire. Salt quickly proved to be the medium of

[345]

exchange. A number of natives agreed to help build the airstrip in return for one spoonful of salt per day in wages.

After radioing their home base for several kegs of salt, the Americans gave the villagers a demonstration of their firearms. Never having seen a rifle or pistol, the Kukukukas were astonished at how a shot from these weapons could burst open a large melon.

Three days after their arrival in the valley the Americans, ably assisted by the Kukukukas, had roughed out an airstrip large enough for a C-47. A few small L-5 airplanes landed on the new strip and took the eight glider pilots back to Nadzab. The rest of their party remained in Hidden Valley until the end of the war, coexisting peacefully with the Kukukukas and providing vital weather data to passing Allied aircraft. The four gliders used in this mission were later retrieved from the valley.

Earlier in the war, the British had set two very impressive records for long-distance glider towing. Their first record mission took place in April, 1943, when a single CG-4A glider was towed from Montreal, Canada, to Land's End, England, a distance of 3,220 miles. The trip had to be made in five separate legs, the longest of which was 875 miles. That historic Canada-to-England glider tow was strictly an experimental mission. It took 28 hours of flying time to complete and was the only transatlantic tow made during the war.[2]

Just two months after that epic flight, during Operation Turkey Buzzard, the British set the all-time long distance record for a combat glider tow in a special mission that involved the towing of 30 Horsa gliders from England to Africa. The first leg of that flight extended from Portreath in Cornwall to French Morocco, a distance of 1,300 miles. It took 10 hours of flying to complete that first leg; it still stands as the greatest long-distance combat glider tow of all time.

The closest the Americans ever came to these two incredible British records was on October 22, 1944, when Lieutenant F. Sunderman and Lieutenant Earl F. Simson of the 1st Provisional Glider took off from Nadzab for Biak, a distance of 840 miles. No other American combat glider had ever flown this distance without making at least one rest stop, but this mission was to be flown non-stop. Parked in the cargo compartment of the big CG-13 was a 1941 Oldsmobile sedan – the personal staff car of Brigadier General Warren Carter, the commanding general of the 54th Wing. Carter's headquarters was on Biak. He was completely unaware that his car was about to be delivered to him on that remote island; the trip had

[346]

been arranged secretly by some members of the general's staff who were eager to please him.

During most of the trip to Biak, the C-46 tow-plane cruised at 2,000 feet, staying close to the shoreline of northern New Guinea. However, on a few occasions it became necessary for the tow-plane to move far inland to avoid heavy rainstorms encountered along the route. Those sudden inland detours were very unpopular with the glider pilots, who had to worry constantly about the tow-line breaking. If that happened, they would be forced to make an emergency crash landing in dense jungle terrain occupied, more than likely, by Japanese units that had been bypassed by the Allies.

Fortunately the nylon held. Exactly seven hours after they had taken off from Nadzab, the glider pilots saw the shoreline of Biak dead ahead. They made their cutaway on the first pass over the island and rolled to a smooth stop on the largest of three coral airstrips constructed by the Japanese. A small welcoming party was on hand to greet the glider pilots. Its highest ranking member was General Carter. The unsuspecting general had been taken to the airstrip by his chief of staff, who told him that the incoming glider contained a visiting dignitary.

By the time General Carter arrived out at the glider, Lieutenants Sunderman and Simson had raised its nose section, and his staff car was being driven down the ramp. Seeing the car, Carter broke into a broad smile and exclaimed, 'I just don't believe it – a staff car here in Biak!' Later that evening he invited all of the pilots who had taken part in this mission to his command post, where he gave them mixed drinks and a steak dinner. Lieutenants Sunderman and Simson enjoyed their sumptuous meal, unaware that they had just set a long-distance flight record for the CG-13 glider, one that would remain unbroken for all time.[3]

Not all of the gliders ferried from New Guinea's east coast to Biak had an uneventful trip. The Battle of the Bulge was just drawing to a close in Europe when, on January 26, 1945, a brand-new Waco was towed into the air at Nadzab for the long trip to Biak. The flight plan for this mission called for a short stopover at Hollandia. Sitting at the controls were Lieutenant Raymond Nutting and his copilot, Flight Officer David S. Kaufman. Only 10 days earlier, Kaufman had received a telegram at Nadzab informing him that his wife, Doris, had presented him with twin baby boys. The pilots, as well as the three passengers directly behind them, Flight Officer Harold N.

Wallace, Corporal Louis C. Robinson and Private Elliot V. Paris, were members of the 68th Squadron, 433rd Troop Carrier Group.

After hauling the glider up to an altitude of 5,000 feet, the tow-plane stayed one mile out to sea and began skirting the coastline toward Hollandia. Shortly after passing the town of Wewak the tow-line suddenly and inexplicably broke loose from the tugship. Lieutenant Nutting made a quick 90 degree turn toward shore and plopped the glider down neatly on a sandy beach.

The tow-plane pilot circled until he saw that everyone was safe and then continued on to Hollandia. As the sound of the tow-plane's engines faded in the distance, the five stranded Americans saw movement coming through the jungle toward the beach. Instinctively, everyone drew weapons, thinking that they were about to be attacked by a Japanese patrol. They were soon greatly relieved to see that the visitors were a group of friendly natives. Within moments of their arrival the natives were smoking American cigarettes and climbing all over the glider.

A few hours later, the tow-plane returned and dropped two bundles, containing food, blankets and mosquito nets. Tied to one of the bundles was a note which said that a patrol boat would come by in the morning to pick up everyone. At dusk an Australian patrol plane flew over the survivors. It was flashing a message in Morse code at a rate so fast that it made all three pilots on the ground wish they had paid better attention during their code classes back in the States. None of them could read a word of the message.

About noon the next day an Australian rescue vessel arrived 500 feet off shore and launched a small boat containing two sailors. The boat had got about one-third of the way to shore when it capsized in the tall waves. After righting their small craft, one of the sailors, Seaman Tommy Ryan, dived back into the water and swam to shore, nearly drowning in the process.

Waving his shirt as a signal flag, Seaman Ryan informed his shipmates that he and all of the survivors would attempt swimming out to the ship. When their third attempt to swim through the extremely rough surf ended in failure, the exhausted survivors and Seaman Ryan regretfully decided they would have to walk through the jungle to the nearest Australian Army outpost, some 50 miles away. With their newly acquired local friends as guides, the party reached safety four days later.[4] One of the survivors of this harrowing experience, Flight Officer Wallace, was destined to be killed four months later in a glider crash.

By the end of January, 1945, American ground units in the Philippines had liberated the island of Leyte and were advancing toward the capital of Manila on Luzon. This fortunate turn of events prompted General MacArthur to issue instructions for all units of the 54th Wing still based on Biak to begin deploying on up to Leyte so as to be in position for the final phases of the Philippine campaign. It was during the 54th Wing's northward move that Brigadier General Carter's staff car advanced its standing as the most widely travelled military automobile of World War II. On March 17, the car was driven into the same CG-13 glider that had delivered it to Biak from Nadzab five months earlier. The destination this time was the American airstrip at Tacloban in northeastern Leyte, 1,200 miles away.

Major Edward C. Milau, the commanding officer of the 1st Provisional Glider Group on Biak, was chosen to be chief pilot of the CG-13. His copilot was Lieutenant Wolfram F. Sexaur. Before coming to Biak, Sexaur had taught advanced glider flying techniques at Laurinburg-Maxton Army Airfield in North Carolina. During the first leg of its flight up to the Philippines, the single C-46 and CG-13 glider combination made a scheduled overnight stop on Morotai in the Halmahera Islands. Early the next morning the combination set out on its second and, at 650 miles, longest leg. Some five hours later, Major Milau cut loose from the straining tug and landed the big glider without incident.[5] Milau and Sexaur remained on Leyte only a few days before they were returned to Biak to help prepare the remaining elements of their unit for shipment to the Philippines.

Even though the war had left New Guinea, thousands of American supply and administrative troops were kept there to ensure uninterrupted logistic support to the units fighting on Okinawa and in the Philippines. Life for the American forces on New Guinea was dull. Unlike many of their counterparts in Europe, who were quartered in regular military barracks and who could enjoy an occasional visit to cities like Paris and London, these troops were living in small tents and had virtually no entertainment available. The highlight of their stay on that hot, humid island was an occasional outdated movie which they could watch while sitting on empty bomb crates in a makeshift open air theatre. More often than not, those movies were rained out by evening thunderstorms.

[349]

Many unit commanders on New Guinea tried to raise the morale of their troops by organizing baseball games and other sporting events. Colonel Peter J. Prossen, of the Far East Air Service Command Headquarters based at Hollandia, went one step further. Because he was a command pilot and had access to a C-47, Prossen arranged to take 19 members of his Engineering Section on a Sunday afternoon flight over the towering peaks of the Oranje Mountain Range for a close look at Shangri-La Valley. Positioned 130 air miles southeast of Hollandia, the valley and its surrounding mountains were in one of the remotest places on earth. The formal name of this area was Grand Valley. It had never been explored except from the air. On maps of New Guinea the entire region was blank, and printed inside those large white blank spots were the words, 'unexplored', and 'estimated 14,000-foot peak.'

American pilots who had earlier conducted survey flights of a proposed north-south air route across New Guinea had named the valley Shangri-La after the mythical Himalayan retreat described in James Hilton's popular 1933 novel, *Lost Horizon*.[6] Pilots had spread a number of wild rumours about the valley. Some had it that the natives living there were fierce headhunters who averaged seven feet in height and were nearly white. Another rumour was that the valley contained a lost civilization which had developed an efficient irrigation system and practised the modern agricultural technique of crop rotation.

The valley soon developed such a mystique that Colonel Ray T. Elsmore's 332nd Troop Carrier Group at Hollandia established a Shangri-La Club. To qualify for membership, each candidate had to undergo an initiation ceremony which included a flight over the valley. After the candidates had met all of the entry requirements, Colonel Elsmore would present them with a fancy membership certificate.

Sunday, May 13, was the day Prossen had selected for the recreational outing. Shortly after 2:00p.m., he taxied his fully loaded C-47 to the downwind end of the Santani airstrip at Hollandia and requested permission from the tower to take off. Counting the five crew members, there were 24 persons on board the airplane. Eight of them were enlisted WACs of the Far East Air Service Command, eight were enlisted men, and eight were officers.[7] As soon as he got clearance from the tower, Prossen pushed the throttle forward and the big ship began racing down the runway. Soon they were airborne and those passengers fortunate enough to have a seat by a window were staring down at the thick jungles of New Guinea.

To one of the passengers, Technical Sergeant Kenneth W. Decker, this was a very special day. It was his 34th birthday. Just across the way from Decker was his boss, Lieutenant John S. McCollom. Because they were among the last few people to board the aircraft, McCollon and Decker had to take seats in the tail section. McCollom was a bit disappointed with this arrangement; he had wanted to sit beside his twin brother, Lieutenant Robert E. McCollom, who was up forward.

One hour after leaving Hollandia, the C-47 approached the northern side of the Oranje Mountain Range. Just as it had cleared the initial line of mountain peaks and was preparing to cross a second set of barriers, it suddenly lost altitude in an overpowering downdraft and crashed some 300 feet below the top of a ridgeline. On impact the airplane's tail section snapped off and came to a stop. The remainder of the aircraft slid a short distance up the slope, halted, and burst into flames.

When he crawled out of the wreckage, Lieutenant John McCollom thought he was the only one who had survived the terrible crash. But then he saw another survivor, Sergeant Decker, come staggering around the side of the flaming wreckage. Decker had sustained several burns on his back and ankles, plus a large gash on his forehead. He also had a broken right arm. Right behind Decker came a third survivor, Corporal Margaret J. Hastings, a young WAC who weighed less than a hundred pounds. She too was suffering from extensive injuries. Most of her hair had been burned off, and both of her legs and the left side of her face had been blistered by the flames. She had lost both of her shoes in the crash.

The fire was spreading as McCollom dashed into the burning fuselage to look for his twin brother and other survivors. A few seconds later he emerged from the inferno dragging two WACS, Sergeant Laura E. Beasley and Private First Class Eleanor P. Hanna. Both had been very severely injured and were near death. There were no other survivors.

Because they were all battered and emotionally drained, the survivors decided to stay put until they could figure a way out of their predicament. Soon the daily rains of New Guinea closed in on the mountain peaks, adding to their misery.

When the flames died down, McCollom made several trips into the

[351]

wreckage to see what could be salvaged. There he found two inflatable life rafts, two large yellow tarpaulins, several cans of drinking water, a dozen pieces of hard candy, an emergency signal kit, and one first aid box. It was nearly dark before McCollom finished administering morphine to the injured and inflating one of the life rafts. The two most severely injured WACs were placed on the raft and covered with a tarpaulin. McCollom, Decker and Hastings then covered themselves with the other tarp.

The crash had occurred at about 3.30 in the afternoon. When the plane failed to return on time to Hollandia, officials there began radioing all other airstrips where it could have made an emergency landing. The negative results led Hollandia to launch a search plane.

It rained all night, but the morphine enabled the injured survivors to drift off to sleep. McCollom stayed awake most of the night. Several times during the night he could hear a search plane overhead and could see some of the parachute flares it was dropping into the valley, but he had no means of answering the signals.

At dawn, McCollom checked on the two WACs on the life raft. One of them, Private Hanna, had died during the night.

For breakfast the survivors each had a piece of hard candy and a ration of fresh water. They agreed that they would spend the rest of the day on the peak, trying to recover from shock. Then, in the morning, they would start down the mountain. They knew that other search planes would come looking for them and that they would stand a better chance of being spotted down in the valley than up on a jungle-covered slope.

The first plane passed over the crash site at 10:00 a.m. McCollom snatched the mirror from the emergency kit and tried to signal it. Though the aircraft did not see his frantic signals, the survivors felt good just knowing that a search was in progress.

New Guinea's daily dose of mist and rain began closing in on the mountains at mid-afternoon, causing the survivors to become disheartened. Things went from bad to worse for them when they discovered that the other critically injured WAC, Staff Sergeant Beasley, had died while McCollom was trying to signal the search plane. Later that night, for the first time, the survivors heard the voices of natives calling to each other. That struck terror into their hearts; the natives in this area were supposed to be vicious headhunters, and not one of the survivors was armed. However, the night passed without any further signs of visitors.

[352]

Early in the morning they began making their way toward a clearing lower down the ridge where they hoped to be spotted by a search plane. During this march, Margaret Hastings wore the shoes of her deceased friend, Laura Beasley. The going was so rough on the trail that they did not reach the clearing until noon on Wednesday. It had taken them a day and a half to march only two and a half miles.

Only one hour after Lieutenant McCollom spread a bright yellow life raft tarpaulin out on the ground, they were spotted by a B-17 bomber that had joined the search team. The pilot acknowledged their presence by dipping his wings. Then he dropped two life rafts as markers and flew off toward Hollandia, where he reported their location as being on the uphill side of a ridge about 10 miles northeast of Shangri-La Valley. The survivors were so thrilled at being found that they celebrated by eating all but the last few pieces of their candy. Their outburst of joy was quickly dampened, quite literally, by a violent rainstorm which closed in on them, ruling out any further flights until morning.

About an hour after the B-17 left the valley area the survivors were startled to see a group of 100 natives emerge from the edge of the clearing and start walking toward them. Several of the natives were carrying large stone axes over their shoulders. None of them looked friendly. On seeing the visitors approaching, McCollom whispered, 'We've got to act friendly. So stand up and smile!'

When the natives were about 15 feet from the survivors, they halted and gathered around. Their chief then walked up to McCollom and greeted him with a broad smile. All three survivors heaved a sigh of relief. The rumours about fierce, light-skinned, seven-foot-tall headhunters had just been proven false. These people were about five feet tall and quite black.

Both groups tried sign language, without success. After a while, several of the natives built a campfire and began roasting some sweet potatoes over the coals. This was welcomed by the hungry survivors, who were by now tired of their candy and water diet. Things were proceeding nicely when a rainstorm suddenly blew in from the west and put an end to the cookout. When that happened the natives formed up into a marching column. There were several warm smiles and friendly waves from the natives, and then they departed as quickly as they had arrived, taking their half-cooked sweet potatoes with them.

Then next morning another airplane dropped in a parachute

[353]

supply bundle containing a first aid kit, some canned food, and a small radio. The bundle landed almost on top of the survivors. They quickly established communications with the airplane. During his conversation with the pilot, Lieutenant McCollom explained what had happened during the crash, and gave a detailed explanation of each survivor's injuries.

Later that afternoon there was a second supply drop. When they completed unpacking all of the parachute containers, the survivors had enough camping equipment, clothing, canned food and weapons to stock a small sporting goods store.

While these supply drops were taking place, officials back at Hollandia were trying to figure out how they could rescue the three survivors from the remote and difficult area in which they had crashed. One possibility was having a team of trained volunteers march into the area to lead the survivors back to civilization. But when local government authorities pointed out that such an expedition would require at least 150 men and a month's marching time each way, the idea was scrapped. U.S. Navy air-sea rescue pilots were brought in to see if it would be possible to land a seaplane on the Baliem River that flowed through Shangri-La Valley, or on Lake Archbold which was 18 air miles northwest of the crash site. But the pilots reported that both of those places were far too risky to attempt a landing.

The next plan considered by officials at Hollandia required the injured crash survivors to hike down off the mountain to the floor of Shangri-La Valley. There they would be met by a lightweight L-5 airplane which would land and return them to Hollandia. It was estimated that a one-way flight to the valley for an L-5 would take three hours and would consume all of its fuel. Therefore a parachute delivery of fuel would have to be made into the valley for the return trip.

The only aviators in the vicinity of Hollandia who were both immediately available and thoroughly familiar with L-5 airplanes were the few glider pilots still stationed out on Biak Island. One of those pilots, Lieutenant Henry E. Palmer, was placed on board a B-25 bomber and taken on a reconnaissance flight to the valley to see if an L-5 could safely land and take off there. One low level pass over the valley floor convinced Palmer that its condition was too dangerous for L-5 operations, but safe enough to accept a glider.

Palmer returned to Hollandia and used a blackboard and a piece of

[354]

chalk to show officials how a glider could land in the valley and then be snatched back into flight. Palmer closed his argument by volunteering to fly the rescue glider himself.

After hours of consultation and coordination with numerous rescue operations experts, the officials at Hollandia decided to accept Lieutenant Palmer's suggestion. Their plan was simple but would take considerable time to execute because it contained three separate phases, the timings of which were predicted on the recovery rate of the injured survivors, the weather and the availability of the equipment needed for the glider portion of the plan.

Phase One called for a small team of U.S. Army medics to parachute in to the survivors, administer first aid and set up a tent campsite. The medics were to continue caring for the survivors until their injuries had partially healed and they were strong enough to travel on foot. In Phase Two, a second group of parachutists would jump into the widest part of Shangri-La Valley, 10 miles from where the survivors were encamped. Their mission would be to set up a second campsite to receive the survivors when they marched down off the moutain, and to clear an area large enough for a glider to land in. Phase Three required the 433rd Troop Carrier group to land a glider in the valley, load up the survivors, medics and parachutists, and then snatch them out with a tow-plane for the return to Hollandia. Lieutenant Palmer, the originator of the glider idea, was designated chief pilot.

A U.S. Army paratrooper, Captain Cecil E. Walter, Jr., volunteered himself and his men for the Shangri-La Valley rescue mission. Walter was chief jumpmaster of the 1st Reconnaissance Battalion based at Hollandia. This battalion, unique in the U.S. Army, was the only one comprised entirely of Filipino-American men who had been recruited for cloak-and-dagger missions behind Japanese lines in the Philippine Islands. When formed in 1942, the battalion was trained to be put ashore at night from U.S. Navy submarines. Several small detachments had already used that method to infiltrate Japanese strongholds along the coasts of Leyte and Luzon. However, in May 1944, Captain Walter had been sent to Hollandia to jump train some 100 members of the battalion so that they would have the additional capability of reaching objectives deep inside the Philippines.

On May 18, five days after the plane crash, a pair of medics from the 1st Reconnaissance Battalion, Staff Sergeant Benjamin C.

Bulatao and Corporal Camilo Ramirez, jumped into the area where the survivors had been sighted. This initial parachute operation miscarried, in that the jumpers landed two miles away from the survivors and Corporal Ramirez sustained several cuts and bruises on his right leg. Nevertheless, the medics reached the survivors and began treating their burns, which had become badly infected. The medics then set up a small campsite, which they christened 'Mike 1.'

Two days later, Captain Walter and eight more of his men parachuted into the valley to establish the larger 'Mike 2' campsite and select the best spot for the glider to land. Moments after collapsing his parachute, Walter established radio contact with his troopers up at Mike 1 campsite. He designated three men to remain at Mike 2 to set up the encampment that was to receive the survivors when they came down off the mountain. Then he and the other five men started up through the jungle toward Mike 1.

It took them three days to make their way through difficult jungle terrain to the Mike 1 campsite. There they found the survivors resting comfortably and the two aid men busy fixing a multi-course meal with the fresh food supplies that were now being dropped in daily by parachute to both campsites.

Two days after Walter reached the survivors, an Army airplane dropped a parachute supply bundle containing several shovels, 20 wooden crosses and one Star of David for the burial of the seven women and 14 men who had perished in the accident. Walter then took a burial detail farther up the mountain to the crash site. As he and his men were placing the star and crosses at the head of each grave, a lone C-47 circled above them. On board were three Army chaplains, one Catholic, one Protestant and one Jewish. As each chaplain intoned his services for the dead, his words were broadcast by radio to everyone on the mountain. It was a sorrowful experience, especially for Lieutenant McCollom who had lost his twin brother.

Meanwhile, on the isolated island of Wakde east of Hollandia, Lieutenant Palmer was busy conducting glider landing and snatch take-off rehearsals in preparation for the actual rescue. Palmer had picked Wakde for the rehearsals because it was far away from Hollandia and Biak, both of which had occasional heavy air traffic flows which could have interrupted his training flights.

However, frequent rainstorms on Wakde caused him much lost time, and Palmer was handicapped by the unavailability of some special machinery which had to be installed in the snatch airplane.

The hardware was up in the Philippines, and only after many urgent requests to the advance headquarters of the 54th Wing at Clark Field, near Manila, was the special equipment finally flown back to Biak and delivered to Palmer on Wakde.

During one of the first snatch take-off practice runs, the steel cable being reeled back inside the airplane suddenly snapped in two. Thrashing around the interior of the airplane like a bullwhip, the cable inflicted several cuts on Privates James Howell and Frederick Baron. The glider went on to make a safe emergency landing.

The injuries suffered by Howell and Baron and the faulty cable drum mechanism caused yet another delay in glider training activities on Wakde. It was a week after this mishap before a second cable drum was delivered directly from the Philippines.

Not until June 15 – 33 days after the crash – did the medics caring for the survivors pronounce all three of them fit enough to make the arduous foot march down into the valley. By this time many of the local natives had become regular visitors to the Mike 1 campsite. Several of them volunteered to carry equipment for the Americans. It took three days to complete the downhill move to Mike 2.

At Mike 2, the survivors were pleased to see an elaborate series of tents erected for them. The camp even had a large private boudoir and bath for Corporal Margaret Hastings. Just beyond the campsite, a 400-yard runway area had been cleared to receive the glider.

A siege of torrential rains on Wakde and another broken cable delayed the actual rescue attempt until June 28. On that day a single CG-4A glider took to the air from Hollandia behind a powerful C-46 airplane. Only a few days earlier, Lieutenant Palmer, the originator of this glider rescue idea, had been angered when his boss, Major Milau, informed him that he was being relegated to the position of copilot on the mission and that a new officer, Captain George R. Allen, would take over as chief pilot. One hour after departing Hollandia the combination passed over the Oranje Mountain Range and descended into Shangri-La Valley. Having already made a reconnaissance flight over this area, Palmer knew exactly where and when to signal the cutaway. On sighting the checkpoint he had earlier selected, Palmer nodded to Allen, who punched the release knob immediately. A few moments later the glider skidded to a smooth stop, right beside the wide-eyed group of survivors and natives.

Because of the valley's altitude – 5,000 feet – authorities at rescue control headquarters in Hollandia had decreed that three separate flights would have to be made to extract the crash survivors, Captain Walter, and his men. The passengers chosen to go out on this first run were the three survivors: Lieutenant McCollom, Sergeant Decker and Corporal Hastings.

The natives in the valley did not know what to make of this strange contraption that had landed silently in their midst, but they knew instinctively that it had come to take away the pretty WAC corporal and all of the other Americans with whom they had become good friends. As McCollom, Decker and Hastings bade them farewell, several of the natives could be seen with tears streaming down their faces. All three survivors had to fight back the same emotions.

Less than half an hour after it touched down in the valley, the glider was snatched into flight by a C-47 airplane that had trailed it during the flight up from Hollandia. It took an hour and a half to complete the return trip to Hollandia, and it ended on a confused note. Instead of landing on Cyclops airstrip where a bevy of generals, doctors and newspaper reporters were waiting to welcome the survivors, Captain Allen set the glider down on Sentani Airstrip, the same place where, 47 days earlier, the three survivors had taken off for what was supposed to have been a three-hour pleasure trip to Shangri-La Valley.

A lingering rainstorm ruled out any further rescues that day. Early the next morning, Captain Allen and Lieutenant Palmer performed another successful snatch mission, returning five of Captain Walter's troopers to Hollandia. A series of additional downpours delayed the final extraction mission until Sunday, July 1. On that day Captain Walter and the balance of his men were safely returned to Hollandia. During this final flight, Captain Allen had a new copilot in Lieutenant Nicholas P. Kimler.

Within a week of their return to Hollandia, all three survivors of the crash were flown home to the United States. After a brief rest period with their families, Lieutenant McCollom and Corporal Hastings were placed on temporary duty with war bond rally teams that were travelling about the United States. The third survivor, Sergeant Decker, was sent to Barnes Army Hospital in Vancouver, Washington, for treatment of the extensive injuries which were still troubling him.

In a rare show of appreciation for the kind of exceedingly dangerous flying duty being performed throughout New Guinea by the

American glider pilots, the Army Air Force awarded the Distinguished Flying Cross to the three who had participated in the Shangri-La Valley mission.

For the part they played in the rescue, Captain Walter, Sergeant Bulatao and Corporal Ramirez were presented the Soldiers Medal, the highest decoration awarded for non-combat heroism. After the war had ended, the U.S. Army made two attempts to retrieve the remains buried on the mountain. The first attempt was scheduled to be made in January 1948. It had to be cancelled when the two civilian airplanes that were to be used in the operation were destroyed by a typhoon. The second attempt, made in December 1958, was successful. The remains of 20 of the 21 crash victims were casketed and returned to the United States for internment in the Jefferson Barracks National Cemetery, St. Louis, Missouri, on June 29, 1959. The 21st victim, WAC Staff Sergeant Laura E. Beasley, was buried in the Punchbowl Cemetery, Honolulu, Hawaii, on May 13, 1959, 14 years to the day from the tragic plane crash in the valley of Shangri-La.

# Chapter 13

# *Luzon – The Last Glider Mission*

THE TUMULTUOUS VICTORY CELEBRATIONS that accompanied U.S.
President Truman's May 8 announcement of V–E Day did not
extend as far as the embattled Philippine Islands. On the day
Truman made the announcement, General Joe Swing and his 11th
Airborne Division were just moving into a new base camp which had
been built around the former Japanese airstrip at Lipa, some 45 miles
below Manila. Swing and every one of the men in his division were
exhausted. For the last 10 weeks they had been engaged in heavy
infantry combat in southern Luzon. Swing's troopers were happy to
hear of Germany's surrender, but with most of northern Luzon and
large areas of China still occupied by Japanese they could not bring
themselves to shout for joy as the rest of the Allied world was doing.
Instead, they began again the monotonous routine of pitching pup
tents and cleaning weapons. Rumours were circulating about a possible airborne combat assault on the China mainland.

Lipa's three concrete runways had been built by Japanese engineer
units in 1942. It was from this airfield that Japanese paratroopers had
taken off on December 6, 1944, for their ill-fated night combat jump
on General Swing's command post at San Pablo Airstrip on Leyte.
During that attack the 200-man Japanese airborne detachment managed to set fire to only a few planes parked on the airstrip. But by
noon the following day, all of the attackers had been killed in a series
of counterattacks which General Swing threw against them. When,
in mid-May, the 11th Airborne's engineer battalion began lengthen-
ing the runways, and one CG-13 glider and 10 of the smaller CG-4A
Waco gliders arrived from Tacloban Airfield, new rumours concerning the division's future were born. Scuttlebutt had the division
making an airborne assault on the Japanese mainland in support of a
gigantic amphibious invasion, similar to the one the Allies had made
at Normandy. Because all of the Japanese they had encountered in

the Philippines had fought to the death, the 11th Airborne troopers found this easy to believe. Japan, they realized, would have to be devastated and occupied if the war was ever to end.

All of the newly arrived glider pilots at Lipa were members of Major Edward C. Milau's 1st Provisional Glider Group and had come to the Philippines with him from Biak. With the exception of the one CG-13, which had earlier been ferried up from Biak by Milau, all of their gliders were brand new ones that had just been shipped from U.S. factories and assembled at Tacloban Airfield. Upon their arrival at Lipa, the pilots were placed on temporary duty with the 11th Airborne Division. Their living quarters consisted of several tents located right beside the main runway and half a mile away from the division's bivouac area which was comfortably situated in a shady palm forest. This quarters arrangement was a bit disconcerting to the pilots, who correctly reasoned that the runway would be the primary target for Japanese bombers.

Fortunately, no bombers put in an appearance at Lipa to interrupt the vigorous training programmes that were being inaugurated by the 11th Airborne Division. Utilizing airplanes from the various troop carrier squadrons based up at Clark Field, the 11th Airborne was soon engaged in a brisk series of parachute and glider landing exercises.

Back in the United States, meanwhile, the tactical glider manufacturing programme had survived three years of indecision, often stymied by confusion on the basic issue of glider requirements, and was still going forward at full steam. By this time, the Army Air Force's Materiel Command at Wright Field had awarded 24 separate manufacturing contracts to 16 different companies who were producing both training and tactical gliders. To date, the Air Force had taken delivery of 10,879 combat CG-4A gliders, 52 of the larger CG-13s, and 20 of the newer CG-15A models.

In Washington, the overall control of the glider programme was now being administered by the Glider Branch, a subsection of General Arnold's Operations, Commitments, and Requirements (C&R) Division at the Pentagon. The Glider Branch was activated in November 1943, shortly after Richard DuPont and four other men were killed at March Field, California, during a demonstration flight of the experimental MC-1 glider. Serving as chief of the Glider Branch was Major A. Felix DuPont, Richard's older brother. At the time he was picked by General Arnold for that assignment the elder

DuPont had been an active duty Air Force officer serving in the Air Transport Command.

Under supervision of the Glider Branch, several new gliders had been developed during the past year. One of them was the CG-15A, which was almost identical in appearance to the CG-4A glider. The CG-15A project had been conceived by Major Floyd J. Sweet, a design and development engineer and chief test pilot at Wright Field. The CG-15A incorporated all of the improvements that glider pilots and Air Force commanders had recommended for the CG-4A, plus a number of refinements that Sweet himself had originated. The two most significant changes in this new model were its reduced wing-span, which was 21 feet 5 inches shorter than that of the CG-4A, and its weight carrying ability, which was 1,000 pounds greater.

Major Sweet instituted several other improvements in the CG-15A. One was a more aerodynamically shaped nose section which contained an elaborate built-in crash protection device similar to the one previously designed for CG-4A gliders by Roger W. Griswold II. The noses of the CG-15As contained far more plexi-glass, affording the pilots a greatly improved field of vision. Another modification that increased pilot vision was the positioning of the tow-line. Instead of having it connect to the top of the nose section, as on the CG-4As, Major Sweet positioned the tow-line coupler in the centre of the glider's nose and well below the instrument panel. He also added new ailerons to the CG-15A for improved flight control, new landing gear with stronger brakes, and a set of wing flaps which reduced the amount of power required to tow the glider at speeds in excess of 120 mph. Another outstanding feature of the CG-15A was its maximum towing speed of 180 mph – 60 mph faster than the CG-4A. Despite all of those improvements, the cost of the CG-15A crated for export was only $511 more than the price of the standard model CG-4A.[1]

Another more unusual glider that had been developed recently was the XCG 17, one of America's largest cargo-carrying gliders during the war years. Actually, this glider was simply a C-47 airplane that had been stripped of its engines and modified to lift 15,000 pounds of cargo – almost four times as much as one Waco CG-4A could haul.

The XCG-17 had been developed during the summer of 1944 at the urging of American Air Force officials in India, who desperately needed more cargo capacity for hauling supplies over the Himalayas to China. Gliders were an obvious solution, but because all of the combat models then being manufactured were urgently needed for tactical operations, none could be spared.

Experimentation with the XCG-17 was carried out at Clinton Country Army Air Field in Ohio by military glider specialists. Using cutting torches and other tools, they stripped the aircraft's interior of its radio and navigation compartments and all other bulkheads which separated various sections of the fuselage. This created a cavernous space measuring 30.4 cubic feet, enough to accommodate three jeeps or 27 combat soldiers. Next they removed the two engines and covered the nacelles with rounded caps made of aluminium. The nacelles and outer wing panels were then modified to carry cargoes of gasoline and oil. Although they had made a number of radical changes in creating the XCG-17, the glider specialists left enough critical parts in place so that it could be reconverted into a powered C-47 in only eight hours.

During the fall of 1944, several flight tests were conducted with the XCG-17 using a four-engined C-54 as a tow-ship. All of those tests were successful, but by that time the supply situation in China had improved and there was no longer a desperate need to convert whole fleets of C-47 airplanes into gliders. The project was halted, and the single XCG-17 returned to service as a powered airplane.

Another interesting experiment converted combat gliders into powered airplanes. As originally conceived, these aircraft were to be standard-model gliders with low-power engines mounted on them. The Army Air Force classified all of these experimental aircraft as powered gliders rather than powered cargo airplanes because 'they retained the appearance, function, and many of the characteristics of ordinary gliders.'[2]

Three experimental powered gliders were developed. The North-western Aeronautical Corporation produced the XPG-1, a standard CG-4A glider that had been equipped with two 125 hp Franklin engines.

The XPG-2, developed by the Ridgefield Manufacturing Corporation of Ridgefield, New Jersey, was also a standard CG-4A glider, powered in this case by two 175 hp Ranger engines.

The third powered glider, the XPG-3, was a product of the Waco Aircraft Company. It was a standard CG-15A that had been equipped with a pair of Jacobs R-755-9 engines.

Though all three of the experimental powered gliders passed their flight tests at Clinton County Army Air Field, none of them was

[363]

ever put into production. For a brief period in November 1944, the Air Force considered building 60 XPG-2 gliders for use in the European theatre. But by that time there was a dramatic increase in the production of C-47 airplanes and the project was scrapped. At the time the experimental powered glider programme was cancelled, the Army Air Force had expended $246,000 on it.

The only one of the new tactical glider models to see overseas service during the war was the CG-15A. Shortly after Operation Varsity, in March 1945, several of them were shipped to France for field testing by American troop carrier units stationed there. That field testing was still in progress when, on June 9, Lieutenant General 'Vinegar Joe' Stilwell, who had won fame in the China-Burma-India theatre, paid a visit to the 11th Airborne Divison in the Philippines. In honour of Vinegar Joe's visit, General Swing and his troopers put on the most spectacular show they had staged since arriving overseas. It began with a formal parade on the Lipa airstrip. Before the division passed in review, Stilwell presented 15 Silver Star Medals to troopers who had displayed exceptional heroism during the 11th Airborne's numerous battles in Manila and on southern Luzon.

General Swing was prepared to give the 'pass in review' command when nine C-47 jump planes zoomed overhead and dropped two companies of paratroopers in a field behind the runway on which the division was standing at attention. Leaving their parachutes where they had fallen, the paratroopers assembly quickly and joined the tail end of the parade. Not to be outdone by the theatrical performance of the paratroopers, eight gliders suddenly landed and screeched to a halt at the far end of the runway. Out of them poured four jeeps and a battery of artillerymen pulling their howitzers. Within minutes the howitzers were connected to the jeeps. The artillerymen then leaped into the jeeps and rolled past the reviewing stand, sitting proudly at attention.

Elsewhere on Luzon, the remnants of 140,000 Japanese troops from the Shobo Group that were defending against the Americans had withdrawn into strongholds on the island. Those forces were all under the command of 59-year-old General Tomoyuki Yamashita, Japan's most popular combat general. Yamashita was known throughout the Japanese army as the 'Tiger of Malaya' for his drama-tic capture of Singapore in 1942. There his forces had succeeded in forcing over 90,000 British, Indian and Australian soldiers defending that island fortress to lay down their arms in unconditional surrender. In his war memoirs, Prime Minister Churchill described that stunning Japanese victory as the worst British military disaster in history.

Only eight months earlier, when the American forces first returned to the Philippines, Yamashita had boasted to his staff that he would soon be demanding MacArthur's unconditional surrender. Yamashita, of course, never got the opportunity to make that demand. Now he was hiding out with his troops, who had brought large stores of ammunition and food with them during the retreat. Yamashita estimated that he had sufficient food supplies to last his troops until mid-September. At that time he would launch one last massive banzai suicide charge against the Filipino guerrillas and American forces that were pursuing him.

General Walter Krueger, one of America's finest, although least known, combat commanders of World War II, was directing operations of the Sixth Army on Luzon. Unlike his boss, General MacArthur, Krueger shunned publicity throughout the war. Born on January 26, 1881, in Flatow, West Prussia (today a part of East Germany), Krueger came to the United States with his family when he was eight years old and was educated in state schools in the Midwest. At the age of 17, he enlisted in the U.S. Volunteers and saw combat in Cuba during the Spanish-American War. Returning from Cuba he joined the regular Army and was assigned to duty in the Philippines, where he rose to the rank of sergeant. In 1901 he was commissioned a second lieutenant in the 30th Infantry Regiment. Following a second tour in the Philippines, Krueger took part in the 1916 Mexican Punitive Expedition with General Pershing. He also saw combat in France during World War I. As commander of the Sixth Army, Krueger had seen combat in this war on Kiriwina and Woodlark islands, New Britain, the Admiralty Islands, Biak Island, New Guinea, Morotai, Leyte and Luzon.

As a tactician, Krueger was more of a staunch pragmatist than a theoretician. A review of the many campaigns that he so skilfully directed during the war reveals that his methods were nearly identical to those of England's Field Marshal Montgomery. Krueger never made his move until he was certain that he had the requisite strength at hand to prevail.

Having previously spent six years on Luzon, Krueger was thoroughly familiar with every corner of the big island. It was his

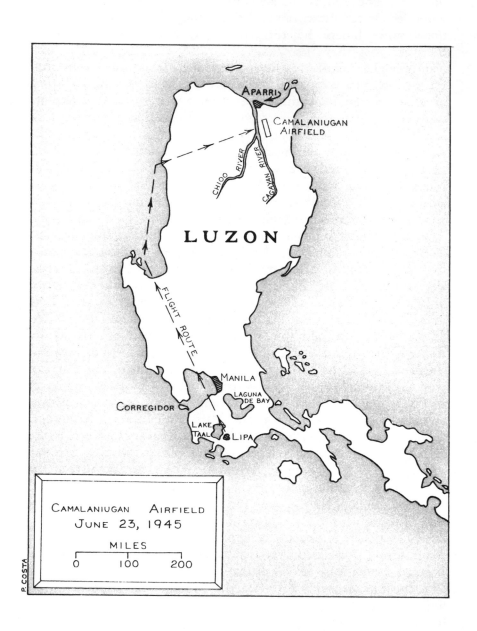

APARRI

CAMALANIUGAN
AIRFIELD

CHICO RIVER

CAGAYAN RIVER

LUZON

FLIGHT ROUTE

MANILA

LAGUNA
DE BAY

CORREGIDOR

LAKE
TAAL   LIPA

CAMALANIUGAN   AIRFIELD
JUNE 23, 1945

MILES

0      100      200

P. COSTA

opinion that the remaining Japanese troops under Yamashita were going to retreat all the way to Appari, a small seacoast town on the north shore. There, he estimated, Japanese ships would evacuate them so that they might survive to fight elsewhere. To deny Yamashita the use of Appari as a port of escape, Krueger dispatched Task Force Connolly[3] up Route 3 along the island's west coast with orders to occupy the town and make contact with Filipino guerrilla units operating in that area 'as soon as possible'. Next, he instructed General Swing to drop a battalion combat team on Camalaniugan Airstrip, located 10 miles south of Appari. After they had seized the airstrip, the paratroopers were to march south and make contact with Major General Robert S. Beightler's 37th Infantry Division, attacking up the Cagayan Valley toward Appari.

For the Appari airborne mission, General Swing organized a special unit called Gypsy Task Force. It consisted of Lieutenant Colonel Henry A. Burgess's 1st Battalion, 511th Parachute Infantry; Companies G and I of the same regiment; Battery C, 457th Parachute Field Artillery Battalion; 1st Platoon, Company C, 127th Engineers; and miscellaneous division signal and medical detachments. Swing appointed Burgess the Task Force Commander.[4] Originally, Swing set June 25 as D-Day for the Camalaniugan Airstrip drop, but due to the 37th Division's rapid advance up the Cagayan Valley, he was forced to move it up to Saturday, June 23.

In a move that surprised his division staff officers, General Swing directed that gliders be included in Gypsy Task Force for the Camalaniugan combat drop. No gliders had ever been used in a Pacific battle action, but on this mission six CG-4As and one CG-13 were going to deliver artillery pieces and communications jeeps into the airhead. Also allocated to Gypsy Task Force were 54 C-47s and 13 C-46s from the 317th and 433rd Troop Carrier groups based at Clark Field.

The glider pilots and paratroopers at Lipa were busily preparing for combat when, on June 21, Task Force Connolly entered Appari unopposed. There was now little reason for going ahead with the drop, since it was just a matter of time before the still marching 37th Division linked up with Task Force Connolly. When news of the sooner-than-expected seizure of Appari reached General Krueger at his headquarters in Manila, his staff expected that he would call off the airborne attack mission. But he did not.

On June 22 – one day before D-Day – word reached Krueger's headquarters that a reconnaissance patrol from Task Force Connolly

[367]

had just swept across the Camalaniugan Airstrip and found it devoid of enemy troops. Again, Krueger's staff expected him to cancel the airborne mission. But the general was leaving nothing to chance. With Task Force Connolly, and the Filipino guerrilla units, he had already closed the only door of escape for the Japanese at Appari. Now he was going to methodically nail it shut with an airborne strike.

On D-Day the glider pilots and paratroopers were awakened at 4:00 a.m. to complete final preparations for their mission. The day began with a hearty breakfast of bacon and eggs, a rare treat for combat troops in the Philippines. Next came the long walk out to the airstrip where the great fleet of dew-covered jump planes and gliders basked in the warm rays of the rising sun. As the troops were strapping on parachutes and checking their glider loads, Generals Krueger and Swing strolled among them, making frequent stops to chat with individual officers and soldiers. At 6:00 a.m. sharp the jump planes began rolling down the runway. While the last few were still roaring into their take-offs the C-47 glider tugs began rolling into position behind them. All aircraft cleared the ground without incident.

During the three-hour flight up to the Camalaniugan Airstrip objective, the six CG-4A gliders were arranged in a column of twos. Directly in front of them flew the paratroop planes, arranged in a V of Vs formation, and the single CG-13 glider piloted by Major Edward C. Milau and Lieutenant Maxwell Cone. This was the same CG-13 that Milau had earlier ferried to Leyte from Biak with General Carter's staff car on board. It was the only CG-13 in the Philippines.

Upon their arrival in the objective area at 9:00 a.m., the jump planes and gliders were to climb to an altitude of 10,000 feet and orbit west of Camalaniugan Airstrip for half an hour while several Fifth Air Force planes bombed and strafed the drop and landing zones. As soon as the bombers completed their preparatory fires the jump planes descended and made their drops, right on target. Although all parachutes opened properly, the jump casualty rate was fairly serious. Seven per cent of the paratroopers suffered serious injuries while making rough landings in a 25-mile-per-hour ground wind.

Hundreds of discarded parachutes were still billowing on the ground when the glider tugs zoomed over the LZ at an altitude of 400 feet. One by one the glider pilots made their cutaways and began lining up their aircraft on the bomb-cratered LZ. Pilots of the leading CG-13 and the first three of the CG-4As managed to avoid all the craters and make smooth landings. However, as the fourth glider was preparing to land, its two pilots, Flight Officers Robert J. Meer and Harold N. Wallace, had to use all of their skill and strength to throw on the spoilers to skip over an enormous crater that would certainly have caused them and their passengers serious harm.

The fifth glider, piloted by Flight Officers William Bartz and Robert Brook, ran out of air speed as it was approaching another crater. Both of its belly skids caught on the lip of the crater, forcing the glider to lurch to one side and crash. Fortunately, neither Bartz, Brook, or their lone passenger, Flight Officer Harold Picker, was seriously injured. Picker was also a glider pilot; he had gone along on this mission as an observer and to drive the jeep being carried in the glider.

The sixth and final CG-4A, flown by Lieutenant John J. Booth and Flight Officer Emil D. Doty, narrowly missed crashing into yet another crater.

Less than an hour after his troops and gliders had landed, Colonel Burgess had all of Gypsy Task Force assembled. Leaving the glider pilots and his injured troopers at Camalaniugan Airstrip, he started pushing south to link up with the ground column advancing up the Cagayan Valley. Some three days later, after marching 35 miles and encountering only light enemy forces, Gypsy Task Force reached the Paret River. There the paratroopers met the lead foot patrols of the 37th Infantry Division. Burgess and his men were picked up and flown back to the 11th Airborne's base camp at Lipa.

Retrieval of the Gypsy Task Force gliders actually began on D-Day. Colonel Burgess and his troops had been gone from Camalaniugan Airstrip only one hour when two C-47s arrived to snatch out a pair of CG-4As that had landed well clear of the bomb craters. As soon as the snatches had been completed, a third C-47 landed to return all of the injured paratroopers and remaining glider pilots to Lipa. Two weeks after D-Day a third CG-4A was also snatched up and returned to Lipa. All other gliders used on this mission were left where they had landed. It was indeed an ignominious end for the $55,000 CG-13 that had been flown first from Nadzab, New Guinea, to Biak Island, thence northward to Morotal and the Philippines, only to be left to rot in an open field. The CG-13 so wastefully abandoned, was just 10 months old and had logged only 42 flying hours.

By the first week in July, General MacArthur was able to wire

U.S. President Truman that the liberation of the Philippines was complete. During the Philippine campaign, MacArthur's forces had killed 317,000 and captured 7,236 Japanese troops against American casualty figures of 59,000 killed, wounded, and missing, of which about 10,000 were killed.

In a 3,000-mile-long campaign that stretched from New Guinea up to the Philippines, General MacArthur had outguessed and out-fought the military might of the Japanese Empire. By constantly 'hitting them where they ain't', in a series of leapfrog and bypass attacks, he had succeeded in draining Japan's strength by cutting her long supply lines and isolating her from critical raw-material reservoirs. In so doing he kept his promise to return to the Philippines, and captured more territory with less loss of life than any military commander since ancient Persia's emperor, Darius the Great.

Though victory was his in the Philippines, MacArthur knew the war had not yet been won. The Japanese home islands were still bristling with defence works and millions of civilians who had vowed to repel all invaders. Accordingly, MacArthur turned Luzon into a huge training camp and supply base from which he would eventually launch the invasion of Japan. In his initial plan for that undertaking, MacArthur had designated General Krueger's Sixth Army to lead the attack.

As part of its invasion training programme, the 11th Airborne Division conducted a series of glider and parachute exercises at Lipa. On July 22, six C-47s and six gliders took off on a navigation flight that was to take them southward to the island of Mindoro, then northeast to Clark Field, and back again to Lipa. Everything went well during this exercise until the tugs and gliders were approaching Manila. A tremendous rainstorm had blown in from the north, completely obscuring Clark Field. Soon all of the aircraft were overtaken by the storm. During the resultant turbulence and confusion two gliders collided and crashed into Manila Bay. Killed in the crash were eight members of the 11th Airborne who had been riding in the gliders. Also dead were the four pilots: Lieutenant Daryl E. Drummond and Flight Officers Donald Orkney, Harold Picker and Harold N. Wallace, all of whom had taken part in the Appari mission with Gypsy Task Force. They were the last four glider pilots to be killed in World War II.

At the time of the atomic holocausts at Hiroshima and Nagasaki, early in August 1945, the 11th Airborne Division was still undergoing intensive glider and parachute training at Lipa. On August 14 – five days after the second atomic bomb had obliterated Nagasaki – Emperor Hirohito made a radio announcement to his nation and its armed forces that Japan was surrendering unconditionally to the Allies, effective that day. Some two weeks later, the entire 11th Airborne Division, along with several of its attached glider pilots, was airlifted to Japan to begin the formal American occupation.

When news of the Emperor's announcement reached General Yamashita in the mountains of northern Luzon on September 2, he and 50,500 of his remaining troops surrendered to the Americans. Yamashita's soldiers were permitted to return to Japan, but he was imprisoned in Manila to await trial as a war criminal. On December 7, the fourth anniversary of the surprise Japanese attack on Pearl Harbor, a commission of five generals found Yamashita 'guilty of failing to discharge his duties as Commanding General of the Japanese 14th Army by permitting the members of his command to commit atrocities against Americans and Filipinos in the Philippine Islands during the period 9 October 1944 to 2 September 1945.' Following a review of his case by the Supreme Court of the United States, General Yamashita was hanged on February 23, 1946.

Brooke County Library
945 Main Street
Wellsburg, W. Va. 26070

# Epilogue

By the time World War II ended in August 1945, the United States had built 14,612 gliders and had trained over 6,000 pilots to fly them. But having just concluded the second war to end all wars, the American military planners saw no need to maintain enormous and expensive Army, Navy and Air Force combat units. So along with the rest of America's giant military machine of 1945, the glider fleets were drastically reduced in size, to the point that there were only enough CG-15s left to lift the 82nd Airborne Division's 325th Glider Infantry, the only such regiment retained on active duty in the postwar years.

All other combat gliders were declared war surplus items. As early as November, 1945, the U.S. Government started selling crated CG-4A gliders – for which it had paid some $20,000 apiece – for $75. The five huge crates required to ship one of those aircraft were made with over 10,000 board feet of Grade A lumber – enough to build a small modern ranch house – and surplus gliders sold like hot cakes. The people who purchased them did not want an aircraft; what they really wanted was the first-quality wood of the crates. The surplus gliders were sold with such haste that Air Force officials neglected to keep even one for display in its aviation museum.

The thousands of American glider pilots who survived hazardous crash landings during their U.S. training, and behind enemy lines in combat, returned home at the end of the war. And though it was difficult for them to do so, they picked up the pieces of their interrupted civilian careers and got on with the task of earning a living in the world they had helped restore to peace.

Many of the recently discharged pilots had hopes of getting a job with commercial airlines that were then widely expected to use gliders to haul everything from the U.S. Mail to heavier freight cargoes, such as household furniture, from city to city. But the

[372]

freight glider industry failed to materialize. Only one firm, the Wing Cargo Company of Philadelphia, made a serious attempt to use gliders. Headed by Colonel James Dolenberg, a former troop carrier power pilot, Wing Cargo utilized two surplus gliders in 1946 to pick up cargoes of strawberries in Georgia and oranges in Florida and deliver them to wholesale grocery warehouses in Philadelphia. Only three months after it began operating, Wing Cargo was forced out of business by truck companies and the railroads, both of which transported the fruit at cheaper rates and in larger quantities.

The majority of the few hundred glider pilots who remained on active duty after WW II were assigned to Pope Air Force Base, North Carolina, for duty with the 82nd Airborne Division at neighbouring Fort Bragg. Other pilots were assigned to Fort Benning, Georgia, where student paratroopers at the U.S. Army Parachute School were required to take glider orientation flights as part of their airborne training up until 1949. Still other pilots were stationed at Wright Field, where they flew experimental models of the new aluminium-skinned gliders being developed there.

In April 1949, the U.S. Army conducted Operation Tarheel, the last American training manoeuvre in which gliders were employed. Tarheel was a sizeable month-long tactical exercise that took place near Fort Bragg and involved the 82nd Airborne and the 28th and 43rd National Guard Infantry divisions. During the manoeuvre the 82nd Airborne was resupplied by waves of CG-15A gliders. Though gliders were never used again during training manoeuvres, it was not until January 1, 1953, that the U.S. Army formally deleted glider landings from the list of capabilities of its airborne units.

The glider test pilots at Wright Field literally worked themselves out of a job by helping to perfect the new XCG-18A and XCG-20 gliders, both of which had been produced by the Chase Aircraft Company of New York City. Each of those modern, state-of-the-art gliders was constructed entirely of metal and had a smooth outer skin of sheet aluminium. During its late 1947 experimental flight trials, the 30-passenger XCG-18A was outfitted with two Wright R-1850 engines and transformed into a C-122 powered airplane, the U.S. Air Force's first large tactical aircraft capable of short field take-offs and landings. In October 1949, the 60-passenger XCG-20 glider was equipped with two wing-mounted Pratt and Whitney R-2800 Double Wasp radial piston engines and transformed into the versatile C-123 Provider tactical transport aircraft. Hundreds of C-123s were later

[373]

used extensively as combat support aircraft during the Vietnam War (1964-1975) and the Arab-Israeli Yom Kippur War of 1973. With the conversion of the XCG-18A and XCG-20 gliders into powered airplanes, the drastically reduced American military glider programme passed into history.

Several of the American glider pilots who remained on active duty after World War II volunteered to become power pilots in the U.S. Air Force, and subsequently saw more combat in the Korean War (1950-1953), and the Vietnam War. David H. Trexler, a veteran of service as a glider pilot in Europe, flew an F-82 twin Mustang fighter in Korea where, in June 1950, he was credited with a possible kill of a North Korean Yak-9 fighter. Later, during the Vietnam War, Trexler won the Distinguished Flying Cross while commanding the 421st Fighter Squadron at DaNang. With that unit he flew 116 combat missions in an F-4 Phantom jet fighter over North Vietnam, Cambodia and Laos. When he retired in 1974 at the rank of Lieutenant Colonel, after 33 years of service, Trexler had logged over 6,000 hours of flying in every kind of aircraft from towed gliders to supersonic jet fighters.

When the U.S. Army's 187th Regimental Combat Team made the second, and largest, parachute assault of the Korean War behind enemy lines at Munson-Ni, on March 23, 1951, Lieutenant John Huska, another ex-glider pilot, was on board the leading jump plane. Huska, a communications specialist, had left the service after World War II. However, when war broke out in Korea, he was involuntarily recalled to active duty. Huska remained in the service after the Korean War, retiring in 1966 at the rank of major.

British forces, like the Americans, gradually began to phase their gliders out of service shortly after the end of World War II.

In September 1945, the Glider Pilot Regiment was dispatched to Palestine minus its gliders for duty with the 6th Airborne Division. By 1948, the regiment had returned to England and had been reduced in size to a headquarters and training squadron stationed at Aldershot and two tactical squadrons of Horsas and Hamilcars based at Waterbeach, Netheravon and Fairford.

In 1950, England's Glider Pilot Regiment was further reduced to a single squadron, and the training of new glider pilots was discontinued. One year later, the RAF terminated its glider programme and reassigned the 30 remaining pilots to other flying duties in powered aircraft. Many of those pilots later logged a considerable number of combat flying hours in the Korean War with Great Britain's Commonwealth Division, and in Malaya (1951-1954) during the attempted communist take-over of that country. It was not until August 31, 1957 – one day prior to the birth of England's new Army Air Corps – that the proud Glider Pilot Regiment was formally disbanded.

World War II had barely ended when, in 1945, the surviving veterans of England's Glider Pilot Regiment established the Glider Pilot's Regimental Association. Today the association still has more than 700 members, publishes its own magazine, *The Eagle*, and holds annual reunions in London.

In recent years, the World War II German glider pilot veterans have also formed their own Luftland-Fliegerkameradschaft (Glider Pilot's Association). Annual reunions of the Luftland-Fliegerkameradschaft are held in various West German cities.

It is ironic that the Soviet Union – the country that first pioneered the development of large transport gliders – never used them during World War II. In 1946, however, the Soviets began developing two types of large troop-carrying gliders for its new post-war airborne divisions. The first of those gliders was the Ts-25, which could accommodate 25 combat troops or 4,806 pounds of cargo. The other was the Yak-14, a large, square wooden craft capable of hauling 35 troops or slightly more than four tons of cargo. Using those two types of gliders, the Soviets maintained an impressive airborne strike force of three glider infantry regiments until 1965.

The Soviets had just discontinued the use of gliders in their armed forces when, in 1965, an American combat veteran glider pilot by the name of Earl Dust took the first steps to organize what is now known as the National World War II Glider Pilots Association. Since 1971, the association has been holding annual national reunions in various cities around the United States. At those reunions, the ex-glider pilots, many of whom still suffer disabilities from World War II wounds and injuries, gather to renew old acquaintances and honour friends who did not survive the war. Since 1976, a large group of World War II British glider pilots have been attending the reunions. Since 1980, several German glider pilots have also been in attendance.

Each year more and more American ex-glider pilots make pilgrimages back to England and to the European and Pacific combat areas. There they stroll through towns where they were once

[375]

stationed and walk across battlefields where their lives almost ended abruptly many years before. In Holland, Normandy, and the Philippines they are greeted warmly by grateful citizens who still remember their brave deeds during World War II.

Apparently, glider pilots never lose their love of flying, because many of them are members of the various soaring clubs. While researching the tragic story of the XCG-16 glider crash in which Richard C. DuPont and others were killed, I called the home of Harry N. Perl, one of two men who survived that air disaster. Before telephoning Perl, I had assumed that after his narrow escape in the crash of the XCG-16, he had probably never dared enter another glider. But when I called and asked, 'Is Mister Perl there, please?' his wife replied, 'No, he's out doing some flying at our local airport.' With her assistance, I finally got in touch with Perl at the airport later that day.

What became of the thousands of combat gliders that were built during World War II by the United States (14,612), England (5,935), Germany (3,995), Italy (18), and Japan (825)? Today there are only five complete combat gliders in existence, and most of them restored from bits and pieces of wreckage found rotting and rusting in junkyards.

The Caproni Museum in Milan, Italy, has on display a Caproni TM-2 glider, an all-wood aircraft first developed in 1943 to haul 20 troops or two tons of cargo. All of the remaining four combat gliders are American CG-4As. One is located in France's Ste. Mère-Église airborne museum. That glider was originally restored in the United States and shipped to England in 1960 for use in the movie, *The Longest Day*. However, the glider did not appear in the film, and was subsequently purchased by the French museum. Another CG-4A is on display in the 101st Airborne Museum at Fort Campbell, Kentucky. That aircraft bears the same markings as the Fighting Falcon glider which carried General Donald F. Pratt to his death in Normandy on June 6, 1944. A third CG-4A can be seen at the U.S. Air Force Museum at Wright Patterson Air Force Base in Ohio where it hangs from the ceiling in an attitude of flight. The final and most completely restored CG-4A is on display at the Silent Wings Museum in Terrell, Texas, 25 miles east of Dallas, on Interstate Highway 20. First opened in April 1983, the Silent Wings Museum was established by the Military Glider Pilots Association, Inc., an affiliate of the National World War II Glider Pilots Association. The glider itself was restored with funds donated by the American World War II glider pilots and various other persons and organizations. All of the restoration work on this glider was performed by volunteer ex-glider pilots of WW II.

In addition to those whole gliders, there is the cockpit of a Horsa on display in England's Airborne Forces Museum at Aldershot, and two-thirds of a Horsa fuselage, including the cockpit, in the Museum of Army Flying at Middle Wallop.

In the United States, the 82nd Airborne Museum at Fort Bragg, North Carolina, exhibits the forward half of a CG-15A fuselage. and at the National Soaring Museum in Elmira, New York, visitors can see the front end of a CG-4A fuselage, complete with a jeep emerging from its upraised nose section.

In addition to the museums just mentioned there are two others, both located in Holland, that contain extensive displays of combat equipment used by British and American glider pilots during World War II. The first is the former Hartenstein Hotel in Oosterbeek, which served as the headquarters of General Urquhart's British 1st Airborne Division during Operation Market-Garden.

The other is the Netherlands Liberation Museum, currently under construction near Nijmegen in an area that the Dutch have named Little America, encompassing the area in which the 82nd Airborne Division's glider and parachute troops landed during Operation Market-Garden. This museum commemorates the freeing of the Netherlands by its own brave people with the decisive assistance of American, English and Polish troops.

Gliders, outlawed for use by American military personnel in the 1930s, hurriedly pressed into combat in World War II, and phased out of military service in the early 1950s, have silently returned to the modern U.S. Air Force. Today, the Air Force Academy in Colorado operates one of the largest sailplane schools in the world, flying more than 13,000 sorties annually. Each year some 400 cadets are enrolled in the Academy's Airmanship Program, where they learn the basics of flying in sleek new Schweizer 2-23 two-place gliders.

In a 1976 interview, Lieutenant Colonel Richard Williams, chief of the airmanship programme at the Air Force Academy, said that 'soaring is one of the best tools available for giving cadets a general understanding of aviation while at the same time equipping them with some basic flying skills.'

Those were the very words Captain Ralph S. Barnaby of the U.S. Navy had said to his superiors in 1935, just before they ordered the glider programme at Pensacola Naval Air Station to be discontinued.

Brooke County Library
945 Main Street
Wellsburg, W. Va. 26070

[377]

# *Notes*

Chapter 2. Better Late Than Never

1.  The term 'shock cord' is of German origin. Americans were to later change its name to 'bungee cord'. Depending on its manufacturer, each cord measured between three-quarters to one inch in diameter and consisted of over 100 individual thin rubber strings, the whole item being covered by a cotton fabric skin.

2.  For the record, the original German glider launch commands were: (1) *'Haltenmannschaft fertig?'* (Holding team ready?). To which the two anchor men holding ropes attached to the tail section were to reply: *'Fertig'* (Ready). (2) *'Startmannschaft fertig?'* (Start team ready?). To which the eight or more men holding the shock cord in front of the glider were to reply: *'Fertig'* (Ready). (3) *'Laufen!'* (Walk). At this command the start team was to begin walking away from the glider, drawing the cord taut. When the launch director saw that the cord had been drawn completely taut he would shout: (4) *'Rennen!'* (Run). When the cord had been stretched sufficiently to provide a good take-off the launch director would turn around to face the two men positioned at the tail and command: (5) *'Los!'* (Let go). The start team, meanwhile, would continue running until the cord automatically fell away from the glider. When carrying the cord back up the hill the start team would hold it above their heads to keep it from dragging on the ground and being damaged.

3.  Rickenbacker, Captain Edward V., *Seven Came Through* (New York: Doubleday 1943) page 104.

4.  Both the *Akron* and the *Macon* were fitted with a hangar inside their spacious bellies that could accommodate five Curtis F9C-2 Sparrowhawks, a light biplane fighter originally

[378]

designed for naval aircraft carriers. The U.S. Navy solved the problem of how to get an airplane into the hangar while it and the airship were in flight by means of a special trapeze-like device. When retrieving an airplane in flight, the device would be lowered beneath the airship. The pilots manoeuvred their planes so that a hook affixed to the upper wing could clip onto the trapeze bar. Once the airplane was hooked on, a mechanical arm dropped over the aft end of its fuselage to hold it steady while it was winched up into the hangar. For take-off, the airplane was simply lowered by the same device and released.

5.  The *Eaglet* is on permanent display at the Smithsonian Institution in Washington, DC.

6.  The Condor Legion was an all-German Luftwaffe (Air Force) unit that served on the side of General Franco and his Nationalist Forces during the Spanish Civil War.

7.  The Japanese never employed their glider troop units in combat during World War II. However, their parachute units did make combat jumps on the Netherlands East Indies island of Celebes (January 11, 1942), Sumatra (January 14, 1942), and Timor (February 21, 1942). They also jumped on Leyte Island in the Philippines (December 6, 1944) in an unsuccessful attempt to capture an airfield being guarded by troops of the American 11th Airborne Division.

8.  No other type of German tank was produced in as many variations as the Pz. Kw IV. In service throughout World War II, this versatile tank was armed with a short-barrelled 75 mm gun and an MG 34 (7.92 mm) machine gun. It had a crew of five and top speed of 20 mph. Initial production models of the Pz. Kw IV weighed 20 tons.

9.  Army Air Forces Historical Study No. 47; *Development and Procurement of Gliders in the Army Air Forces 1941-1944,* p. 5.

Chapter 3. Growing Pains

1.  Army Air Forces Historical Study No. 1: *Development and Procurement of Gliders in the Army Air Forces 1941-1944* (Washington, DC: A.A.F. Historical Office, 1946), p. 4.

2. Robinson went on to become the first three-time consecutive winner of the U.S. National Soaring Competitions. He won again in 1941 and for the third time in 1946. (No contests were held in 1942-1945 because of the war.) In 1949 he won lasting international fame when he became the first pilot in the world to be awarded the coveted Diamond C badge by the Federation Aeronautique Internationale, the governing body of flying. The Diamond C is still the world's foremost soaring achievement badge. To earn it, a sailplane pilot must (1) achieve an altitude gain of 5,000 metres during a single flight after release from the tow-plane. This altitude gain must be verified by a sealed onboard barograph; (2) complete a goal flight of 300 kilometres. Prior to take-off on a goal flight, a pilot must state, in writing, the names of various points (airports or cities) at which turns are to be made. The pilot must carry a camera to photograph each goal, or turning point. The sailplane's wing must appear in each photo for verification by officials; (3) complete an all-out distance flight of at least 500 kilometres. Pilot must obtain sworn statements from witnesses at take-off and landing points for presentation to officials.

3. Sir B. H. Liddell Hart, *History of the Second World War* (New York: G. P. Putnam's Sons, 1970), p. 136.

4. Army Air Forces Historical Study No. 1: *Developoment and Procurement of Gliders in the Army Air Forces 1941-1944* (Washington DC: A.A.F. Historical Office, 1946), p. 11.

5. Those bases were located in the First Corps Area at: Westover Field, Massachusetts; in Second Corps Area at: Mitchel Field, Long Island, New York; in Third Corps Area at: Olmstead Field, Middletown, Pennsylvania, and Langley Field, Hampton, Virginia; in Fourth Corps Area at: Shaw Field, Sumter, South Carolina, Kessler Field, Biloxi, Mississippi, and Army Air Base, Orlando, Florida; Fifth Corps Area at: Bowman Field, Kentucky; in Sixth Corps Area at: Chanute Field, Rantoul, Illinois; in Seventh Corps Area at: Sherman Field, Fort Leavenworth, Kansas, Lowry Field, Denver, Colorado, and Jefferson Barracks, Missouri; in Eighth Corps Area at: Randolph Field, Texas; in Ninth Corps Area at: McChord Field, Washington, Army Air Base, Salinas, California, Army Air Forces Base, Salt Lake, Utah, and March Field, Riverside, California.

6. Those 18 schools were: (1) Jolly Flying Service, Grand Forks, North Dakota, (2) L. Miller-Wittig, Crookston, Minnesota, (3) Fontana School of Aeronautics, Rochester, Minnesota, (4) Hinck Flying Service, Inc., Monticello, Minnesota, (5) Morey Airplane Company, Janesville, Wisconsin, (7) Anderson Air Activities, Antigo, Wisconsin, (8) McFarland Flying Service, Pittsburg, Kansas, (9) Ong Aircraft Corp., Goodland, Kansas, (10) Hunter Flying Service, Spencer, Iowa, (11) Sooner Air Training Corp., Okmulgee, Oklahoma, (12) Harte Flying Service, Hays, Kansas, (13) Anderson and Brennan Flying Service, Aberdeen, South Dakota, (14) Kenneth Starnes Flying Service, Loanoke, Arkansas, (15) Plains Airways, Ft. Morgan, Colorado, (16) Cutter-Carr Flying Service, Clovis, New Mexico, (17) Big Spring Flying Service, Big Spring, Texas, and (18) Clint Breedlove Aerial Service, Plainview, Texas.

7. Army Air Forces Historical Study No. 47: *The Glider Pilot Training Program 1941 to 1943* (Washington, DC: Assistant Chief of Air Staff, Intelligence Historical Division, 1943), p. 78.

8. Those 16 companies were: (1) Waco Aircraft Co., Troy, Ohio, (2) General Aircraft Corp., Astoria, New York, (3) National Aircraft Corp., Elwood, Indiana, (4) Robertson Aircraft Corp., St. Louis, Missouri, (5) Laister-Kauffmann Aircraft, St. Louis, Missouri, (6) Porterfield Aircraft Co., (formerly Ward Furniture Manufacturing Co.), Ft. Smith, Arkansas, (7) Jenter Corp., (formerly Ridgefield Manufacturing Corp.), Ridgefield, New Jersey, (8) Pratt, Reed and Co., Deep River, Connecticut, (9) Timm Aircraft Co., Los Angeles, California, (10) AGA Aviation Corp., (later known as G&A Aircraft, Inc.), Willow Grove, Pennsylvania, (11) Rearwin Aircraft and Engines, Inc., (later known as Commonwealth Aircraft, Inc.), Kansas City, Kansas, (12) Babcock Aircraft Corporation, Deland, Florida, (13) Northwestern Aeronautical Corp., Minneapolis, Minnesota, (14) Ford Motor Co., Kingsford, Michigan, (15) Gibson Refrigeration Co., Greenville, Michigan, and (16) Cessna Aircraft Co., Wichita, Kansas.

9. Army Air Forces Historical Study No. 7: *The Glider Pilot*

*Training Program 1941 to 1943* (Washington, DC: Assistant Chief of Air Staff, Intelligence Historical Division, 1943), p. 151.

10. Especially designed for transport in Hamilcar gliders, the Tetrarch Mark IV was primarily a light reconnaissance tank used by British airborne troops until such time as heavier tanks effected ground link-up with them. Operated by a three man crew, the Tetrarch was armed with one 37 mm or one 40 mm gun and one machine gun. Its 12 cylinder, 165 hp engine enabled it to reach a top speed of 37 mph. A total of 171 Tetrarchs were manufactured during WW II, 20 of them being sent to Russia on lend-lease.

11. Army Air Forces Historical Study No. 1: *Development and Procurement of Gliders in the Army Air Forces 1941-1944* (Washington, DC: A.A.F. Historical Office, 1946), p. 20.

12. James E. Mrazek, *The Glider War* (New York: St. Martin's Press, 1975), p. 45.

13. Army Air Forces Historical Study No. 1: *Development and Procurement of Gliders in the Army Air Forces 1941-1944* (Washington, DC: A.A.F. Historical Office, 1946), p. 82.


Chapter 4. Disaster Over Sicily

1. The proper phase of the moon was critical in that it would provide illumination for a pre-dawn attack and would also influence the tides upon which the amphibious troops were dependent in getting to the beaches.

2. A crate apiece for the: (1) nose section, (2) cargo section of the fuselage, (3) left and right inboard wing panels, (4) left and right outboard wing panels, and (5) the empennage consisting of the rudder, vertical and horizontal stabilizers, elevator, dorsal fin, and the tail wheel.

3. Gavin's combat team was made up of the following units: his own 505th Parachute Infantry Regiment: 3rd Battalion of the 504th Parachute Infantry: 456th Parachute Field Artillery Regiment; Company B, 307th Airborne Engineer Battalion; plus signal, medical and naval gunfire support detachments.

4. Tucker's combat team was comprised of his own 504th Parachute Infantry (less his 3rd Battalion loaned to Gavin); the 376th Parachute Field Artillery Battalion; and Company C, 307th Airborne Engineer Battalion.

5. The proper position for American gliders was at an altitude just slightly higher than the tow-plane. In that higher position the glider avoided the prop-wash of the airplane. When being towed by a C-47, a CG-4A glider pilot was supposed to be able to see the top of the tow-plane's tail in a direct line with its plexiglass astrodome.

6. A 'stick' is comprised of an arbitrary number of paratroopers who jump out of a plane in one group.

7. Charles Leslie Keerans, Jr. was born in 1899 in North Carolina. He graduated from West Point in the class of 1919 and was commissioned a second lieutenant in the infantry. During the 1920s and 1930s Keerans served in a number of infantry assignments with various units stationed in the United States.

   Prior to joining the 82nd Airborne Division as a newly promoted brigadier general in August of 1942 at Camp Claiborne, Lousiana, Keerans had been a colonel serving as chief of staff of the 101st Airborne Division, also stationed at Camp Claiborne. One of Keerans's last official acts as chief of staff in the 101st Airborne was to be the officer in charge of the ceremony in which Colonel Pratt was promoted to the rank of brigadier general. As fate would have it, Pratt was the only American general to be killed during the June 1944 invasion of Normandy.

## Chapter 5. Aftermath of Sicily

1. *Sicily and the Surrender of Italy*, p. 425.

2. *St. Louis Post-Dispatch*, May 4, 1975, p. 12.

3. Army Air Forces Historical Office, Headquarters A.A.F., Army Air Forces Historical Studies: No. 47 (unpublished); *Development and Procurement of Gliders in the Army Air Forces 1941-1944*, p. 295.

4. The Smithsonian Institution has one of Murphy's stunt planes on permanent display in Washington, DC.

5. Generally considered the grandfather of modern short-field and vertical take-off airplanes, the Fiesler Fi 156 Storch (Stork) was a high winged, single-engine monoplane that was used on every battle front by the Germans for artillery spotting, evacuation of walking wounded, and general liaison work. Developed in 1935, it had a 240 hp Argus eight-cylinder inverted-V engine which enabled it to fly between 30 and 105 mph. Its wooden wings were particularly aerodynamic. Moveable flaps were installed the full length of the leading edges of both wings. Trailing edges of the wings were also completely mobile and contained a number of braking flaps which allowed the Storch to remain all but motionless in the air. These aerodynamic features permitted it to land in a space of only 50 feet, the equivalent of its wingspan, and likewise enabled it to take off in a little over 50 yards. The Storch could carry a pilot and two passengers. Its range was 240 miles; ceiling was 17,061 feet.

6. The regiments were numbered the 88th, 187th, 188th, 189th, 190th, 193rd, 194th, 325th, 326th and 401st. Three of them (the 88th, 189th and 190th) were eventually consolidated with the 326th glider regiment. During the closing days of World War II the 188th Glider Infantry was converted to a parachute regiment.

7. The separate glider battalion was the 550th Airborne Infantry Battalion.

8. Glider Field Artillery Battalions were the 319th, 320th, 321st, 602nd, 675th, 676th, 677th, 680th, 681st and 907th.

9. Army Air Force pamphlet, *I Troop Carrier Command, The Operational Training Program*, 1944, pp. 296-297. On file in the base library at Maxwell Field in Montgomery, Alabama.

10. Like sailors, army glidermen were trained extensively in the use of rope and complicated knots. They used the baker bowline knot almost exclusively because it enabled them to quickly tighten loads loosened during turbulent flights. Unse cured cargo was a serious hazard for everyone aboard the

glider. Well known to sailors and Boy Scouts, the baker bowline knot is similar to the 'trucker's hitch' commonly used by truck drivers to secure canvas coverings on their vehicles.

11. The C-47 airplane was equipped with a transparent astrodome on top of the fuselage, directly above the navigator's seat, from which navigational observations could be made. During night-time paratroop and glider missions, coloured lights were often displayed in the astrodome of the formation's leading airplane to signal the start of the jump or glider-release to trailing aircraft.

12. During a later return trip to the crash scene, Hoyt had his left shoe given back to him by the farmer. It was completely broken in half at the instep.

13. Lesley James McNair graduated from West Point in the class of 1911, taking his commission in the field artillery branch. He saw his first combat in 1914 as a member of General Frederick Funston's command during the Vera Cruz Expedition in Mexico. During WW II, McNair took very seriously his job as chief of Army Ground Forces. He twice left the security of his Washington office to visit battlefronts in Africa and Europe to see how well American soldiers were applying the tactics his instructors had taught them in U.S. training camps. In April 1943, he got so close to the fighting in Tunisia that he was wounded by German shellfire. One year later, at the age of 61, he was killed while observing American forces near St. Lo, France, during the breakout from the Normandy beachhead. Ironically, his death was caused by an American bomber which accidentally dropped its full bomb load on American troop positions. Fort McNair, in Washington, DC., was named in his honour.

14. Edward M. Flanagan, *The Angels, a History of the 11th Airborne Division*, Washington DC: Infantry Journal Press, 1948, p. 11.

Chapter 6. The Forgotten War in Burma

1. Started in 1920, and completed in 1939, this famous highway

followed the route used by Genghis Khan's messengers and the ancient tea and spice caravans travelling between China and Burma. Measuring 717 miles in length, the road extended between Kunming, China, and the Burmese city of Lashio. When Japanese troops sealed all of China's seaports in 1942, the Burma Road became China's only land supply route.

2. Yust, Walter (ed.): *Ten Eventful Years* (Chicago: Encyclopedia Britannica 1947) Vol. 4, p. 164.

3. In Southeast Asia, the monsoon season extends from April to October. Throughout that period the weather is typified by torrential rainstorms and sweltering heat, both of which seriously impede large military operations.

4. During their first and second campaigns in Burma the Chindits used over 3,000 horses and mules, of which 2,216 were flown in aboard gliders and powered airplanes. Very few survived, most dying of disease, exhaustion, starvation, injuries, battle wounds – or being shot and eaten. The Chindits camouflaged pale coloured mules by painting them green.

5. The 5037th Provisional Unit (Merrill's Marauders) was organized in India from volunteers obtained in the United States, the Caribbean area and the Southwest Pacific. In preparation for combat in Burma, this force underwent an intensive training programme that was supervised by British General Orde Wingate. Wingate's training methods apparently were effective, because the 5037th was later awarded the Distinguished Unit Citation by President Roosevelt for exceptional gallantry at Walawbum, Inkangahtawng, Nhpum Ga, and Myitkyina. General Merrill, the 5037th's commander, graduated from West Point in 1929. He retired from the U.S. Army in 1948 with the rank of major general; he died on December 11, 1958.

6. This was done because if the glider on the right side (short tow position) cut off first there was a danger that its tow-line would shoot forward like a rubber band and wrap itself around the wings of the other glider.

7. Slim, Field Marshal the Viscount William J., *Defeat Into Victory*, (Chicago: David McKay Company, 1961), p. 224.

8. General Alison told me that at the time he was picked to lead the Broadway mission he had never before flown a glider of any type. Only two nights before the operation was to be launched, he got checked out in a CG-4A at Hailakandi.

9. Thomas, Lowell, *Back to Mandalay* (New York: The Greystone Press, 1951), p. 197.

10. I asked Turner what prevented the Gurkha from bursting through the thin canvas flooring. He replied that the exterior air pressure pushing against the glider's frail canvas skin must have enabled the canvas to support the Gurkha's weight.

11. Bartlett told the author that the sword was later stolen from him as he was returning home after the war.

12. Turner still has the bullet. He keeps it on his desk top as a reminder of how close he came to being killed in Burma.


Chapter 7. Cross-Channel Attack

1. Each American troop carrier group was comprised of a headquarters unit with four aircraft and four squadrons with 12 planes apiece.

2. The 6th Air Landing Brigade was made up of the 2nd Battalion Oxfordshire and Buckinghamshire Light Infantry, the 1st Battalion of the Royal Ulster Rifles, and the 12th Battalion of the Devonshire Regiment.

3. Bradley, General Omar N., *A Soldier's Story* (New York: Henry Holt, 1951), p. 239.

4. Those air units were task-organized as follows: the 50th Troop Carrier Wing had command of the 439th, 440th, 441st and 442nd Groups; the 52nd Wing commanded the 61st, 313th, 314th, 315th and 316th Groups; and the 53rd Wing commanded the 434th, 435th, 436th, 437th and 438th Groups.

5. The 50th Wing had its aircraft at these RAF bases: Exeter, Merryfield, Up Ottery and West Zoyland. Meanwhile, the 53rd Wing occupied these bases: Aldermaston, Greenham Common, Membury, Ramsbury and Welford Park.

6. The term 'pair of pairs in echelon to the right' is unique to airborne operations. It means that all aircraft participating in a given mission are to fly in a column which is slanted to the right and consists of groupings of four aircraft flying abreast with each succeeding grouping positioned to the right of the one it is following. This echeloning, or slanting, of the column is done to avoid air turbulence being generated by the leading aircraft. Using this easily controlled formation, an airborne force commander can rapidly deliver large numbers of glider and parachute troops in a short period of time.

7. Army Group B was comprised of the Seventh and Fifteenth German Armies. Seventh Army was deployed from the Loire River all the way up through western France to the Dives River at the point where it empties into the Bay of Biscay east of Caen. Fifteenth Army occupied Belgium and northern France – including the Pas de Calais area – to the Scheldt estuary.

8. Dupuy, Colonel R. Ernest and Dupuy, Trevor N., *Military Heritage of America* (New York: McGraw Hill Book Co., Inc., 1956), p. 529.

9. A serial is an arbitrary number of aircraft operating under one commander and flying in a formation as part of an airlift. The formations are separated by predesignated time intervals.

10. Each pathfinder team consisted of one officer and nine enlisted men who had been training in secret together in England since March of 1944. Team members were handpicked volunteers, trained and equipped to jump into enemy territory ahead of the main airborne assault forces and mark both glider LZs and parachute DZs with lights and radar. Glider LZs were marked with seven coloured lights laid out in a straight line pointing downwind. Going downwind, the first light was red, the next five amber, and the last green. Parachute DZs were marked with five white lights placed to form a T. Eureka radar devices were used to guide incoming paratroop planes and glider tugs to their respective zones. Their signals were received by a Rebecca unit mounted in the nose of each airplane.

11. During the peak war years, Gibson employed some 4,400 men and women. The Company built a total of 1,078 gliders, a production record second only to the Ford Motor Company.

[388]

Gibson also manufactured the incendiary bombs that were dropped on Tokyo by Doolittle's raiders in April 1943.

12. William J. Delp to author.

13. Don Forrest Pratt was born in Brookfield, Missouri, a few miles from the birthplace of General John J. Pershing. Upon graduating from the University of Wisconsin in 1917, Pratt entered the U.S. Army as an infantry officer and was assigned to training duties in California. During World War I, he tried without success to obtain a transfer to a combat unit in France. In 1932 Pratt graduated from the Command and General Staff College and was assigned to a three year tour in China with the 15th Infantry. Graduating from the War College in 1937 as a lieutenant colonel, he was next assigned to Fort Benning, Georgia, for a four-year teaching assignment. Shortly after Pearl Harbor he was promoted to colonel and reassigned first to the 43rd Infantry Division and then, in 1942, to the newly activated 82nd Infantry Division at Camp Claibourne, Louisiana. While serving as chief of staff of the 82nd he was promoted to brigadier general in August 1942 and transferred to the new 101st Airborne Division, also at Camp Claibourne. Pratt remained with the 101st until his death in Normandy on June 6, 1944.

14. That unit was part of the Light Armoured Reconnaissance Regiment. It was equipped with Tetrarch tanks, which had been specially designed for transport in Hamilcar gliders, and standard production models of mechanized Bren gun carriers.

15. General Order Number 33, Headquarters Ninth Air Force, APO 133, U.S. Army. Dated July 5, 1944. In possession of author.

Chapter 8. Operation Dragoon

1. Pritchard's unit had originally been the 2nd Parachute Brigade of the 1st Airborne Division. But as the 1st Airborne was preparing to return to England, in November 1943, the brigade was increased in size, separated from the division, and detailed to remain behind in Italy under the new name of 2nd

Independent Parachute Brigade Group. Its combat elements consisted of the 4th, 5th (Royal Welch) and 6th (Scots) Parachute Battalions, plus five batteries of Royal Artillery, and the 23rd Independent Parachute Platoon. The latter unit was a pathfinder detachment that was extremely well trained and proficient in marking glider and parachute zones.

2.  The airborne training centre on Sicily was nothing more than a large piece of real estate adjacent to the Allied airfield at Trapini. Unlike the American airborne training centres, it had no formal schools or training staff. From time to time various airborne units were rotated in and out of the centre to conduct practice glider landings, parachute jumps, and live-fire training manoeuvres. Not far from Trapini is Mount Saint Giuliano where, on an exceedingly windy day late in 1943, a pilot from the 45th Squadron of the 316th Troop Carrier Group managed to soar along the high southern bluff in a CG-4A glider for a record-setting four and one-half hours.

Chapter 9. Costly Setback in Holland

1.  Liddell Hart, B. H., *History of the Second World War*. (New York: G. P. Putnam's Sons, 1970), p. 562.

2.  Browning had held the rank of lieutenant general since December 1943. Brereton was promoted to that same rank in April 1944.

3.  Such a piecemeal insertion violated several of the fundamental principles of war: Surprise, Simplicity, Mass and Manoeuvre.

4.  Gavin had only been commanding the 82nd Airborne since August 15. He was given command of the division when its original commander, General Ridgway, was promoted to take over the XVIII Airborne Corps Headquarters in the 1st Allied Airborne Army.

5.  Ryan, Cornelius, *A Bridge Too Far*. (New York: Simon and Schuster, 1974), p. 159.

6.  Officially known as the 17-pounder (76.2 mm) AT (anti-tank) Mark I, this extremely accurate and lethal weapon had been

especially developed by the British in 1942 to deal with Rommel's Afrika Korps tanks. It had a low profile (5 feet 6 inches), a double-baffle muzzle break which considerably reduced its recoil, and a spaced protective armour shield for its crew. The shield consisted of two layers of steel separated by a 2-inch space. When large calibre shells struck the first (outer) layer of armour, they would usually explode, and the resultant fragmentation would be insufficient to penetrate the second layer and cause harm to the guncrew. The 17-pounder weighed 6,700 pounds and had a range of 11,500 yards. Its outstanding feature was that the shell it fired could penetrate 9.13 inches of steel at 1,100 yards, enough to knock out any German tank.

7.  Ryan, Cornelius, *A Bridge Too Far*. (New York: Simon and Schuster, 1974), p. 217.

8.  Browning was not the only ranking Allied officer eager to be first to relieve himself on German real estate. When Patton reached the Rhine on March 7, 1945, the first thing he did was to urinate in it. Then he sent a top secret message to Eisenhower which read: 'Dear Ike, today I pissed in the Rhine.'

9.  Warren, John C., *U.S.A.F. Historical Study No. 97: Airborne Operations in World War II, European Theater*. (Maxwell Air Force Base, Alabama, 1956), p. 129.

10. General Gavin to author.

11. This division should not be confused with the 6th German Parachute Regiment which was operating further south against the American 101st Airborne Division.

12. Letter, Gavin to Williams, dated September 25, 1944. In possession of author.


Chapter 10. Battle of the Bulge

1.  In France the headquarters of the 50th Troop Carrier Wing was located in Chartres; the 439th Group at Chateaudun; the 440th Group at Bricy and Orleans; the 441st Group at Dreux, and the 442nd Group at Saint Andre-de-l'Eure.

2.  SHAEF was one of the most famous acronyms of the war,

standing for Supreme Headquarters, Allied Expeditionary Forces. Eisenhower had moved his headquarters to France from England on September 1, 1944. Before his arrival, operational control of the battle on the Continent had been under Montgomery's direct supervision.

3.  Bradley, General of the Army, Omar N., *A Soldier's Story*, (New York: Henry Holt, 1951), p. 462.

4.  Those non-airborne units were the 755th and 969th Field Artillery Battalions, both of which were composed mainly of black soldiers manning powerful 155 mm howitzers. Also present was Combat Command B, 10th Armored Division, and Combat Command R of the 9th Armored Division. All told, these two armoured units only had forty operable medium tanks among them. The final non-airborne unit in Bastogne was the 705th Tank Destroyer Battalion.

5.  Much later in his military career, in 1968, Abrams would succeed his 1936 West Point classmate, General William C. Westmoreland, as the supreme commander of all American troops fighting in Vietnam. From that post, Abrams would go on to become Army Chief of Staff, the highest-ranking officer in the U.S. Army. Abrams died on September 4, 1974.

6.  The vital contribution made by the glider pilots toward the winning of the Battle of the Bulge is generally unknown to military history buffs and even to some professional military historians. Indeed, all but a very few of the combat infantry veterans of the Bulge interviewed by the author were unaware that gliders had landed at Bastogne during the height of the battle.


Chapter 11. Crossing the Rhine

1.  Lieutenants Barker and Doyle were both veterans of the southern France and Holland missions. At the time they began working on this project, Barker was the Squadron Glider Engineering Officer, Doyle was his assistant, and Krause a chief glider mechanic. During the writing of this book, Mr. Barker kindly sent a copy of the blueprints that he and his companions had used.

2.  The British 6th Airborne had a solid combat record. While the two American airborne divisions (the 82nd and 101st) that had jumped into Normandy with it on June 6, 1944 were returned to England early in July, the 6th Airborne remained on the Continent to fight as an infantry division. It was kept in the line until September, then returned home. The division was just about fully refitted and trained again for airborne work when, on December 26, 1944, it was hurriedly airlifted to Europe to defend bridges crossing the Meuse in Belgium. During the Battle of the Bulge the division fought against German units in the tip of the salient. In the last week of January, the 6th Airborne was trucked to Holland. There it occupied defensive positions between Roermond and Venlo. From Holland it was redeployed to England during the middle of February to again refit for combat.

3.  All of those CG-13 gliders were assigned to the 313th Troop Carrier Group which was then based at Achiet, France. The 313th was the only unit in Europe to be equipped with the large CG-13 gliders.

4.  Because more Allied glider and parachute troops were dropped into Holland after Market-Garden's D-Day, that operation still stands as the largest airborne assault in the history of warfare.

5.  Julian told the author that he later went looking for the jeep driver who had refused to stop. 'It's just as well that I never found him', said Julian, 'for I know I would have shot him for sure.'

6.  After the war, Jaisonkowski had his surname changed to Jason.

7.  The British still hold the record for the highest combat glider release. They set that record during the June 1944 Normandy invasion when six Horsas of their two *coup de main* parties made their cutaways at 5,000 feet.

8.  While relating this incident to the author General Miley said that General Ridgway was the only American still standing at this time. All others had hit the dirt to avoid getting shot. Still speaking of his former boss, Miley went on to say: 'I've never quite seen anyone so cool under fire as General Ridgway. It's a wonder that he didn't get killed during that war.'

9. When interviewed at his home in Pittsburgh, Pennsylvania in 1977, General Ridgway still had the fragment in his shoulder. He shrugged it off, saying, 'Bothers me once in a while during rainy weather, but other than that I never know it's there.'

10. Colonel Pilling buried Model in an unmarked grave. After the war he identified the grave site for the field marshal's son, Major Hansgeorg Model. He in turn reinterred his father's remains in a German military cemetery located in the Huertgen Forest. There the Lion of Defence rests among the graves of soldiers he had commanded in battle.

Chapter 12. Deliverance From Shangri-La

1. This is the same William T. Sampson, II who, earlier in 1942, had achieved modest fame by having his glider pilot's wings pinned on by the film star, Marlene Dietrich. Further information concerning Sampson will be found in Chapter 3.

2. The CG-4A glider used on this transatlantic flight had been manufactured by Pratt, Read and Company of Deep River, Connecticut. A short length of the tow-line used in the mission is on display today at that company. The pilot of the glider was Squadron Leader R. G. Seys of the R.A.F. His copilot was Squadron Leader F. M. Goebeil of the Royal Canadian Air Force. The longest (875-mile) leg of their trip extended from Newfoundland to Iceland.

3. Sunderman told the author that the thing he remembers most about his record flight is that the drinks he and his companions were given at the general's quarters actually contained ice cubes, an unheard of luxury on New Guinea.

4. One of the survivors, David S. Kaufman, informed the author that just before he and his party struck out through the jungle on foot, he climbed up on the glider and cut away that piece of the fabric containing its serial number of 341111. He kept that fabric until 1981 when he donated it to the glider pilots' museum in Terrell, Texas.

5. Milau and Sexauer were the only ones aboard the glider during this mission. Each wore an inflatable Mae West life preserver

throughout the trip. In the event the glider had to ditch at sea, the pilots were supposed to use a six-man rubber life raft that was secured to the floor of the glider, directly in front of the general's staff car. Sexauer told the author that the raft was so large and bulky that they never could have got it out of the side emergency exit door before the glider sank. Fortunately, it never had to be used.

6. When President Roosevelt was asked by newspaper reporters in April 1942 where the six American bombers that attacked Japan took off from he evasively replied, 'Shangri-La'. Actually, that attack originated from the carrier *Hornet* which had steamed undetected to within 670 miles of Tokyo to launch the strike force.

7. The five crew members were: Col. Peter J. Prossen, pilot, Maj. George H. Nicholson, copilot, S/Sgt. Hilliard Norris, PFC Melvin A. Mollberg, and PFC George R. Newcomer. The 19 passengers were: Maj. Herman F. Antonio, S/Sgt. Laura E. Beasley (WAC), Maj. Phillip J. Dattilo, T/Sgt. Kenneth W. Decker, PFC Alethia M. Fair (WAC), Capt. Louis E. Freyman, PFC Marion C. Gillis (WAC), Capt. Herbert G. Good, PFC Eleanor P. Hanna (WAC), Cpl. Margaret J. Hastings (WAC), Lt. Lawrence F. Holding, Sgt. Helen G. Kent (WAC), PFC Mary M. Landau (WAC), Lt. John S. McCollom, Lt. Robert E. McCollom, T/3 Marion W. McMonagle (WAC), Cpl. Charles R. Miller, Sgt. Belle G. Naimer (WAC), and Cpl. Melvyn A. Weber.

Chapter 13. Luzon – The Last Glider Mission

1. Originally, the Army Air Force planned to have only the North-western Aeronautical Corporation of Minneapolis, and the Waco Aircraft Company of Troy, Ohio, build the new CG-15A gliders. However, in October, 1944, procurement officials at Wright Field, Ohio, decided to limit production of the CG-15A to Waco Aircraft, the primary engineering contractor for that glider. Waco eventually built 427 CG-15A gliders, many of which saw postwar service. Waco charged the U.S. Government $20,548 for a new CG-15A. The 82nd

Airborne Division Museum at Fort Bragg, N.C. has on display the fuselage of a CG-15A, the only one in existence.

2. Army Air Forces Historical Study: No. 47, p. 57.

3. So named for its commander, Maj. Robert V. Connolly. This force was comprised of the following units: 6th Ranger Battalion, one rifle company from the 32nd Infantry Division, a 105 mm howitzer battery, plus medical and engineer units. The entire force was truck-mounted during its advance on Appari.

4. Colonel Burgess was a native of Sheridan, Wyoming. After graduating from Harvard in 1940, he was commissioned a Lieutenant and entered the U.S. Army. Thus far while serving with the 11th Airborne's 511th Parachute Infantry Regiment, Burgess had made a combat jump on Tagaytay Ridge, near Manila, and had seen considerable ground combat on Leyte and Luzon. He also participated in the daring Los Banos Prison raid of February 23, 1945, wherein a combined American and Filipino force liberated 2,147 civilian men, women and children internees from a prison camp located 40 miles behind Japanese lines on Luzon. In 1946, he left the service, went on to obtain a law degree from the University of Michigan, and is currently practising law in his home town of Sheridan.

Brooke County Library.
945 Main Street
Wellsburg, W. Va. 26070.

# Bibliography

Adleman, Robert H., and Walton, George, *The Champagne Campaign*. Boston: Little, Brown and Company, 1969.

Ambrose, Stephen E., *The Supreme Commander: The War Years of General Dwight D. Eisenhower*. New York: Doubleday, 1970.

Ansel, Walter, *Hitler and the Middle Sea*. Durham: Duke University Press, 1972.

Army Air Forces Historical Study No. 1. *The Glider Pilot Training Program, 1941 to 1943*. Washington, D.C: Assistant Chief of Staff, Intelligence Historical Division, 1943.

Army Air Forces Historical Study No. 47. *Development and Procurement of Gliders in the Army Air Forces*. Washington D.C: AAF Historical Office, 1946.

Barnaby, Captain U.S. Navy Ralph S., *Gliders and Gliding*. New York: The Ronald Press Company, 1930.

Barringer, Lewin B., *Flight Without Power*. New York: Pitman Publishing Corporation, 1940.

Bekker, Cajus, *The Luftwaffe War Diaries*. New York: Doubleday, 1970.

Belote, James H. and William M., *Corregidor: The Saga of a Fortress*. New York: Harper and Row, 1967.

Berry, Capt. John T., *The 509th Parachute Battalion in North Africa*. Privately published. Headquarters Airborne Command, 1943.

Bidwell, Shelford, *The Chindit War*. New York: MacMillan Publishing Company, Inc., 1979.

Blumenson, Martin, *U.S. Army in WW II: Salerno to Cassino*. Washington, D.C: Office of the Chief of Military History, Dept. of Army, 1965.

―――――, *The U.S. Army in WW II: Breakout and Pursuit*. Washington, D.C: Office of the Chief of Military History, Dept. of Army, 1961.

————, *The U.S. Army in WW II: Sicily and the Surrender of Italy*. Washington, D.C: Office of the Chief of Military History, Dept. of Army, 1965.

————, *The Patton Papers 1885–1940*. Boston: Houghton Mifflin, 1972.

Blyle, Col. William J., *The 13th Airborne Division*. Atlanta: Albert Love Enterprises, 1947.

Bradley, General of the Army Omar N., *A Soldier's Story*. New York: Henry Holt, 1951.

Brereton, Lt. Gen. Lewis H., *The Brereton Diaries*. New York: William Morrow, 1946.

Breuer, William B., *Bloody Clash At Sadzot*. St. Louis: Zeus Publishers, 1981.

Carr, William H.A., *The DuPonts of Delaware*. New York: Dodd, Mead and Company, 1956.

Cave, Floyd A. and Associates, *The Origins and Consequences of WW II*. New York: The Dryden Press, 1948.

Cole, Hugh M., *U.S. Army in World War II: Battle of the Bulge*. Washington, D.C: Office of the Chief of Military History, Dept. of Army, 1965.

Craig, Gordon A., *The Politics of the Prussian Army*. New York: Oxford University Press, 1956.

Craven, Wesley F. and Cate, James L., *The Army Air Force in WW II: Europe – Torch to Point Blank*. Chicago: University of Chicago Press, 1949.

————, *The Army Air Forces in WW II: The Pacific – Guadalcanal to Saipan*. Chicago: University of Chicago Press, 1950.

————, *The Army Air Force in WW II: The Pacific – Matterhorn to Nagasaki, June 1944 to August 1945*. Chicago: University of Chicago Press, 1953.

————, *The Army Air Force in WW II: Men and Planes*. Chicago: University of Chicago Press, 1955.

Dank, Milton, *The Glider Gang*. Philadelphia: J. B. Lippincott Company, 1977; London: Cassell, 1978.

Davin, Daniel M., *Official History of New Zealand in the Second World War 1939-1945*. New Zealand: New Zealand War History Branch, 1953.

Dawson, W. Forrest, *Saga of the All-American (82nd Airborne Div.)*. Privately printed.

Deakin, F. W., *The Brutal Friendship: Mussolini, Hitler and the*

*Fall of Italian Fascism*. New York: Harper & Row, 1962.

Department of the Army Pamphlet 20-260, *Historical Study: The German Campaign in the Balkans (Spring, 1941)*. Washington, D.C: Dept. of Army, 1963.

Dorian, Max, *The DuPonts*. Boston: Little, Brown and Company, 1962.

Dupuy, Col. R. Ernest and Dupuy, Trevor N., *Military Heritage of America*. New York: McGraw Hill Book Company, Inc., 1956.

Eisenhower, Dwight D., *Crusade in Europe*. New York: Doubleday, 1948.

Erickson, John, *The Soviet High Command*. New York: St. Martin's Press, 1962.

Farrar-Hockley, A. H., *Student*. New York: Ballantine Books, Inc., 1973.

Flanagan, Maj. Edward M., *The Angels: A History of the 11th Airborne Division*. Washington D.C: Infantry Journal Press, 1948.

Foley, Charles, *Commando Extraordinary: The Exploits of Otto Skorzeny*. New York: Ballantine Books, 1957.

Gavin, Lt. Gen. James M., *Airborne Warfare*. Washington D.C: Infantry Journal Press, 1947.

————, *War and Peace in the Space Age*. New York: Harper & Bros., 1958.

————, *On to Berlin*. New York: Viking, 1978; London, Leo Cooper, 1979.

Glavin, John R., *Assault*. New York: Hawthorn Books, Inc., 1969.

Goerlitz, Walter, *History of the German General Staff 1657-1945*. New York: Praeger, 1953.

Guild, Frank Jr., *Action of the Tiger: The Saga of the 437th Troop Carrier Group*. Nashville: The Battery Press, 1980.

Harrison, Gordon A., *U.S. Army in WW II: Cross-Channel Attack*. Washington, D.C: Office of the Chief of Military History, Dept. of Army.

Hooftman, Hugo, *Russian Aircraft*. Fallbrook, California: Aero Publishers, 1965.

Horrocks, Lieutenant General Sir Brian, *Corps Commander*. New York: Charles Scribner's Sons, 1977; London, Sidgwick & Jackson, 1977.

Huston, James A., *Out of the Blue*. West Lafayett, Ind.: Purdue University Studies, 1972.

Jacobson, H. J. and Rohwer, J., *Decisive Battles of World War II*. New York: G. P. Putman's Sons, 1965.

*Japanese Parachute Troops Special Series No. 32*. Washington, D.C: Military Intelligence Service, U.S. War Department, 1944.

Keitel, Wilhelm, Field Marshal, *The Memoirs of Field Marshal Keitel*; Walter Gorlitz, editor. New York: Stein & Day, 1965.

Kenney, Gen. George C., *General Kenney Reports*. New York: Duell, Sloan and Pierce, 1949.

Krueger, Gen. Walter, *From Down Under to Nippon: The Story of the Sixth Army in World War II*. Washington, D.C: Combat Forces Press, 1953.

Kusman, Michael, *Register of Graduates and Former Cadets of the U.S. Military Academy*. West Point: Association of Graduates of U.S.M.A., 1975.

Liddell Hart, Captain B. H., *History of the Second World War*. New York: William Morrow 1970.

————, *The German Generals Talk*. New York: William Morrow, 1948.

*Life*, editors of, *Life's Picture History of World War II*. New York: Time, Inc., 1950.

Lord, W. G. II, *History of the 508th Parachute Infantry*. Privately printed, n.d.

MacDonald, Charles B., *Command Decision*. Kent Greenfield, editor. London: Methuen, 1960.

————, *The Mighty Endeavor*. New York: Oxford University Press, 1969.

————, *U.S. Army in World War II: The Siegfried Line Campaign*. Washington, D.C: Office of the Chief of Military History, Dept. of the Army, 1963.

————, *U.S. Army in WW II: The Last Offensive*. Washington, D.C: Office of the Chief of Military History, Dept. of the Army, 1972.

Mahon, John K., and Danysh, Roman A., *Army Lineage Series, Infantry, Part I*. Washington, D.C: Office of the Chief of Military History, Dept. of the Army, 1972.

Marshal, Gen. S. L. A., *Night Drop*. Boston: Little, Brown and Company, 1962.

McDonough, James L. and Gardner, Richard S., *Sky Riders – History of the 327/401 Glider Infantry*. Nashville: The Battery Press, 1980.

Miller, John Jr., *The U.S. Army in WW II: Cartwheel: The Reduction of Rabaul*. Washington, D.C: Office of the Chief of Military History, Dept. of the Army, 1958.

Montgomery, Field Marshal Sir Bernard, *Despatch of Field Marshal The Viscount Montgomery of Alamein*. New York: British Information Services, 1946.

———, *The Memoirs of Field Marshal The Viscount Montgomery of Alamein*. London: Collins, 1958.

Morison, Samuel Eliot, *The Battle of the Atlantic Sept. 1939-May 1943*. Boston: Little, Brown and Company, 1948.

———, *The Two Ocean War*. Boston: Little, Brown and Company, 1963.

Morton, Louis, *U.S. Army in World War II: The Fall of the Philippines*. Washington, D.C: Office of the Chief of Military History, Dept. of the Army, 1953.

Morzik, Major General Fritz, *German Air Force Airlift Operations*. New York: Arno Press, 1968.

Mrazak, Col. James E., *The Glider War*. New York: St. Martin's Press, 1975.

———, *Fighting Gliders*. New York: St. Martin's Press, 1977.

———, *The Fall of the Eben Emael*. Washington, D.C: Robert B. Luce, Inc., 1971.

Pay, Don R., *Thunder from Heaven – A History of the 17th Airborne Division*. Birmingham: The Airborne Quarterly, 1947.

Pogue, Forrest C. *The Supreme Command*. Washington, D.C: Office of the Chief of Military History, Dept. of the Army, 1946.

Raff, Edson D., *We Jumped to Fight*. New York: Eagle, 1944.

Rapport, Leonard, and Northwood, Arthur, Jr., *Rendezvous with Destiny: A History of the 101st Airborne Division*. Washington, D.C: Washington Infantry Journal Press, 1948.

*Reports of General MacArthur, Vol. I: The Campaigns of MacArthur in the Pacific. Prepared by his General Staff*. Washington, D.C: U.S. Government Printing Office, 1960.

Rickenbacker, Captain Edward V., *Seven Came Through*. New York: Doubleday, 1943.

———, *Fighting The Flying Circus*. New York, Doubleday, 1965.

Ridgway, General Matthew B., *Soldier: The Memoirs of Matthew B. Ridgway*. New York: Harper Bros., 1956.

Rola, Charles J., *Wingate's Raiders*. New York, Viking Press, 1944.

Romanus, Charles F. and Sunderland, Riley, *U.S. Army in World*

*War II: China-Burma-India Theater*. Washington, D.C: Office of the Chief of Military History, Department of the Army, 1956.
————, *U.S. Army in World War II: Time Runs Out in the CBI*. Washington, D.C: Office of the Chief of Military History, Department of the Army, 1959.

Ruppenthal, Maj. Roland G., *The U.S. Army in WW II: Utah Beach to Cherbourg*. Washington, D.C: Office of the Chief of Military History. Dept. of the Army, 1947.

Rust, Kenn C. *The 9th Air Force in World War II*. Fallbrook, California, Aero Publishers, 1967.

Ryan, Cornelius, *The Longest Day*. New York: Simon and Schuster, Inc., 1959.

————, *A Bridge Too Far*. New York: Simon and Schuster, 1974; London, Hamish Hamilton, 1974; Coronet, 1975.

Slim, Field Marshal the Viscount William J, *Defeat Into Victory*. New York: Davis McKay Company, 1961; London, Cassell, 1956.

Smith, Joseph H., *Small Arms of the World*. Harrisburg: The Stackpole Company, 1976.

Smith, Robert R., *U.S. Army in WW II: Triumph in the Philippines*. Washington, D.C: Office of the Chief of Military History, Dept. of the Army, 1961.

Sowards, Kelly, *Western Civilization to 1660*. New York: St. Martin's Press, 1964.

Speer, Albert, *Inside the Third Reich*. New York: Macmillan, 1970.

Swiecicki, Marek, *With the Red Devils at Arnhem*. London: Max Love Publishing, 1945.

Swinson, Arthur, *The Battle of Kohima*. New York: Stein and Day, 1967.

Taylor, Maxwell D., *Swords and Plowshares*. New York: W.W. Norton & Co., Inc., 1972.

Thomas, David A., *Nazi Victory – Crete 1941*. New York: Stein and Day, 1972.

Thomas, Lowell, *Back to Mandalay*. New York: The Greystone Press, 1951.

Toland, John, *The Rising Sun: The Decline and Fall of the Japanese Empire 1936-1945*; Volumes 1 and 2. New York: Random House, 1970.

Turbiville, Graham H. *Soviet Airborne Troops*. Fort Leavenworth: Military Review, Professional Journal of the U.S. Army, 1973.

*United States Marine Corps Parachute Units.* Historical Branch, G-3 Division, Headquarters, U.S. Marine Corps, Washington, D.C: 1962.

Warren, John G. *U.S. Air Force Historical Study No. 97: Airborne Operations in World War II, European Theater.* Maxwell Air Force Base, Alabama, 1956.

Wright, Lawrence, *The Wooden Sword.* London: Elek Books, Ltd., 1967.

Yarborough, Lt. Gen. William P., *Bail Out Over North Africa.* New Jersey: Phillips Publications, 1979.

————, *U.S. Airborne Operations In North Africa. A Personal Account.* England: Privately printed, 1943.

Young, Brig. Gen. Gordan R., *The Army Almanac.* Harrisburg: The Stackpole Company, 1959.

# Index

Brooke County Library
945 Main Street
Wellsburg, W. Va. 26070